SPECIAL PUBLICATION
of CARNEGIE MUSEUM OF NATURAL HISTORY

WEST VIRGINIA BIRDS
Distribution and Ecology

GEORGE A. HALL
Research Associate, Section of Birds
(Address: West Virginia University, Morgantown, West Virginia 26506)

THIS SPECIAL PUBLICATION IS PUBLISHED
IN COOPERATION WITH THE WEST VIRGINIA
DEPARTMENT OF NATURAL RESOURCES
NONGAME WILDLIFE PROGRAM

NUMBER 7   PITTSBURGH, 1983

SPECIAL PUBLICATION OF CARNEGIE MUSEUM OF NATURAL HISTORY

Number 7, pages 1–180, 12 figs., 21 plates

Issued 15 April 1983

Price: $20.00 a copy

DEDICATION

This book is dedicated to Maurice Brooks and to the memory of Charles L. Conrad, each of whom in greatly different ways has contributed much to the advancement of the knowledge of West Virginia birds.

CARNEGIE MUSEUM OF NATURAL HISTORY, 4400 FORBES AVENUE
PITTSBURGH, PENNSYLVANIA 15213

CONTENTS

Foreword v

Acknowledgments. vi

The Environment—A Description of the State 1

History of West Virginia Ornithology 7

Analysis of the West Virginia Avifauna 11

Species Accounts 21

Gazetteer 167

Uncited Literature 170

Literature Cited. 172

Index to Bird Names 177

LIST OF PLATES

Plate   Page

Frontispiece: *Dendroica potomac* Sutton's Warbler—watercolor by George M. Sutton

1. Virgin Red Spruce, Pendleton County 16
2. Young Red Spruce Forest, Randolph County 16
3. Virgin Northern Hardwoods Forest, Nicholas County 17
4. Top of Allegheny Front Mountain, Tucker County 17
5. Grass-covered Mountain top ("sods"), Pocahontas County 18
6. View from Bickell's Knob, Randolph County 18
7. The Cranberry Glades, Pocahontas County 19
8. Mixed farmland and forest, western part of the Ridge and Valley Region, Pendleton County ... 19
9. Brown Creeper 94
10. Nest of Swainson's Thrush 94
11. Swainson's Thrush 95
12. Nashville Warbler 95
13. Nest of Northern Parula in a piece of burlap lodged in a tree 96
14. Chestnut-sided Warbler 96
15. Magnolia Warbler 97
16. Black-throated Blue Warbler 97
17. Yellow-throated Blue Warbler 98
18. Mourning Warbler 98
19. Swainson's Warbler 99
20. Nest of Swainson's Warbler 99
21. Summer Tanager 100

LIST OF ILLUSTRATIONS

Figure   Page

1. County Map of West Virginia 2
2. The Avifaunal Regions of West Virginia 12
3. Breeding Season Records for the Solitary Vireo 113
4. Breeding Season Records for the Magnolia Warbler. The distribution of many other typical Allegheny Mountains Region birds would be nearly the same as this 121
5. Breeding Season Records for the Black-throated Blue Warbler 122
6. Breeding Season Records for the Blackburnian Warbler 125
7. Breeding Season Records for the Yellow-throated Warbler 126
8. Breeding Season Records for Swainson's Warbler 133
9. Breeding Season Records for the Rose-breasted Grosbeak 141
10. Breeding Season Records for the Blue Grosbeak 142
11. Breeding Season Records for the Savannah Sparrow 148
12. Breeding Season Records for the Swamp Sparrow 152

FOREWORD

Since the last catalog of the birds of West Virginia was published in 1944, the total amount of effort devoted to the study of birds in the state probably has exceeded all that went before. The habitat changes that have occurred in these three decades probably have had a more profound effect on the birdlife than did those changes accompanying the clearing of farms by the first settlers and the deforestation in the heyday of the lumber industry. Those changes proved to be largely transitory, but today's changes may be more permanent. Parts of West Virginia no doubt eventually will be included in the "megapolis" predicted for the eastern United States, and in places the changes made by the strip-mining industry are nearly "geological" in nature. It seems desirable to put on record the status of the birds of the state in the third quarter of the 20th Century to serve as a benchmark for future generations. This book attempts to be such a benchmark.

As Robert Mengel pointed out in his monumental *Birds of Kentucky* (1965), the day is past when one man can monograph the birds of a region as large as a whole state, and produce a book in the tradition of the "State Bird Books" of past generations. Such a job would have to be done by a committee and, even if it were completed, the present-day publishing costs would result in a publication too expensive for the average student of birds, as witnessed in a recent publication from a southwestern state.

For this book, therefore, I have selected only certain phases of the birdlife for presentation. The existence of inexpensive and excellent field guides makes it unnecessary to give descriptions of the birds. The details of the nesting cycle have been omitted, as has practically all information about bird behavior. In a zone of ecological tension, such as exists in West Virginia, the behavior and nesting biology of many species may indeed be different than they are elsewhere. Such topics do deserve attention, but I have deliberately left them for another time and another author. This compilation concentrates, as the subtitle indicates, on the general distribution and on the ecology of the species as we presently understand these topics. Much use has been made of numerical population data.

During the preparation of this work I have read all of the published material on West Virginia birds of which I am aware and have examined most of the specimens of birds collected in West Virginia. Several of the bird students of the state have given me abundant information from their personal notes and recollections. But even with all this material and my own extensive fieldwork, it is evident that the book cannot be complete. Many areas of the state, particularly some west of the Great Kanawha River, are still *terra incognita* from an ornithological standpoint. It is to be hoped that future studies will concentrate in these areas.

In recent years, West Virginia has become a vacationland for many persons from elsewhere. Some of these, whose very existence is unknown to me, have no doubt made significant observations on the birds of the state. Despite these limitations, I feel that the book does give an accurate picture of the birdlife of the state to the present. All information known to me in the autumn of 1976, when this manuscript was completed, has been included. Additional information has been added since then; consequently, the account is essentially complete to the early summer of 1982. No literature appearing after 1 May 1982 has been included.

I made my first observations on birds in West Virginia on 28 April 1940, a meager list of 16 species seen on a short walk. However, I did not begin intensive and systematic study of the birds of the state until I returned to West Virginia permanently in 1950. Since that time, I have visited all 55 counties of the state and have made at least some observations on the birds in about 35 of these counties.

In the spring of 1968, Chandler S. Robbins asked me to be the summarizing speaker for a symposium on state bird books that he was organizing for the annual meeting of the Wilson Ornithological Society. He suggested that the title of my talk be "The State Bird Book of the Future." Perhaps Robbins was just hard up for a speaker, but perhaps he had a vision of the future, since my participation in that symposium, as the only speaker who had not written a regional bird book, started the final processes that led to this book. I must admit, however, that the present work bears little resemblance to the visionary "book of the future" that I described in that talk.

George A. Hall

ACKNOWLEDGMENTS

This book could not have been written without the dedicated work over many years of the members of the Brooks Bird Club. The raw data assembled here were collected by them, and many offered suggestions and encouragement. Unfortunately many of these people must go unnamed.

However, there are people who must be named and acknowledged for their help. Of special importance are Maurice Brooks, who over the years has given me much advice and more help than he perhaps realizes, and who made available to me a series of notebooks belonging to his uncle E. A. Brooks containing much valuable information on early records; the late Charles O. Handley, Sr., supplied me with a copy of a then-unpublished manuscript by him and J. L. Smith on the birds of the Kanawha Valley, and was a source of much other information; Karl W. Haller offered many suggestions based on his extensive collecting in the state in the 1930s; Lloyd F. Kiff supplied a detailed critique of my comments on the birds of the Mason-Cabell Counties region, where my own field experience has been limited and gave me access to the records of S. S. Dickey; Glen Phillips carefully compiled and organized the data from the Singing Male Censuses taken over the years by members of the Brooks Bird Club; and Chandler S. Robbins supplied a summary of the Breeding Bird Survey data taken in the state, gave invaluable help in setting up the definitions of the abundance categories, and supplied many other useful data from the files of the Fish and Wildlife Service.

For supplying help of various kinds or information of many sorts, I am indebted to Lawrence E. Bayless, Daniel D. Berger, John Bull, Roger B. Clapp, Mary H. Clench, Eugene Eisenmann, Richard L. Hall, Charles O. Handley, Jr., Janet Hinshaw, J. Russell Hogg, George Innarone, W. K. Igo, Ned K. Johnson, Roxie C. Laybourne, Walter Lesser, Daniel McKinley, Sheldon Miller, James Morash, Allan R. Phillips, Joseph C. Rieffenberger, Frederic R. Scott, Lester L. Short, George M. Sutton, Duane A. Tolle, Milton B. Trautman, John S. Weske, Thomas Wray, and Peter E. Zurbuch.

Detailed data on distribution and migration at various local areas were supplied by William H. Armstrong, Pollye Ballowe, A. R. Buckelew, Jr., Kyle Bush, E. R. Chandler, Charles L. Conrad, Sue Edmonds, George F. Flouer, Paula Gale, Norris Gluck, C. O. Handley, Sr., Eugene E. Hutton, Wilda Jennings, Oliver Johnson, Robert C. Kletzley, Nevada Laitsch, Clark Miller, Stauffer Miller, Ephe Olliver, Glen F. Phillips, Thomas E. Shields, Anne Shreve, Harry S. Slack, L. John Trott, and Leon P. Wilson.

I am indebted to the following curators of various museums for permission to examine specimens under their care: Richard C. Banks and Richard L. Zusi, National Museum of Natural History; Robert W. Storer, University of Michigan Museum of Zoology; Wesley E. Lanyon, American Museum of Natural History; Raymond A. Paynter, Jr., Museum of Comparative Zoology; Rollin Bauer, Cornell University; David M. Niles, Delaware Museum of Natural History; Robert L. Birch, West Virginia University; W. Gene Frum and Michael Seidel, Marshall University; and especially to Kenneth C. Parkes, Carnegie Museum of Natural History for his advice on many matters over many years.

The penultimate draft of the manuscript was read and criticized by Ralph K. Bell, George H. Breiding, Maurice Brooks, A. R. Buckelew, Jr., Charles L. Conrad, Greg E. Eddy, Norris Gluck, Karl W. Haller, C. O. Handley, Sr., George F. Hurley, Constance Katholi, Lloyd F. Kiff, George Koch, and Nevada Laitsch. Charles H. Baer, Earl L. Core, James L. Hall, John F. Hall, and Kenneth C. Parkes read and commented on some of the preliminary chapters. The final work has benefited greatly from the suggestions of these people, but any errors or misstatements remaining must remain my responsibility.

The West Virginia University Senate Research Committee provided financial support in the form of summer salary during the period of actual writing. The Frank M. Chapman Fund of the American Museum of Natural History gave a grant that enabled me to visit several museums. The Christmas Count data used were obtained from the data files at the University of Colorado through the courtesy of Carl E. Bock and financed by the Department of Chemistry, West Virginia University.

The Frontispiece was printed through the courtesy of the Leigh Yawkey Woodson Art Museum of Wausau, Wisconsin, through George Harrison, and George M. Sutton. The line drawings, originally drawn by George M. Sutton for W. E. C. Todd's *Birds of Western Pennsylvania* and now a part of the collections of the Carnegie Museum of Natural History, have been used by arrangement with Dr. Sutton. Hal H. Harrison supplied the photographs of birds, and additional photographs came from the files of the U.S. Forest Service. Nancy Perkins drew the maps and Chuck Ripper drew the cover design.

The final manuscript was typed by Anne B. Drake with the support of the College of Arts and Sciences, West Virginia University. Additional typing was done by Duana Nacarate. Editing was done by James A. Carte with the assistance of Pam Delardas.

Publication of this book was partially financed by the Nongame Wildlife Fund of the West Virginia Department of Natural Resources.

Finally, some mention should be made of my wife and son who spent many long husbandless and fatherless hours during the writing of this book.

Dendroica potomac Sutton's Warbler. Male (upper); female (lower). Watercolor by George M. Sutton.

THE ENVIRONMENT—A DESCRIPTION OF THE STATE

It is difficult to summarize the geographical location and the general environmental picture of West Virginia in a few words. Geographers commonly place the state in the Middle Atlantic Region, but the highly irregular boundaries, most of which are determined by streams and mountain ridges, produce some strange contrasts. Thus, the northernmost point in the state is almost at the latitude of New York City; the easternmost point lies within 40 miles of the longitude of Washington, D.C.; the southernmost point is 60 miles south of the latitude of Richmond, Virginia; and the westernmost point is 40 miles farther west than Cleveland, Ohio. The wide variation in latitude and longitude and the great variation in elevation make West Virginia a "transition state" between the north and the south, and to some extent between the east and midwest. This transitional nature extends beyond geological and biological matters into many aspects of human culture.

West Virginia is the only state that lies solely within the Appalachian upland. With a mean elevation of 450 meters (1,500 feet), it is the most elevated state east of the Mississippi River, and with small exceptions the topography of the whole state is rugged. The secondary continental divide separating the Atlantic drainage from the Mississippi drainage divides the state into two unequal parts, each of which has a character of its own. It has been remarked in the past that a line drawn from just east of Morgantown in Monongalia County to Bluefield in Mercer County divides the state into two sections. "To the east of that line the area abounds in huckleberries and rattlesnakes and to the west it abounds in blackberries and copperheads." Plant succession has gradually reduced the area covered by the two plants, but this aphorism does contain a certain amount of merit and truth.

On the basis of both physiography and phytogeography, we can divide the state into the three regions discussed below under separate subheadings, i.e., the Unglaciated Allegheny Plateau, the Allegheny Mountains, and the Ridges and Valleys. As shown in a later section, the distribution of birds in the state parallels these three divisions.

THE UNGLACIATED ALLEGHENY PLATEAU

The greater part of the state falls in the physiographic section known as the Unglaciated Allegheny Plateau (Fenneman, 1938). This area includes all of the state west of a line drawn from eastern Monongalia County southwest to central Pocahontas County, and thence south along the Greenbrier River to the state border in Monroe County, except

for a small portion of Mercer County. The surface rocks of this region are largely of the Pennsylvanian age and consist mostly of shales and sandstones. The rock strata are essentially horizontal. Much of this area is underlain by extensive coal beds, a fact of considerable importance to the ultimate fate of the natural biota. The surface rocks are of Permian age in the Ohio Valley from Ohio County to Mason County and extending east of the valley for several miles. In the north, the rocks are poorly resistant to erosion, the terrain is highly dissected, and the drainage is of the dendritic pattern. The hills are usually steep and the valleys separating them narrow. Most of these hills are below 450 meters (1,500 feet) in elevation and the maximum relief is usually from 150 to 250 meters (500 to 800 feet). The general aspect is of a jumble of hills, all of more or less the same elevation, forming no definite orderly pattern. In the south, the rocks are more resistant to erosion and the major streams have cut deep, narrow canyons into a rather gently rolling upland. The elevations and the relief are higher than in the north. The hills here occasionally rise as high as 1,000 meters (3,200 feet) above sea level with the relief being from 300 to 400 meters (1,000 to 1,300 feet). A few isolated knobs with elevations of around 1,070 meters (3,500 feet) are located in Mercer County. The lowest elevations in the hill country are about 155 meters (500 feet) where the Ohio River leaves the state in Wayne County.

The principal stream in this region is the Ohio River with its two main tributaries, the Monongahela in the north and the Kanawha in the south. The Kanawha has important tributaries in the Gauley, the Greenbrier, and the New Rivers. The whole region has little flatland except in the flood plains of the Ohio and Kanawha Rivers and in the Teays Valley, an abandoned streambed of an extinct river dating from Pleistocene time.

This physiographic region coincides almost exactly with the Allegheny Plateau Section of the Mixed Mesophytic Forest Region in the classification of Braun (1950). This forest region is also known as the Central Hardwoods Region. As the name implies this forest is a highly mixed one, with the exact composition depending upon the amount of moisture, the soil character, and the direction of the slope. When the first settlers came to the state, this area was covered by a forest in which oaks (*Quercus* spp.) of several species were predominant and hickories (*Carya* spp.) were quite important. American chestnut (*Castanea dentata*) was an important species and numerous other species occurred. In the more sheltered and moister ravines, tulip poplar

Fig. 1.   County Map of West Virginia.

(*Liriodendron tulipifera*) was an important tree in the so-called Cove Hardwoods forest. In the southern part of the region and near the eastern border, as in Raleigh County, the steeper moister ravines had fine stands of white pine (*Pinus strobus*) and eastern hemlock (*Tsuga canadensis*). Hemlock also occurred in ravines all along the eastern border of the region. Rainfall in this area was adequate, and most of this forest was lush and had a well-developed understory. On the drier slopes, and particularly on the ridge tops, the oaks were mixed with pines, Virginia (*Pinus virginianus*) and short-leaved (*P. echinata*), forming an oak-pine forest similar to that in the eastern part of the state. In a few places on the river terraces of the main rivers, these pine forests were almost pure stands. In the lower Ohio Valley, a few species characteristic of the Southern Hardwoods forest such as red gum (*Liquidambar* *styraciflua*) occur. In the presettlement days, probably no non-forested land existed except small transitory areas resulting from fires, and possibly areas of cultivation by the pre-Columbian Indians who inhabited some areas.

Practically all of the original forest in this region had been removed by the latter part of the 19th Century, and at one time most of the land except for the steeper slopes had been converted to farmland. In the central part of the state, this farmland—particularly open grassy, heavily grazed slopes—still is common, but reforestation has occurred in much of the rest of the region. A second-growth woodland consisting largely of black locust (*Robinia pseudoacacia*) is an important and widespread early stage in the succession. In many parts of the state, now 75 years after the cutting, mature forests of approximately the original type, except for the absence of the chestnut, have come back, particularly on the steeper slopes unsuitable for farming.

Of major importance to the physiographic and floristic aspect of the Unglaciated Allegheny Plateau Region is the advent of widespread strip-mining operations, particularly in the last two decades, in which whole mountain sides have been removed and large areas denuded of vegetation. Although some effort at reclamation of these areas has been made by planting grass and pines, most of them may be many years in returning to a natural state.

The southeastern part of this region in southern Greenbrier and Monroe Counties presents a much different aspect. This is the only part of the Plateau where Mississippian limestone is exposed to any extent, and much of the area is currently in grassland and cropland.

THE ALLEGHENY MOUNTAINS

The area bounded on the west by Chestnut Ridge in Monongalia County, south to Laurel Ridge in Randolph County, further south to the junction of Cheat and Back Allegheny Mountains in Pocahontas County, and then north along the crests of Back Allegheny Mountain, and the Allegheny Front to the Potomac River and the Maryland border is considered by physiographers (Fenneman, 1938) to be the Allegheny Mountain section of the Appalachian Plateau.

The surface rocks of this section are largely from the Mississippian and Devonian ages with a lesser amount from Pennsylvanian. The rock strata are tilted from horizontal because of folding. The general aspect of this region is one of a high plateau carrying numerous higher ridges, often of great length. These ridges are fairly uniform in height, but occasionally rise to higher peaks called "knobs." The plateau is usually from 750 to 1,000 meters (2,500 to 3,000 feet) high in the north and slightly higher in the south. Many of the ridges and knobs are above 1,200 meters (4,000 feet) in elevation. The relief is usually about 300 to 500 meters (1,000 to 1,600 feet) except along the eastern margin of the region where there is often a drop of over 600 meters (2,000 feet) to the valley below.

Spruce Knob on Spruce Mountain, Pendleton County—the highest point in the state—reaches 1,480 meters (4,860 feet), but many other high points are above 1,300 meters (4,250 feet). This region is drained by the headwaters of the Monongahela system through the two main branches, the Tygart's Valley River and the many forks of the Cheat River, as well as the headwaters of the Greenbrier River, which ultimately flows into the Kanawha. The North Branch of the Potomac River originates in the region and a few other streams flow into the Potomac, but

the secondary continental divide forms much of the eastern boundary of the section.

Braun (1950) included all the Allegheny Mountain Physiographic Section as well as a strip from the eastern boundary of that section to the crest of Allegheny Mountain on the Virginia border in the Allegheny Mountain section of the Mixed Mesophytic Forest Region. The narrow valleys of the westernmost part of the Ridge and Valley Province do not differ significantly in their floristic composition from the easternmost ridges of the Allegheny Mountains and more elevated portions of the Unglaciated Allegheny Plateau along the southeastern border of West Virginia.

The lower slopes in the Allegheny Mountain Region originally were covered with a rich mixed mesophytic forest in which sugar maple (*Acer saccharum*), beech (*Fagus grandifolia*), American chestnut and red oak (*Q. rubra*) predominated. The western slopes of the mountains received abundant rainfall, and this forest was lush with a well-developed understory. Hemlock was common in the moister ravines cutting the main slopes. An extensive belt of white pine was along the western edge of the region from Tucker to Greenbrier Counties. White oak (*Q. alba*) was the dominant tree on some slopes. On higher ground, the maple-beech combination became more predominant and red maple (*A. rubrum*) and yellow birch (*Betula lutea*) became important components of the forest on moist cool slopes. This maple-beech-birch forest usually is referred to in the accounts that follow as the Northern Hardwoods forest. Red spruce (*Picea rubra*) occurred in places as low as 750 meters (2,500 feet), but usually did not occur below 1,000 meters (3,250 feet). With increasing elevation, the amount of spruce increased, forming a mixed coniferous-hardwoods belt between the pure hardwoods and a pure spruce forest that occurred above 1,200 meters (4,000 feet). It has been estimated that red spruce originally covered about 189,000 hectares (467,000 acres) of the state, but this forest has largely been removed. Balsam fir (*Abies balsamea*), the common associate of spruce in the true boreal forest, was essentially missing from the West Virginia forest, although a few small isolated stands are in Tucker, Grant, Randolph, and Pocahontas Counties.

In some of the high mountain valleys, there is much level, or near-level, land and here mountain bogs and swamps are frequent. The outstanding example of this is the large Canaan Valley, an anticlinal valley, in Tucker County. The wetland areas are often enlarged by the flooding associated with beaver dams. There are many small sphagnum bogs, which usually are relict communities. The most noted and most extensive of these is the Cranberry Glades in Pocahontas County.

The original forest of the Allegheny Mountain Region was almost completely removed in the lumbering operations which reached their peak in the early years of this century. However, a few remnant stands of virgin forest, usually small in area, do give us some inkling of what the country was like 200 years ago. The northern hardwoods forest has regenerated in essentially the same composition as it was, and in many places this second-growth forest is approaching maturity. Except in a very few places, the white pine and spruce forest has not regenerated to the present, although it may come back in the future. In some places, e.g., the top of the Allegheny Front, there were extensive fires shortly after the forest was cut over, and often these fires so destroyed the organic matter in the soil that little plant growth has occurred in these areas. Extensive fields of blueberries (*Vaccinium*), huckleberries (*Gaylussacia*), and other heaths interrupted by a scrubby deciduous growth mixed with a little spruce cover these areas today. Some of the higher mountain slopes are so heavily grazed by livestock that they remain today as grasslands. A few small areas of grassland (often called "sods") were on some of the heights when the first settlers reached the area. The origin of these treeless areas has been a matter of debate.

In West Virginia much of the Allegheny Mountain Region lies within the boundaries of the Monongahela National Forest, large parts of which can be considered to be true wilderness.

In the accounts that follow the Allegheny Mountain Region refers to the area based on the forest types rather than on the strict physiographic area.

THE RIDGES AND VALLEYS

All of the state that lies east of the Allegheny Mountains is included in the Ridge and Valley Province of the physiographers (Fenneman, 1938). A small portion of southern Mercer County also belongs in this province. This is a region of extreme folding of the rock strata. The surface rocks over the largest part of the province are of Devonian age, but some outcrops of Silurian, Ordovician, and Cambrian rocks also are present. This area has more outcroppings of limestone than any other part of the state, but shale outcroppings and sandstone also are common. Pre-Cambrian metamorphic rock is present on the Blue Ridge in eastern Jefferson County, and the area usually is considered to be a separate physiographic province. However, no apparent biological difference exists in this small area; consequently, it is included in the Ridge and Valley Province.

The terrain of this region consists of long, narrow mountain ridges and valleys running from northeast to southwest more or less parallel to each other. The area has a trellis drainage pattern. The Shenandoah Valley, the easternmost valley, is a portion of the Great Appalachian Valley, a prominent topographic feature of eastern United States. North Fork Mountain, the westernmost ridge, reaches heights in excess of 1,200 meters (4,000 feet) with some knobs to 1,375 meters (4,500 feet). The relief in the area is from 450 to 600 meters (1,500 to 2,000 feet). Shenandoah Mountain on the Virginia border also rises above 1,200 meters (4,000 feet), but most of the ridges are much lower, and in the north and the east they seldom rise above 600 meters (2,000 feet). The valleys usually are about 300 meters (1,000 feet) lower. The lowest elevation in the state is reached at Harper's Ferry, Jefferson County, where the Potomac River leaves the state at an elevation of 75 meters (247 feet). This province is drained by the Potomac River and its two branches east of the Allegheny Front. The area in Mercer County is drained by tributaries of the New River.

The Ridge and Valley province lies in the rain shadow of the higher mountains to the west and much of the region is quite dry, producing a much different forest cover. Braun (1950) places all of this area in the Oak-Chestnut Forest Region. The American chestnut is essentially all gone and the present forest perhaps is more nearly described as being oak-pine forest. Several species of oak, chestnut (*Q. montana*), white (*Q. alba*), scarlet (*Q. coccinea*), and black (*Q. velutina*) predominate, mixed with Virginia and pitch (*Pinus rigida*) pines. On some of the drier slopes, pines are in almost pure stands, although this is only a developmental stage eventually to be invaded by oaks and other hardwoods. In most of this forest, the undergrowth is fairly sparse.

The shale barrens are of particular botanical interest in this region, but these areas are too small in extent to influence the bird life.

The valleys, particularly the broader ones, at present are largely unforested and are farmlands of a varied nature. Grazing is important in the region, but many agronomic crops are raised and extensive orchards are found in the eastern part of the region.

CLIMATE

As expected from its location, West Virginia has a continental-type climate with hot summers and cold winters. The largest part of the state falls within the Mesothermal Hot Summer Climate [Cfa climate in the Köppen System (Koeppe and Delong, 1958)], which signifies that the coldest month averages between 18 and −3°C, precipitation is well distributed throughout the year, and the mean temperature of the warmest month is above 22°C. The Allegheny Mountain Region belongs in the Mesothermal, Warm Summer Climate (Cfb) in which the warmest month averages below 22°C but at least four months are over 10°C.

All parts of the state receive adequate rainfall that is distributed through the year with no dry season. The average rainfall for the whole state is somewhat above 100 cm, but this varies greatly from place to place. In the Allegheny Plateau section, the upper Ohio Valley averages 105 cm, the lower Ohio and Kanawha Valleys 108 cm, the central part of the state 117 cm, and the extreme south 99 cm with an overall average for the region of 108 cm. The Allegheny Mountains average 128 cm and the Ridge and Valley region 92 cm. (Environmental Data Service, 1968). The difference is even more pronounced than the above data show. Pickens in Randolph County on the western slopes of the Alleghenies has received a long-term average of 174 cm. The higher mountains must have even greater rainfall, but no data are available. Upper Tract, Pendleton County, at about 450 meters in South Branch Valley and about 80 km east of Pickens has received an average of only 64 cm.

LIFE ZONES

In the past, faunal summaries such as this one carefully analyzed the bird distribution on the region under consideration on the basis of Merriam's Life Zones. Under this system, most of West Virginia falls in the Transition Zone (called the Alleghanian Zone in eastern United States); the red spruce forest belongs to the Canadian Zone, perhaps better referred to as the quasi-Canadian Zone; and the lower river valleys of the southwest and Eastern Panhandle belong to the Carolinian Zone. While these divisions may have been appropriate in the past, they do not seem very useful at present. With the general deforestation of the state as well as the warming trend in the climate of the mid-20th Century, many species, particularly those of the brushy seral stages and of the grasslands, have expanded their ranges throughout the state. Many so-called Carolinian species now occur at very high elevations, and at the same time some species thought to be limited to the high mountains have extended their ranges to lower elevations. In light of these events it does not seem desirable to use the Life Zone concept, and the distributional material in this book makes no reference to it.

AVIAN HABITATS

The foregoing discussion has outlined with a broad brush the general picture of the original forests of the state, but it is of even more concern to discuss types of habitat that occur within these broad regions.

Mature Forest

As indicated above, practically all of West Virginia was originally covered by forest when the earliest settlers arrived, and while essentially all of the original forest has now been removed, approximately 74% of the state remains forest covered. Only a few remnant stands of uncut virgin forest remain, but much of the second-growth forest is now in a stage that can be called mature. Except for the small remaining patches of spruce forest, the forest is essentially deciduous forest with small amounts of pine, but several of the different types occur.

Young Forest or Brush Habitats

After the deforestation the land not converted to agricultural purposes passed through a series of successional stages from weed fields to great tangles of briars (*Rubus* spp.) and finally into a brushy young forest. Much of the western part of the state remains covered with a growth of black locust and wild cherry (*Prunus* spp.). Many abandoned pastures are now in a stage consisting of tangles of briars and copses of sumac (*Rhus* spp.). Between 1958 and 1967, the amount of forested land increased by about 10% and this increment is currently in the brushy stage. However, there is much less of this habitat than there was 40–50 years ago, and the growth of the forests has had an important effect on the populations of certain bird species.

Grassland

With a few almost negligible exceptions, the state had no areas of grassland when the first settlers arrived. Today about 12% of the land area is pastureland and additional acreage may be in meadow or ungrazed grassland such as occurs on some of the higher mountains. Most of this grassland occurs on steep hillsides unsuitable for agronomic crops.

Agricultural Land

Besides the pastureland, approximately 7% of the land is covered by cropland or orchards. The latter represent moderately important bird habitats, but while croplands may offer feeding sites they are of little use for nesting. The amount of farmland in the state has steadily decreased over the last half-century.

Urban and Industrial Land

Except for a very few places, West Virginia has so far escaped the urban sprawl that has afflicted much of the northeast. Some of the larger cities show signs of this, but the irregular terrain consisting of steep hillsides will prevent extensive development in most places. Even the largest cities today offer good bird populations in the residential areas. Some parts of the state, particularly the river valleys, have been highly developed as industrial sites. Approximately 3% of the state may be classified as urban and industrial.

Wetlands

The numerous mountain swamps and bogs mentioned above are interesting places to visit, but their total area is so small that they do not represent important bird habitats. Some marshes of rather limited area occur a few places away from the high mountains. These are most notable in the Eastern Panhandle and in the lower Kanawha Valley in Mason County. Although they provide the only nesting habitat in the state for several species, these marshes cannot be considered as important habitats. As with all wetlands everywhere, the marshes are in constant threat of being drained. Most of the streams of the state are too rapid in flow to have much floodplain swamp, but such wooded swamps do occur along the Ohio River. The most noteworthy of these was the Beech Bottom Swamp in Brooke County, which in its time provided a number of unique bird records but which was filled in the early 1950s. Another interesting floodplain swamp is at Boaz, Wood County.

Aquatic Habitats

In the past, aquatic habitats—and consequently aquatic birds—were of almost no importance in the state. Except for a small pond in Hardy County there are no natural lakes in the state, and aquatic habitat was limited to the larger streams: the Potomac, the Ohio, and the Kanawha. The total area under water is about 0.3% of the state's land area. Over the years, however, numerous large artificial impoundments have been made for a variety of reasons. The most important of these are Cheat Lake, Monongalia County; Stony River Reservoir, Grant County; Tygart Reservoir, Taylor County; Sutton Reservoir, Braxton County; Summersville Reservoir, Nicholas County; Bluestone Reservoir, Summers County; East Lyne Lake, Wayne County; and other very new impoundments in the southwest. All of these artificial lakes provide resting places for migrating waterfowl, but are usually very poor for feeding purposes. Most of them are in steep valleys and lack extensive shoreline flats; consequently, shorebird occurences are of little importance in the state. In the mid-20th Century, thousands of small farm-ponds were established, and these have had a small effect on nesting waterfowl.

Mine-Residue Habitats

In areas where deep mining of coal has been carried out for many years, there are often large mounds, or small hills, of accumulated mine-waste material. These areas are almost true deserts with little vegetation growing on them, and no bird life. Early strip-mining operations were small in scale but did make marked alterations on the habitat. Highwalls were left and the barren subsoil was exposed. The modern strip mine procedures, however, are on a very large scale and great areas of the state have been denuded of vegetation and have had the soil structure altered. Between 1930 and 1971, 79,300 hectares of land were surface-mined and in 1981 nearly 41,000 hectares were still under bond. In some places the changes in terrain have been so marked as to almost come under the heading of a "geological" change. Since the passage of a strict reclamation law in 1972, many of these sites have been planted in grassland. Between 1972 and 1977, some 43,000 hectares of new grassland were created.

HISTORY OF WEST VIRGINIA ORNITHOLOGY

The earliest explorers and settlers in the area that is now West Virginia reported very little about the bird life of the region except for casual mention of the game birds, particularly the turkey and waterfowl. Typical of such reports are the brief notations of waterfowl seen on the Ohio and Great Kanawha Rivers in the diary of George Washington.

Access to the west in the early 19th Century was largely by way of the Ohio River from Pittsburgh or Wheeling, and many early naturalists and others interested in wildlife briefly passed through this part of West Virginia. Meriwether Lewis, on his way to join William Clark at the start of their famous exploring expedition, reported seeing flocks of Passenger Pigeons somewhere below Wheeling.

The first person who can be called an ornithologist to visit the area now included in the state was Alexander Wilson, often called the Father of American Ornithology. When he first arrived in this country from Scotland, Wilson lived for a short time in Shepherdstown in what is now Jefferson County. Undoubtedly the young Scot had many of his first experiences with American birds in this state, but his later writings make no specific mention of this. In 1810, Wilson descended the Ohio River, alone, in a small boat in the early spring. His great work, *American Ornithology,* makes note of several species occurring in the West Virginia (then Virginia) portion of the Ohio River, e.g., Bald Eagle, Snowy Owl, and Carolina Parakeet.

In 1808, John J. Audubon had also gone down the Ohio on his way to take up residence in Kentucky, and in later years he apparently crossed the southern part of the state. However, in his writings Audubon made little mention of the birds seen in the (West) Virginia part of his journey. Such noted naturalists as Thomas Say, Thomas Nuttall, Prince Maxmilian von Wied-Neuwied, Titian Peale, and others travelled down the Ohio, but these men were headed for the glamorous West and they reported very little of what they saw in the prosaic East.

Essentially nothing was published on West Virginia birds during the middle years of the 19th Century. Undoubtedly many local residents had, as most country people do have, a working knowledge of the local birds and their habits, but this information was unpublished. The establishment of popular "watering places" such as the one at White Sulphur Springs in Greenbrier County brought many people interested in botany to the state, and these visitors contributed much to the growth of knowledge of West Virginia flora, but apparently few if any people interested in birds visited these places. However, there is a very old record of a visitor collecting a "mottled" Screech Owl at White Sulphur Springs in

1837 (Cabot, 1839) and another report (Stark, 1874) of the nest of a Chestnut-sided Warbler (earliest state record) at White Sulphur Springs.

In the summer of 1872, a young Harvard student, William Earle Dodge Scott, later to become a prominent ornithologist at Princeton University, spent the summer visiting a classmate, W. S. Edwards, at Coalburg, Kanawha County. These two young men made an extensive collection of birds of the area, and Scott's paper (1872) is the first publication describing a local avifauna in the state. This paper has been commented on and the conditions reported then have been compared with those of the present by Gluck and Handley (1973). Scott's collection of birds is still extant at the Harvard Museum of Comparative Zoology, but the present location of the Edwards collection is unknown.

Three other Cambridge, Massachusetts, youths—Ernest Ingersoll, Ruthven Deane, and William Brewster—spent two weeks in the spring of 1874 in Ritchie County (Brewster, 1875). The report of this trip by Brewster, destined to become one of the leading ornithologists of his day, is most valuable in giving a clear picture of the bird life in the state at that time. Brewster's collection of birds from West Virginia is still in the Museum of Comparative Zoology. In 1974 a group of present-day bird students spent the same period of time in Ritchie County making comparisons of a century of change (Koch, 1975).

At about this same time, the Rev. W. E. Hill of Fairview, Hancock County, published several papers on the birds of the Northern Panhandle, the first ornithological papers by a person residing in the state. In the 1880s a young man living at White Sulphur Springs, Thaddeus Surber, began to publish a number of valuable observations from that area, culminating in a full-scale faunal list of the birds of Greenbrier County (Surber, 1889). Besides adding several unique species to the state list (Swallow-Tailed Kite, Swainson's Hawk), Surber published the first ornithological journal to be written in the state. This journal, called *The Loon,* existed for 10 issues from January to October 1889. A number of specimens collected by Surber are in the American Museum of Natural History, New York.

The first catalog of the birds of the whole state appeared in 1888 as the now infamous Bulletin Number 3 of the West Virginia Agricultural Experiment Station (Doan, 1888). William D. Doan was hired to make a survey of the state, and he visited various areas in the late summer and autumn. Doan claimed that his specimens were lost, and his report contained many records that are scarcely credible at this late date. Earle A. Brooks considered most of Doan's report to be unreliable largely on the basis of his first-hand observations of Doan's field-work methods. Brooks hinted that he might someday reveal the true story of this Bulletin, but to our present-day regret he never did.

In 1890 W. C. Rives of Washington, D.C. published his *Catalog of the Birds of the Virginias.* At this time Rives had apparently not visited West Virginia, and his notes for this state consisted largely of assembling the records of Scott, Brewster, and Doan; however, Rives's list does represent the first reliable attempt to catalog the birds of the whole state. Later Rives made two trips to the spruce forest area in Tucker County and left a graphic account of conditions in that area both before and immediately after the intensive lumbering operations that so altered the natural conditions in that region (Rives, 1898). Robert B. McClain of Wheeling published a number of papers on the birds of that region in the 1890s, and this decade also saw the first ornithological publications of Earle A. Brooks.

The last few years of the 19th Century and the first quarter of the 20th Century may well be called the era of the Brooks family in the history of biological studies in West Virginia. This remarkable family of naturalists from Upshur County, largely self-taught, contributed much to the knowledge of both the flora and the fauna of the state. The principal ornithological contributions came from the four brothers, Earle A., Fred E., C. Linn, and Alonzo B. (AB). Earle Brooks was the ornithological specialist of the family and until he left the state he was considered to be the principal authority on the birds of West Virginia. Besides numerous short papers, Earle Brooks published three catalogs of the birds of West Virginia (E. A. Brooks, 1909, 1912, 1929), but perhaps his most valuable contribution was a detailed annotated bibliography of the ornithological literature of the state complete to the date of publication (E. A. Brooks, 1938). The present writer acknowledges a great debt to this bibliography. Prior to this time, most of the people who had published on West Virginia birds had reported on only very small areas, usually their home grounds, but despite obvious difficulties Earle Brooks and his brothers made journeys to various parts of the state, hitherto unexplored. Their discoveries laid the broad groundwork for our present-day understanding. The Brooks brothers were all-around naturalists; consequently, their work had a very distinct ecological flavor, which has permeated the study of West Virginia birds down to the present.

Several other workers were active in the early part of the 20th Century. The most important of these were the Morgan brothers, Albert Sydney and Thomas A., of Poca, Putnam County. For many years these two men made interesting and important observations and valuable collections of waterbirds and shorebirds along the Kanawha River. A. S. Morgan lived until 1972 and this writer had the great pleasure of spending a part of one day with him in 1971, at which time his grasp of things as they once were was firm and clear. His important collection, which contained many unique items, was maintained for many years as a private museum, but upon his death it has been transferred to Milton, Cabell County, where it is a part of a tourist attraction. C. W. G. Eifrig, who later became a well-known ornithologist in the Chicago region, was for a time pastor of churches in Cumberland and Accident, Maryland. During his stay there, he collected birds and made many observations. It is not always clear from the titles of his papers that many of his important records were made on the West Virginia side of the North Branch of the Potomac River. Ralph B. Simpson, a prominent Pennsylvania ornithologist and oologist, made a number of important studies in Doddridge County at this time, and another Pennsylvania man, J. Warren Jacobs of Greene County, made a number of important contributions to the knowledge of the birds of Monongalia County.

In the 1920s, I. H. Johnston for a time held the formal position of State Ornithologist, and he devoted much time to spreading the knowledge of birds in the schools of the state. In 1923 Johnston (1923) published a catalog of the birds of the state as known to that time.

In the late teens and early twenties of this century, three young men who were to be a most important part of the history of West Virginia ornithology began work and to publish. These were Charles O. Handley, George Miksch Sutton, and Maurice Brooks, the son of Fred E. Brooks. In these early days, Handley published a few notes from his home area in Greenbrier County, including the first state record of the Black Vulture. After a prolonged absence from West Virginia, he returned in the late 1940s to work for the Conservation Commission (as then designated) and to become the mentor of the active group of bird students in the Kanawha Valley. George Sutton reported on a number of interesting records from his home in Brooke County and later published an important listing (1933) of the birds of the Northern Panhandle; however, he eventually left the state and went on to ornithological fame elsewhere. Maurice Brooks became the successor to his uncle, and for almost the last half century he has been the acknowledged authority on the birds of West Virginia, and indeed the birds of the whole southern Appalachian region.

The 1930s were a time of great ornithological activity in West Virginia in three diverse ways.

Maurice Brooks and his students at West Virginia University were extremely active and the work of this group shed light on much that had been previously unknown. A number of species were added to the state list, but more important much was learned about the distribution of many species and this distribution was beginning to be understood on the basis of the ecology of the state.

In 1937 a party of collectors from the Smithsonian Institution, under the general direction of Alexander Wetmore, spent most of the year traveling around the state making a very large general collection of birds from all areas. This collection is currently housed in the National Museum of Natural History. Wetmore's report (1937) is a detailed treatment of the taxonomy of many species and is almost a statewide catalog.

However, the event that was of the greatest importance to West Virginia ornithology was the formation of the Brooks Bird Club (named for A. B. Brooks) in Wheeling in 1932. This group of spirited and dedicated young people—of whom we can mention John Handlan, Charles Conrad, Harold Bergner, George Flouer, Dorothy and Carolyn Conrad, and Thomas Shields—under the guidance of A. B. Brooks founded an organization that has grown from a small local bird club to a statewide organization. Early in the history of this club it was decided to start a journal for the publication of information gathered, and in 1933 *The Redstart* was founded. At present (1982), it is in its 49th volume. This publication has become the most important single source of published information on the birds of the state.

The year 1934 produced another catalog of the birds of the state in the form of a West Virginia University Agricultural Station Bulletin by P. C. Bibbee (1934). This Bulletin was a condensation of a thesis written for a master's degree (Bibbee, 1929). Bibbee taught for many years at Concord College and amassed valuable data, as well as a small collection from the extreme southern part of the state. Another college teacher, E. R. Grose at Glenville, did valuable work in Upshur and Gilmer Counties at this time.

The years just preceding World War II saw a climax in ornithological work in the state. It was at this time that the Brooks Bird Club initiated the series of Annual Forays, week-long campouts devoted to the study of the natural history of selected areas in the state. The major portion of the distributional information given in this work comes from the data gathered on these Forays. Important work was being done at this time by some of the younger men such as William C. Legg, who discovered the mountain population of Swainson's Warbler, Wil-

liam A. Lunk, Lloyd Poland, and especially Karl W. Haller, who made a very valuable study of the birds of the lower Kanawha and Ohio Valleys (Haller, 1940a) and amassed the largest recent collection of West Virginia birds, now at the University of Michigan. Haller's work climaxed in 1939 with the discovery, along with Poland, of the enigmatic form known as Sutton's Warbler.

Relatively little work was done in the state during the war years, but in 1944 Maurice Brooks published the first really good catalog of the birds of the state (Brooks, 1944). Although forced by the exigencies of wartime publication to condense and abbreviate the vast amount of information at his disposal, Brooks managed to present a great amount of information. This 1944 Check-list has provided the foundation for the present account.

In the 30 odd years that have followed World War II, the amount of ornithological work done in the state has probably exceeded all that had been done before. The Brooks Bird Club has grown both in membership and in area covered until at present it is more than a statewide organization. A daughter group, the Handlan Chapter of the Brooks Bird Club, was founded at Charleston and has served as centralizing influence for the many bird students of that area. A number of bird clubs or natural-history clubs have been founded in other cities, such as Huntington, Morgantown, and Franklin, and in the Eastern Panhandle.

At Marshall University students under the direction of R. M. Edeburn and N. B. Green compiled valuable data from the lower Ohio Valley culminating in an important account of the birds of that area (Edeburn et al., 1960). Ornithology at West Virginia University has gone through a series of ups and downs, but by the early 1980s important work was being done by the staff and students of Wildlife Biology.

The Brooks Bird Club Forays have continued and have more or less covered the whole state. These Forays have been supplemented by a series of shorter explorations called the Sorties, carried out by the Handlan Chapter of Charleston. One of the most important steps in accumulating ecological data for the state was the introduction to the Foray program of the Singing Male Census technique by the late W. R. DeGarmo. More of these censuses have been made in West Virginia than in any other state, and the species accounts in this work have drawn heavily on this data source.

Samuel S. Dickey of Waynesburg, Pennsylvania, was an oologist who did a certain amount of collecting in West Virginia in the 1930s to the 1950s. After the bulk of this manuscript had been written, his data slips became available through the courtesy of the Western Foundation of Vertebrate Zoology, Los Angeles, California. His egg collection is now at that institution.

Table 1 describes many of the earlier catalogs of the birds of West Virginia.

Table 1.—*Earlier catalogs of the birds of West Virginia*

DOAN, W.D.

1888. Birds of West Virginia. Bull. 3, W. Va. Agri. Exp. Sta., Morgantown.

Lists 200 species but cannot be considered a reliable source of information.

RIVES, W. C.

1890. A catalogue of the birds of the Virginias. Proc. Newport Nat. Hist. Soc., Newport, R.I.

Contains mostly information on Virginia, but lists over 200 species for West Virginia.

BROOKS, E. A.

1909. List of birds found in West Virginia. Report of W. Va. State Board of Agriculture, Charleston.

Contains brief annotations on 192 species that were contained in an Ornithological Exhibition of the Board of Agriculture.

BROOKS, E. A.

1912. Game birds of West Virginia. Second Biennial Report of the Forest, Game and Fish Warden., Belington. Pp. 87–94.

The non-game birds of West Virginia. Second Biennial Report of the Forest, Game and Fish Warden. Belington. Pp. 95–106.

These two reports list more than 50 species of game birds and 193 species of non-game birds, together with brief annotations. Game birds are discussed in some detail.

BROOKS, E. A.

1916. The game birds of West Virginia. Fourth Biennial Report of the Forest, Game and Fish Warden. Pp. 87–106.

Some material on other species included.

JOHNSTON, I. H.

1923. Birds of West Virginia. State Dept. of Agriculture. 140 pp.

Accounts of 40 common species, together with a checklist of all species, and some migration data.

BROOKS, E. A.

1926. A check-list of the birds of West Virginia. W. Va. Wildlife, 3:18–22.

BROOKS, E. A.

1929. The birds of West Virginia. The West Virginia Encyclopedia pp. 60–74.

Contains very brief annotations and lists 264 species.

BIBBEE, P. C.

1929. Birds of West Virginia. Unpubl. M.S. Thesis, West Virginia Univ.

Good annotations on 266 species.

BIBBEE, P. C.

1934. Birds of West Virginia: A check-list. Bull. 258, W. Va. Agri. Exp. Sta., Morgantown.

A formal publication, with much condensation, of the 1929 thesis.

BROOKS, M. G.

1944. A check-list of West Virginia birds. Bull. 316, W. Va. Agri. Exp. Sta. Morgantown.

The first detailed summary of the distribution of the birds of the state. Lists 283 species. Additions to this list through 1968 (Hall, 1969a) brought the list to 298.

HALL, G. A.

1971. The list of West Virginia birds. Redstart, 32:2–18.

Accepts 295 species for the state. Contains only minimal annotations, mostly on seasonal status. Two supplements to this list (Hall, 1973 and 1982) consider 304 species to have been located in the state.

ANALYSIS OF THE WEST VIRGINIA AVIFAUNA

The Species Accounts of this work list 304 species for which adequate information is available to admit them to the state list. Two of these species, the Passenger Pigeon and the Carolina Parakeet, are extinct. Fourteen additional species have been reported under circumstances that do not permit them to be added to the list and have been designated as Hypothetical.

Of the 302 extant species on the list, 33 have been reported fewer than five times and another 35 must be considered to be of only casual occurrence. Thus 234 species are known to occur in the state in essentially every year. These can be classified as: 73 species present the year around; 99 summer residents; 55 known only as passage migrants or sometime winter residents; and 7 present only in the winter. A total of 176 species has been known to nest in the state at least once and 4 other species can be considered to probably have nested, although definite evidence is lacking for them.

Avifaunal Regions

I have made an attempt to analyze the list of 180 breeding species (this total includes the ones for which definite evidence is lacking) on the basis of their geographical distribution. Twenty-five species must be placed in an "Unanalyzed" category. These include 15 aquatic species that may nest wherever in the state suitable habitat occurs. Such aquatic habitat is very limited in West Virginia and these species are not important members of the avifauna. Seven other species have nested so few times in this state that it is impossible to clearly assign them to any particular geographical area, and three species are managed by the Department of Natural Resources to such an extent that the "normal" ranges are no longer apparent.

Sixty-seven species (38.1%) nest in all parts of the state and at all elevations, although their populations may vary widely from one location to another. Thus, the following analysis is based on only 86 species (48.9%). The large number of state-wide species (many of the unanalyzed species no doubt should also fall into this category) is a good indicator of the relative homogeneity of the state.

On the basis of the 86 species whose distribution can be analyzed, I believe that it is possible to recognize three Avifaunal Regions in the state. These regions very closely approximate the three divisions of the deciduous forests in the state discussed above. The three Avifaunal Regions are (Fig. 2): The *Western Hills Avifaunal Region*; the *Allegheny Mountains Avifaunal Region*; and the *Ridge and Valley Avifaunal Region*. The Allegheny Mountain Region

is quite distinct from the other two, which are only rather subtly distinguishable from each other.

The Western Hills Region has a list of 143 species known to have nested at least once in the region. This figure may be corrected to a breeding list of 122 species by subtracting those that nest only in a few isolated places or those that have nested on only a few occasions. The Allegheny Mountains Region has a breeding list of 124 species (122 corrected) and the Ridge and Valley Region has a list of 122 species (113 corrected).

In order to test the distinctness of these regions, I computed a "Percentage of Resemblance" between the regions by the following formula:

$$\text{Percentage Resemblance} = \frac{c \times 100}{a + b - c}$$

where a and b are the number of species breeding in each of any two regions and c is the number of species found in both regions. The results of this calculation are given for the corrected breeding lists with the values for the total breeding list in parentheses. The Western Hills Region shares 107 species (122) with the Ridge and Valley Region giving a Resemblance of 82.3% (84.7%) and the Western Hills Region also shares 80 species (94) with the Allegheny Mountains Region giving a Resemblance of 48.2% (53.7%). The Allegheny Mountains Region shares 78 species (86) with the Ridge and Valley Region giving a resemblance of 49.6% (53.4%). We can conclude from the calculations that the Allegheny Mountains Avifaunal Region is safely separable from the other two, but that these latter are perhaps doubtfully separable.

The Allegheny Mountains Avifaunal Region

This Avifaunal Region includes the Allegheny Mountains physiographic section of the Appalachian Plateau Province and portions of the Ridge and Valley physiographic province east to Allegheny Mountain and the Virginia border, as well as some of the Unglaciated Plateau Section south into Greenbrier County. Thus, it is essentially the same as the Allegheny Mountain Forest Section of Braun (1950). The western boundary of the Region might be selected as the 750-m (2,500-ft) contour in the south declining to the 600-m (2,000-ft) contour in the north. There are elevations above 600 m in Raleigh and Mercer Counties that are not contiguous with this region, but since these areas lack most of the characteristic mountain species they are not included.

Forty-one species (Table 2) may be said to be characteristic of the Allegheny Mountains Region,

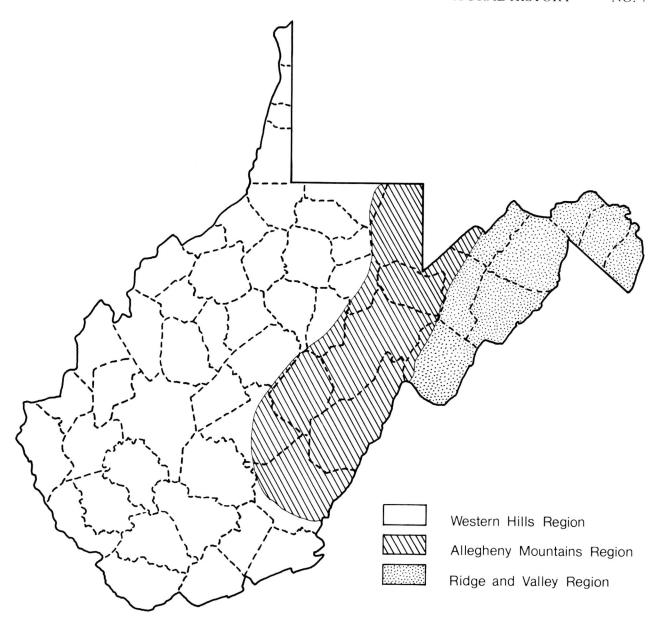

Fig. 2.   The Avifaunal Regions of West Virginia.

including four species whose nests have not actually been found. Several of these species do nest in small numbers in other parts of the state—for example, in the high country to the southwest or in the extreme Northern Panhandle—but the populations in the Allegheny Mountains are usually much larger than in these other places. Twenty-five of these 40 species (marked * in Table 2) are not known to nest outside of the Mountain Region. Indeed, 14 (marked with a † in Table 2) of these species reach the southern extremity of their range in West Virginia.

Since the Appalachians are higher in North Carolina and Tennessee and the boreal forest is more extensive there, it is puzzling that these species do not nest farther south. In a few cases, we may speculate as to the reasons. Such species as the Common Snipe, the Nashville Warbler, the Northern Water-

thrush, and the White-throated Sparrow probably are missing from south of West Virginia, since their semi-wetland habitat is essentially missing there. Indeed the White-throated Sparrow has been known to nest in West Virginia only once, and then only in the extreme north of the state. The red spruce forest in West Virginia is disjunct, being separated from the spruce forest in northeastern Pennsylvania and from that in the mountains of North Carolina and Tennessee. These southern spruce forests may be treated as ecological islands.

MacArthur and Wilson (1967) have shown that the number of species inhabiting an island varies inversely with the distance of the island from the continental mainland. If the spruce forest of the southern Appalachians can be considered to form a chain of islands extending from the boreal forest "mainland" in New York and New England, we should expect some "mainland" species to be missing even from the closest "islands" and additional species would be absent from the more distant islands. Thus the Yellow-rumped Warbler until recently has been absent and, for practical purposes, the White-throated Sparrow is absent from the closest "island," the Allegheny Mountains in West Virginia, while other species such as the Swainson's Thrush occur in West Virginia but are missing from the farther "island" in North Carolina.

However, the island analogy does not explain the limitations in range in all cases. The habitats for the Magnolia Warbler and for the Black-throated Blue Warbler are very similar and these habitats appear to be essentially continuous from New York (and farther north) to Georgia along the main Appalachian backbone. The Black-throated Blue Warbler does occur as a nesting species as far south as Georgia, but the Magnolia Warbler reaches its limit of range in West Virginia. The reason for this difference is not apparent. (In 1974 and 1975, Magnolia Warblers were found for the first time in the summer in southwestern Virginia and northeastern Tennessee.) Two grassland species, the Bobolink and the Savannah Sparrow, are no doubt very recent invaders into the southern Appalachians from the north and west, and perhaps they have not had time enough since the clearing of the forests to extend their ranges farther south, although the sparrow has been found sparingly in Tennessee since the mid-1970s.

The majority of the species characteristic of the Allegheny Mountains Region are forest species and have the centers of their distributions to the north of West Virginia. They have probably been in the state for a very long time, and indeed during the Pleistoscene glaciation these species had a much wider distribution than at present and occurred at lower elevations. The West Virginia boreal forest not only occurred at lower elevations but was continuous with the boreal forest to the north. No doubt certain boreal species that are not now present in West Virginia did occur here at that time. The remains of Spruce Grouse (*Dendragapus canadensis*) and the Gray Jay (*Perisoreus canadensis*) have been found at Natural Chimneys, Virginia (Guilday, 1962) and no doubt these occurred in West Virginia. Such species as the Black-backed Woodpecker, Boreal Chickadee, Yellow-bellied Flycatcher, Philadelphia Vireo, and several of the northern warblers may also have occurred here. The factors that eliminated these species as nesting birds in the southern Appalachians but allowed others to survive are unknown. It is noted, however, that all the nonmigratory species (such as the woodpecker, jay, and chickadee) are gone and only species that migrate south in winter remain. The nonmigratory species

Table 2.—*Species characteristic of the Allegheny Mountains Avifaunal Region.*

Northern Harrier*†	Hermit Thrush*†
Sharp-shinned Hawk	Solitary Vireo
Northern Goshawk*	Nashville Warbler*†
Golden Eagle	Chestnut-sided Warbler
Common Snipe*†	Magnolia Warbler*†
Northern Saw-whet Owl	Black-throated Blue Warbler*
Yellow-bellied Sapsucker*	Yellow-rumped Warbler*
Olive-sided Flycatcher*	Blackburnian Warbler
Alder Flycatcher*†	Northern Waterthrush*†
Least Flycatcher	Mourning Warbler*†
Tree Swallow*	Canada Warbler*
Cliff Swallow	Rose-breasted Grosbeak
Common Raven	Savannah Sparrow
Black-capped Chickadee*	Swamp Sparrow†
Red-breasted Nuthatch*	White-throated Sparrow*†
American Brown Creeper	Dark-eyed Junco*
Winter Wren*	Bobolink†
Sedge Wren	Purple Finch*†
Golden-crowned Kinglet*	Red Crossbill*
Veery*	Pine Siskin*
Swainson's Thrush*†	

* Species that are not known to nest outside of the Allegheny Mountains Region.

† Species that reach the southern limit of their range in West Virginia. (Two of these, Magnolia Warbler and Savannah Sparrow, occurred south of West Virginia in 1975.)

may have been eliminated in the period of warm dry climate which is thought to have occurred from about 9,000 to 2,500 years ago.

The Bobolink, Rose-breasted Grosbeak, and Savannah Sparrow have small nesting populations in the Northern Panhandle in the Western Hills Region that are contiguous, or nearly so, with the main breeding range of these species. The sparrow also occurs along the western boundary of the Allegheny Mountains at elevations lower than 600 m at least as far south as Raleigh County. Bobolinks also have been found in small numbers in the higher country of Raleigh County.

The Western Hills Avifaunal Region

The Western Hills Avifaunal Region shares most of its species with the Ridge and Valley Avifaunal Region. Besides the 67 statewide species, 20 species (Table 3) occur nearly statewide except in the higher mountains. Although a few of these may occur at times as high as 900 m the greatest populations will be below 600 m. Fourteen of these species have ranges that extend for some distance both north and south of West Virginia. Many of these species are distinctly southern in origin and have invaded our area from the south long enough ago to now extend well north of West Virginia. Five southern species (marked *) are actively extending their ranges north at present. The northern limits of their ranges are either now in West Virginia or else have only in recent years been extended beyond the state. The

Table 3.—*Species found statewide except in the Allegheny Mountains.*

Black Vulture*	White-eyed Vireo*
Northern Bobwhite	Yellow-throated Vireo
Red-bellied Woodpecker	Yellow-throated Warbler*
Acadian Flycatcher	American Redstart
Eastern Kingbird	Worm-eating Warbler
Purple Martin	Louisiana Waterthrush
Carolina Chickadee	Summer Tanager*
Carolina Wren	Blue Grosbeak*
Blue-gray Gnatcatcher	Orchard Oriole
Northern Mockingbird	Northern Oriole

* Southern species whose northern limit of range occurs in West Virginia or has done so until relatively recently.

White-eyed Vireo has advanced well to the north of West Virginia. The Black Vulture occurs only in the lower Potomac drainage in the Eastern Panhandle and in parts of the New River drainage in the Western Hills, indicating that it has invaded the state from the south along these river systems.

Only three, or possibly four, species may be said to characterize the Western Hills Region. These are the Cerulean, Kentucky, and Hooded Warblers, and possibly the Blue-winged Warbler. The first three of these do occur sparingly in the Ridge and Valley Region, but they reach very high populations in the forested areas of the Western Hills. One or the other of them may be the most numerous breeding warbler in many places. The Hooded and Kentucky Warblers are southern species that have been in this area for a long time, possibly since the mixed mesophytic forest succeeded the northern hardwoods forest in post-glacial times. Presumably they entered the state from the southwest, possibly along the Ohio River, and have been present long enough to have spread throughout the region. The Cerulean Warbler is a midwestern deciduous forest endemic, and indeed probably this species originated in this general area. The Blue-winged Warbler is a much more recent invader from the southwest and probably has arrived only since the removal of the forest in the last two centuries. This species is common only in the lower Kanawha and Ohio Valleys, which suggests that it has entered the state along the Ohio River but has not had time to spread from that valley. It has not, as yet, become numerous in the Monongahela Valley.

Swainson's Warbler is a species found only in certain parts of the Western Hills, notably in the Kanawha Valley. This southern species may also have entered the state along the New River Valley. If so, it is remarkable that only this warbler, possibly the Yellow-throated Warbler, and the Black Vulture have entered the state along this river which originates in the Blue Ridge Province in North Carolina and cuts a low-elevation pathway through the Appalachians.

At one time, I thought it might be possible to divide the Western Hills into a northern and a southern subregion. Other than the rather nebulous line that marks the area to the south where the Summer Tanager is more common than the Scarlet Tanager in contrast to the reverse situation to the north, no possible boundary suggested itself. This separation is highly unsatisfactory; consequently, I do not recognize any subregions.

The Ridge and Valley Avifaunal Region

As noted earlier, the Ridge and Valley Region is barely distinct from the Western Hills Region. No species occur on the complete list for this region that do not also occur in the Western Hills Region. The four warbler species that characterize the Western Hills are essentially absent from this region. Several species of transient warblers (e.g., Nashville, Tennessee, and Cape May) are uncommon in this region. However, several species do occur elsewhere in the state, but at present reach their greatest numbers in the Ridge and Valley Region. These are the Upland Sandpiper, Red-headed Woodpecker, Bewick's Wren, Loggerhead Shrike, Pine Warbler, Blue Grosbeak, and Lark Sparrow. Of these the woodpecker, wren, and sparrow once had a much wider distribution in the state, and indeed all three probably entered the state from the west. Within the last half century all three have declined and at present their stronghold is in the dry valleys of the Ridge and Valley Region. The Red-headed Woodpecker population has been seriously compromised by the presence of the introduced Starling. The Bewick's Wren does still occur in small numbers in the western part of the state, even in the high mountains, but it has been eliminated from much of its range by the influx of the House Wren, which has occurred within the memory of persons still living. The Lark Sparrow was once extremely common west of the mountains and scarce east of them. The western population has disappeared, except for a few still nesting in Jackson County and possibly nearby counties. There the habitat is not unlike that in the east.

The Pine Warbler, which is almost totally restricted to stands of Virginia and pitch pines, also has good populations in those parts of the Western Hills Region where these pines are common. The Upland Sandpiper, a bird of the grasslands, has reached West Virginia only recently and has presumably come from the grasslands to the north along the Great Appalachian Valley. At present, its range does not go south of West Virginia.

Prior to about 1950, the Common Grackle might have been considered to be a species characteristic of the Ridge and Valley Region, while being in low numbers elsewhere, but in the last 25 years this species has staged a great population explosion and now is common throughout the state in suitable habitat.

The above analysis has accounted for all but 13 of the analyzed species. Four of these 13 species are grassland species that entered the state only after the settlement of the area converted the original forest to grassland in places. These are the Dickcissel, Vesper Sparrow, Henslow's Sparrow, and Bachman's Sparrow. The Vesper Sparrow occurs almost statewide but seems to be very scarce in the southwest for reasons that are not apparent. Bachman's Sparrow invaded the state from the west in the early part of this century. It was extremely common for several years, but at present it has almost disappeared. Henslow's Sparrow was first found in the state only about 40 years ago. It reaches peak numbers in habitats representing the very earliest stages in plant succession; consequently, its populations are subject to sudden ups and downs in given areas. The Dickcissel presumably has never been very common in the state and today is only of sporadic occurrence.

Two warbler species, the Golden-winged and Black-throated Green, have distributions that do not fit any neat pattern. The Golden-winged Warbler is most common in parts of the Western Hills, away from the major river valleys, but it does occur in the Allegheny Mountains and in the western part of the Ridge and Valley Region. It does not occur in the upper Ohio Valley and in the Eastern Panhandle. The Black-throated Green Warbler, which is often considered to be a northern species, nests throughout the state except in the extreme Eastern Panhandle, the lowlands of the Ridge and Valley Region, and the Ohio Valley, including the lowlands of the Monongahela drainage. However, this species reaches its greatest numbers in the Allegheny Mountains, particularly in the mixed spruce-hardwoods forest.

Several other species defy easy classification. The Bank Swallow and the Prothonotary Warbler are found in various parts of the state at low elevations, but apparently their distribution is limited more by the availability of suitable nesting habitat than by any other factor. The Whip-poor-will was once common throughout the state except in the mountains, but its population has been declining for several years and it has disappeared from many of its former stations. The two cuckoo species occur almost statewide and are sympatric in many places. The Yellow-billed is not generally found at high elevations (above 800 m) and the Black-billed is seldom found at the lowest elevations.

ECOLOGICAL ANALYSIS

The breeding species in West Virginia may also be analyzed on the basis of the ecological situation

Table 4.—*Distribution of breeding species in broad ecological categories.*

Habitat	No. of species	Percent of total
Forest	82	46.6
Open land	21	11.9
Park and urban	31	17.6
Aquatic	33	18.8
No preference	9	5.1
Total	176	100.0

preferred for nesting. Table 4 shows the distribution of the 176 nesting species according to five more or less subjective ecological categories: Forest Birds; Open Land Birds; Park and Urban Birds; Aquatic Birds; and birds of No Preference. It is seen that 46.6% of the species are Forest Birds.

The list contains 64 non-passerine species, including most of the aquatic species known to nest in the state. Most of these either nest in so few places or else have nested on so few occasions that their contribution to the avifauna is quite small. The large raptors, both hawks and owls, are difficult to place in tidy little classifications. For these reasons, it seems reasonable to examine in detail the ecological distribution of only the 112 passerine species.

For this purpose the habitats of the state are divided into the following eight categories:

1. *Mature Forest:* Forest with a closed crown and either an open understory or one with plant species differing from the trees. Not necessarily a climax forest.
2. *Seral Forest:* Seral stages of development from small shrubs until the lower branches of trees die and the crown closes.
3. *Park and Residential:* Habitat with widely spaced trees mixed with grassy areas, shrubs, and buildings. A habitat with much "edge."
4. *Savannah:* Widely spaced trees mixed with grassland. Much of the pastureland in the state falls in this category.
5. *Grassland or Other Openland:* Meadow, pasture, weedfields, golf courses, airports, cropland, and recovered surface mines.
6. *Wet Woodland:* Mature swamp forest, wet brushy areas, wooded streambanks and small bogs surrounded by forest.
7. *Wet Meadow or Marsh:* Marshes and low-lying meadows that may be flooded.
8. *Aquatic Habitats:* Large streams or ponds.
9. *No Preference:* Species that seem to be equally at home in a wide variety of habitats.

Each species has been assigned to one, two, or three of these habitats; if found in more than one, these have been ranked as first, second, or third choices. The number of species in each category is

Plate 1.   Virgin Red Spruce, Pendleton County. Blackburnian Warblers and Golden-crowned Kinglets will be abundant in this habitat. *U.S. Forest Service.*

Plate 2.   Young Red Spruce Forest, Randolph County. Magnolia Warblers and Dark-eyed Juncos are the most common species in this forest. *U.S. Forest Service.*

Plate 3.   Virgin Northern Hardwoods forest, Nicholas County. Red-eyed Vireos, Ovenbirds, and Black-throated Green Warblers are abundant in this habitat. *U.S. Forest Service.*

Plate 4.   Top of Allegheny Front Mountain, Tucker County. Stunted Red Spruce mixed with areas covered with grass or with heath scrub. Chestnut-sided Warblers and Dark-eyed Juncos are the most abundant in the scrub. Hermit Thrushes are common in the larger spruce groves. *U.S. Forest Service.*

Plate 5.   Grass-covered Mountain top ("sods"), Pocahontas County. Rather few species of birds will nest in these areas when the grass is this high. Areas that are more heavily grazed have Savannah Sparrows and Vesper Sparrows. *U.S. Forest Service.*

Plate 6.   View from Bickell's Knob, Randolph County. Typical Allegheny Mountain scene, with mixed grassy areas ("sods") and northern hardwoods. *U.S. Forest Service.*

Plate 7.   The Cranberry Glades, Pocahontas County. *U.S. Forest Service.*

Plate 8.   Mixed farmland and forest, western part of the Ridge and Valley Region, Pendleton County. *U.S. Forest Service.*

Table 5.—*Distribution of passerine species in habitat categories.*

Habitat	First	(%)	Second	Third	Total	(%)	Corrected	(%)
Mature forest	37	(33.0)	8	2	47	(29.0)	37.5	(33.5)
Seral forest	25	(22.3)	10		35	(21.6)	20.5	(18.3)
Park and residential	16	(14.2)	11	2	29	(17.9)	15	(13.3)
Savannah	7	(6.3)	6	4	17	(10.4)	10-1/6	(9.1)
Grassland and openland	12	(10.7)	2		14	(8.6)	12.5	(11.2)
Wet woodland	7	(6.3)	2	1	10	(6.2)	7-5/6	(7.0)
Wet meadow or marsh	3	(2.7)	1		4	(2.5)	3	(2.7)
Aquatic	1	(0.9)	1		2	(1.2)	1.5	(1.3)
No preference	4	(3.6)			4	(2.5)	4	(3.6)

given in Table 5. The total number of species in the first three choices is tabulated for each habitat as well as a corrected (weighted) figure for each habitat. Thus the Chipping Sparrow, for example, was assigned first choice in the Park and Residential, second in the Seral Forest, and third in the Savannah. The corrected number of species for each of these habitats thus includes one-third of a species for each as the contribution of the Chipping Sparrow.

Perhaps the most important point to be derived from these data is that 55.3% of the nesting passerines have a first choice in forested habitats (both mature and seral) and that 51.8% of the species (corrected) are Forest Species. This result is certainly not surprising considering the preponderance of forest habitat in the state at present and the fact that when the first settlers came to the state forest covered almost all of the state. These forest species have presumably been present in this region for a long time, possibly since post-glacial times. A few of the species found in the seral stages have invaded the state in historic times since the removal of the forest cover.

The 35 species found in the Park and Residential habitat, the Savannah, and the Grassland are of two groups. Some of these have been present in the state for a long time. Presumably they arrived in the dry-warm period mentioned above when grassland probably occurred more extensively. When the forest returned, these species were reduced to small remnant populations that have again expanded with the opening of the forest. The other group of species have arrived only since the clearing of the forests in the last 200 years. Indeed, some have arrived in the state within the memory of persons still living.

CHANGES IN BIRD HABITATS AND BIRD POPULATIONS

The major change in habitat in the state within historic times has been the removal of much of the forest from the lowlands and the conversion of these areas into farmland and, at a somewhat later date, the removal of the mountain forests by the lumber industry—a process that still continues. The major effect of this deforestation has been the homogenization of the bird distribution. Over the years the lines of demarcation, which were never too sharp in any event, between the different floristic areas of the state have been blurred. We have no data about the distribution of birds in the state at about 1800, but it seems likely that fewer than the 67 species outlined above would have been statewide species at that time. The removal of the original forest and the conversion of much of the state into a fairly uniform seral condition permitted many southern species to move to higher elevations than they had occupied before, and also permitted some northern species to move to lower elevations. At the same time the deforestation occurred there was a warming trend in the climate, which allowed many of the species to remain throughout the state even when the northern forests began to return.

The latter half of the 20th Century, however, is experiencing changes in habitat that may be more profound than any that have gone before. Many areas are becoming extensively urbanized. The amount of land that has been covered with pavement, both in the huge parking lots currently being built and the extensive amount of new highways represents a not inconsiderable area. Modern highways introduce not only several strips of pavement but an even broader strip of relatively sterile grassland in the right of way. Few species of birds utilize these areas.

The surface-mining operations throughout the state have removed sizeable acreage from almost any biological productivity. In some places, these operations have altered the terrain to an extent that is almost geological.

An unknown fraction, but not a small one, of the streams of the state have been polluted to the extent that no aquatic life remains, and the other wetland habitats, always scarce in West Virginia, remain in danger of being drained.

This book attempts to describe the bird life of the state as it was in the third quarter of the 20th Century. It will remain for ornithologists of the future to record the changes produced by these major habitat changes in the last quarter.

SPECIES ACCOUNTS

The species of birds are recognized to be valid members of the state list according to the following set of criteria (Hall, 1971). A species is accepted for the regular list if: (1) A specimen has at some time been collected in the state and has been examined by a competent ornithologist. Some of these specimens apparently are no longer in existence or cannot now be located. Species for which no specimen is known are marked with (*); (2) a recognizable photograph has been taken of the bird in the state and has been examined by a competent ornithologist; (3) the bird has been handled by a bander and released, providing the bander and his associates have been judged competent to identify the species; (4) one or more sight records, each of which involved at least three persons having previous experience with the species, have been made in the state; and (5) there have been repeated sight records over the years by persons having previous experience with the species, but for which fewer than three persons were involved in each sighting.

These criteria represent a middle ground of acceptance. A strict standard would not recognize species unless specimens had been taken, but in the 1980s it seems more realistic to realize that specimen records are not always possible for some species. Species that probably have been reported correctly, but which do not meet one of these criteria, are classified as "Hypothetical."

NOMENCLATURE AND ARRANGEMENT

The nomenclature and sequence of families and species within families follows the forthcoming Sixth Edition of the American Ornithologist's Union Check-list of North American Birds (A.O.U., 1983) as given in the 34th Supplement to the Check-list (A.O.U., 1982). This sequence and some of the names vary from the more familiar 5th Edition of the Check-list (A.O.U., 1957).

DEFINITION OF TERMS

Terms Denoting Status

Permanent Resident.—A species for which individual birds are to be found in a given place throughout the year. Not applied to species for which different individuals are present in the summer than in the winter.

Summer Resident.—Species found throughout the summer, usually on established territories, but for which the same individuals are not present in winter. Such species are understood to migrate into and out of the state and may be more numerous during the migration seasons than in the summer.

Summer Visitant.—A species found in the sum-mer, but not known to establish breeding territories. Difficult to separate from some migrants.

Winter Visitant.—A species that nests elsewhere, but spends all or part of the winter in the state. Also applied to those species for which different individuals are present in winter than in summer.

Migrant.—A species to be found in the state only during a period of migration, although occasional individuals may remain in the state after the migration season is over.

Local.—A species occurring only in a restricted part of the state.

Accidental.—Those species for which there are fewer than four or five records.

Casual.—Those species that have been recorded more frequently than the "Accidentals" but which cannot be expected every year, or even in a period of years.

Terms Describing Populations

Very Abundant.—Species for which more than 1,000 individuals can be seen by a single observer in a full day's work in the field in a suitable habitat. A species for which more than 300 individuals can be listed on a 24.5-mile Breeding Bird Survey.

Abundant.—A species for which an observer can see between 201 to 1,000 in a full day's work in a suitable habitat. A species for which 101 to 300 individuals can be listed on a 24.5-mile Breeding Bird Survey. A species for which a Singing Male Census has a density of more than 100 males per 100 ha.

Very Common.—A species for which an observer can see between 51 and 100 in a full day's work in a suitable habitat. A species for which between 31 and 100 individuals can be listed on a 24.5-mile Breeding Bird Survey Route. A species which has a density of between 51 and 100 males per 100 ha on a Singing Male Census.

Common.—A species for which an observer can see between 21 and 50 individuals in a day. A species for which between 11 and 30 can be listed on a Breeding Bird Survey, a species with a density between 26–50 males per 100 ha on a Singing Male Census.

Fairly Common.—A species for which an observer would list between 7 and 20 in a full day. A species for which between 4 and 10 would be listed on a Breeding Bird Survey Route. A species with a density of between 11 and 25 males per 100 ha on a Singing Male Census.

Uncommon.—A species for which an observer will list between 1 and 6 in a full day's work. A species for which between 1 and 3 individuals will be listed on a Breeding Bird Survey Route. A species with a density of between 6 and 10 males per 100 ha on a Singing Male Census.

Rare.—A species for which an observer can expect to list between 1 and 6 birds per season, but which is found in every appropriate season.

MIGRATION DATES

The arrival and departure dates for most migrants is highly variable from place to place. In the accounts, the broad picture of the migration period for each species is sketched out and then average arrival and departure dates are given for several locations. I have used the average dates rather than extreme dates, since I fully agree with the viewpoint on extreme dates expressed by Trautman and Trautman (1968). West Virginia bird observers have not been especially diligent about keeping migration dates; consequently, there are fewer of these data than might be desirable.

DEFINITE NESTING RECORDS

Most species that are present throughout the summer can be considered to nest in the state, but I give definite breeding records only in those cases where an occupied nest was found or parent birds were seen feeding recently fledged young. In a few cases, it is not known whether or not the nest found was actually occupied (e.g., too high in a tree to be investigated), but in these cases the benefit of doubt is given.

QUANTITATIVE DATA

Four sets of numerical data have been used where appropriate and where available:

Singing Male Censuses

Since 1948, between two and six censuses made by the Singing Male Method (also known as the Spot-mapping Method) have been made on each of the Brooks Bird Club Forays. Other such censuses have been made on the small-scale replica of the Foray known as the Sortie, and by single individuals. These data have been summarized for each species, and an average density (males per 100 hectares) is given for those species that have occurred on these studies. The habitat types having the highest populations for each species are then listed, together with the location, elevation, and population density as number of males per 100 ha.

Breeding Bird Surveys

Between 1966 and 1974, a total of 155 counts over 29 different routes representing all parts of the state had been carried out as a part of the Breeding Bird Survey program sponsored by the United States Fish and Wildlife Service. These counts follow a carefully specified and uniform procedure over the same 24.5-mile route each year, recording the birds identified during a three-minute stop at each of 50 stops located one-half mile apart. The data from these counts have been extracted from the computer files of the Wildlife Service and have been reported for each appropriate species as the average number listed per count per year for those counts that list the species, together with the averages for the routes having the highest and lowest averages.

Banding Data

Since about 1960, some rather extensive bird-banding programs have been carried out in various parts of the state, particularly at Charleston, Inwood, Morgantown, Wheeling, and Ona. The State Department of Natural Resources also has done some banding of waterfowl and woodcock. Records obtained from these operations have been used, but no attempt has been made to summarize them or examine them in detail. The exception has been the major project that has been studying the fall migration along the Allegheny Front in Grant-Tucker Counties each fall since 1958. Through the fall of 1981, a total of 76,091 birds of 110 species have been banded there. The data from this station, known as the Allegheny Front Migration Observatory (designated as A.F.M.O.), have been extensively used under the Fall Migration heading, both as to numbers banded and the migration dates.

Christmas Counts

For 46 species (Mourning Dove, woodpeckers, and passerines), Christmas Count data are given for the years 1963 to 1972 for eight different stations. So that meaningful comparisons can be made, the data are given as the 10-year average of birds seen per party-hour, together with the extreme range of this value. The Counts included, with the number of years of the count in parentheses, are: Charleston, Kanawha County (10); Charles Town, Jefferson County (9); Huntington, Cabell County (10); Inwood, Berkeley County (9); Mason County (9); Ona, Cabell County (10); Pendleton County (2); Lewisburg, Greenbrier County (7); and Hampshire County (3).

For waterfowl and other non-passerines, the total number of birds seen on each count is used rather than the birds per party-hour. A few Christmas Counts have been made elsewhere, but these counts were omitted since they were made only once in the 10-year period analyzed.

In the accounts under the heading of "Specimens," I have listed the museums in which specimens taken in the state have been preserved. I have personally examined almost all of these specimens, particularly those of the rarer or more unusual species.

The museums are designated by the following initials: AMNH—American Museum of Natural History, New York; BC—Bethany College, Bethany, West Virginia; CM—Carnegie Museum of Natural History, Pittsburgh, Pennsylvania; CU—Cornell University, Ithaca, New York; DMNH—Delaware Museum of Natural History, Greenville, Delaware; MCZ—Museum of Comparative Zoology, Harvard University, Cambridge, Massachusetts; MU—Marshall University, Huntington, West Virginia; OP—Oglebay Park, Wheeling, West Virginia; OSM—Ohio State Museum, Columbus, Ohio; S—Sunrise, Charleston, West Virginia; UMMZ—University of Michigan Museum of Zoology, Ann Arbor, Michigan; USNM—National Museum of Natural History, Washington, D.C.; WVU—West Virginia University, Morgantown, West Virginia; WVUM—West Virginia University Mounted Collection; and WFVZ—Western Foundation for Vertebrate Zoology, Los Angeles, California.

Three private collections also have been referred to: WAL—William A. Lunk Collection, currently at Ann Arbor, Michigan; ASM—Albert Sydney Morgan Collection, currently at Milton, West Virginia; GMS—that portion of the George M. Sutton Collection, currently at Bethany College.

The largest collections of West Virginia material are at The University of Michigan Museum of Zoology, the National Museum of Natural History, and West Virginia University, with many of the rarer specimens at Carnegie Museum. The mounted collection of West Virginia University has been poorly cared for, and some specimens are missing, possibly vandalized.

SUBSPECIES

In the section on "Specimens," I also have commented on the subspecies of the various species that have been identified from specimens collected in West Virginia. In a few cases, I am responsible for these identifications, but in most cases I have utilized the identifications made on specimen labels by competent authorities, although these authorities are not usually named. If no subspecies is mentioned under a polytypic species, it can be assumed that the one occurring in West Virginia is the expected one occurring in eastern North America.

Family Gaviidae   LOONS

RED-THROATED LOON

Gavia stellata (Pontoppidan)

Status: Casual local spring and fall migrant.

Records: Most of the reports of Red-throated Loons come from Cheat Lake, Monongalia County, where it was of fairly regular occurrence until the late 1960s. These records come in both spring and fall and as many as three birds were seen in a single day. From 1949 through 1956, it occurred every year, but since that time, it has been less frequently reported and the last report I have was 25 April 1965. Away from Cheat Lake it is accidental. A few scattered records exist from Cabell County, including 29 December 1963 (T. Igou) and 2 January 1967 as winter records. Three records exist from the Ohio River at Mason County; 22 November 1952 and 14 March 1953 (H. C. Land) and 6 October through 9 November 1970 (H. Slack). A. S. Morgan collected one at Poca, Putnam County, on 25 October 1932. One was seen on the Ohio River at Wheeling on 1 May 1966 (P. and F. Temple) and there are reports from Randolph (E. Hutton) and Greenbrier (C. Handley) Counties. One was seen in November 1980 at Harper's Ferry, Jefferson County (C. Miller).

Specimens: ASM (there are two specimens in this collection, one of which was the local specimen, but they were unmarked when examined by me).

COMMON LOON   *Gavia immer* (Brünnich)

Status: Uncommon to common spring migrant; uncommon to very common fall migrant; rare winter visitant.

Spring: The Common Loon migrates throughout the state, but it is rare or casual away from the larger bodies of water. It appears to be most common on Cheat Lake (originally called Lake Lynn), Monongalia County, and the other bodies of water in the northeastern part of the state. The species is rare on the Ohio and Kanawha Rivers and uncommon in the Potomac drainage. There are a few reports from some of the mountain ponds, such as Spruce Knob Lake, Randolph County. The usual arrival time in spring is about the first of April and most will have departed by 1 May. On Cheat Lake, loons frequently remain until mid-May and often give the yodeling call. On occasion, a loon will remain in the state well into June, and there is a late date of 23

June 1964 at Tygart Reservoir, Taylor County (R. T. Butterfield).

First-seen Spring Dates: Monongalia County, 1 April; Greenbrier County, 12 April; Mason-Cabell Counties, 14 April.

Fall: The loon generally arrives in late October and moves through the state until early December. As in spring, it is most common in the northwest and on occasion over 1,000 birds have been seen in one day on Cheat Lake. On the Ohio and Kanawha Rivers, it is more common than in spring but never reaches large numbers.

First-seen Fall Dates: Greenbrier County, 14 October; Cabell-Mason County, 23 October.

Winter: A few loons may winter in the state where there is open water. There are winter records from Jefferson, Monongalia, Randolph, Mason, Kanawha, and Cabell Counties.

Remarks: Occasionally during foggy rainy nights, loons are forced down, or perhaps mistakenly alight on wet pavement. These "crashes" have occurred in all parts of the state and sometimes involve sizeable numbers.

Until the 1960s, the Common Loon was a frequent and numerous migrant in both spring and fall on Cheat Lake, but in recent years the numbers have declined drastically and it is now unusual to see one. The cause of this is unknown.

Specimens: WVU, ASM, BC, MU.

Family Podicipedidae   GREBES

PIED-BILLED GREBE

Podilymbus podiceps (Linnaeus)

Status: Fairly common to common migrant (occasionally becoming abundant); rare local summer resident; uncommon winter visitant.

Spring: The Pied-billed Grebe migrates throughout the state and may be found on most bodies of water, including farm ponds and beaver ponds. However, the greatest numbers occur on the larger lakes and rivers. Since many birds winter or move into the state with the first mild weather, arrival dates are difficult to determine, but by early April peak numbers are present. Most of these have departed by early May.

Last-seen Spring Date: Cabell County, 6 May.

Summer: The Pied-billed Grebe is present in scattered places in summer and indeed may be more common than reports indicate. Many of these summer visitants are probably non-breeders who fail to migrate, but there are scattered breeding records. A nest was found at Leetown, Jefferson County, in 1939 (L. Poland) and elsewhere in Jefferson County (C. Miller). Downy young were found at Lake Avalon, Ohio County, in 1935 (R. West). An adult with young was found in Canaan Valley, Tucker County, in 1951 (W. R. DeGarmo) and birds have been seen in summer in a beaver pond atop the Allegheny Front (elevation, 1,100 m), Tucker County (Hall). There are several summer records from the McClintic Wildlife Station, Mason County, and young birds were seen there in 1972 (Matthews). Other June records come from Ridge, Morgan County; Gap Mills, Monroe County; Lake Terra Alta, Preston County; Cranberry Glades, Pocahontas County; Beaver Lake, Raleigh County; and Wood County.

Fall: In the fall this grebe occurs throughout the state, and large concentrations sometimes occur on the larger streams and lakes. On 13 October 1949, for example, a total of 347 were seen on the Kanawha River at Charleston (C. Handley), and similar concentrations have been reported from the Ohio River and from Cheat Lake. The birds begin to appear in mid-September (some of these may represent unrecognized breeders), but the peak comes in late October and early November.

First-seen Fall Date: Cabell-Mason County, 11 October.

Winter: A few Pied-bills may spend the winter on any of the ice-free larger streams in the state, and there are Christmas Count records on a regular basis from all localities having such a stream in the count area. In the case of freeze-up, these birds depart only to appear again when the ice melts.

Specimens: WVU, MU.

HORNED GREBE

Podiceps auritus (Linnaeus)

Status: Fairly common to common spring and fall migrant (occasionally abundant); casual to rare winter visitant.

Spring: The Horned Grebe migrates throughout the state, but most reports come from the areas with large bodies of water. The greatest numbers are to be seen at Cheat Lake, Monongalia County; Lake of the Woods, Preston County; the southern Ohio River in Mason and Cabell Counties; and on the Kanawha River in Kanawha and Putnam Counties. It is less common on the northern Ohio River and in the Potomac and Shenandoah Valleys. Away from these places, it becomes uncommon to casual.

Arrival dates are usually from mid-March to 1 April and a few birds may remain until mid-May.

First-seen Spring Dates: Monongalia County, 18 March.

Fall: The Horned Grebe is more common in fall than in spring, and sometimes impressive numbers occur. Rafts of several hundred have been seen on Cheat Lake, the Ohio River at Huntington, and the Kanawha River at Charleston. Most of the fall reports come from the same places as do the spring reports. It may appear as early as mid-October, but most records are in late October or early November.

Winter: There are numerous late December reports, particularly on Christmas Counts, from Jefferson, Pendleton, Monongalia, Ohio, Summers, Kanawha, Mason, and Cabell Counties. These reports may be of belated fall migrants, but there are a few records for January and early February in places that contain open water.

Specimen: WVU.

RED-NECKED GREBE *Podiceps grisegena* Boddaert

Status: Casual migrant.

Records: From 1948 to 1959, the Red-necked Grebe was seen almost annually on Cheat Lake, Monongalia County, in both spring and fall. Usually, the records were of single birds but in March 1948 Red-necked Grebes were present for nearly two weeks and up to nine were seen at one time (Frazier, 1948). Another influx, which coincided with a general "invasion" throughout the east, occurred from 14 March to 5 April 1959 when as many as 14 were seen on one day (Hall). There were a number of records on Cheat Lake in the late 1930s. Since 1960, it has seldom been reported from Cheat Lake, but one was seen on nearby Lake of the Woods, Preston County, on 19 March 1972 (R. Oades).

Elsewhere, there are only a few records. Doan (1888) reported that J. R. Mathers collected one near Buckhannon, Upshur County, in November 1884; T. Surber collected two at White Sulphur Springs, Greenbrier County; A. S. Morgan collected one at Poca, Putnam County, in February 1914; and P. C. Bibbee (1929) tells of an attempt to collect one in Wood County in April 1924. More recently there have been records from Cabell County, 24 May 1925 (Waldron); and 3 November 1951 (H. C. and H. K. Land) (Edeburn et al., 1960); Kanawha County, 3 December 1954 (C. Handley and C. Johnson) (Handley, 1976); Jefferson County, 20 March 1940 (Poland, 1941); Cacapon State Park, Morgan County, 26 March 1938 (Flouer, 1938); and Brooke County, 17 February 1934 (collected) (Weimer, 1935).

Specimens: WVU (unsatisfactory data), CM, ASM.

*EARED GREBE *Podiceps nigricollis* C. L. Brehm

Status: Hypothetical. Accidental visitant.

Record: There is one sight record for the Ohio River at Wheeling, Ohio County, 12 February 1955 (Shields, 1955).

Family Pelecanidae   PELICANS

AMERICAN WHITE PELICAN
Pelecanus erythrorhynchos Gmelin

Status: Accidental visitant.

Records: Two specimens were taken in Braxton County in late April 1910, one of which was examined by E. A. Brooks. During the same week, R. B. Cook noted a flock on the Ohio River in Wood County (M. Brooks, 1944). Brooks (1944) reported a specimen in the West Virginia University Museum taken on the Cacapon River, Morgan County. One was present on the Kanawha River at South Charleston from 30 October to 3 November 1943 and was seen by hundreds of people (Handlan, 1944). W. Argabrite found one on the Ohio River at Huntington, which was later seen by Edeburn, Kiff, and Igou on 1 November 1963 (Kiff, 1965).

Specimen: A specimen in the West Virginia University Museum (WVUM) may be the one referred to above but no data are given for it. Bibbee (1929) was doubtful that this specimen came from West Virginia.

Family Phalacrocoracidae   CORMORANTS

GREAT CORMORANT
Phalacrocorax carbo (Linnaeus)

Status: Accidental visitant.

Record: P. C. Bibbee (1929) reported that one was shot on the Ohio River at Parkersburg in November 1914 and was brought to him for mounting.

Specimen: The present location of this specimen is unknown.

DOUBLE-CRESTED CORMORANT
Phalacrocorax auritus (Lesson)

Status: Rare spring and fall migrant. Accidental to casual winter visitor.

Records: As with some of the other unusual waterbirds, most of the records of cormorants have come from Cheat Lake, Monongalia County. Until the late 1960s, this cormorant was of fairly regular occurrence there in both spring and fall. Most of these reports were of single birds, but small flocks were seen on occasion. The spring dates were from mid-April to mid-May, and the fall dates ranged from late October to early December. Elsewhere the bird is much less common. There are a few records for the Ohio River in the Northern Panhandle, and a few more from the Mason-Cabell County area.

There are three records from Kanawha County and reports from Jefferson, Barbour, Raleigh, Lincoln, Mercer, Summers, and Putnam Counties. In the spring of 1952, they were found at the old Stony River Reservoir, Grant County (DeGarmo). There is one December record from Cheat Lake and one December and one January record from Ohio County.

Remarks: Since the mid-1960s, there have been very few reports of cormorants, which parallels the general decline in population of this and other fish-eating birds concomitant with the pollution of the aquatic food chains with biocides. However, on Cheat Lake the decline in reports may be due to a totally different factor. Most of the cormorant sightings came from a portion of the lake that is no longer accessible by shore. This may also be an important factor in the decrease in reports of other species from that lake.

Specimens: WVU, MU.

Family Ardeidae   HERONS

AMERICAN BITTERN
Botaurus lentiginosus (Rackett)

Status: Uncommon migrant; rare to uncommon summer resident; casual winter visitor.

Spring: The American Bittern probably migrates throughout the state, arriving in mid-April. It usually occurs in marshy areas that would be suitable for breeding, but occasionally may be found at the edge of farm ponds, in wet meadows, or may be seen flying overhead. However, unlike most herons, this species is usually secretive and will stay concealed in the marsh vegetation. Because of this habit, it may appear to be less numerous than it really is.

First-seen Spring Date: Cabell-Mason Counties, 5 April.

Summer: The American Bittern has been found in summer in most of the marshy areas of the state. It is quite numerous in the Canaan Valley, Tucker County, where the only definite nesting record was made (Breiding, 1971). It has been found regularly at Ashton and the McClintic Wildlife Station in Mason County, at the Boaz marsh, Wood County, and at Altona Marsh, Jefferson County. Other summer records come from Berkeley Springs, Morgan County; Cranesville, Preston County; Randolph County; Greenbrier County; Gap Mills, Monroe County; on the Little Kanawha, Gilmer County; Jackson's Mill, Lewis County; Coonskin Park, Kanawha County; Hurricane, Putnam County; and Wayne County. Bitterns nest in marshes, particularly cat-tail marshes, that offer tall dense cover, but

in many cases they select marshes of surprisingly small size.

Fall: Fall records come from the same places where summer records have been made and most of the birds move through in late September and early October.

Winter: There have been several recent records on the Christmas Count at Ona, Cabell County, and there are winter records from Greenbrier County (C. Handley).

Specimens: USNM, MU.

LEAST BITTERN   *Ixobrychus exilis* (Gmelin)

Status: Uncommon, very local summer resident. Uncommon migrant.

Spring: The Least Bittern is present on the breeding marshes by mid-May, although there is a date of 27 April in Mason County. A Kanawha County record for 5 May, and one from Ohio County on 16 May are probably migration records. It probably migrates throughout the state, although it is seldom seen away from marshes of various kinds. Once in a while one will be found dead in an odd place away from water.

First-seen Spring Dates: Wood County, 11 May; Cabell-Mason Counties, 14 May.

Summer: The Least Bittern nests fairly regularly at three or four places in the state and may be more widespread than is known. In recent years it has been present every summer in the Boaz Marsh in Wood County. It nests, probably in every year, at the McClintic Wildlife Station, Mason County, and perhaps in a few other marshy areas of Mason County. Formerly it nested at the Federal Fish Hatchery at Leetown, Jefferson County, but changes in hatchery operation have changed the habitat for waterbirds there and the bittern may no longer nest; however, it probably does nest in the Altona Marsh, Jefferson County, in some years at least. The species was found on occasion, and may have nested at the former marsh at Beech Bottom, Brooke County. Other summer records come from Kanawha County (nest found by A. B. Brooks); Mercer County (P. Bibbee); Greenbrier County (near Alvon); and Tucker County (near Parsons).

Fall: A record from Jackson's Mill, Lewis County on 3 August (M. Brooks) may be of a migratory bird. Two seen in the remarkable concentration of shorebirds in Barbour County on 5 September 1936 (M. Brooks, 1936) were no doubt migrants. There is a September record for Cabell County. Two very late records come from Nicholas County (one found moribund on 9 November 1944) and one found dead in Preston County on 8 January 1967 (WVU specimen).

Populations: A wooded marsh in Mason County had a population of 32 males per 100 hectares (two males on the 6-hectare plot).

Specimens: WVU, MU.

GREAT BLUE HERON   *Ardea herodias* (Linnaeus)

Status: Uncommon to fairly common spring, summer, and fall visitant. Rare or casual summer resident; rare to locally fairly common winter visitant.

Spring: The Great Blue Heron may occur in almost any part of the state from March through mid-May. They are most numerous along the major streams and in the major marshy areas, but also often occur on small streams and ponds, and frequently can be seen flying overhead, far from any water.

First-seen Spring Dates: Summers County, 25 March; Ohio County, 5 April.

Summer: There are summer records from Jefferson, Berkeley, Hardy, Preston, Tucker, Randolph, Greenbrier, Monroe, Hancock, Brooke, Ohio, Wood, Upshur, Lewis, Webster, Summers, Kanawha, Putnam, Mason, Wayne, and Cabell Counties. It is fairly common in the Kanawha and Ohio Valleys, but elsewhere it is only occasionally seen. There are very few suitable nesting sites in the state and there are few actual nesting records. Bibbee (1929) quotes Surber as to its former nesting in Greenbrier County. A pair apparently nested near the East Lynn Reservoir, Wayne County in 1972 (W. Smith). There is an uncertain report of nesting near Vadis, Lewis

County, in recent years and E. A. Brooks had a report of half-grown birds seen near Weston many years ago.

Fall: In late July and August, the Great Blue Heron again may occur throughout the state in suitable habitat. Most of these birds are post-breeding wanderers from the south. At this time maximum numbers are reached and groups of 10 to 20 are occasionally seen. Most of these reports come from the lower Ohio and Kanawha Valleys and from the Eastern Panhandle. Many of the "summer records" given above no doubt fall in this category.

Winter: Many of the fall birds remain in the early winter, and a few spend the entire winter in places having open water and unfrozen marshes. They are found almost annually, sometimes in numbers, on the Christmas Counts at Charles Town, Jefferson County; Ona, Cabell County; Huntington, Cabell County; and Charleston, Kanawha County. There are other winter records from Berkeley, Pendleton, Hampshire, Hardy, Randolph, Greenbrier, Summers, Hancock, and Ohio Counties.

Specimens: WVU, OP, MU. The subspecies occurring is the nominate one, *herodias.*

GREAT EGRET   *Casmerodius albus* (Linnaeus)

Status: Rare to uncommon summer visitant.

Records: The Great Egret has occurred in all parts of the state in spring, summer, and fall. As with other waterbirds it occurs on the larger streams, except in densely forested areas, on farm ponds, and in the few marshes in the state. There are records for April and May in most places with an early date of 22 March in Putnam County. In the Kanawha Valley, it is regular in the spring. There are few reports from June, but it does occur from time to time in the early summer. Most of the records come from late July through September when the birds-of-the-year raised in the south wander northward. At this time it may occur throughout the state, but once again the greatest number of reports comes from the lower Kanawha Valley and the Eastern Panhandle. In the mountain areas and in Monongalia and Preston Counties, it is, at best, rare.

Although there are a few June records, there is no evidence that this species ever nested in the state.

Specimens: WVU, S.

*SNOWY EGRET   *Egretta thula* (Molina)

Status: Casual summer visitant.

Records: One was collected on the New River in Mercer County in July 1934 (P. Bibbee). One occurred at Lake Terra Alta, Preston County, during most of September 1936 (M. Brooks, 1938c). More recent records are: one in Cabell County, 2 May

1948 (Edeburn, et al., 1960); one in Wheeling, 20 August 1956 (T. Shields); one at McClintic Wildlife Station, Mason County, 13 May 1959 (C. Handley); one in Cabell County, 17 April 1974 (H. Slack); and one north of Wheeling, May 1975 (N. Laitsch).

Specimen: I have been unable to locate Bibbee's specimen, apparently the only one ever taken in the state.

LITTLE BLUE HERON *Egretta caerulea* (Linnaeus)

Status: Casual to rare late summer visitant.

Records: Immatures of this species wander on occasion into the state in late summer, with some records as early as late June. They are most common around large farm ponds and in the few marshes in level non-forested areas. There are records from Jefferson, Berkeley, Brooke, Ohio, Marshall, Preston, Randolph, Greenbrier, Monroe, Mercer, Lewis, Gilmer, Ritchie, Kanawha, Putnam, Mason, and Cabell Counties. These late-summer influxes were apparently more common in the 1930s than they have been recently.

There are spring records for adults from: Monongalia County, 11 May 1923 (M. Brooks); Ritchie County, 30 April 1874 (Brewster, 1875); and Mason County (McClintic Wildlife Station), 23 April 1974 (J. Stewart).

Specimens: WVU, CM.

CATTLE EGRET *Bubulcus ibis* (Linnaeus)

Status: Casual visitant.

Records: The Cattle Egret was first reported in the state from Kanawha County on 24 April 1967 (Shreve) (Anon. 1967). Since that time there have been other records from Kanawha County, 22 May 1972 (C. Katholi and D. Shearer) and 4 April 1974 (N. Gluck). There are spring reports from Nicholas County, 3 May 1970 (M. Trowbridge); Mason County, 12 May 1970 (H. Slack); Wayne County, 1 May 1971 (S. C. Church); Kearneysville, Jefferson County, 21 April 1972 (N. Dorsett); Hancock County, May 1974 (N. Laitsch); Preston County 4 June 1974 (D. Samuel); Greenbrier County, 20 April 1980 (C. Lanham); and Monroe County, spring 1967 (E. Bradley), spring 1969 (B. Bradley), spring 1974 (B. Walker). There were three fall records: near Buckhannon, Upshur County, 24 November 1967 (R. and M. Brooks), one shot by a hunter in Preston County in December 1967, and from Franklin, Pendleton County, 15 November 1979 (C. Ruddle).

Remarks: This species can be expected to appear more regularly, particularly in the agricultural land of the Eastern Panhandle and the lower Kanawha River.

Specimen: WVUM.

GREEN-BACKED HERON
Butorides striatus (Linnaeus)

Status: Fairly common migrant. Uncommon to fairly common summer resident. Accidental winter visitant.

Spring: The Green-backed Heron arrives from mid-April to early May and the migratory movement lasts until the third week in May. At this time, they may be found along any stream in the state except the high mountain streams, as well as on farm ponds and other lakes.

First-seen Spring Dates: Cabell-Mason Counties, 19 April; Monongalia County, 6 May.

Summer: The Green-backed Heron probably nests in every county in the state. It does not frequent the rocky streams in the heavily forested mountains, but does occur in the mountain valleys. As with most other fish-eating birds, the population has probably declined as the result of the pollution of many small streams by acid run-off of mine waters. Green-backed Herons will nest singly or in small loose colonies in the trees along streams of nearly any size or near lakes or farm ponds. There are definite nesting records from Hardy, Preston, Lewis, Randolph, Greenbrier, Summers, Raleigh, Brooke, Ohio, Wood, Jackson, Lincoln, Kanawha, Mason, and Cabell Counties.

Fall: The Green-backed Heron departs in mid-September and most will be gone by early October, although a few may remain until late November. On the night of 14 September 1974, a large number of calling Green-backed Herons was noted flying over Blackwater Falls State Park, Tucker County. The flight lasted for several hours and several thousand birds were thought to have passed over this site (Wylie, 1974).

Last-seen Fall Date: Cabell-Mason Counties, 20 September.

Winter: There are several Christmas Count reports in recent years; Charles Town, 1967, Charleston, 1971 and 1974, and Wheeling.

Remarks: This species is called Green Heron in earlier literature.

Specimens: WVU, OP, CM, MU. West Virginia specimens are the subspecies *virescens*.

BLACK-CROWNED NIGHT-HERON
Nycticorax nycticorax (Linnaeus)

Status: Uncommon to fairly common migrant; uncommon summer visitant; rare winter visitant.

Spring: Night Herons begin to migrate in late February or early March and most records come in late March or April. Besides those counties having summer records, there are spring records from Kanawha, Raleigh, Berkeley, and Monongalia Counties. A group of 15 roosted near Nitro, Kanawha County, in March and April 1950. The birds are most often seen roosting in streamside trees or else are heard giving their characteristic calls as they fly overhead at night.

Summer: There are summer records for Jefferson, Hardy, Tucker, Barbour, Greenbrier, Summers, Hancock, Brooke, Ohio, Wood, Mason, and Cabell Counties. The only nesting records come from Wheeling Island, Ohio County, and Short Creek, Brooke County in the 1930s (T. Shields). It is possible that a few pairs nest along the Potomac or Shenandoah Rivers in the Eastern Panhandle. Adults and young flying birds were seen at Leetown, Jefferson County, on 23 August 1953 (C. Miller), but these may have been reared in Maryland or Virginia.

Fall: There are fall or late-summer records from Jefferson, Berkeley, Monongalia, Ohio, Wood, Kanawha, Mason, and Cabell Counties. Grose (1945) reports one from Troy, Gilmer County, without date.

Winter: A few birds may spend the winter in the state on occasion from along the Ohio and Kanawha Rivers in Mason, Cabell, and Kanawha

Counties. They were seen in Wheeling on 4 December 1955 and 29 December 1956 (T. Shields).
Specimens: WVU, UMMZ, MU.

YELLOW-CROWNED NIGHT-HERON
Nycticorax violacea (Linnaeus)

Status: Casual spring and summer visitant.
Records: There are five spring records: McClintic Wildlife Station, Mason County, 16 April 1966 (G. Hurley); Dailey, Randolph County, 14 April 1961 (R. Britten); Morgantown, 15 April 1925 (WVU specimen) and 15 April 1973 (Hall); and Parkersburg, 10 May 1978 (Means). All other records are for late summer or early fall and come from Leetown, Jefferson County (specimen—L. Poland); Wheeling (specimen—A. B. Brooks, 1930); Boaz, Wood County (J. Stewart); Poca, Putnam County (specimens—Morgan); and several records from near Charleston, Kanawha County, from late June to mid-September. There are no breeding records for the state, but it may have nested on occasion in Kanawha County.
Specimens: WVU, USNM.

Family Threskiornithidae   IBISES

*WHITE IBIS   *Eudocimus albus* (Linnaeus)

Status: Accidental visitant.
Record: Two immature birds were seen and photographed on the South Branch of the Potomac River near Franklin, Pendleton County, on 29

August and 7 September 1980 (C. Ruddle). These birds were a part of a major influx of this species along the East Coast, which brought many sightings north of the usual range.
Specimen: A photograph is on file in the U.S. National Photoduplicate File at Laurel, Maryland.

Family Ciconiidae   STORKS

WOOD STORK   *Mycteria americana* Linnaeus

Status: Accidental visitant.
Records: One was collected by A. Wall at Bloomery, Hampshire County, in 1884 (Wall, 1884). This record is presumably the basis for the listing of the species for the state by Rives (1890). A. S. Morgan collected one on Coal River, Kanawha County, in July 1928 (E. A. Brooks, 1934). One was seen by WVU Forestry students and M. Brooks on

Anthony Creek, Greenbrier County, in July 1949. One was present and was photographed in Pendleton County from 17 August to 7 September 1973 (C. Ruddle).
Specimen: The Kanawha County specimen collected by Morgan is mounted in the Center for Culture and History adjacent to the State Capitol Complex in Charleston. A photograph of the Pendleton County bird was published in *American Birds,* 28: 52, 1974.

Family Anatidae

Until rather recently West Virginia, with its lack of natural lakes, was an almost "duckless" state. Waterfowl certainly flew over the state, but except on the larger rivers few ever landed. Waterfowl have become more common since the construction of several large artificial reservoirs, which give the birds a place to rest, if not to feed. The advent of the farm pond in the years just after World War II served to further increase the number of ducks seen in the state, and the return of the beaver to the mountain areas also provided ponds.

Most of the state lies outside of the main migratory flyways for waterfowl; as a result, large numbers are seldom seen except at a few places. Bellrose (1968) has given the most recent analysis of waterfowl flyways east of the Rocky Mountains based on a variety of data sources including radar observations, censusing by aircraft, and visual observation from aircraft. This treatment shows that a major flyway used by some 101,000 to 350,000 dabbling ducks and 251,000 to 500,000 diving ducks crosses the northern part of the Northern Panhandle, the Monongalia-Preston County area, and the Eastern Panhandle as far west as Mineral County. Two lesser flyways, carrying from 31,000 to 100,000 dabbling ducks each, cover the southern part of the state west of a line from about Jackson County to Greenbrier County, and these intersect in the Cabell-Mason-Kanawha County area. A flyway carrying from 76,000 to 250,000 diving ducks just misses the western portion of the state, but stragglers from this route do occur in the Cabell-Wayne County area. Thus, we see that only relatively few waterfowl will fly over much of the state, and suitable resting grounds are scarce even along the major flyways.

One can expect to see good numbers of waterfowl only in a few places in the state. These are: the Potomac and Shenandoah Rivers in the Eastern Panhandle; Cheat Lake, Monongalia County; Lake of the Woods and Lake Terra Alta, Preston County; Tygart Reservoir, Taylor County; the Ohio River Valley in the extreme north and in the Cabell-Mason County area; and the Kanawha River as far south as Charleston.

Even at these places large concentrations are not usually found unless the weather conditions prevent the birds from flying over without stopping. Consider, for example, Cheat Lake in Monongalia County (also known in the literature as Lake Lynn), which is a large, mostly sterile, body of water situated at the foot of the westernmost ridge of the Allegheny Mountains. If migrating waterfowl on a flight path from the Great Lakes to the Carolina and Virginia capes encounter a storm system centered over the higher mountains, large numbers of them may come down to rest on Cheat Lake rather than cross the mountains. Deep Creek Lake in Garrett County, Maryland, also shows this phenomenon. Under these circumstances, many thousands of waterfowl have been seen in one day on Cheat Lake. Noteworthy flights occurred in October 1936, when about 10,000 birds were present, and in October 1951 and November 1955. Most of these birds departed as soon as the weather changed, often on the next day. In the late 1960s and 1970s, the flights reported at Cheat Lake were not as large as formerly. The reduced continental waterfowl populations, the increased use of the lake by speedboaters, and the fact that much of the lake is not now accessible to the land-based observer all are factors contributing to this decline.

In the years just following World War II, the State Conservation Commission (as it was then called) established a game-management area now known as the C. F. McClintic Wildlife Station on the site of an abandoned munitions plant near Point Pleasant, Mason County. A portion of this area was managed for waterfowl by construction of ponds, and for several years this area produced many interesting records of both waterfowl and shorebirds. A rather extensive waterfowl banding program was carried out (Appel, 1957). In recent years, the increased use of this area by people, and the establishment of some more secluded ponds on a power-plant site across the Ohio River, have served to decrease the number of records at the McClintic Station, but it is still an important waterfowl location for the state.

Subfamily Anserinae   SWANS AND GEESE

TUNDRA SWAN   *Cygnus columbianus* (Ord)

Status: Rare to common migrant; occasionally locally abundant.

Spring: The migration route of the Tundra Swan

from Chesapeake Bay and the Carolina-Virginia capes to its Arctic breeding ground is a narrowly defined path that lies to the north of West Virginia. During certain weather conditions, this flight may be deflected southward and sizeable flocks may be seen flying over or resting on the lakes in north-eastern West Virginia. While numerous records come from the Eastern Panhandle, most of the birds apparently fly over this area which is close to the starting point. Cheat Lake, Monongalia County, situated at the foot of the westernmost Allegheny ridge, often is visited by large numbers of swans. Flocks of over 1,000 have been seen and flocks numbering in the hundreds are often present. It is not unusual to hear flocks of swans flying over the vicinity of Morgantown. The big flights come in a rather narrow time pattern, usually in mid-March to early April depending on the availability of open water. A few birds have remained in the Monongalia-Preston-Garrett County (Maryland) area until mid-May. The Tundra Swan is known only as a rare to casual stray away from this area, with scattered records coming from locations throughout the state. There are spring records from Berkeley, Grant, Randolph, Hancock, Wood, and Kanawha Counties.

Fall: Fall migration usually occurs in late October or November and is largely the reverse of the spring migration. In most years the birds miss the state completely, but when a severe storm system is present in the Allegheny Mountains to the north of West Virginia the flight may be deflected to the south and the birds may alight on Cheat Lake rather than head across the stormy mountains. Often this deflection is greater in the fall and the birds may appear more commonly at other locations. There are fall records from Brooke, Randolph, Greenbrier, Monroe, Upshur, Gilmer, Wood, Ohio, Mason, Cabell, Putnam, and Kanawha Counties as well as the northern counties where the flights are more common. An occasional bird may remain well into winter with December records from Randolph and Barbour Counties, and reports on the Ona, Cabell County, Christmas Counts in 1967 and 1972.

Remarks: This species is called Whistling Swan in earlier literature.

Specimen: WVU.

TRUMPETER SWAN *Cygnus buccinator* Richardson

Status: Accidental visitant.

Record: One was shot at Letart Island on the Ohio River in Mason County on 30 November 1875.

Remarks: This bird was preserved in a collection of mounted birds at the State Capitol Building in Charleston, where it was examined by E. A. Brooks. It has been commonly supposed, as mentioned by M. Brooks (1944), that this specimen was destroyed in the fire that burned the Capitol in 1923. However, at present there is a mounted swan specimen in the Center for Culture and History in Charleston bearing the data usually associated with the Letart Island specimen except that the date is

given as 19 September 1905. Bibbee (1929) remarks that, since the mount is in a sealed case, it is not possible at this time to check the true identification of the specimen, an idea with which I agree. Handley (in litt.) also expressed doubt as to the identification. According to J. L. Smith, A. S. Morgan was convinced that this was the original specimen. The Trumpeter Swan formerly wintered in some numbers in North Carolina and undoubtedly migrated over parts of West Virginia in the early days. Trumpeter Swan bones have been found in an archaeological site in Putnam County (Guilday, 1971).

*MUTE SWAN   *Cygnus olor* (Gmelin)

Status: Casual visitant.

Records: From time to time, Mute Swans are seen in West Virginia, but it is never possible to tell whether the birds are truly feral or whether they have just recently escaped from captivity. For example, a flock of eight appeared on the Ohio River at New Cumberland, Hancock County, on 13 December 1934. One of these was shot near Wellsburg, Brooke County, and the specimen was examined by T. Shields and R. Hogg (Brooks, 1944). However, these birds were probably a flock that had been liberated from captivity near Akron, Ohio, that fall, since they appeared on the Ohio just three days after they disappeared from the liberation area (Hicks, 1935). J. L. Poland recorded Mute Swans in Jefferson County. One was seen on the Kanawha River at Charleston on 6 November 1958 (Handley, 1976). One was seen on the Monongahela River near Morgantown on 14 April 1973 (G. Sanderson and R. Sanderson), and one was present in Hampshire County in the winter of 1977–78. There have been more sight records of this species in inland United States in recent years, and additional records may be expected from West Virginia.

GREATER WHITE-FRONTED GOOSE
                                   Anser albifrons (Scopoli)

Status: Accidental visitant.

Records: T. A. Morgan collected one from a flock of five seen at Poca, Putnam County, in the fall of 1893. A White-fronted Goose was shot by a hunter on the Ohio River near Belleville, Wood County, on 14 December 1977. A wing of this bird was preserved by Department of Natural Resources employee J. McCready.

Remarks: Six White-fronted Geese were seen on 13 March 1971 on the ponds at the power plant at Kyger Creek, Ohio, just across the River from Point Pleasant, Mason County (Anderson and Hurley, 1974).

Specimen: CM (Wing). The whereabouts of the Morgan specimen is not known at present.

SNOW GOOSE   *Chen caerulescens* (Linnaeus)

Status: Casual spring migrant; rare to uncommon fall migrant; casual winter visitor.

Spring: This species seldom moves through West Virginia in the spring. I find only two reports of the white phase ("Snow Goose"); Parsons, Tucker County, 27 March 1949 and Canaan Valley, Tucker County, 28 March 1949. Several records exist for the blue phase ("Blue Goose") from Beverley, Randolph County, 10 May 1951 (W. DeGarmo); from Huntington, 1953; from Charleston, 28 February 1960 (C. Handley); and from McClintic Wildlife Station, Mason County, 25 March 1960 (R. Kletzley). There are also reports (unidentified as to color phase) from Summers and Greenbrier Counties.

Fall: West Virginia is outside of the regular migration routes of this species. The Greater Snow Goose (*C. c. atlantica*) migrates off the Atlantic Coast and the Lesser Snow Goose (*C. c. caerulescens*), which has two color phases, migrates through the Mississippi Valley. Prior to 1944, there were only two records for the blue phase: one in Morgantown 21 November 1914 (WVU specimen) and one in Mercer County, accompanied by a white-phased bird, in the winter of 1942. There were a few other records of white-phased birds on Cheat Lake. Since that time, there has been some shift in migration pattern and both forms have become more common. Both phases, with the blue predominating, are almost annual visitors in small numbers to the Cabell-Mason-Kanawha County area. There are also several records of "Blue Geese" from Ohio County in fall and early winter. Other records come from Monongalia (Morgantown) (M. Brooks), Tucker, Upshur (French Creek), Randolph (Beverly), Monroe (Pickaway), (P. Handlan), and Wetzel Counties. On 25–26 October 1949, great flocks of Snow Geese were precipitated onto West Virginia by a storm system. A total of 1,500 were seen on the lower Kanawha River near Point Pleasant (the white to blue ratio was about 100 to 8) (Handley). Other Ohio River Counties such as Marshall, Jackson, Cabell, Roane, Putnam, and Kanawha also had great numbers.

Winter: A few blue-phased birds and an occasional white phase have wintered at the McClintic Wildlife Station and on the Ohio River in Cabell County.

Remarks: The literature prior to about 1960 considered that the Snow Goose (*Chen hyperborea*) and the Blue Goose (*C. caerulescens*) were distinct species. However, information obtained on the breeding ground showed conclusively that the two forms interbreed freely and so they constitute a single species with two color phases.

*BRANT   *Branta bernicla* (Linnaeus)

Status: Accidental fall visitant.
Records: Eight were seen on Cheat Lake, Monongalia County, on 23–24 October 1936 in the large concentration of waterfowl present at that time (J. T. Handlan, 1938). One was present on a small pond near Beverly, Randolph County, on 1 November 1951 during the great flight of waterfowl to eastern West Virginia in that year (W. R. DeGarmo). Five were seen on the Tygart Reservoir, Taylor County, on 7 November 1959 and one on 9–10 November 1959 in Doddridge County (photographed) (W. Lesser, 1960).
Specimen: No specimen has been taken but Lesser's photograph is on file at the U. S. National Photoduplicate File.

CANADA GOOSE   *Branta canadensis* (Linnaeus)

Status: Common to very common migrant. Introduced summer and permanent resident.
Spring: The Canada Goose migrates in late February and early March. Most of West Virginia is outside of the main goose flyways, but migration does occur across the Eastern Panhandle and the mountainous areas of Grant and Mineral Counties. In spring, geese are most commonly reported from Cheat Lake, Monongalia County, Lake of the Woods, Preston County, and along the Ohio and Kanawha Rivers. Away from these waterways, geese are only casual or rare.
Summer: Canada Geese may have nested in West Virginia in pre-settlement days, but there is no evidence for this. In 1955 the Department of Natural Resources (then called the Conservation Commission) liberated 24 wing-clipped subadult geese at the McClintic Wildlife Station, Mason County. These geese had been trapped from the wild geese at the Horseshoe Lake National Wildlife Refuge in southern Illinois. In the next few years, a few more geese were liberated. This captive flock nested successfully and the progeny remained at the Station. In the fall of 1974, the population was estimated to be from 400 to 425 freely flying birds, and from 50–70 goslings are hatched each year (W. K. Igo, in litt.). In 1981 it was estimated that the McClintic area had about 50 nesting pairs, and a fall population of about 250 to 300 geese (W. Lesser, in litt.). From 1967 to 1971, 72 geese live-trapped at McClintic Station were liberated in the Canaan Valley, Tucker County. This introduction was also successful and the birds have nested there. In the fall of 1981, approximately 100–125 birds made up

this population. Canada Geese, probably from the Canaan Valley introduction, have nested at Silver Lake, Preston County. For several years a pair of geese nested at Lake of the Woods, Preston County. These birds, which are now thought to have been shot out, may have originated from the introductions in Canaan Valley, but prior to 1967 summer residents of the Lake of the Woods colony had told me of seeing young geese on the lake.

In 1976 an extensive program of introductions was initiated using birds from Connecticut, Delaware, and New York. Transplants were made every year since that time, and by the end of 1981 a total of 4,125 birds had been released. Banding returns indicate that less than 1% of these birds have returned to their place of origin. Liberations were made in about 25 counties mostly on major streams, such as the Ohio from Tyler County south to the Kentucky border; the Tygart and Monongahela system; the Greenbrier, New, Kanawha system, and on the South Branch of the Potomac. Breeding and production of young have occurred at all release sites; for example, the South Branch population (from Petersburg to Romney) has been producing about 25 broods of young a year (W. Lesser, in litt.). Summering Canada Geese may now be encountered in many places in the state except in the high mountains, and in the wooded areas of the southern part of the Hill Section.

Fall: The fall flight of geese begins in October, usually with the first genuine cold wave of the season. Resting flocks are often seen on Cheat Lake, Lake of the Woods, and the lower Ohio River. The resident population at McClintic Wildlife Station attracts many transients, often numbering to 200. Flocks of migrating geese are frequently seen flying southwest along the Allegheny Front at A.F.M.O., and I have seen flocks flying up (south) the Monongahela River at Morgantown as well as heard them overhead at night. The introduced population in Canaan Valley, winters, at least in part, in eastern North Carolina as determined by marked birds.

Winter: A few geese may winter in the lower Ohio and Kanawha Valleys, and there is a record of a small flock in Hampshire County on the Christmas Count. The resident flock at McClintic Wildlife Station seems to winter at the warm water tailing ponds of the power plant at Kyger Creek, Ohio, just across the river from the Station. Seven Christmas counts at McClintic have averaged 260. A flock of up to 300 has been wintering in recent years at the City Park in Chester, Hancock County (Chandler and Chandler, 1980).

Specimens: WVU, MU. There are too few specimens from the state to establish which subspecies normally migrate through the area. According to the A.O.U. Check-list (1957), the subspecies expected would be *interior* Todd. A specimen from the resident Mason County flock has been identified as *maxima* Delacour by H. Hanson (Waggy, 1973), as expected from the original source of these birds.

In the winter of 1955–56, a small Canada Goose was present for some time in a farmyard in Berkeley Springs, Morgan County. This bird, which was photographed, was clearly a representative of one of the small forms of white-cheeked goose which has sometimes been separated as a distinct species, *Branta hutchinsi* (Richardson), the Cackling Goose.

Subfamily Anatinae	DUCKS

WOOD DUCK   *Aix sponsa* (Linnaeus)

Status: Fairly common to common summer resident; rare winter visitant.

Spring: The Wood Duck first appears in late February, but the general arrival is in the first half of March. At this time it may occur on any stream in the state. It appears not to be very common in the southern hill country nor in the high mountains.

First-seen Spring Dates: Cabell-Mason Counties, 28 March; Randolph County, 15 March; Greenbrier County, 3 March.

Summer: The Wood Duck probably nests, at least sparingly, throughout the state and may occur in every county. It does not occur in very large numbers in the higher mountains. There are definite nesting records for Jefferson, Berkeley, Hampshire, Hardy, Pendleton, Randolph, Pocahontas, Green-

brier, Monroe, Preston, Upshur, Lewis, Summers, Hancock, Brooks, Ohio, Wood, Ritchie, Kanawha, Mason, Cabell, and Wayne Counties. Nesting populations seem to depend largely upon the availability of nesting sites, and nest boxes have been installed in several places in the state. This project has been most successful at the McClintic Wildlife Station where, for example, 1,346 young were raised in the years 1950–57 with 379 in 47 broods in 1957 (Appel, 1957). Handley (1976) remarks that good production depends not only on nesting sites but also on the absence of snapping turtles (*Chelydra*). Nest boxes also have been placed near the beaver ponds on some of the higher mountains, but here predation by raccoons (*Procyon*) becomes important.

Fall: The Wood Duck may begin to congregate in flocks in favored spots, usually in shallow tree-lined pools, in late August and the migration occurs in October with most birds being gone by mid- to late November. Over 1,000 Wood Ducks were reported as resting on a single pond at McClintic Wildlife Station in the fall of 1963.

Last-seen Fall Dates: Cabell-Mason Counties, 23 November; Randolph County, 1 November.

Winter: There are a few late-December records from Jefferson and Monongalia Counties. A few Wood Ducks may winter in the lower Kanawha and lower Ohio Valleys, and on the Potomac and some of its tributaries.

Remarks: In the early days, the Wood Duck must have been at least a fairly common summer resident in most of the state, but it was easily shot, and overhunting together with the loss of habitat almost eliminated it. Bibbee (1929) remarked that he had seen it on only three occasions. With the passage of the Migratory Bird Act, this species was placed on the completely protected list and with protection, and lately, the installation of nest boxes it has returned to most of its former range. Limited hunting has been permitted.

Specimen: WVU, MU.

GREEN-WINGED TEAL　　　*Anas crecca* Linnaeus

Status: Fairly common to common migrant; casual summer resident; rare winter visitor.

Spring: The Green-winged Teal arrives after mid-March and becomes most numerous in early April. Most of them depart by late April. It usually occurs in small flocks of 5 to 10, and is found on the larger ponds and lakes. It is more common in the lower Ohio-Kanawha Valleys than elsewhere. It is rather rare in the Monongalia-Preston County area, but is somewhat more numerous in the Eastern Panhandle.

Summer: I found a male on a beaver pond on the Allegheny Front, Tucker County, in June 1965, but saw no female or brood. Harwood (1974) found a brood on a beaver pond near the same place in August 1972. A brood was seen at the Tygart Reservoir, Taylor County, in 1971 (D. Mathews).

Fall: A few Green-winged Teal arrive in late

August, but the main flight will be in late October to early November. Small numbers can be seen in all parts of the state, but as in spring it is most common in the lower Ohio-Kanawha Valley region. Small flocks are the rule, but a flock of 62 was reported from McClintic Station in 1960.

First-seen Fall Date: Cabell-Mason County, 30 September.

Winter: Surber (1889) considered this species to be a common wintering bird along the Greenbrier River in the last century, but it apparently no longer winters there. There are December records from Leetown and Charles Town, Jefferson County, Lewisburg, Greenbrier County, and McClintic Wildlife Station.

Specimens: WVUM, UMMZ, MU.

AMERICAN BLACK DUCK　　　*Anas rubripes* Brewster

Status: Common to very common migrant; rare to uncommon local summer resident; common winter visitant.

Spring: Migrant Black Ducks join the winter flocks in late February and early March and most of them are gone by late March. The Black Duck migrates throughout the state, but is generally less numerous than the Mallard. It is less frequently seen on small ponds and streams than is the Mallard.

Summer: The Black Duck nests in small numbers on the beaver ponds in the Canaan Valley and on the Allegheny Front, and is probably as common there as anywhere in the state. A few nest along the Shenandoah and Potomac Rivers in the Eastern Panhandle and in the marshes of Jefferson and Berkeley Counties. There are also summer records from Hampshire, Wetzel, Upshur, Wood, Fayette, and Mason Counties, but definite nesting records come only from Berkeley, Hardy, Hancock, Tucker, Summers, and Cabell Counties.

Fall: The Black Duck arrives later than most other species and does not appear in force until late October. It may be found in all parts of the state, but is usually only on larger bodies of water. Large concentrations occur only in such favored spots as the McClintic Wildlife Station, Cheat Lake, or the Potomac River.

Winter: The Black Duck winters in some numbers along all the major streams of the state and at such favored locations as the McClintic Wildlife Station, where the Christmas Counts (7) have averaged 366 (572–150). Christmas Counts at Ona in Cabell County (7) averaged 37 (128–9) and at Charles Town in Jefferson County (7) averaged 12 (33–1). As mentioned below, the Black Duck at one time outnumbered the Mallard in winter in northern West Virginia, but this ratio has changed and the Black Duck has become rather uncommon there.

Remarks: Some authorities would consider the Black Duck and the Mallard to be conspecific. Hybridization is quite common in some nesting areas. The Black Duck, as we have known it, may be a vanishing species. For many years the Mallard has been increasing in population to the east, and interbreeding has now widely contaminated the Black Duck stock with Mallard genes. The Black Duck genetic makeup may ultimately be completely swamped out by that of the Mallard. The changes in relative numbers of the two species mentioned above may be due in part to this.

Specimens: WVUM, MU. Contrary to the older literature, no subspecies are currently recognized in the species.

MALLARD   *Anas platyrhynchos* Linnaeus

Status: Common to very common migrant; uncommon summer resident; common to abundant local winter resident.

Spring: Because of the large wintering population, it is difficult to date the spring migration of the Mallard, but the influx from the south occurs from mid-February to early March, depending on the late-winter weather. By the first week in April, most of the migrants are gone. The species probably migrates throughout the state and it is often seen on small ponds and streams, although the largest numbers will be on the bigger bodies of water. The largest numbers are found in the lower Ohio and Kanawha Rivers and along the Potomac drainage.

Summer: An occasional Mallard pair may nest at a farm pond or similar place almost anywhere in the state. Many of these may be of semi-domesticated stock. There are definite nesting records from Jefferson, Preston, Randolph, Greenbrier, Summers, Barbour, Lewis, Hancock, Ohio, Mason, Cabell, and Kanawha Counties. Additional summer records come from Morgan, Grant, Pendleton, Pocahontas, Upshur, and Gilmer Counties.

Fall: A few Mallards may appear in early September, but the main influx begins in mid-October and builds up in November. As in the spring, Mallards may be seen in almost any part of the state.

Winter: Large concentrations of Mallards winter in the lower Ohio Valley and the Kanawha Valley. Seven Mason County Christmas Counts (largely at McClintic Wildlife Station) have averaged 550 (709–302). At Ona, Cabell County, the Christmas Counts (7) have averaged 37 (128–5) and at Charles Town the average was 114 (444–1). Other Christmas Counts have averaged less. Much smaller numbers winter on Cheat Lake and on the Monongahela and Tygart Rivers in the north, and on the Ohio at the northern Panhandle. In the early 1950s at Morgantown, the wintering birds were largely Black Ducks

with only a few Mallards, but this ratio reversed in the 1970s.
Specimen: WVU, MU.

NORTHERN PINTAIL   *Anas acuta* Linnaeus

Status: Fairly common to common migrant; uncommon local winter resident.

Spring: The Pintail is one of the earliest ducks to arrive in the spring, and it usually appears in late February or early March and departs by the end of March. It usually occurs only on the larger streams and lakes. It is rare in northern West Virginia and uncommon in the Eastern Panhandle and the northern Ohio Valley. The greatest numbers occur in the Ohio Valley from Wood County south and in the lower Kanawha Valley, where flocks of 15–30 are sometimes seen.

First-seen Spring Date: Cabell-Mason Counties, 11 March.

Last-seen Spring Date: Cabell-Mason Counties, 6 May.

Fall: The status in fall is similar to that in spring, with the Pintail being found at the same places in about the same relative numbers, although total numbers in the fall may be somewhat less than in spring. Arrival is in late October and early November with some birds remaining into December.

First-seen Fall Date: Cabell-Mason Counties, 29 October.

Last-seen Fall Date: Cabell-Mason Counties, 17 December.

Winter: The Pintail winters in small numbers at the McClintic Wildlife Station with a maximum of 32 on Christmas Counts. There are a few other winter records from the Ohio and Kanawha Rivers.

Specimens: WVUM, UMMZ, MU.

BLUE-WINGED TEAL   *Anas discors* Linnaeus

Status: Common migrant; casual summer resident; casual winter visitant.

Spring: The Blue-winged Teal begins to arrive in mid-March, but the peak of migration is in mid-April and some birds will remain until late May. It migrates throughout the state, but as with other dabbling ducks the teal is most common in the Kanawha and southern Ohio Valleys. It generally frequents small and shallow bodies of water; consequently, it is most commonly seen on farm ponds, particularly in the southwestern part of the state.

First-seen Spring Dates: Cabell-Mason Counties, 23 March; Brooke County, 16 April.

Last-seen Spring Dates: Ohio County, 28 April; Cabell-Mason Counties, 16 May.

Summer: The first nesting record for the state was reported by G. M. Sutton in Brooke County in

1912 (Sutton, 1933). There are also nesting records from the Great Cacapon River in Hardy County (Brooks, 1944); Hancock County, in 1980 and 1981 (Chandler and Chandler); Ohio County in 1961 (Breiding, 1962a) and 1964; Putnam County in 1976 (Shreve, Katholi, and Gluck); Pleasant County in 1982 (Jones); and Wood County (Armstrong). There are summer records from the McClintic Wildlife Station, but as yet no definite nesting records. Blue-winged Teal were reported from near the Sinks of Gandy, Randolph County, in the summer of 1968 (B. Greenlee and E. Chandler).

Fall: The Blue-winged Teal is the earliest of migrating waterfowl in autumn, and it begins to arrive in numbers in August, builds up to a peak in early September, and is practically gone by mid-October. It migrates throughout the state, frequenting, as in spring, shallow ponds and streams, but also as in spring it is most common in the southwestern part of the state.

First-seen Fall Date: Cabell-Mason Counties, 8 September.

Last-seen Fall Date: Cabell-Mason Counties, 11 November.

Winter: There are a few scattered records from Kanawha and Cabell Counties in winter.

Specimens: WVU, UMMZ, MU.

NORTHERN SHOVELER   *Anas clypeata* Linnaeus

Status: Uncommon to fairly common migrant; accidental winter visitant.

Spring: This is the least numerous of the dabbling ducks that normally appear in the state. It migrates in late March or early April and occurs on shallow ponds and streams, perhaps throughout the state. As with the other dabbling ducks, it is most common in the southwest where flocks of up to 20 are sometimes seen. Elsewhere it is uncommon. Apparently it has always been uncommon since Bibbee (1929) mentioned that his father (in Wood County) had shot only two in all of his years of wildfowling on the Ohio.

First-seen Spring Date: Cabell-Mason Counties, 23 March.

Last-seen Spring Date: Cabell-Mason Counties, 25 April.

Fall: The Shoveler generally migrates in late October and early November, but there are August records for Mason County. It is less numerous in fall than in spring everywhere, and is seldom seen in most of the state. I have never seen it in fall in the Monongalia-Preston Counties area.

First-seen Fall Date: Cabell-Mason Counties, 3 September.

Last-seen Fall Date: Cabell-Mason Counties, 11 November.

Winter: The Shoveler has been found in Leetown, Jefferson County, in winter.

Specimen: WVUM.

GADWALL   *Anas strepera* Linnaeus

Status: Uncommon to fairly common migrant; rare winter visitant.

Spring: The Gadwall is one of the less frequently reported species of ducks that migrate through the state, although it is possible that some individuals are not identified as Gadwalls. Most of the records come from the usual waterfowl localities: McClintic Wildlife Station, Mason County; Cheat Lake, Monongalia County; and Lake of the Woods, Preston County. They arrive in early March and may remain through April. I have seen individuals on the Monongahela River at Morgantown in mid- to late May. Besides these places, there are occasional records from the Eastern Panhandle, Randolph, Greenbrier, Brooke, Ohio, Wood, Upshur, Kanawha, and Putnam Counties.

First-seen Spring Date: Cabell-Mason Counties, 19 March.

Last-seen Spring Date: Cabell-Mason Counties, 12 May.

Fall: The fall migration takes place in late October or early November, and the status of the bird is similar to that in spring.

First-seen Fall Date: Cabell-Mason Counties, 6 October.

Last-seen Fall Date: Cabell-Mason Counties, 17 December.

Winter: A few Gadwall winter from time to time at the McClintic Wildlife Station, and occasionally on Cheat Lake, Monongalia County.

Specimen: WVUM.

*EURASIAN WIGEON   *Anas penelope* Linnaeus

Status: Casual migrant.

Records: One was seen on the Ohio River at Huntington by E. Seeber on 8 March 1952. R. Kletzly saw one at the McClintic Wildlife Station on 1 April 1960 and G. Hurley reported two from there on 18 March 1967. Brooks (1944) mentioned several records for Cheat Lake. These are all the West Virginia records, but the following three records come from within a few miles of the West Virginia border: the Land brothers saw one in Gallia County, Ohio, across the Ohio River from Point Pleasant on 14 March 1953; I saw this species at Deep Creek Lake, Garrett County, Maryland, on 8 April 1956 and near Farmington, Fayette County, Pennsylvania on 14 March 1965. This species should perhaps be considered as hypothetical, but I am convinced that it has occurred in West Virginia, possibly more often than reported.

Specimens: None.

AMERICAN WIGEON   *Anas americana* Gmelin

Status: Common to very common migrant; uncommon local winter visitor.

Spring: The American Wigeon migrates throughout March and early April and may remain in favored spots until early May. It occurs throughout the state, but generally is found on the larger streams and lakes. It is the only dabbling duck that normally migrates through our region in large flocks and is perhaps the most abundant dabbling duck in most parts of the state. Unlike some of the other dabblers, it is quite common in the northeastern part of the state as well as in the southwest.

First-seen Spring Date: Cabell-Mason Counties, 5 March.

Last-seen Spring Date: Cabell-Mason Counties, 11 May.

Fall: The American Wigeon passes through the state in October and early November. As with other dabbling ducks, a few stragglers may appear rather early but the main flight comes after the advent of the first cold weather. At this time it will be found on farm ponds as well as the larger lakes and streams throughout the state, but as with other species it often does not occur in as large numbers as in spring.

First-seen Fall Date: Cabell-Mason Counties, 3 October.

Winter: A few wigeon winter in the lower Ohio Valley. The Mason County Christmas Counts have ranged from 2 to 15. Other winter records come from Cabell, Kanawha, Greenbrier, and Jefferson Counties.

Specimens: WVUM, MU.

CANVASBACK   *Aythya valisneria* (Wilson)

Status: Uncommon to common migrant; rare to uncommon winter visitor.

Spring: The Canvasback arrives in late February or early March and is gone by mid-April. It occurs only on the larger bodies of water, and the greatest concentrations are seen on the Ohio River in the north. As with the other diving ducks, the Canvasback is less numerous in the southwest than in the north.

First-seen Spring Date: Cabell-Mason Counties, 1 March.

Last-seen Spring Date: Cabell-Mason Counties, 26 April.

Fall: The Canvasback is somewhat less common in fall than in spring, and it occurs in numbers only when storms prohibit the crossing of the mountains to the main wintering grounds on Chesapeake Bay. Under these circumstances, large flocks have been seen on Cheat Lake and on the upper Ohio River. Most of these flights are in late October and early November.

First-seen Fall Date: Cabell-Mason Counties, 11 November.

Winter: Good-sized flocks sometimes remain on the Ohio River, both in the north and the south, through the winter. It is much less common elsewhere.

Remarks: Overshooting and drought on the prairie breeding grounds reduced the continental population of Canvasbacks to extremely low numbers in the late 1950s. A partial closure of the hunting season resulted in a slow increase, but numbers never approached those obtaining before the 1930s. In the 1980s, populations were again low and the species has been placed on the "Blue List" by the National Audubon Society—the list of species that may become endangered and whose status should be carefully watched. It is now a great rarity to see a large flock in this state.

Specimen: WVUM.

REDHEAD   *Aythya americana* (Eyton)

Status: Common to very common migrant; uncommon winter visitor.

Spring: In the south the Redhead arrives in late February and in the north it appears as soon as the lakes are free of ice. The peak of migration is in late March or early April. While small groups of from two to six are most frequent, on occasion large rafts of several hundred can be seen on the Ohio River or Cheat Lake. The species migrates throughout the state and occasional pairs may occur on farm ponds, but large concentrations occur only on the lower Ohio-Kanawha Rivers and at the Cheat Lake-Lake of the Woods area in the northeast. During March 1959, a total of 282 were banded at the McClintic Station. Most are gone by mid-April.

Fall: The Redhead is not as common in fall as in spring, but small numbers pass through the state in late October and early November. As in spring, the largest numbers are seen on the lower Ohio River and on Cheat Lake. Elsewhere it is only casual or rare.

First-seen Fall Date: Cabell-Mason Counties, 30 October.

Winter: Winter records come only from the McClintic Wildlife Station (where seven Christmas Counts have averaged about 10 per season), Cabell County, and Kanawha County.

Specimens: WVUM.

RING-NECKED DUCK   *Aythya collaris* (Donovan)

Status: Fairly common to very common migrant; uncommon winter visitant.

Spring: A few Ring-necked Ducks may arrive in late February, but the main migration comes in mid-March and many may remain in numbers until mid-May. Migrant flocks tend to remain for several weeks in favored spots. The species migrates throughout the state, but the largest numbers are found in the Monongalia-Preston Counties area where flocks of 40 to 50 each, totaling several hundred birds, can be seen in a day. Small parties of one or two males with three to six females are of frequent occurrence on many small bodies of water, even farm ponds. Unlike the dabbling ducks, this species is rather less numerous in the southwestern part of the state and along the entire Ohio River. There are several records of stragglers in the state throughout the summer.

First-seen Spring Dates: Cabell-Mason Counties, 16 March; Monongalia-Preston Counties, 13 March.

Fall: In the northeastern part of the state, the Ring-neck is a common to very common migrant, and in some years it is the only common duck in autumn. Perhaps this species does not take as much hunting pressure as some others. In the southwest and in most of the Western Hills and the Allegheny Mountain Regions, it is much less numerous, being casual to uncommon at most places. The peak of migration will be in late October and early November.

First-seen Fall Date: Cabell-Mason Counties, 1 November.

Winter: There are Christmas Count records from Ohio, Summers, Mason, and Cabell Counties. Single individuals or pairs may turn up on any open water during the winter.

Specimens: WVU, MU.

GREATER SCAUP   *Aythya marila* (Linnaeus)

Status: Rare to uncommon migrant; may be present in winter.

Spring: Most of the few reliable reports of this species are in March and April. Edeburn, et al. (1960), comment that a few may be seen in the lower Ohio Valley area in any migration season and give spring dates from 13 February to 7 May (a May date for this species is highly unlikely). One was banded at the McClintic Wildlife Station in 1957 (season not given) (Appel, 1957) and three were banded there in March 1959 (Handley, 1976). C. Miller reported them from the Eastern Panhandle on 24 March 1953. Two specimens (WVU) were collected in Putnam

County by A. S. Morgan on 6 March 1911 and 29 March 1913.

Fall: Edeburn, et al. (1960), give fall dates from 1 November to 1 January for the lower Ohio Valley. Two were seen at Charleston on 1 January 1947 (W. Strunk). Three were present at Lake of the Woods, Preston County, on 6 December 1964 (Hall). These last are my only Morgantown records in 25 years. One was seen on the Ona, Cabell County, Christmas Count on 31 December 1972.

Winter: Poland (1941) reports that they are rather common throughout the winter along the Potomac River in the Eastern Panhandle.

Remarks: I am convinced that this species is much less common in the state than the literature and observer reports would indicate. In poor light conditions, many scaup cannot be identified at a distance, but of the several thousand scaup that I have carefully examined under strong light conditions the three mentioned above were the only ones that could be definitely called Greater Scaup. Given the normal winter and summer ranges of this species, the most likely place for them to appear in the state would be in the Monongalia-Preston area and in the Eastern Panhandle, but as pointed out above they are extremely rare in the Monongalia-Preston area. Field guides stress the green gloss on the head of the Greater as opposed to the purple gloss of the Lesser, but in my experience, in some lights, there is a decided greenish tint to the head of the Lesser Scaup. In good light the head of the Greater is very green, so much so that the Lake of the Woods birds mentioned above were thought by an inexperienced observer to be Mallards before examination with binoculars. It seems likely that an undetermined number of records of Greater Scaup are misidentifications.

Specimen: WVUM.

LESSER SCAUP   *Aythya affinis* (Eyton)

Status: Common to abundant migrant; casual summer visitant; uncommon winter visitant.

Spring: The Lesser Scaup is the most common diving duck to migrate through the state. It probably passes through the whole state, and while a few pairs may be seen on farm ponds it will be most numerous on the larger bodies of water. Flocks numbering over 100 are occasionally seen. Migration starts in late February, but the peak does not come until late March or even early April. A few remain until mid-May.

First-seen Spring Date: Monongalia-Preston Counties, 2 March.

Summer: Occasional birds of this species are seen in June or even later in the summer in the state. These birds are probably incapacitated in some way but there is evidence of breeding in the state. Thaddeus Surber reported (fide Brooks, 1944) an adult with downy young on the Greenbrier River in Greenbrier County in 1907. Rives (1898) took a female in breeding condition on the Blackwater River in Tucker County. Young birds were seen on Lake Terra Alta, Preston County, in the summer of 1936 (Brooks, 1936c).

Fall: The Lesser Scaup appears in small numbers in September, but the main flight does not take place until the lakes in the far north freeze, which is usually from mid- to late-November. At this time large flocks, numbering 100 or more, are common on the Ohio, Kanawha, and Monongahela Rivers and on the larger reservoirs such as Cheat Lake and the Tygart Reservoir. Many of these birds remain until mid- or late-December.

First-seen Fall Date: Cabell-Mason Counties, 8 September.

Winter: A few scaup may winter anywhere in the state. Mason County Christmas Counts have averaged six (10–3) birds per count, but many of these may really be late fall migrants.

Specimens: WVU, UMMZ, MU.

KING EIDER   *Somateria spectabilis* (Linnaeus)

Status: Accidental visitant.

Record: T. Milewski and F. Fitch shot one on the Ohio River at Huntington on 28 November 1953 (Edeburn, 1954).

Specimen: MU.

*HARLEQUIN DUCK

          Histrionicus histrionicus (Linnaeus)

Status: Hypothetical; accidental winter visitant.

Record: One was present on the New River near Hinton, Summers County, from 22 January to 15 February 1974 (J. L. Smith, 1976). Interestingly enough, one had spent the late winter of 1973 at Blacksburg, Virginia, just about 40 airline miles from Hinton (*American Birds,* 27:615, 1973).

Specimen: None.

OLDSQUAW   *Clangula hyemalis* (Linnaeus)

Status: Rare spring migrant; rare to uncommon (but occasionally very common locally) fall migrant; uncommon winter visitant.

Spring: Males in breeding plumage have been seen in April on Lake Terra Alta, Preston County, and on several occasions on Cheat Lake, with a date as late as 30 April for the latter place (Hall). Other spring records come from Charleston, 13 April 1966 (G. Hurley), Wheeling, March 1954 (C. Conrad),

and several records from Jefferson County (C. Miller). In early April 1972, there was a small influx in the southern part of the state with records coming from Lewisburg, Greenbrier County; Bowden, Randolph County; Pipestem, Summers County; and Spencer, Roane County.

Fall: There are a few records in early November but most arrival dates are in late November or December. On Cheat Lake there are sometimes sizeable flocks and while a few probably occur there every year, the large numbers appear only after storm conditions. In the fall of 1951 and in December 1953, such sizeable influxes occurred and several hundred birds were seen. The influx of November 1951 also produced records over many other parts of the state, but away from Cheat Lake, which is on the main flight line from the upper Great Lakes to Chesapeake Bay, the species is uncommon or rare, and away from large bodies of water it is only accidental. There are fall records from Monroe, Randolph, Mason, Taylor, and Preston Counties.

Winter: A few Oldsquaws have been reported occasionally at most of the places favorable to waterfowl. There are winter records from Cheat Lake, the Ohio River at Wheeling and Huntington, and the Kanawha River at Charleston.

Specimen: WVUM.

BLACK SCOTER   *Melanitta nigra* (Linnaeus)

Status: Casual migrant.

Records: R. B. Cook reported one from the Huntington area in 1904 (Brooks, 1944) and the Morgan brothers collected it on several occasions at Poca, Putnam County (Haller, 1940a). Boggs saw two on 18 October 1936 and one on 5 November 1936 on Cheat Lake (Brooks and Boggs, 1938); Handley saw five at Charleston on 2 November 1951 (Handley, 1976): J. Casto saw six at Willow Island, Pleasants County on 29 October 1956; Booth saw them on the Tygart Reservoir, Taylor County on 7 November 1959; and I saw one on Lake of the Woods, Preston County, on 30 October 1966. In November 1975 a lone bird, possibly wounded, was present for some time on Cheat Lake.

Remarks: Prior to 1973, this bird was called *Oidemia nigra,* and in all the literature before that time as well as in the current field guides the English name has been either Common Scoter or American Scoter.

Specimen: No specimens were evident in the A. S. Morgan collection when I visited it in 1971.

*SURF SCOTER *Melanitta perspicillata* (Linnaeus)

Status: Casual local migrant.

Records: There are six sight records, all but one

from the Monongalia-Preston County area. M. Brooks and I. B. Boggs saw nine on Cheat Lake on 5 November 1936 (Brooks and Boggs, 1938). I saw three on Cheat Lake on 9 November 1952 (Hall, 1954b) and two there on 23 November 1969. G. Knight and I saw six on Lake of the Woods on 18 and 25 October 1959 (Hall, 1960). J. Phillips saw this species at Athens, 1–2 November 1980, and Gary Felton saw one near Rowlesburg, 16 November 1980.

Specimens: None.

WHITE-WINGED SCOTER
Melanitta fusca (Linnaeus)

Status: Uncommon local migrant and winter visitant.

Spring: The White-winged Scoter is casual to rare in spring. There are several late-February records from the Ohio River at Wheeling and from the Potomac River in Jefferson County, 16 February 1941; Shepherdstown and Harpers Ferry, Jefferson County, 16 February 1961 (P. Anderson); Mason County, March 1940 (K. Haller); McClintic Wildlife Station, 18 May 1961 (R. Kletzley); Bluefield, Mercer County, 10 February 1951 (M. Dickinson); and South Charleston, Kanawha County, 14 March 1977 (N. Gluck).

Fall and Winter: Small flocks of White-winged Scoters are reported regularly in fall and early winter on Cheat Lake, and at least a few probably occur there every year. Arrival there has been as early as 16 October but most records are in November and December. As with several other species large numbers will occur only when storms force the birds down. Away from Cheat Lake (and Lake of the Woods), this species is only casual. There are fall records from French Creek, Upshur County, 25 October 1913 (collected); Brooke County, 5 February 1941 (collected); Mason County, March 1940 (Haller, 1940a), 13 February 1954 (Lands), and 12 January 1971 (H. Slack); New Cumberland, Hancock County, 27–28 December 1969 (O. Johnson); Taylor County, 7 November 1959 (Booth); and Kanawha County, 2 December 1954 (C. Handley). The Morgans collected several at various times on the Kanawha River at Poca, Putnum County.

Remarks: The writer (Hall, 1960) has discussed in detail the occurrence of all three scoter species prior to 1960.

Specimens: UMMZ, ASM.

COMMON GOLDENEYE
Bucephala clangula (Linnaeus)

Status: Very common migrant and winter visitant in the north; less common in the south.

Spring: In the north the Goldeneye appears as soon as there is open water on the larger lakes. The winter flocks are augmented by these migrants but most of the birds seen have wintered nearby. Courtship is at a high level at this time and various displays of males to females, and males to males will be seen. Most of these birds depart by late March, but a few, usually females, remain until late April or even early May.

Fall: The Goldeneye is among the last ducks to arrive in the fall, and usually does not appear before late November or early December. At this time of year, it occurs only on the larger rivers and lakes.

Winter: The main winter range of the Goldeneye is to the north of West Virginia, but it does winter commonly in flocks as large as 50 to 60 on the Ohio River in the Northern Panhandle, on the Monongahela River at Morgantown, and on Cheat Lake if this does not freeze over. It is also numerous along the Shenandoah and Potomac Rivers in the Eastern Panhandle. To the south it is less numerous and more variable in occurrence. On the southern Ohio River, it is common in some years and scarce in others. This probably is correlated with the severity of the winter and the lack of open water to the north, but no study has been made of the matter. It is infrequent and usually in low numbers on the Kanawha River. Mason County Christmas Counts (7) have averaged about 15 (38–5) per count.

Specimens: WVU, MU.

BUFFLEHEAD
Bucephala albeola (Linnaeus)

Status: Uncommon to very common migrant; uncommon to fairly common winter visitant.

Spring: Small parties of five or six Buffleheads appear in late February and early March, and continue to pass through the state until mid-April. A few may stay as late as early May. These attractive little ducks may occur on farm ponds or small streams, but are most common on the larger bodies of water. Most flocks contain fewer than 10 birds but on a given day there may be many such flocks, and occasionally larger flocks of 50 to 100 occur. The Bufflehead is most common in the northeastern part of the state, Monongalia-Preston area, and the Eastern Panhandle, with smaller numbers in the southwest. It becomes uncommon to rare away from the principal bodies of water on the main flyways.

First-seen Spring Date: Monongalia-Preston Counties, 2 March.

Fall: The Bufflehead does not appear in numbers until the freezeup in the north; consequently, most of the arrival dates are in November. In fall the small groups are augmented by the immature birds, resulting in both larger flocks and more total birds being seen than in spring. As in the spring, it is most common in the northeast and east.

First-seen Fall Date: Cabell-Mason Counties, 8 December.

Winter: A few small groups (usually a male and two or three females or immatures) remain for most of the winter wherever there is open water, but the numbers are largest in the lower Ohio Valley and on the Kanawha River. As with other diving ducks, wintering birds are not easily separated from late-fall or early-spring migrants by dates alone.

Specimen: WVU.

HOODED MERGANSER
Lophodytes cucullatus (Linnaeus)

Status: Uncommon to fairly common migrant; uncommon winter visitant; casual summer resident.

Spring: Along with the other diving ducks, the Hooded Merganser begins to appear in the state in early March and the peak of migration is in late March, although a few may remain until the first of May. It probably occurs throughout the state, but it is fairly common only in the Monongalia-Preston area. Elsewhere it is found in small numbers, but unlike the other mergansers it may occur on rather small lakes or streams, resulting in a fairly wide distribution. The birds usually occur in small "courting parties" of one or two males and five to six females. These small groups seldom aggregate into large flocks.

First-seen Spring Date: Monongalia-Preston Counties, 20 March.

Summer: From 1956 through 1962, Hooded Mergansers nested at McClintic Wildlife Station, raising seven to eight young per year (Handley). However, since 1962 no broods have been seen there. In 1952 a brood of seven young was seen on the Tygart's Valley River near Elkins, Randolph County (W. R. DeGarmo). Sutton (1933) observed apparently mated pairs along Buffalo Creek in Brooke County on several occasions in late spring but no nesting was proven. The species may nest along some of the mountain streams, or some of the tributaries of the Potomac River more frequently than we know. The limiting factor may be lack of suitable nesting sites.

Fall: The Hooded Merganser does not arrive until early November and then it is usually found only on the larger bodies of water. It usually occurs in family-sized groups and may remain until the end of December unless the water freezes earlier. As in spring, it is most common in the northeast, but becomes more numerous in fall than in spring along the lower Ohio River.

Winter: The Hooded Merganser is not uncommon in late December on Christmas Counts, but

these records may be of birds that would best be called late migrants. Such records are available from Jefferson, Monongalia, Summers, Ohio, Mason, Kanawha, and Cabell Counties. Smaller numbers do winter on the lower Ohio, the Kanawha, and the Potomac. There are winter records also from Cheat Lake.

Specimens: WVUM, S, CU, MU.

*COMMON MERGANSER
Mergus merganser Linnaeus

Status: Uncommon migrant and winter visitant.

Spring: The winter population of Common Mergansers leaves almost as soon as the first weather warm enough to assure open water in the north arrives. Few remain in our region after early March. It occurs only on the bigger lakes and reservoirs, and the larger rivers. It is probably more numerous on the Ohio River than elsewhere, but it is seldom numerous at any place.

Fall: The Common Merganser arrives in November and December and is found only on the larger bodies of water such as the Ohio and Kanawha Rivers. It is seldom numerous but flocks of 10 or so have been seen.

First-seen Fall Date: Cabell-Mason Counties, 17 November.

Winter: The Common Merganser winters in small numbers on the lower Ohio River and on the Potomac and Shenandoah Rivers in the Eastern Panhandle. Seven Christmas Counts have averaged two at Charles Town (5–1) and 4.5 at Mason County (8–1). It is more unusual on the Kanawha where Handley (1976) listed only six records. It also occurs occasionally on Bluestone Reservoir, Summers County. Unlike most of the other diving ducks, this species is only casual or rare on Cheat Lake.

Specimen: I am unable to locate a specimen for the state.

RED-BREASTED MERGANSER
Mergus serrator Linnaeus

Status: Uncommon to fairly common migrant; casual winter visitant.

Spring: The Red-breasted Merganser arrives in late February, but the main migration is usually in late March or early April. It is seldom found away from the larger bodies of water such as the Ohio River, the Potomac River, Cheat Lake, and the other large reservoirs. Most of the birds depart in late April, but it is not unusual to find a few birds, most commonly females, still present in mid-May. This species seems to be more common in the Monongalia-Preston area than in the lower Ohio-Kanawha area.

First-seen Spring Date: Cabell-Mason Counties, 25 February.

Last-seen Spring Date: Cabell-Mason Counties, 7 May.

Fall: The Red-breasted Merganser arrives in the second half of November and may be numerous through December. It does not seem to be as common anywhere in fall as in spring, and as in that season it is found only on the larger lakes and streams.

First-seen Fall Date: Cabell-Mason Counties, 19 November.

Last-seen Fall Date: Cabell-Mason Counties, 26 December.

Winter: There are occasional winter records from the lower Ohio River and the Kanawha River, but most of the late-December birds will not spend the winter in the state.

Specimens: WVUM, MU.

RUDDY DUCK   *Oxyura jamaicensis* (Gmelin)

Status: Common migrant; casual winter visitant.

Spring: The Ruddy Duck arrives in early or mid-March and generally remains in the state until mid-April. It usually occurs in pairs or in small groups, but sometimes flocks of as many as 10 to 20 are seen. It usually occurs on the larger lakes and streams and only occasionally will occur on small ponds. The Ruddy Duck probably migrates through the whole state, but it is rare or uncommon away from the favored duck localities in the northeastern and southwestern parts of the state.

First-seen Spring Dates: Cabell-Mason Counties, 3 March; Monongalia-Preston Counties, 27 March.

Fall: The Ruddy Duck arrives in late October or early November and remains until early or mid-December. It is somewhat more numerous in fall than in spring, and flocks as large as 100 have been seen on Cheat Lake and the Kanawha River.

First-seen Fall Date: Cabell-Mason Counties, 5 November.

Last-seen Fall Date: Cabell-Mason Counties, 30 November.

Winter: A few Ruddy Ducks remain throughout the winter on the larger bodies of water that remain ice-free. There are winter records from Monongalia, Ohio, Mason, Cabell, and Kanawha Counties.

Specimens: WVUM, MU.

Family Carthartidae   NEW WORLD VULTURES

*BLACK VULTURE   *Coragyps atratus* (Bechstein)

Status: Uncommon to fairly common local summer resident; uncommon to fairly common winter resident.

Distribution: The Black Vulture was not known for the state prior to 3 July 1930 when C. O. Handley saw eight near Lewisburg, Greenbrier County (Handley, 1931). At present, it occurs sparingly throughout eastern West Virginia east of the main Allegheny Divide in the Ridge and Valley Avifaunal Region from Mercer to Jefferson Counties. It is not as common as the Turkey Vulture. It has penetrated the area west of the divide by means of the New River passageway (Brooks, 1952) and occurs in good numbers in the southern Greenbrier Valley, but becomes rare in the higher, more northern part of that valley. In recent years, it has advanced farther down the New River drainage and is now occasionally seen in the Kanawha Valley near Charleston. According to Edeburn, et al. (1960), it occurs in Wayne County as far north as Wayne and one was seen at Cabwaylingo State Forest in May 1948, but it was not recorded there during the 1952 Brooks Bird Club Foray. There is a June sighting for the Canaan Valley, Tucker County (1951 Foray), which was probably of a stray bird. The birds may be seen elsewhere in spring and fall. There are records from the Point Pleasant area in March 1968, the only ones I find from the Ohio Valley. In September 1972, two were seen from the hawk-watching station at Bear Rocks, Tucker County, the first local record (W. Wylie and H. Heimerdinger) and they have been reported from there from time to time since 1972. In the early winter of 1974–75, Black Vultures were found to out-number Turkey Vultures near Lewisburg, Greenbrier County (C. Handley). The only nesting records for the Black Vulture come from Monroe County (G. Flouer), Morgan County (R. Bartgis and R. Dean), and Berkeley County (Bartgis and S. Roach).

Specimen: I am unable to locate any specimens taken in the state.

TURKEY VULTURE   *Cathartes aura* Linnaeus

Status: Fairly common to common summer resident; uncommon to fairly common local winter visitant.

Spring: Turkey Vultures begin to appear north

of the winter range in late February and early March when they are seen on warm sunny days in most of the state where they commonly nest.

First-seen Spring Dates: Kanawha County, 15 February; Cabell-Mason Counties, 27 February; Summers County, 28 February.

Summer: The Turkey Vulture is most common in the southern and eastern parts of the state, particularly where the forest is greatly interrupted by open land. The greatest numbers are in the Ridge and Valley Region. It inhabits the mountain valleys as well as the broader lowland valleys. It becomes less numerous toward the Ohio River, and in most of the upper Ohio Valley it is uncommon or almost absent. It is somewhat more numerous in the lower Ohio and Kanawha Valleys. Nests have been found in Jefferson, Berkeley, Morgan, Hampshire, Randolph, Greenbrier, Monroe, Preston, Monongalia, Marshall, Wirt, Braxton, Summers, and Cabell Counties.

Fall: Flocks of vultures are common at the autumn hawk-watching stations, but most of these birds are not migrating. In the northern part of the range, departure takes place in late October and November after the hawk watchers have ceased activity.

Last-seen Fall Date: Cabell-Mason Counties, 10 October.

Winter: In the southern part of the state, the Turkey Vulture is virtually a permanent resident. Some large winter roosts are known from Jefferson, Greenbrier, and Monroe Counties. It occurs sparingly elsewhere in the state, but is rarely found in the Upper Ohio Valley or in the higher mountains during the winter.

Populations: One hundred fifty-five Breeding Bird Survey Routes have average 1.1 (12.30–0.1) birds per route. The highest counts have been in Pendleton County. Christmas Count averages have been: Lewisburg, 35 (79–31); Charles Town, 20 (40–6); Inwood, 6 (41–2); and Hampshire County, 25 (69–1). No other counts have reported vultures.

Remarks: Turkey Vulture populations have gradually declined for a number of years. Such factors as changing farming practices as well as pesticide effects on breeding success are probably responsible.

Specimen: WVU.

Family Accipitridae

One of the ornithological attractions of the Appalachians is the southbound migration of large numbers of raptors along the mountain ridges. In West Virginia, flights of varying size occur along all of the ridges of the Ridge and Valley Region as well as those in the Allegheny Mountains from the Blue Ridge on the Virginia border in Jefferson County to Chestnut Ridge in Monongalia-Preston Counties. The mountains that have the largest flights are those of the Ridge and Valley Region, the Blue Ridge, North Mountain, Berkeley County, Great North Mountain on the Virginia border in Hampshire County, North River Mountain, Hampshire County, the Allegheny Front in either Mineral or Tucker Counties, Backbone Mountain, Tucker County, and in particular Peters Mountain in Monroe County. Some details of these flights have been published by DeGarmo (1953) and Hurley (1970, 1975).

These flights start in mid-September and at that time the principal species is the Broad-winged Hawk, which comes in large numbers each day. Such species as Red-shouldered Hawks, Northern Harriers, Ospreys, American Kestrels, and occasionally both species of eagle are also present at this time. After the Broad-winged flight has passed, large numbers of Sharp-shinned Hawks come through in early October, and later in the month good numbers of Red-tailed Hawks migrate.

OSPREY   *Pandion haliaeetus* (Linnaeus)

Status: Uncommon spring migrant; casual to rare summer resident; uncommon to fairly common fall migrant.

Spring: The Osprey migrates throughout the state during the latter half of April and early May. At this time it may be seen over the larger streams and almost any good-sized lake. At some places the birds remain for a few days before passing on.

First-seen Spring Date: Cabell-Mason Counties, 11 April.

Summer: There are only six definite nesting records: Alton, Upshur County in 1894 (F. E. Brooks); Tomlinson Run State Park, Hancock County in 1968 and 1969 (E. R. Chandler); Tygart Reservoir, Taylor County in 1971 (D. Mathews); East Lynn Reservoir, Wayne County in 1973 (R. Hogg); and Marshall County in 1975 (A. Dunnell). There are many summer records from Preston County and nesting has

surely taken place there at times. Other summer records come from Morgan, Mineral, Hardy, Greenbrier, and Kanawha Counties.

Fall: The Osprey is a regular migrant along the eastern mountain ridges during all of September and early October. In the early 1950s, as many as 26 were seen at a single location in one day, but with the general decline in the continental Osprey population today's counts are lower. In the mid-1970s, there was some indication of an upturn in numbers. Away from the mountain ridges, the Osprey is occasionally seen near the larger streams and lakes. There is a late-December record from Huntington, but in general the species does not winter in our area.

First-seen Fall Date: Kanawha County, 10 September.

Last-seen Fall Date: Kanawha County, 24 September.

Specimen: WVU.

AMERICAN SWALLOW-TAILED KITE
          Elanoides forficatus (Linnaeus)

Status: Accidental visitant.

Record: T. Surber reported one collected by F. McConnell near Mill Hill, Greenbrier County, on 3 September 1908 (in litt., to F. E. Brooks). The Swallow-tailed Kite seen by many observers at Cumberland, Maryland, in the fall of 1974 almost certainly occurred over West Virginia at times.

Specimen: The location of the Greenbrier County specimen is unknown.

BALD EAGLE   *Haliaeetus leucocephalus* (Linnaeus)

Status: Rare to casual visitant at all season; casual summer resident.

Records: The Bald Eagle has been reported in the state in every month except January. Most of these records come from the mountain hawk-watching stations during the fall migration and from one to five or six are reported annually at these stations. At other times of the year, it is most commonly seen over the major streams, the Ohio, the Kanawha, the Monongahela, and the Cheat, but there are scattered reports from throughout the state. Most of these reports come in late winter and early spring.

There are summer records from Wetzel, Berkeley, Hardy, Pendleton, and Webster Counties. After

wintering in the South Branch Valley, a pair of eagles nested along this river in Hardy County in the spring of 1981, the first known nesting for the state (B. Levaas). This nest was again active in 1982. Brooks (1944) mentions a "somewhat uncertain" record from the Greenbrier River. Most summer birds probably represent the usual post-breeding-season wandering of southern birds.

The general decline in the continental Bald Eagle population since the 1940s does not seem to have been reflected in West Virginia records.

Specimens: WVU, USNM, MU, S. No subspecific examination has been made of the West Virginia specimens, but it is probable that the northern subspecies *alascanus* Townsend occurs in fall migration and in winter, and the southern form *leucocephalus* occurs in summer.

NORTHERN HARRIER   *Circus cyaneus* (Linnaeus)

Status: Uncommon spring migrant; uncommon to fairly common local fall migrant; rare local summer resident; rare to uncommon local winter visitant.

Spring: The Northern Harrier probably migrates throughout the state but generally does not occur over forested land. Most spring observations come from marshy areas or the wet open fields such as are selected for nesting, and are made from late March or early April.

First-seen Spring Dates: Kanawha County, 15 March; Cabell-Mason Counties, 6 April.

Summer: Harriers nest sparingly in some of the mountain bogs. A nest was found at Terra Alta, Preston County, in 1936 (F. Conner) and another at Cranesville Bog, Preston County, in 1944 (W. R. DeGarmo). Nests were found in the Canaan Valley, Tucker County, in 1948 (Ward, 1948) and in 1953. One or more pairs usually summer in the open boggy areas atop the Allegheny Front, and young birds were seen there in 1973 (N. Laitsch). Prior to the 1950s, Harriers probably nested at the McClintic Wildlife Station, but the increased human activity following the opening of the area resulted in the disappearance of the species. In some years, at least, it may nest in the Altona Marsh, Jefferson County. One was seen in Greenbrier County 30 May 1981 (BBC Foray).

Fall: Hawk watchers on the eastern mountain ridges can expect to see one or two Northern Harriers on almost any day in September and early October. There is some suggestion that it may be more common later in the season. Elsewhere the species is occasionally seen over wet open or marshy areas with most of the records coming from Cabell and Mason Counties.

Winter: There are Christmas Count records from Jefferson, Berkeley, Hampshire, Mason, Ohio, Cabell, and Kanawha Counties. Most Counts will report one or two but usually not in every year. Northern Harriers may winter elsewhere in the state where there is suitable habitat.

Remarks: This species is called Marsh Hawk in almost all the literature.

Specimens: WVU, UMMZ, MU.

SHARP-SHINNED HAWK *Accipiter striatus* Vieillot

Status: Rare to uncommon permanent resident; fairly common to very common fall migrant in the mountains.

Distribution: The Sharp-shinned Hawk probably occurs in every county, although the populations are usually small at most places. There are nesting records from Preston, Randolph, Pendleton, Greenbrier, Monroe, Wirt, Upshur, Summers, Kanawha, and Cabell Counties. The Sharp-shinned Hawk inhabits any forested habitat but at present it is probably most numerous in the northern forest at higher elevations. As with most other raptors this species has declined greatly in population in recent years.

Sharp-shins may be seen in any month of the year, but they migrate from the Northern Panhandle and from the higher mountains during the coldest part of the winter. There is some hint of a spring migration in April.

Fall Migration: The Sharp-shinned Hawk moves south along the Allegheny Mountains in considerable numbers during the fall. The heaviest movement takes place in October, after the majority of the hawk watchers have ceased operations. During September counts have averaged about seven birds per day per station (range 54–0), while in October a small sample of counts averaged 90 (146–14). Sharp-shins do not form flocks but come as individuals, usually flying rapidly at rather low elevations just above the treetops.

Winter: Twenty-one Christmas Counts reporting the Sharp-shinned Hawk have averaged 1.7 per count (8–1).

Remarks: At A.F.M.O., it has been a rather common occurrence for Sharp-shins to "patrol" the net lanes, but only 27 have been captured. A Sharp-shinned Hawk that had been banded at Point Pelee National Park, Ontario, the previous fall, was recaptured at A.F.M.O. in the fall of 1969. One banded at Ona, Cabell County, on 31 December 1963 was recovered in North Carolina the following spring.

Specimens: WVU, UMMZ, USNM, CU, MU.

COOPER'S HAWK *Accipiter cooperii* (Bonaparte)

Status: Rare to uncommon permanent resident; uncommon to fairly common fall migrant in the mountains.

Distribution: The Cooper's Hawk occurs throughout the state. It does not require as continuous a forest as does the Sharp-shinned Hawk, and is more widely distributed through the farmlands of the state, providing there are woodlots for nesting. It is not common in the dense northern forest at high elevations and is apparently missing from the spruce forest. Definite nesting records come from Hampshire, Tucker, Greenbrier, Monongalia, Hancock, Brooke, Wirt, Summers, Kanawha, and Cabell Counties. Cooper's Hawk populations have declined greatly in the last 10 to 20 years, and the species should be considered almost endangered.

Fall Migration: The Cooper's Hawk migrates in small numbers along the mountain ridges, but never becomes so common at this time as does the Sharp-shin. This migration takes place throughout September and October, and a few birds may still be moving in November. Daily counts have averaged about four birds per station.

Winter: Twenty-two Christmas Counts have averaged 1.5 bird per count (3–1).

Remarks: At one time this may have been the most common hawk in the state, except possibly for the Kestrel. This situation does not hold today. Accipiters are not as likely to be shot as "vermin" as are the soaring hawks; consequently, the decline may be due to more subtle environmental factors. The food chain, insect-small bird-accipiter, may result in a greater concentration of pesticide in the raptor than does the chain, grass and herbs-mouse-buteo.

Specimens: WVU, UMMZ, OP, CU, MU.

NORTHERN GOSHAWK *Accipiter gentilis* (Linnaeus)

Status: Rare winter visitant; accidental or casual summer resident.

Records: The Goshawk enters the state in winter sporadically, but occasionally some numbers are present. A major invasion took place in 1926–27 (Brooks, 1944) when records came from all parts of the state. However, the very heavy fall migration in 1973 observed at many places in the northeast was unnoticed in West Virginia. This may have been because little hawk watching was being done at the time of the flight, but there were also very few reports during the winter. There are winter records from Monongalia, Barbour, Nicholas, Hancock, Brooke, Ohio, Gilmer, Putnam, Kanawha, and Cabell Counties. Most of these have been of single birds. Fall reports have come from Jefferson, Mineral, and Kanawha Counties and some late-spring reports come from Kanawha and Cabell Counties.

There have been a sprinkling of reports from the mountain counties during the summer and nesting has been suspected. One was collected near Glady, Randolph County on 18 April 1951 by J. Rhodes. Goshawks were reported from the Canaan Valley in June of 1956 (T. Shields) and May of 1972, but nesting was not established until May 1975 when a nest was found in Canaan Valley, Tucker County by J. Rawson and R. Hall.

When the field notes of S. S. Dickey became available, it was learned that he had taken sets of Goshawk eggs near Bemis, Randolph County, in 1951 and 1959.

Remarks: Goshawks are difficult to identify, and some sight records are undoubtedly in error. Unusually large female Cooper's Hawks may approach *gentilis* in size, or may appear to when seen at a distance.

Specimens: WVU, CM, Center for Culture and History in Charleston.

RED-SHOULDERED HAWK *Buteo lineatus* (Gmelin)

Status: Uncommon migrant; uncommon to fairly common summer resident; rare to uncommon winter visitant. Some birds are permanent residents.

Spring and Summer: The Red-shouldered Hawk appears in areas where it has not wintered in late February or early March. Nest building has been

observed in February. In summer it is distributed throughout the state in moderate numbers. The Red-shouldered Hawk is most common in the eastern part of the state and in the mountains, but it also occurs in the lowlands. The Red-shouldered Hawk is almost entirely a forest bird and is seldom seen away from extensive wooded areas, although it is most commonly seen soaring over such areas. At present, the Red-shouldered is probably more common than the Red-tailed at most places. Definite nesting records are available for Randolph, Greenbrier, Barbour, Monongalia, Nicholas, Wirt, Wood, Raleigh, Kanawha, McDowell, Lincoln, Mason, and Cabell Counties. This species is not as common in the Northern Panhandle as elsewhere.

Fall: In the autumn a few Red-shouldered Hawks move along the mountain ridges, but a count of two a day per station is about par. This movement is spread throughout September and October.

Winter: Red-shouldered Hawks winter in small numbers in the lower Ohio and Kanawha Valleys, and more sparingly in the eastern valleys. They are not found at this time in northern West Virginia or in the high mountains.

Specimens: USNM, CU, MU. All specimens belong to the subspecies *lineatus*.

BROAD-WINGED HAWK *Buteo platypterus* (Viellot)

Status: Fairly common spring migrant; rare to fairly common summer resident; very common fall migrant, becoming abundant to very abundant along the mountain ridges; casual winter visitant.

Spring: The Broad-winged Hawk appears in the second week in April and the peak of migration probably comes in the third week of April. At this time, it migrates throughout the state, and does not seem to be concentrated on the mountain ridges as in fall, nor does it occur in the large flocks so common in fall. In some locations there seem to be regular flight paths that produce local concentrations, but there has been essentially no "hawk watching" on the mountain ridges in the spring.

First-seen Spring Dates: Kanawha County, 9 April; Summers County, 12 April; Brooke County, 20 April; Monongalia County, 25 April; Ohio County, 26 April.

Summer: The Broad-winged Hawk is now probably the most common and widely distributed buteo in the state. As a summer resident, it is apparently not very common in the Cabell-Mason Counties area, and in years past it was uncommon in the Northern Panhandle (Sutton, 1933). In Hancock County, however, it has become more numerous than it was 40 years ago. Elsewhere in the state it is found in almost any deciduous woodland, being most numerous in the major river valleys, and in the

Allegheny Mountains. The Broad-winged Hawk requires a sizeable woodlot with mature trees for a nesting site and hunting territory; as a result, the population of a given area depends on the abundance of this sort of habitat. Definite nesting records come from Hampshire, Pendleton, Randolph, Pocahontas, Greenbrier, Nicholas, Preston, Monongalia, Hancock, Ohio, Wirt, Summers, McDowell, Lincoln, Kanawha, and Cabell Counties.

Fall: From mid- to late-September, extensive flights of Broad-winged Hawks occur along the mountain ridges in the east. At this time, the birds come in large aggregations, which are probably not properly called flocks, that may vary in size from half a dozen to a thousand or more. Daily counts in the hundreds are commonplace and on many occasions the daily total will go over 1,000. The highest count on record was 2,686 Broad-wings on 20 September 1974 at Hanging Rocks on Peters Mountain, but an earlier, unreported count was above 3,000. The Peters Mountain station has averaged 5,155 Broad-wings per year over the period 1972 to 1975 in 10 days of observation per year (Hurley, 1975). Away from the mountains Broad-wings may be uncommon or even missing in the fall. There is some evidence of a movement through the Ohio Valley, and in recent years there have been good flights at Charleston totalling several thousand birds in a year. The flights in the Kanawha Valley have occasionally been correlated with weather conditions that produce heavy fog in the eastern mountains for several days, thus causing a change from their normal flight path. By the last week in September, the heavy Broad-wing flight is essentially over, but a few stragglers may be present in early October.

Winter: There are a few reports of wintering Broad-wings in the lower Ohio and Kanawha Valleys, and more rarely in the Eastern Panhandle. The A.O.U. Check-list (1957) considered that no Broad-winged Hawks wintered north of southern Florida, but either this is in error or the bird has changed some of its habits. Most of our reports of wintering Broad-wings are undoubtedly misidentifications, but it is possible that the species does winter in the state on occasion.

Specimens: USNM, MU, GMS.

SWAINSON'S HAWK   *Buteo swainsonii* Bonaparte

Status: Accidental fall visitor.
Record: One was collected on 16 September 1897 near White Sulphur Springs, Greenbrier County, by M. M. Collins (Surber 1898).
Specimen: The present location of this specimen is unknown.

RED-TAILED HAWK   *Buteo jamaicensis* (Gmelin)

Status: Uncommon to fairly common spring migrant; rare to uncommon summer resident; fairly common to very common fall migrant; uncommon to fairly common winter visitant. Many birds are probably permanent residents.

Spring and Summer: There is a small movement of Red-tailed Hawks through the state in March, and many of the winter visitants depart at that time. The resident birds may also start to nest in March.

The Red-tailed Hawk breeds throughout the state, but it is not common in the northern forest, nor indeed in any of the densely forested areas. It is most numerous in the lowlands and in farming areas where woodlots suitable for nesting are mixed with grazing and farmlands. Formerly, this bird was quite numerous, but it has suffered greatly from the indiscriminant shooting of raptors. It is an easy target as it is easily seen as it soars over open country.

Definite nesting records come from Hampshire, Greenbrier, Monroe, Preston, Monongalia, Lewis, Summers, Hancock, Brooke, Ohio, Wood, Wirt, Doddridge, Kanawha, McDowell, Mason, and Cabell Counties.

Fall: In October there is a good migration of Red-tailed Hawks along the mountain ridges. Redtails do not form "kettles" as do Broad-wings but come in singles or in twos or threes. Rather few hawk counts have been made in October, but six counts from the Bear Rocks, Tucker County, average 50 birds per day. Two November counts averaged 56. A few birds pass through in September during the Broad-wing flight, but the counts will rarely average 10 in a day.

Winter: Red-tailed Hawks winter in small numbers throughout the state, and in some of the broader river valleys at low elevations there may be good-sized populations of both permanent residents and visitants from the north. Fifty Christmas Counts have averaged about four birds per count.

Specimens: USNM, UMMZ. All identified specimens are referable to the eastern subspecies, *borealis* (Gmelin). There are at least two sight records for Red-tailed Hawks with much white in the plumage that may have been the western form, *krideri* Hoopes, and an occasional darkly colored bird may represent the western subspecies, *calurus* Cassin, or may simply be a melanistic eastern bird.

ROUGH-LEGGED HAWK
   Buteo lagopus (Pontoppidan)

Status: Casual to rare migrant; casual winter visitant.

Spring: There are very few reports of this species in spring, but single records come from Canaan Valley, Tucker County, April 1938 (I. B. Boggs); Marshall County, 20 April 1941 (B. Waterman); Ohio County, 18 April 1937; Kanawha County, 1 March 1939 (C. Upton); and McClintic Wildlife Station, Mason County, 17 March 1963.

Fall: One or two Rough-legged Hawks are seen almost every year from some of the hawk-watching stations on the eastern mountain ridges. Most of the records are from the Bear Rocks station or from A.F.M.O. Dates of observation range from the last week in September to early October. Away from the mountains, the records are in November and December and come mostly from the Mason-Cabell County area and along the Kanawha River to Charleston. There are a few records from Ohio County.

Winter: A few Rough-legged Hawks winter rather regularly in the Cabell-Mason County area and they are sometimes seen at Charleston. Legg (1944) mentioned them as occasionally wintering in Nicholas County. There are Christmas Count records from Jefferson, Berkeley, Ohio, and Hampshire Counties.

Remarks: Both color phases of this hawk have been seen in the state during migration. The two reports of Rough-legged Hawks in the state in the summer (Reddish Knob, Pendleton County, 1963 and Bear Rocks, Tucker County, 1960) are almost certainly misidentifications. The birds seen are much more likely to have been Golden Eagles than Rough-legged Hawks.

Specimen: USNM.

GOLDEN EAGLE   *Aquila chrysaetos* (Linnaeus)

Status: Rare fall migrant; rare winter visitant; rare local permanent resident.

Records: The Golden Eagle has been seen in the mountain areas throughout the year. Most of

these reports come from the Canaan Valley and the Allegheny Front area in Tucker County, and from the mountainous parts of Pendleton County. There is no definite evidence that the species has ever nested in the state, but four young birds were captured by a hunter near Dunmore, Pocahontas County, in 1934 (Brooks, 1944) and there are many summer reports. One was seen near Morgantown on 16 June 1976 (G. A. Hall). In 1965 a Golden Eagle was seen at the Bear Rocks from August through October. It seems likely that even now in the 1980s this species does on occasion nest on some remote mountain cliff. A bird seen at the Pipestem State Resort, Summers County, on 17 September 1972 (O. Johnson) seems rather early for a migrant as does the one seen at A.F.M.O. in early September 1973 (J. Findley and G. Hall).

Golden Eagles are seen from the hawk-watching stations in almost every year from late September to Early October. An unusually early migrant was seen at McClintic Wildlife Station on 18 August 1958 (G. Hurley). During the winter, Golden Eagles may be seen in the mountains and nearby with reports coming from Greenbrier, Monroe, Hampshire, Pendleton, Summers, and Gilmer Counties. In 1974 one spent part of the late winter in the Chestnut Ridge area near Morgantown. Three and possibly five Golden Eagles, feeding on sheep carcasses, were seen near the Sinks of Gandy, Randolph County, on 4 March 1976 (E. Olliver). A. S. Morgan tells of seeing one at Poca in 1939 and in his collection were the tail feathers of one shot many years ago by his father. The Smithsonian party saw one near Huntington on 27 October 1936 (Wetmore, 1937).

Specimens: WVU, CM. (Numerous mounted Golden Eagles are on display in a variety of public places throughout the state.)

Family Falconidae   FALCONS

AMERICAN KESTREL   *Falco sparverius* Linnaeus

Status: Uncommon to common permanent resident. More numerous in the winter.

Distribution: The Kestrel probably occurs throughout the state. It is most common in the Ohio River Valley and the Kanawha Valley and becomes rather scarce or absent in the higher mountains and mountain valleys. It favors open country and the largest populations will be in those farming areas of the state that supply this habitat. In winter, it is more numerous in all parts of the state, and in the mountain valleys it seems to occur only at that time.

During this season, it is conspicuous along the highways, particularly when snow covers the fields.

There is a considerable movement of Kestrels along the mountain ridges in fall and several may be seen in each day of observation. At some lookouts, they will be missed due to their habit of flying rapidly past the observation point at low elevations.

There are definite nesting records from Jefferson, Hampshire, Grant, Randolph, Pocahontas, Greenbrier, Monroe, Preston, Monongalia, Lewis, Summers, Hancock, Brooks, Ohio, Marshall, Wood, Ritchie, Mason, Kanawha, and Cabell Counties. It nests in towns and cities upon buildings, and nests have been found on the State Capitol Building in Charleston.

Despite the common occurrence of this species, 108 Breeding Bird Survey routes in seven years listed only 21 Kestrels.

Remarks: Most of the literature refers to this small falcon as the Sparrow Hawk.

Specimens: WVU, MU.

MERLIN   *Falco columbarius* Linnaeus

Status: Rare migrant; casual winter visitant.

Spring: The Merlin may occur throughout the state during the spring migration with records coming from Monongalia, Randolph, Mason, Kanawha, and Cabell Counties. Most of these records are in April and early May.

Fall: A few Merlins are reported by the hawk watchers each fall. As many as four have been seen in one day. One was banded at A.F.M.O. in 1980. There are a few scattered records away from the eastern ridges from Jefferson, Monongalia, Braxton, Mason, Kanawha, and Cabell Counties. Some birds may remain as late as early November.

Winter: One wintered in Berkeley County in 1957–58; there is a January record from the McClintic Wildlife Station and a February 1975 record from Elkins (E. Olliver).

Remarks: There have been a few early August reports from the Allegheny Front and other mountain areas that seem a little early for fall migrants. This implies that occasional birds may summer in the high mountains and that nesting may occur at times.

In most of the literature prior to 1973 this species was called Pigeon Hawk.

Specimen: WVU.

PEREGRINE FALCON   *Falco peregrinus* Tunstall

Status: Casual to rare migrant and winter visitant; formerly a rare local summer resident, but the breeding population is now extirpated.

Migration: In the pre-pesticide days when the Peregrine was widely distributed in eastern United States, there were a few records in the state during spring, but the only recent ones have been in April and May of 1961 just across the Virginia line from Jefferson County (C. Miller).

In the fall a few Peregrines are seen each year migrating along the mountain ridges. Even prior to the extirpation of the eastern population the bird was rare; for example, three were seen during a season-long watch at the Bear Rocks, Tucker County, in 1948 (DeGarmo, 1953). During the falls of 1951 and 1952, 83 days of observation at some 30 lookouts on the eastern ridges listed only 10 Peregrines (DeGarmo, 1953). Now in the 1980s few are seen.

The only recent records are: one at Peters Mountain, Monroe County, 24 September 1971; three at Bear Rocks, 25 September 1971 (Heimerdinger, 1974); two there on 19 September 1972; and one each at Bear Rocks on 16 and 19 September 1974. Away from the ridges, the Peregrine was formerly seen in many places in the state on occasion, but the only recent records have been from the McClintic Wildlife Station and from near Charleston. There was a sighting in Raleigh County in June 1975 (H. S. Crawford, in litt.).

Winter: Formerly there were winter occurrences in Jefferson and Berkeley Counties (probably of a resident population), and one was seen in Monongalia County in the winter of 1951–52. In recent years there have been occasional reports from the lower Ohio Valley near Huntington and the McClintic Wildlife Station.

Former Nesting: The Peregrine probably once nested in several places in the mountain area wherever suitable cliffs occur, but there are good records of only five documented eyries (D. D. Berger, in litt., M. Brooks). One of these was along the North Branch of the Potomac in Mineral County near Keyser. Another was in the White Sulphur Springs area in Greenbrier County. The most well-known one was at Ead's Fort on the Great Cacapon River, Morgan County. A photograph of this eyrie was published by F. E. Brooks and A. B. Brooks (E. A. Brooks, 1916). This eyrie was active at least until 1937, and it is probable that this is the one which fledged young in 1949 (DeGarmo, 1950). F. E. and A. B. Brooks found another nest on the "Devil's Nose" also on the Great Cacapon River. There was also a possible eyrie near Petersburg on the road to Moorefield. The Peregrine nested at least as late as 1939 on the bluffs on the Maryland side of the Potomac River at Harper's Ferry (Wimsatt, 1938, 1940), and these birds certainly utilized a portion of West Virginia. The only eyrie west of the mountains was on the Guyandot River near Baileysville, Wyoming County.

Specimens: WVU, MU.

Family Phasianidae

Subfamily Phasianinae	PHEASANTS

RING-NECKED PHEASANT
Phasianus colchicus Linnaeus

Status: Introduced. Uncommon local permanent resident.

Distribution: At present, a population of pheasants is in the Northern Panhandle from Hancock County at least as far south as Ohio County. Besides local introductions, these birds are augmented by wanderers from the populations in southwestern Pennsylvania. Much of the pheasant habitat in this area is threatened by urban and suburban expansion.

Until the 1960s, there was a good population in the Morgantown area, but the prime habitat was eliminated in the construction of the University Medical School, and further expansion of the University and the residential areas of the city have all but eliminated this population.

There is a population in the far eastern Panhandle Counties, particularly Jefferson County. Pheasants have been introduced in Mason County, particularly at the McClintic Wildlife Station, and have persisted for a few years, even raising young, but all have now disappeared. Introductions have been attempted in other parts of the state without permanent success. The Department of Natural Resources has established an open season on these birds.

Specimens: WVU, USNM.

Subfamily Tetraoninae	GROUSE

RUFFED GROUSE   *Bonasa umbellus* (Linnaeus)

Status: Uncommon to fairly common permanent resident.

Distribution: The Ruffed Grouse occurs throughout the state in suitable forested habitat. It has become scarce along the Ohio River where its habitat has been eliminated. The greatest populations are probably found in the mountain counties, although few occur in the pure spruce forest.

Much of the forest in the state has matured beyond the state that makes optimum grouse habitat, and it is probable that populations are less than they were in the recent past. The population picture is difficult to interpret, since West Virginia grouse undergo a cycle in population of about 10-year periods, as do the more northern populations. The mid-1970s seemed to represent a low point in this cycle.

Specimens: WVU, USNM, CM, MU. Specimens of grouse from the Allegheny Mountains and from most of the Western Hills Region are all of the subspecies *monticola* Todd, which has its type locality near Cheat Bridge, Randolph County. Two specimens that I have examined from Cabell County (MU) are closest to the subspecies *umbellus*. This latter race might be expected to occur in Jefferson County, but I have seen no specimens from there.

Subfamily Meleagrinae	TURKEYS

WILD TURKEY   *Meleagris gallopavo* Linnaeus

Status: Fairly common permanant resident.

Distribution: In pre-settlement days, the Turkey occurred throughout the state, but with settlement and overshooting it disappeared from most of its range in the state. By the 1920s it had been eliminated from all but the mountain counties. Efforts were made to restock certain areas with game-farm raised birds and with the so-called "wild-mating" system in the 1930s and 1940s; however, all these efforts failed. In the late 1940s, a program was started to live-trap wild birds in the areas where they were numerous for transfer to other areas, which has met with great success (Bailey and Rinell, 1968).

At the present (1982), Turkeys are found in all counties except Wayne and probably Logan (W. K. Igo, in litt.). The greatest populations, and the original sources of the transplanted birds, are in the Allegheny Mountain area from western Berkeley County west to eastern Barbour, Upshur, Braxton, Nicholas, and Fayette Counties, from southern Preston County south to southern Pocahontas County. At present, the Turkey stock is somewhat contaminated with domestic genetic material, but most of them represent pure or nearly pure-blooded "wild" stock.

For the years 1977–1981, an average of 4,000 Turkeys were harvested each year in the two open seasons (West Virginia D.N.R., 1982), and D.N.R. biologists estimate that the prime Turkey areas have a population of about 12,000 birds at the beginning of the spring season.

Specimen: WVU.

Subfamily Odontophorinae	QUAIL

NORTHERN BOBWHITE

Colinus virginianus (Linnaeus)

Status: Fairly common to common permanent resident.

Distribution: The Bobwhite occurs throughout the state and is usually numerous except in the heavily forested areas. It is rare in the high mountain valleys, even when these are open, but I have found it in places as high as 1,100 meters. The largest populations probably occur in the farmlands of the Eastern Panhandle, the South Branch Valley, and in the lower Kanawha-Ohio valleys.

At high elevations and in the north, populations oscillate somewhat with lows being reached after particularly cold and snowy winters. The cold winters of 1977–79 almost eliminated the species from most of northern West Virginia.

Specimens: WVU, UMMZ, MCZ.

Family Rallidae	RAILS

YELLOW RAIL

Coturnicops noveboracensis (Gmelin)

Status: Accidental visitant.

Records: A. S. Morgan collected one near Poca, Putnam County, in 1920 (Handley, 1976). R. and M. Brooks saw one near Volga, Barbour County, on 6 September 1935 (M. Brooks, 1936a). G. F. Flouer found one dead at Clinton, Ohio County, on 8 October 1939 (Flouer, 1940).

Specimen: UMMZ.

*BLACK RAIL   *Laterallus jamaicensis* (Gmelin)

Status: Hypothetical. Accidental visitant.

Record: A Black Rail was seen at Bluefield, Mercer County, on 28 April 1955 by M. Dickinson.

*CLAPPER RAIL   *Rallus longirostris* Boddaert

Status: Hypothetical. Accidental visitant.

Record: In the notes of E. A. Brooks, there appears the following statement, "F. J. Frye saw one near the Ohio River. Positively identified the birds. Said it was not a King Rail." This is apparently the source of the statement attributed to E. A. Brooks of one taken at Waverly, Wood County (Brooks, 1944). No dates given.

Specimen: None available.

KING RAIL   *Rallus elegans* Audubon

Status: Rare migrant; rare and very local summer resident.

Spring: The King Rail probably migrates throughout the state, but there are very few records and most of them come from the places where the bird is found in summer in at least some years. The few arrival dates on hand are all in late April.

Summer: There are nesting records, mostly of broods of small young seen, from Jefferson County—Leetown (at least formerly) (Poland 1938c), Altona marsh and Albemarle Marsh (C. Miller); Wood County—Boaz (P. Murphy); Mason County—Ashton (L. Kiff); Putnam County (Morgan brothers); and Wayne County—Lavalette (Green, 1949). There are also summer records from two other marshes in Jefferson County (Shepherdstown and Lake Louise) and another location in Wood County.

Fall: Fall records are mostly in late September and early October. These come from the summering stations at Leetown and Altona Marsh, Jefferson County, Boaz Marsh, Wood County, and the McClintic Wildlife Station, Mason County. There are also reports from Follansbee, Brooke County (Montagna, 1940), and St. Albans, Kanawha County. There is a record from Poca, Putnam County, on 31 December 1930.

Remarks: The number of marshes suitable for the breeding of this species is extremely limited and all of them are in danger of destruction. The changes in the management practices at the Leetown Federal Fish Hatchery have eliminated that station for this and several other species.

Specimens: WVU, UMMZ, S.

VIRGINIA RAIL   *Rallus limicola* Vieillot

Status: Rare to uncommon migrant; rare to uncommon summer resident; casual winter resident.

Spring: The Virginia Rail probably migrates throughout the state; however, besides the summering stations there are records only from Pendleton, Wood, and Kanawha Counties. Spring records are mostly in late April or early May. The average arrival in the Mason-Cabell area is 4 May, and there is an early date of 16 April from Fort Seybert, Pendleton County.

Summer: Records of nests or downy young are available from Jefferson (Leetown, Altona Marsh); Greenbrier (White Sulphur Springs); Putnam (Poca); Brooke (Beech Bottom Swamp); Mason (Ashton, McClintic Wildlife Station); and Summers Counties. Other summer records come from Hancock, Tucker (Yokum Run, Canaan Valley), Wood (Boaz), and Randolph Counties. The record from St. Marys, Pleasants County (J. Stewart), on 11 August 1974 and Jackson's Mill, Lewis County, on 18 August 1934 (M. Brooks, 1934c) may represent summering birds or extremely early fall migrants.

Fall: This rail is a widespread migrant in September and early October and is liable to turn up in any small marsh in the state. There are fall records from Jefferson, Brooke, Preston (Lake Terra Alta), Nicholas (Mt. Lookout), Mercer (Buffalo), Hancock, and Mason Counties.

Winter: A few apparently winter at the McClintic Wildlife Station (Handley, 1976). At least one spent the winter at Altona marsh, Jefferson County, in 1952–53, and the species was reported on the Jefferson County Christmas Counts in 1963 and 1973.

Remarks: As with the King Rail, the amount of suitable habitat in the state is limited and in danger of elimination. The nesting sites at Beech Bottom Swamp and the Leetown Hatchery are no longer available.

Specimens: MU, S.

SORA   *Porzana carolina* (Linnaeus)

Status: Uncommon spring migrant and summer resident; fairly common fall migrant; rare winter resident.

Spring: The Sora probably migrates throughout the state, and it sometimes turns up in very small patches of marshland. Arrival dates vary from mid- to late-April (20 April, Wood County; 26 April Cabell-Mason Counties), and the bird is often present until late May. There are definite spring records from Jefferson (Altona Marsh); Berkeley; Preston (Reedsville); Hancock, Brooke (Beech Bottom Swamp); Ohio (Oglebay Park); Wood; Putnam; Nicholas; and Mason Counties.

Summer: Surber (E. A. Brooks, 1909) found the bird nesting at White Sulphur Springs, Greenbrier County, prior to 1900. Wetmore (1937) believed that they were nesting at Muddlety, Nicholas County, in 1936. W. R. DeGarmo saw an immature Sora along the Tygart Valley River, Randolph County on 20 August 1952, which may have been raised locally. There are June records from St. Marys, Pleasants County; Boaz, Wood County; Summersville, Nicholas County; Monroe County; McClintic Wildlife Station, Mason County; and Putnam County, as well as late-summer reports from Wayne County (Dickson). It is odd that there have been no summer records from the Altona Marsh, Jefferson County.

Fall: This species is much more common in fall than in other seasons and numbers up to 50 have been counted at suitable places. August dates may represent summer records or may be early migrants, but the greatest numbers are present throughout September and into early October, with a few dates as late as 9 November (Kanawha County). There are fall records from Preston (Lake Terra Alta), Brooke (Beech Bottom), Randolph (Cheat Mountain), Upshur (French Creek), Greenbrier (Lewisburg), Raleigh (Ghent), Cabell (Huntington), Mason (McClintic Station), and Kanawha (Charleston, Belle) Counties.

Winter: A few winter at McClintic Wildlife Station, Mason County, and there is an old record for Lewis County in January 1914 (E. A. Brooks, 1929).

Specimens: WVU, USNM, UMMZ, MU.

PURPLE GALLINULE

                    Porphyrula martinica (Linnaeus)

Status: Accidental visitant.

Records: W. S. Edwards reported one from Coalburg, Kanawha County, "some years ago" (E. A. Brooks, 1909). One was collected by H. G. Mansberger at Walkersville, Lewis County, in the spring of 1923 (WVU specimen), and one was collected at the McClintic Wildlife Station, Mason County, in the summer of 1962. One was seen in Cabell County in June 1952 (Edeburn, et al., 1960); and one was captured and later released in Charleston on 15 April 1951. A freshly killed specimen was picked up beneath a window of a residence in St. Albans, Kanawha County, on 10 May 1958 (Handley, in litt.). One was seen near Beckley, Raleigh County, on 15 May 1978 (J. L. Smith).

Specimens: WVUM, S.

COMMON MOORHEN

Gallinula chloropus (Linnaeus)

Status: Rare migrant; uncommon local summer resident; casual winter visitant.

Spring: This is another species that probably migrates throughout the state but has been reported from only a very few places. There are spring records from Jefferson, Ohio, Wood, Kanawha, Cabell, and Mason Counties. An early date is 30 March in Mason County but most arrive in mid-April.

Summer: Broods of downy young have been found in at least three different locations in Jefferson County (Leetown, Albemarle Marsh, and Lake Louise). In 1952 six broods were located in the county (C. Miller). The Morgans report nesting in Putnam County and one summered at Jackson's Mill, Lewis County, in 1934 (M. Brooks). Records from Rupert, Greenbrier County, on 22 August 1943 and Ohio County on 23 August 1955 may be early fall migrants.

Fall: Most fall migrants do not arrive until early October and are gone by the end of the month. There are fall records from Wood, Mercer, Mason, and Greenbrier Counties.

Winter: One was seen on 30 January 1954 near Eureka, Cabell County (H. K. Land).

Remarks: In the literature prior to 1982, this species is known as the Florida Gallinule or the Common Gallinule.

Specimens: WVU, MU.

AMERICAN COOT

Fulica americana Gmelin

Status: Common to abundant migrant; casual summer resident; casual to rare winter visitant.

Spring: The Coot migrates throughout the state and can be found wherever suitable bodies of water occur. Coots do not commonly occur on farm ponds, and the greatest numbers occur on the major rivers where there are often great concentrations. Arrival is in late March or early April and peak numbers are in the last half of April with a few remaining until mid-May. Occasional stragglers may linger until the first of June.

First-seen Spring Date: Mason-Cabell Counties, 20 March.

Last-seen Spring Date: Mason-Cabell Counties, 12 May.

Summer: The first recorded nesting in the state was at the McClintic Wildlife Station, Mason County, where a brood of young was seen on 29 June 1953 (C. O. Handley, Sr., in litt.). It may nest at that station rather regularly, since there are a number of summer records there. A brood of young was seen at South Charleston, Kanawa County, 12 July 1981 (H. and S. Good). Other summer records come from Leetown, Jefferson County; Parsons, Tucker County; and Lewisburg, Greenbrier County, but in most cases these were of single birds and breeding probably did not occur there.

Fall: The Coot arrives in late October and may be present in numbers until late November with stragglers remaining through December. Some very large flocks are sometimes seen on the larger bodies of water. In November 1950, "hundreds of thousands" of Coots were seen on the Ohio River at Huntington (Edeburn et al., 1960).

First-seen Fall Date: Mason-Cabell Counties, 9 October.

Winter: Coots occasionally winter in small numbers on the lower Ohio River and in the Eastern Panhandle.

Specimens: WVU, UMMZ, MU.

Family Gruidae   CRANES

SANDHILL CRANE   *Grus canadensis* (Linnaeus)

Status: Accidental migrant.

Records: There are only six records. Brooks (1944) reported that one had been taken at Point Pleasant, Mason County, in 1934. W. Russell saw one in the Canaan Valley, Tucker County, in the fall of 1967 and A. Shreve saw one at Berry Hills, Kanawha County, on 19 November 1968. T. K. Pauley saw one near Huntington on 9 February 1972, a rather remarkable date (Pauley, 1974). W. Bailey

and B. Bailey saw one in Preston County near Markleysburg, Pa., on 16 May 1981 (photographed). One was seen in the Dolly Sods area 3 May 1981 by Donna Mitchell. The bone remains of possibly three individuals were found during the excavation of a 17th century Indian village in Putnam County (Guilday, 1971).

Remarks: The population of cranes that summer in Michigan and winter in Florida is apparently increasing and more West Virginia records may be expected in the western part of the state.

Specimen: The whereabouts of the specimen collected in 1934 is unknown. A copy of the photographs of the birds seen in 1972 and 1981 are in the National Photoduplicate File. The bone specimens from the archaeological site are in the collection of P. W. Parmalee, University of Tennessee. Without a specimen for examination, it is impossible to assign the records to a definite subspecies, although the most probably form is *tabida* (Peters).

Family Charadriidae   PLOVERS

BLACK-BELLIED PLOVER
Pluvialis squatarola (Linnaeus)

Status: Casual migrant.

Spring: The Black-bellied Plover is a fairly regular migrant in the Cabell-Mason County area but elsewhere it is very irregular, bordering on accidental. Besides being seen at the edges of ponds, it is often found on airport runways and in flat upland fields. There are May records from Jefferson, Pendleton, Randolph, Hancock, Monongalia, and Kanawha Counties.

Fall: There are very few fall records: 5 and 6 September 1936 at Volga, Barbour County (Brooks, 1936a); Charleston, 13 and 26 October 1949 (C. O. Handley); 4 November 1951, Mason County (Edeburn et al., 1960); Lewisburg, Greenbrier County, 21 September and 16 October 1975 (C. O. Handley); and Leetown, Jefferson County, September 1980 (Honig, 1981).

Specimen: Poland collected one at Leetown, Jefferson County, but the specimen is not with the rest of his collection in the West Virginia University Museum.

*LESSER GOLDEN-PLOVER
Pluvialis dominica (Müller)

Status: Casual migrant.

Records: A. S. Morgan took specimens in Putnam County in 1904 and 1915. There are a number of records from Mason County; 1 September 1956 at Mercers Bottom, and 28 August 1960 at McClintic Wildlife Station (Edeburn et al., 1960); 4 November 1966 at McClintic (Handley, 1976); 1 November 1960, 75 birds at Gallipolis Lock and Dam (W. Argabrite). Other records come from Weirton, Hancock County, on 10 September 1974 (R. Rine), Barboursville, Cabell County, on 16 October 1974 (H. Slack), and Lewisburg, Greenbrier County, on 21 September and 16 October 1975 (C. O. Handley). There have been reports almost annually in the 1970s from Canaan Valley State Park, Tucker County, in late September.

Specimens: I saw no specimens in the Morgan Collection when I examined it in August 1971.

SEMIPALMATED PLOVER
Charadrius semipalmatus Bonaparte

Status: Uncommon migrant, mostly in the spring.

Spring: The Semipalmated Plover migrates in the last half of May, and probably occurs throughout the state. It is to be found in flooded fields, on small ponds, or in flooded strip-mine areas, but seldom occurs in groups of more than two or three.

First-seen Spring Date: Cabell-Mason Counties, 7 May.

Last-seen Spring Date: Cabell-Mason Counties, 25 May.

Fall: Arrives in August and may be found throughout the state, although it is less numerous than in the spring.

Specimens: WVU, UMMZ, CM, CU.

PIPING PLOVER
Charadrius melodus Ord

Status: Accidental visitant.

Records: The only definite record is from Leetown, Jefferson County, where Poland collected one on 14 April 1940 (Poland, 1941).

Remarks: There is one other record of uncertain value. A. S. Morgan collected a bird in Putnam County prior to 1916 whose identity has been the subject of much speculation. Unfortunately, the specimen appears not to be extant. E. A. Brooks (1916) and Bibbee (1929) both listed this specimen under *Charadrius hiaticula*, Ringed Plover, an Old World Species. Haller (1940a) and M. Brooks (1944) both listed this species under *C. melodus*, and this may be correct. A third interpretation supported by myself and Poland (1941) is that the bird was actually *semipalmatus* which in some earlier manuals was called the Ringed Plover, and indeed is thought by some people to be conspecific with *hiaticula*.

Specimen: WVU.

KILLDEER
Charadrius vociferus (Linnaeus)

Status: Common spring and fall migrant; Fairly common summer resident; uncommon to fairly common winter resident.

Spring: The Killdeer migrates throughout the state, occurring at the edges of ponds, in wet boggy situations and in upland pastures and on golf courses. Early arrivals appear before the end of February, but the average arrival comes in the last half of March.

First-seen Spring Dates: Monongalia County, 2 March; Cabell-Mason Counties, 25 March.

Summer: This species probably nests in every county of the state although its numbers will be determined by the amount of nonforested land available. Nests have been found in gravel pits, in parking lots, on the borders of country roads, on newly turned soil, and in similar areas containing gravel and very sparse vegetation. There are definite nesting records from Jefferson, Berkeley, Hampshire, Hardy, Pendleton, Randolph, Pocahontas, Greenbrier, Monroe, Upshur, Barbour, Lewis, Nicholas, Webster, Summers, Raleigh, Monongalia, Hancock, Wood, Wirt, Ritchie, Lincoln, Mason, Kanawha, and Cabell Counties, but it certainly nests in many others.

Populations: Breeding Bird Survey routes averaged 2.1 (6.0–0.4) birds per route.

Fall: Beginning in late August, the Killdeer begins to concentrate on pond and lake shores and numbers sometimes build up to several dozen. These birds generally depart in October. At this time of the year the Killdeer is more of a "shorebird" than at other times.

Winter: The Killdeer winters regularly in small numbers in the lower Ohio Valley and in the Kanawha Valley areas. A total of 87 were reported on the 1971 Christmas Count at Charleston. More irregularly, a few may winter in any part of the state where a combination of some open water, usually in the form of boggy springs, and some open grasslands occur.

Remarks: On several occasions Killdeer nests have been found on the gravel roofs of city buildings.

Specimens: WVU, UMMZ, USNM (downy young), MU.

Family Recurvirostridae   AVOCETS AND STILTS

*AMERICAN AVOCET
Recurvirostra americana Gmelin

Status: Accidental.

Records: An injured avocet was found on 6 July 1977 near Cameron, Marshall County. The bird was kept for several days at the Oglebay Park Zoo in Wheeling, but eventually died. Unfortunately, the specimen was not saved (Buckelew, 1978a).

One was seen near Lewisburg, Greenbrier County, on 14 July 1979 (Handley, Jr., 1979) and two were seen and photographed near Princeton, Mercer County, on 28 July 1980 (J. Phillips, 1980).

Specimens: None. Photograph on file at the U.S. National Photoduplicate File.

Family Scolopacidae

Subfamily Scolopacinae   SANDPIPERS

GREATER YELLOWLEGS
Tringa melanoleuca (Gmelin)

Status: Fairly common spring and fall migrant.

Spring: Found in suitable habitat throughout the state, generally arriving in the middle of April and departing by late May.

First-seen Spring Date: Cabell-Mason Counties, 19 April.

Fall: The Greater Yellowlegs migrates throughout the state, usually arriving in late August, peaking in September, with a few stragglers remaining until early November. At this time, it may be found on any shallow-water area having mudflats.

Specimens: WVU, OP, UMMZ.

LESSER YELLOWLEGS   *Tringa flavipes* (Gmelin)

Status: Fairly common spring and fall migrant.

Spring: The Lesser Yellowlegs migrates throughout the state, arriving in early April and departing by late May. It generally remains somewhat later than the preceding species and is probably somewhat more numerous than that species.

First-seen Spring Date: Cabell-Mason Counties, 6 April.

Fall: This species arrives in early August and departs in October, although some will remain into November. Departure is generally earlier than in the case of the Greater Yellowlegs. One spent the winter of 1961–62 at Leetown, Jefferson County (C.

Miller). It occurs throughout the state on suitable mudflat habitat.

Specimens: WVU, UMMZ, CM.

SOLITARY SANDPIPER   *Tringa solitaria* Wilson

Status: Uncommon spring and fall migrant.

Spring: The Solitary Sandpiper migrates throughout the state and usually occurs on the margins of farm ponds, along backwaters, and along small streams. It is seldom seen on larger bodies of water, but is often found in wooded areas. Arrival is in late April and departure is in late May or even early June.

First-seen Spring Dates: Summers County, 25 April; Cabell-Mason Counties, 10 April; Monongalia County, 3 May.

Fall: A few stragglers will appear in early July but arrival is generally in late July and early August. At this time, it may occur on the larger lakes and ponds as well as the sort of places frequented in spring, and probably occurs througout the state. Most migrants will have departed by mid-September, but some remain even as late as November.

Remarks: This species appears to be much less common since 1970 than it was prior to that time. There are a number of mid-summer records, and indeed, as with some other shorebirds, the time between the last spring departures and the first fall arrivals may be less than a month. The presence of Solitary Sandpipers in the state in mid-summer led to some speculation in the past that the species may breed in the state or nearby regions. However, at present the species is not known to nest anywhere south of the Canadian border.

Specimens: WVU, UMMZ, MU.

*WILLET   *Catoptrophorus semipalmatus* Gmelin

Status: Accident visitant.

Records: A. S. Morgan shot one in Putnam County in 1900 and reported that he saw another one there in 1943. There are three recent sight records: (old) Stony River Reservoir, Grant County, 1 May 1952 (W. R. DeGarmo); Berkeley County, 30 September 1952 (C. Miller); the headwaters of the Williams River, Pocahontas County, 5 May 1965 (R. W. Bailey); and the writer has recorded it twice in Garrett County, Maryland, just a few miles from the West Virginia border.

Specimen: The Putnam County specimen was not apparent in the Morgan Collection in August 1971.

SPOTTED SANDPIPER   *Actitis macularia* (Linnaeus)

Status: Fairly common spring and fall migrant; fairly common summer resident.

Spring: The Spotted Sandpiper migrates throughout the state and will be found along almost all sizeable streams and on many farm ponds. Arrival is generally in the last half of April.

First-seen Spring Dates: Summers County, 15 April; Cabell-Mason Counties, 18 April; Wood County, 20 April; Monongalia County, 27 April.

Summer: This species probably nests in every county, although actual breeding records are very few. The only breeding records made on the annual Forays are a nest in Hardy County and downy young birds in Pendleton and Hampshire Counties. Other breeding records come from Berkeley, Hampshire, Brooke, Ohio, and Summers Counties. The species occurs in summer on the banks of almost all fair-sized streams except in heavily forested country, and may also nest near large farm ponds. Populations have greatly declined in recent years as more and more suitable streams have become polluted by acid mine-drainage water. At present, the species is one for which there should be concern and the populations should be carefully watched.

Fall: The Spotted Sandpiper begins to migrate in late August and continues to move through the state in September. Most will be gone by early October, although stragglers may remain as long as there is open water.

Specimens: WVUM, UMMZ.

UPLAND SANDPIPER
          Bartramia longicauda (Bechstein)

Status: Rare migrant; uncommon local summer resident.

Spring: There are very few spring records for this species. It has been reported from the Cabell-Mason County area and from Monongalia County in the second half of April, and from Jackson County in early May. It occurs only in open grassy areas such as pastures, airports, and golf courses. It is possible that it occurs more commonly than we know on many of the open grassy mountaintops.

Summer: The Upland Sandpiper occurs regularly and in some numbers in the Shenandoah Valley in Jefferson and Berkeley Counties. Nests and downy young have been found in both counties (Poland, 1936). Elsewhere it is rather irregular, but breeding records come from Grant (downy young), Monongalia (downy young), Hancock (nest), Greenbrier (prior to 1942—not present there since), Mason (downy young), Kanawha (downy young reported), and Mineral (Eifrig, 1904). Other summer records come from Preston and Grant Counties. There are late-May records from Putnam, Jackson, Tucker, and Kanawha Counties that may also represent breeding rather than migration. There is an uncertain record from Upshur County in June (Bell, 1973).

It should occur in the South Branch Valley as well as on some grassy mountaintops. The nesting habitat is generally a broad open area in which the grass is not very high.

Fall: Several were seen in the phenomenal concentration of shorebirds seen near Volga, Barbour County on 5 and 6 September 1935 (Brooks, 1936a). There is a 13 August record from Greenbrier County and a 31 August record from McClintic Wildlife Station, but most birds will depart by early September and there are very few reports for the fall season.

Specimen: WVU.

WHIMBREL   *Numenius phaeopus* (Linnaeus)

Status: Accidental visitant.

Records: One was collected by the Brookses at Cranberry Glades, Pocahontas County, on 25 May 1926 (Brooks, Brooks, and Brooks, 1926). G. M. Sutton saw one at Bethany, Brooke County, on 24 July 1933 (Sutton, 1933). One was seen in a concentration of shorebirds found on the flood-control project at Elkins in the spring of 1949 by W. R. DeGarmo.

Specimen: WVUM (specimen not located).

HUDSONIAN GODWIT   *Limosa haemastica* (Linnaeus)

Status: Accidental visitant.

Record: An injured bird was seen near Benwood, Marshall County, on 28 September 1967 by J. Cole. The bird was found dead the next day and was given to C. Conrad, who in turn gave it to the writer for preservation (Conrad, 1968).

Specimen: CM.

*RUDDY TURNSTONE   *Arenaria interpres* Linnaeus

Status: Casual migrant.

Records: The Poland brothers found one at Leetown, Jefferson County, on 19 June 1939 (Poland, 1939). One was seen near Elkins on 9 May 1953 (W. R. DeGarmo); two at Mercers Bottom, Mason County, on 19 May 1956; and one there on 27 May 1966 (Edeburn et al., 1960); three near Point Pleasant (T. Igou); one was seen at Warwood, Ohio County, in May 1961 and another there in May 1953 (P. F. Temple); one at Flat Top Lake, Raleigh County, on 24 May 1964 (R. Langdale-Smith); one at Weirton on 22–23 May 1968 (R. Rine and A. Ryan); one there in May 1979 (Rine); and one near Lewisburg, Greenbrier County, on 22 May 1976 (C. Handley).

Specimens: None have been collected in the state.

*SANDERLING   *Calidris alba* (Pallas)

Status: Accidental visitant.

Records: Four were seen on 22 September 1933 at Tennerton, Upshur County (M. Brooks, 1934b). H. K. Land found them in Mason County on 14 September 1954 and 10 October 1954 (Edeburn, et al., 1960) and one was seen by Mrs. D. Cain and Mrs. H. R. Chapman at the McClintic Wildlife Station on 24 August 1961 (Handley, 1976).

Remarks: This species is marginally qualified for the regular list and perhaps should be carried on the hypothetical list.

Specimen: None.

SEMIPALMATED SANDPIPER
Calidris pusilla (Linnaeus)

Status: Common to very common spring and fall migrant.

Spring: The Semipalmated Sandpiper migrates throughout the state, but as with all other shorebirds they will be rare or accidental in those parts of the state lacking suitable habitat. This species seems to require mudflats to a greater degree than does the very similar Least Sandpiper; consequently, it is not as widely reported, although it may be more common than the Least. In the Cabell-Mason County area, as many as 50 birds may be seen in a day but flocks of five or six are more usual elsewhere. They arrive in late April or early May and depart before the end of May. There is an early June record for Preston County (1980 Foray).

First-seen Spring Date: Cabell-Mason Counties, 28 April.

Last-seen Spring Date: Cabell-Mason Counties, 17 May.

Fall: The Semipalmated Sandpiper arrives in late July and departs by the middle of September. It is slightly more numerous in fall than in spring, but in general the status at the two seasons is similar.

First-seen Fall Date: Cabell-Mason Counties, 7 August.

Last-seen Fall Date: Cabell-Mason Counties, 16 September.

Specimens: WVU, UMMZ.

WESTERN SANDPIPER   *Calidris mauri* (Cabanis)

Status: Casual spring and fall migrant.

Spring: There are spring records from Leetown, Jefferson County, on 22 May 1954 and 21 May 1960 (Hall) and in May and June 1981 (Honig, 1981); from Mercer's Bottom, Mason County, on 29 May 1955 and 6 and 19 May 1956 (Land brothers); from Barboursville, Cabell County, on 22 May 1974 (H.

Slack); and from Lewisburg, Greenbrier County, on 22 May 1976 (Handley Sr. and Jr.).

Fall: Most of the fall records come from the Mason County area: McClintic Wildlife Station, 31 August 1961 (L. Kiff), 25 August 1962 (K. Anderson, G. Koch, and J. L. Smith), and 1 September 1974 (H. Slack); Mercer's Bottom, several dates in 1955 and 1956 with 30 birds seen on 19 August 1956 (Edeburn et al., 1960); and Ashton on 3 August 1975 (H. Slack). The only other records come from Leetown, Jefferson County, 21 August 1936 (L. Poland), 1 and 2 September 1937 (collected—K. W. Haller), and August and September 1980 (Honig, 1981), and from Inwood, Berkeley County, October 1959 (C. Miller).

Specimens: UMMZ.

LEAST SANDPIPER *Calidris minutilla* (Vieillot)

Status: Fairly common to common spring and fall migrant.

Spring: Occurs in suitable habitat throughout the state, sometimes in fairly large flocks, but rather uncommon in the Northern Panhandle. It does not seem to require large expanses of mudflats and is occasionally found along streams and ponds with minimal amounts of shore. As with most of the other shorebirds most of our reports have come from the Mason County area. Migration is generally throughout the month of May. There is a record from Tucker County on 15 June 1951, which must be of a delayed migrant, since there is no evidence that this species nests in the contiguous United States.

First-seen Spring Date: Cabell-Mason Counties, 3 May.

Last-seen Spring Date: Cabell-Mason Counties, 22 May.

Fall: The Least Sandpiper occurs throughout the state, in somewhat lesser numbers than in spring, from early August until October.

First-seen Fall Date: Cabell-Mason Counties, 3 August.

Specimens: WVU, UMMZ, CM.

WHITE-RUMPED SANDPIPER
Calidris fuscicollis (Vieillot)

Status: Casual spring and fall migrant.

Spring: There are spring records from Leetown, Jefferson County (one collected, 31 May 1939—K. W. Haller); Nicholas County, 8 May 1945 (Legg, 1945); Randolph County, late May 1949 (W. R. DeGarmo); Brooke County (two collected at Beech Bottom Swamp, 14 May 1949—K. W. Haller); Beckley, Raleigh County, 15 April 1978 (J. L. Smith); Lewisburg, Greenbrier County, 7 May and 21 May 1978 (C. O. Handley, Jr.); Princeton, Mercer County,

30 April 1981 and 19 May 1981 (J. Phillips); Leetown, Jefferson County, June 1981 (Honig, 1981).

Fall: T. A. Morgan took one in Putnam County many years ago. Eleven were seen in the concentration of shorebirds at Volga, Barbour County, on 5 and 6 September 1935 (M. Brooks, 1936a). Other records come from Fields Park Reservoir, Monongalia County, and Silver Lake, Preston County, on 10 August 1953 (M. Brooks); and Mason County on 5 September 1954 (T. Milewski).

Specimens: UMMZ, CM.

BAIRD'S SANDPIPER *Calidris bairdii* (Coues)

Status: Rare to uncommon migrant.

Spring: Poland collected one at Leetown, Jefferson County, on 12 May 1940. R. Langdale-Smith found one at Flat Top Lake, Raleigh County, on 24 May 1963. There are several records, mostly in the early 1950s, from the Mercer's Bottom area of Mason County. Most of these records were on a single pond, since drained. There are a few more recent reports from the McClintic Wildlife Station.

First-seen Spring Date: Mason County, 21 April.

Last-seen Spring Date: Mason County, 30 April.

Fall: This species was seen at Beech Bottom Swamp, Brooke County, on 17 September 1933 and 27 September 1934 (West and Shields, 1935). There is a record from Wheeling Island, Ohio County, on 26 September 1936 (Kehrer, 1936). All other fall records, of which there are fewer than 10, come from the McClintic Wildlife Station, Mason County.

First-seen Fall Date: Mason County, 27 September.

Last-seen Fall Date: Mason County, 2 November.

Specimen: WVU.

PECTORAL SANDPIPER *Calidris melanotos* (Vieillot)

Status: Fairly common to very common spring and fall migrant.

Spring: This species arrives in early April and generally departs in mid-May, although a few may remain after 1 June. It seems to be particularly common in the Mason-Cabell County area where flocks of over 100 have been seen in both seasons (Edeburn et al., 1960). Less numerous at Leetown and Lake Terra Alta, it can only be rated as uncommon in the rest of the state. This species is likely to frequent flooded short-grass meadows as well as the more normal mudflat habitat.

First-seen Spring Date: Cabell-Mason Counties, 27 March.

Last-seen Spring Date: Cabell-Mason Counties, 3 May.

Fall: Fall migrants arrive in late July and may remain until early November, although most will have departed during September. The fall status and distribution is the same as in the spring.

First-seen Fall Date: Cabell-Mason Counties, 30 July.

Last-seen Fall Date: Cabell-Mason Counties, 7 November.

Specimens: WVU, UMMZ.

DUNLIN   *Calidris alpina* (Linnaeus)

Status: Casual spring and fall migrant.

Spring: There are a few spring records from Hancock, Brooke, Ohio, Preston, Randolph, Pendleton, Mason, and Kanawha Counties. The largest count was 26 in Hancock County on 22 and 23 May 1968 (R. Rine). The Ohio County record was a rather early 20 March but all others are May records.

Fall: The Dunlin is recorded from Leetown, Jefferson County, in 1937 (Poland, 1938a) and occasionally in the Mason County area. Most of these are September and October dates, but an occasional bird may remain quite late. One was found dead in Lewis County in November 1914, and one was listed on the Berkeley County Christmas Count in 1964.

Specimens: UMMZ, CM. Haller identified his specimens from Brooke County as the subspecies *hudsonia* Todd.

STILT SANDPIPER *Calidris himantopus* (Bonaparte)

Status: Casual visitant.

Records: The only spring record is of one at Edray, Pocahontas County, on 7 May 1948 (R. W. Bailey). Fall records are from Caldwell, Greenbrier County, on 2 November 1896 (collected by T. Surber) (Rives, 1897); Leetown, Jefferson County, on 19 August 1939 (collected by Poland); Fish Hatchery, Wirt County, on 16 August 1952 (W. Davis); Wheeling on 10 August 1952 (W. Yenke, 1952); Mercer's Bottom, Mason County, on 13–17 August 1955 (H. K. Land and T. Milewski); McClintic Wildlife Station, Mason County, on 6 September 1972 (N. Gluck); and Athens, Mercer County, on 1 November 1981 (J. Phillips).

Specimen: WVU.

*BUFF-BREASTED SANDPIPER

Tryngites subruficollis (Vieillot)

Status: Hypothetical; accidental.

Records: A bird identified as a Buff-breasted Sandpiper was present at the home of A. Shreve in the Middle Ridge section of Charleston on 19 April

1969. C. Davis and I saw a Buff-breasted Sandpiper in the Canaan Valley State Park, Tucker County, on 7 September 1975 (Hall, 1976b).

*DOWITCHER   *Limnodromus* sp.

Status: Accidental spring migrant; casual fall migrant.

Records: There are only four spring records: eight seen at Lake Terra Alta, Preston County, on 5 May 1926 (Bibbee, 1929); six at Mercer's Bottom, Mason County, on 6 May 1956 (Edeburn, et al., 1960); seen in Mason County, 11 May 1969 (H. Slack); and Leetown, Jefferson County, April 1981 (Honig, 1981). There are a number of fall records from Mason County, mostly in recent years. Five flocks totalling about 200 birds were seen on 5 and 6 September 1935 at Volga, Barbour County (Brooks, 1936a). Poland found two at Leetown, Jefferson County, from 14 to 17 October 1937 (Poland, 1938a) and Honig (1981) reported it there in October 1980. There is a record from South Charleston on 23 August 1966 (T. Igou), and three were seen at Barboursville, Cabell County, from 20 to 24 August 1957 (H. Slack).

Remarks: Most of these records were made prior to the separation of the dowitchers into two full species and the observers were not aware of the necessity of distinguishing between the two. In the field, this distinction can be done only on the basis of the alarm callnote (seldom heard) and so all the recent sight records also fail to separate the two. Most of these records probably refer to the Short-billed Dowitcher (*L. griseus*), although the October records at Leetown could represent the Long-billed Dowitcher (*L. scolopaceous*). Slack believes both species may have been present at McClintic Wildlife Station on 25 August 1973. In the absence of a specimen, it seems better to list these records under the generic name only.

Specimen: None has been collected in the state.

COMMON SNIPE   *Gallinago gallinago* (Linnaeus)

Status: Fairly common to common spring and fall migrant; rare or uncommon local summer resident; rare to common local winter resident.

Spring: The Snipe probably migrates throughout the state and occurs wherever the habitat is suitable. It favors areas containing water and dense grassy vegetation such as the edges of mountain bogs, along sluggish streams, and even in damp meadows. Migration is concentrated in April and most are gone by early May.

First-seen Spring Dates: Cabell-Mason Counties, 3 April; Randolph County, 1 April; Wood County, 19 April.

Last-seen Spring Dates: Randolph County, 1 May; Cabell-Mason Counties, 7 May.

Summer: The Snipe nests in small numbers in the Canaan Valley, Tucker County. Haller took a juvenile bird there on 10 July 1937. On 4 June 1971, I was shown a live chick, not more than a few days old, captured in Canaan Valley on 3 June. There are summer records from Cranesville Swamp, Preston County. There is an uncertain report of breeding from the Altona marsh, Jefferson County. It may, at least on occasion, nest on some of the other mountain bogs. Eifrig saw one on Knobley Mountain, Mineral County, on 13 July 1903.

Fall: Fall arrivals generally take place in September, and a few birds may remain until December. It migrates throughout the state, but in a normal fall suitable habitat will be more limited than in spring; consequently, concentrations will build up in favored spots.

First-seen Fall Dates: Randolph County, 15 September; Cabell-Mason Counties, 13 September.

Winter: This species may winter in any place where a flowing spring serves to keep a small boggy area unfrozen. There are winter records from Jefferson, Berkeley, Hardy (S. Miller), Monongalia (R. Oades), Upshur (M. Brooks), Lewis (G. Breiding), Greenbrier (C. O. Handley), Summers (O. Johnson), Nicholas (W. Legg), Brooke, Kanawha, Mason, and Cabell Counties. On the 1971 Christmas Count in Kanawha County, 15 were listed. In the extensive springs of Jefferson and Berkeley Counties, often used as commercial watercress beds, sizeable numbers winter each year. Over 16 seasons, the average count was 84 per year with extremes of 136 and 26 (Miller, 1969).

Specimens: WVUM, UMMZ, CM, MU.

AMERICAN WOODCOCK *Scolopax minor* (Gmelin)

Status: Fairly common spring and fall migrant; uncommon summer resident; rare and local winter resident.

Spring: The Woodcock migrates throughout the state and can be found in almost any moist brushy fields or low woodlands. In the south, it may arrive in late February if the weather is mild, but the usual arrival is in March. The migrants will have departed by mid-April.

First-seen Spring Dates: Cabell-Mason Counties, 11 March; Randolph County, 1 March; Monongalia County, 24 March.

Last-seen Spring Date: Randolph County, 15 April.

Summer: The Woodcock probably nests at least in small numbers in every county in the state, except possibly Jefferson and Berkeley. There are definite nesting records from Hampshire, Tucker, Randolph, Pocahontas, Greenbrier, Monroe, Preston, Monongalia, Marion, Summers, Ohio, Wetzel, Wood, Wirt, Kanawha, Mason, and Cabell Counties. The large population in the Canaan Valley, Tucker County, has been much studied by the wildlife biologists of the Department of Natural Resources, and many birds have been banded there. The late-summer population in Canaan Valley before the arrival of migrants has been estimated at 1,200 to 1,500 birds (J. Rieffenberger, in litt.).

Fall: The Woodcock migrates throughout the state, arriving mostly in October. Very large concentrations sometimes build up in certain favored spots, particularly around mountain bogs. The Canaan Valley is one such favored spot and it is estimated that more than 20,000 individual woodcock use the valley during the fall. At any one time there may be 5,000 to 6,000 birds present (J. Rieffenberger).

First-seen Fall Dates: Randolph County, 20 October; Cabell-Mason Counties, 3 November.

Winter: The Woodcock winters in small numbers in the lower Ohio Valley and in the Kanawha Valley, and occasionally along the South Branch of the Potomac.

Specimens: WVU, MU.

Subfamily Phalaropodinae   PHALAROPES

WILSON'S PHALAROPE

Phalaropus tricolor (Vieillot)

Status: Casual visitant.

Records: A. S. Morgan saw several on the Kanawha River in August 1928 and collected one there in Putnam County in August 1930. Several observers from the Brooks Bird Club saw one at Beech Bottom Swamp, Brooke County, on 4 May 1935. J. L. Poland collected one at Leetown, Jefferson County, on 4 September 1937 (Poland, 1938a). T. Igou, L. Kiff, and W. Argabrite saw one at the McClintic Wildlife Station, Mason County, on 30 August 1960. There is also a recent record from the Kyger Creek area in Ohio opposite Point Pleasant. One was seen near Wellsburg, Brooke County, on 19 April 1967 (W. Jennings). One was seen at Beckley, Raleigh County, 9 May 1979 (J. L. Smith).

Specimen: An unlabelled specimen in the Morgan Collection may be the one referred to above.

Poland's specimen is supposed to be in the West Virginia University collection, but I have not located it.

RED-NECKED PHALAROPE
Phalaropus lobatus (Linnaeus)

Status: Casual visitant.

Records: The files of the U.S. Fish and Wildlife Service contain a record from Wood County in the fall of 1888 (C. S. Robbins, pers. comm.). W. C. G. Eifrig collected one in Mineral County on 23 May 1901 (Eifrig, 1902). Bibbee (1929) reported that two were collected by S. K. Creel at Parkersburg in the fall of 1922, but he expressed some doubt as to the correctness of the identification since he did not see the specimens. One was seen at Huntington on 13 October 1957 (T. Igou). G. Knight, J. L. Smith, and I saw one on Cheat Lake, Monongalia County, on 23 November 1958 (Hall, 1959). More recent records come from Monroe County, Moncove Lake on 13 September 1964 (M. Thacker, B. Greenlee, G. Koch, and G. Hurley), Linside on 23 September 1967 (Thacker, Greenlee, and Hurley); Fayette County, Montgomery, on 24 October 1969 (a moribund bird captured on the Kanawha River, P. Phil-

lips); and Jackson County, Cedar Lakes on 28 September 1975 (H. Good).

Remarks: The title of Eifrig's paper and the label on the specimen would indicate that this was a Maryland record, but a careful reading of his paper shows that the collection was made in Mineral County, West Virginia. This species was known as Northern Phalarope in the earlier literature.

Specimen: Chicago Academy of Science.

RED PHALAROPE   *Phalaropus fulicaria* (Linnaeus)

Status: Accidental visitant.

Records: A Red Phalarope was seen at Oglebay Park, Ohio County, on 3 November 1961 and was found dead there the next day. It was preserved as a specimen (Breiding, 1962c). In 1964 one was present near Charleston from 29 September to 7 October. C. O. Handley, Sr., netted, banded, and photographed this bird on 6 October. Another Red Phalarope was captured and banded at St. Albans, Kanawha County, on 7 March 1976 (J. and R. Ashworth, 1977). There is an uncertain sight record from the Huntington area in 1951 (Edeburn, et al., 1960).

Specimen: CM.

Family Laridae

| Subfamily Stercorariinae | SKUAS AND JAEGERS |

PARASITIC JAEGER
Stercorarius parasiticus (Linnaeus)

Status: Accidental visitant.

Records: An injured bird was found in St. Albans on 14 September 1963 and was turned over to C. O. Handley, Sr. (Shreve, 1964). On 9 October 1973, one was identified by C. W. Nelson on the

East Lynn impoundment in Wayne County (Hall, 1974). This latter identification seemed to be correct, but since the jaeger species are notoriously difficult to separate, some doubt must remain on this record. There is a report of an unidentified jaeger seen over the Ohio River at East Liverpool, Ohio, on 1 December 1971 (N. Laitsch).

Specimen: USNM.

Subfamily Larinae   GULLS

*LAUGHING GULL   *Larus atricilla* Linnaeus

Status: Casual spring visitant; accidental fall visitant.

Records: The Morgans collected this species in Putnam County and Surber collected it in Greenbrier County. M. Brooks saw four near Elkins on 10 May 1917 and one at Volga, Barbour County, during the unusual concentration of waterbirds there on 5 September 1935 (Brooks, 1936a). This last is

the only fall record. J. and P. Handlan saw one at Charleston on 24 March 1948. C. Miller found them near Inwood, Berkeley County, on 25–26 April 1955, and D. Shearer, G. Hurley, and R. Yunick saw two at South Charleston on 18 April 1963.

Remarks: There are a few other reports of less reliability, and there always exists the possibility of confusion with the Bonaparte's Gull.

Specimens: None located. None were evident in the Morgan Collection in August 1971.

BONAPARTE'S GULL *Larus philadelphia* (Ord)

Status: Common to very common local spring migrant; casual fall migrant.

Spring: In the spring, large numbers of Bonaparte's Gulls cross the Appalachian Mountains in the latitude of West Virginia on their way from the wintering grounds along the Virginia-Carolina coast to the Great Lakes and the northwestern breeding grounds. Large numbers may be seen on the bodies of water along this route, particularly after storms, and many birds are seen well away from any water. Cheat Lake, at the foot of the westernmost mountain ridge, and Lake of the Woods, on top of that ridge, are especially favored places for this flight and concentrations of 100 or more occur almost every year. Other records from the mountain counties come from Mineral, Grant, Tucker, Randolph, Pocahontas, and Greenbrier Counties. Elsewhere, the bird occurs in smaller numbers and is not seen every year, although there is a report of 300 at Charleston on 13 April 1966 and of 125 there on 4 April 1972. There is only one spring record from the Huntington area. These big flights generally occur in the last half of April.

Fall: There are very few fall records, and the hawk watchers on the mountain ridges have never reported flights crossing the mountains during September and early October. There are two fall records from Huntington. On occasion, the fall birds have remained until early January. Two were seen at Princeton, Mercer County, on 29 January 1980 (J. Phillips).

Specimens: WVU, UMMZ.

*RING-BILLED GULL *Larus delawarensis* Ord

Status: Common to very common migrant; locally a fairly common winter resident.

Spring: The Ring-billed Gull may arrive in late March but is most common in April. Departure is in early May with stragglers until late May. It usually arrives somewhat later than the Herring Gull, and during the migration is almost always more common than that species. The Ring-billed Gull is most common along the major river systems, but also is often seen in numbers inland from these rivers. There are numerous reports of small groups flying over places well away from large bodies of water, and on occasion after a storm, large congregations may be seen resting on open fields or even paved parking lots far from water.

Last-seen Spring Date: Cabell-Mason Counties, 30 April.

Fall: A few stragglers may appear in early September, but the main movement is in November.

As expected, it is somewhat more common than in spring and as in spring may often be seen in some numbers away from major bodies of water.

First-seen Fall Date: Cabell-Mason Counties, 3 November.

Winter: The Ring-billed Gull winters in fair numbers in the lower Ohio Valley but is less numerous than the Herring Gull at this season. Single individuals or small groups may occur elsewhere during the winter.

Remarks: The Ring-billed Gull is apparently more numerous now than it was in the 1930s. For example, Sutton (1933) had no definite records for the Ohio River in the Northern Panhandle and Haller (1940a) considered it less common than the Herring Gull in the lower Ohio Valley. This apparent increase is probably real, but as mentioned in the following account some of the increase may be due to better identification and finer distinction between the species.

Specimen: None located.

HERRING GULL *Larus argentatus* Pontoppidan

Status: A common to very common local migrant; common local winter resident.

Spring: The Herring Gull is most common on the Ohio and Kanawha Rivers, is less common on the Monongahela and Potomac Rivers, and is almost completely absent away from these river systems. The early migrants will arrive in late February but peak numbers occur in late March and early April, after which the numbers decline with stragglers present in mid-May. An occasional bird may be seen in summer.

Fall: The Herring Gull begins to arrive in mid-October, and the peak numbers in the north will be in late October and early November and in the south in November. Many birds do not depart until freezing weather sets in in December. Gulls often appear in both spring and fall on the Ohio River during or following severe storms on the Great Lakes.

Winter: This species winters in fairly good numbers on the Ohio River south of Parkersburg, with only small numbers north of there. A few may winter along the main Potomac River, particularly near Harper's Ferry.

Remarks: Superficial examination of the records leads one to believe that the number of Herring Gulls occurring in the state has declined since the 1930s, but in view of the overall increase in the continental population this seems unlikely. It is possible that many observers in the past did not sufficiently separate the Herring from the Ring-billed Gull.

Specimens: WVUM, WAL.

*GREAT BLACK-BACKED GULL

Larus marinus Linaeus

Status: Hypothetical; accidental visitor.
Records: M. Brooks saw one on Cheat Lake near Morgantown on 16 February 1945 (Brooks, 1945a), but this record fails to qualify for the accepted list under the rules. There are two less certain sight records: Oglebay Park, Ohio County, on 11 May 1955 (T. Shields) and the Ohio River in Hancock County on 9 April 1957 (C. Conrad).
Specimen: None.

BLACK-LEGGED KITTIWAKE

Rissa tridactyla (Linnaeus)

Status: Accidental visitant.
Record: One was hit by a car near Dunlow, Wayne County, on 25 October 1963 and the specimen was turned over to R. M. Edeburn (Edeburn, 1964). There was a sight report of one seen near Huntington on 30 October 1967 (W. Argabrite), but the similarity of immature Kittiwakes to certain other small gulls makes this record doubtful. Brooks (1944) listed this species on the hypothetical list on the basis of a sight record of two on the Ohio River in Wood County by E. A. Brooks about 1902.
Specimen: MU.

Subfamily Sterninae	TERNS

CASPIAN TERN   *Sterna caspia* Pallas

Status: Casual visitant.
Spring: There are reports from Brooke (Wellsburg); Tucker, (Canaan Valley); Mason (Gallipolis Dam); and Kanawha (five records, Charleston, South Charleston). Most of these are of single birds, but six were seen at one time at Charleston on 12 April 1948 (C. O. Handley). The dates of these records range from 24 March (Brooke County) to 30 May (Kanawha County) and all are after 1947.
Fall: Bibbee collected one at Speedway, Mercer County, on 5 October 1929. All other records are after 1947 and come from Wetzel (New Martinsville); Cabell (Huntington); and Kanawha (four records) Counties. The dates range from 2 September to 30 November.
Remarks: The older record for the "Ohio River" from Dawson's "Birds of Ohio" (1903), which is often attributed to West Virginia, is ambiguous and indeed probably should be assigned more properly to Kentucky.
Specimen: Concord College Biology Department.

COMMON TERN   *Sterna hirundo* Linnaeus

Status: Casual to rare migrant.
Spring: There are scattered records, mostly in early May, from Jefferson (Shepherdstown), Berkeley (Martinsburg), Preston (Arthurdale), Monongalia (Morgantown, Cheat Lake), Brooke (Wellsburg), Ohio (Wheeling, McMechen), Monroe, Wood (Leachtown), Kanawha (Charleston), Mason (Point Pleasant), and Cabell (Huntington) Counties. Sometimes small flocks of up to 10 are seen, but more usually one or two birds are present.
Fall: I find only three fall records: Warwood, Ohio County, 30 August 1967 (C. Conrad), Huntington, 25 November 1952 (H. C. Land), and Charleston, 13 September 1963 (C. Katholi).
Specimen: WVUM.

*FORSTER'S TERN   *Sterna forsteri* Nuttall

Status: Hypothetical; accidental visitant.
Records: The Land brothers saw two on the Ohio River at Huntington on 3 November 1951 and six on the Ohio at Eureka Dam on 28 April 1956 (Edeburn, et al., 1960). C. O. Handley, Sr., recorded the species at Charleston on 5 May 1953 and 9 September 1955. Four were seen near Williamstown, Wood County, 30 April 1981 (C. Bernstein).
Specimen: None.

LEAST TERN   *Sterna albifrons* Pallas

Status: Accidental visitant.
Records: A. S. Morgan collected one at Poca, Putnam County (date not known, but prior to 1912). W. R. DeGarmo saw one on the Kanawha River at Charleston on 6 November 1941 (Handlan, 1941). Two were seen by J. Tinsley at Rocky Fork, Kanawha County, on 21 July 1957. A flock of 10 was seen on a Breeding Bird Survey run in Berkeley County in 1971 (C. Miller).
Specimen: In August 1971 when I inspected the Morgan Collection, I was unable to identify any particular specimen as coming from West Virginia.

Morgan had several Least Terns, some of which had been collected on the lower Mississippi River. The A.O.U. Check-list (1957) records this specimen under the east coast subspecies, *antillarum* (Lesson), and it was so listed by Brooks (1944). The Great Plains race, *athalassos* Burleigh and Lowery, is more likely but in the absence of a specimen no assignment can be made.

SOOTY TERN   *Sterna fuscata* Linnaeus

Status: Accidental summer visitant.

Records: Following a tropical hurricane, a weakened bird was picked up near Charleston on 31 July 1926 and given to I. H. Johnston, who banded it, and released it several days later (Johnston, 1926). One was also found near Wheeling on 2 August 1926. In mid-August 1975, a Sooty Tern that had been banded in the Dry Tortuga islands off Florida was found dead at Gauley Bridge, Fayette County (P. Phillips).

Specimen: CM.

BLACK TERN   *Chlidonias niger* (Linnaeus)

Status: Uncommon migrant.

Spring: Brooks (1944) considered Black Terns to be "fairly common along the lakes and rivers . . ." In recent years, the species has been less frequently reported with records from Jefferson, Mineral, Monongalia, Preston, Greenbrier, Mercer, Kanawha, Mason, and Cabell Counties. The dates range from 1 May to 30 May.

Fall: There are fewer records in fall than in spring. They come from Mason, Summers, Raleigh, and Kanawha Counties. Arrival in the fall has been as early as mid-August.

Remarks: This species has nested in adjacent Garrett County, Maryland but there is no evidence that it has ever done so in West Virginia. One was seen at the Fish Hatchery at Ridge, Morgan County on 11 June 1957.

Specimens: WVU, UMMZ.

Family Columbidae   PIGEONS AND DOVES

ROCK DOVE   *Columba livia* Gmelin

Status: Introduced; common permanent resident.

Remarks: "Pigeons" occur throughout the state as feral populations in most cities, and often reach the status of a pest. Rural birds may or may not be truly feral. It has nested on buildings in most towns, but few people have bothered to record data on such nestings. Rock Doves undoubtedly nest on the steep face of Seneca Rocks, Pendleton County, as well as possibly on other cliff faces in that region, habitats more closely akin to the truly native one. Such a cliff nest was seen at Harper's Ferry in May 1975.

Specimen: WVU.

MOURNING DOVE   *Zenaida macroura* (Linnaeus)

Status: Fairly common to common migrant; fairly common summer resident; uncommon to common local winter resident.

Spring: Birds that are clearly migrants arrive about 1 March, but the presence of many wintering birds makes it difficult to establish an arrival date. The Mourning Dove migrates throughout the state, but is quite uncommon in heavily forested areas and at some high elevations.

Summer: The Mourning Dove nests in every county and at all elevations if suitable habitat is present. It is scarce or missing from areas that are heavily wooded or lack broad open areas. There are breeding records from Jefferson, Berkeley, Hampshire, Hardy, Pendleton, Pocahontas, Greenbrier, Summers, Fayette, Webster, Randolph, Upshur, Tucker, Preston, Monongalia, Hancock, Brooke, Ohio, Marshall, Wetzel, Wood, Wirt, Gilmer, Jackson, Mason, Kanawha, Cabell, and Wayne Counties.

Breeding Populations: The Mourning Dove has been found on 144 Breeding Bird Survey Route counts averaging 9.6 (58.7–0.6) birds per route. The highest counts come from the Eastern Panhandle. Mourning Doves have contributed to the population of only three Singing Male Studies: Second growth pine, Hampshire County, 25 males per 100 ha; Overgrown pasture, Ohio County, 13; and Virgin cove hardwoods, Greenbrier County, 7.5.

Fall: Doves begin to congregate in September and migration occurs in October, but as in spring it is difficult to distinguish migrants from residents.

Winter: A few Doves may winter at any locality in the state except at the higher elevations. Fairly large numbers winter in the broad agricultural valleys such as the Kanawha, the lower Ohio, and the lower Greenbrier. Christmas Count averages (birds per party hour) are: Statewide, 2.85 (6.4–0.6); Lewisburg, 7.44 (13.8–1.0); Charleston, 1.01 (3.07–0.03); Ona, 2.90 (6.6–0.9); Huntington, 1.90 (5.8–0.44);

Charles Town, 3.85 (9.6–0); Mason County, 3.50 (12.3–0); Pendleton County, 5.51 (9.2–0.7); and Inwood, 0.73 (3.9–0).

Remarks: Two factors have served to increase dove populations in recent years in some parts of the state. The replacement of forest and brushland by residential areas accompanied by ornamental conifer plantings has supplied both the open land needed and favorite nesting sites. The construction of super highways with their wide grassy rights-of-way has also provided much open land, and since these highways are often accompanied by utility cables there is an abundance of perching sites.

At the present writing (1982) populations, both in winter and summer, are unusually high in northern West Virginia.

Specimens: WVU, USNM, UMMZ, MCZ.

PASSENGER PIGEON
Ectopistes migratorius (Linnaeus)

Status: Extinct. Formerly, a very abundant migrant and very abundant summer resident.

Remarks: The Passenger Pigeon apparently migrated throughout the state, but most of the reports come from the Western Hills Region, passing through to the north in March and April and returning in October and November (Schorger, 1955). The main breeding range was to the northwest of West Virginia, but some extensive nestings occurred in the valleys of the Ohio and Little Kanawha Rivers. The last great flights apparently took place in 1873 and 1874 with reports from Roane County in 1886 and a nesting of several hundred on the headwaters of the Greenbrier (Sugar Ridge) in 1889. C. L. Brooks saw one in Upshur County in 1898. A. S. Morgan shot one in Putnam County in 1902. The only report available from the territory east of the Allegheny Mountains comes from Hampshire County as late as 1894 when a nest was built on a farm on Short Mountain (Frye, 1967). The latest probable record was in Upshur County in 1903 (Schorger, 1955; Smith, 1965).

Specimens: I have been able to locate only two specimens: a mounted specimen is at the Oglebay Park Nature Center, and the other specimen listed by Hahn (1963) is in the Illinois State Museum, Springfield (collected in 1884, but no other data). A specimen formerly at Bethany College has disappeared.

Family Psittacidae   PARROTS

CAROLINA PARAKEET
Conuropsis carolinensis (Linnaeus)

Status: Extinct. Former status unknown but probably only a casual visitant.

Remarks: A humerus of this species was found in a Putnam County archaeological site which has been dated about 1650 (Guilday, 1971). This may constitute the only valid record for the state. Audubon (1831) remarks that in the past the species had been known to occur as far up the Ohio as the mouth of the Great Kanawha, but he may have been speaking in very general terms. Wilson was told that the birds had occurred at Marietta, Ohio, and Hildreth reported them from the mouth of the Little Hocking River in Washington County, Ohio. Birds present at either of these two places would undoubtedly also have been in West Virginia (McKinley, MS). In the files of the Fish and Wildlife Service, there is a record from Thaddeus Surber of seeing one at White Sulphur Springs in 1881 (Surber was 10 years old at that time). However, he did not mention this species in his later account of the birds of Greenbrier County (1889).

Specimen: The archaeological specimen is in the collection of P. W. Parmalee, University of Tennessee. No other specimen has been preserved. The subspecies *ludoviciana* would have been the one occurring in the state.

Family Cuculidae   CUCKOOS

BLACK-BILLED CUCKOO
Coccyzus erythrophthalmus (Wilson)

Status: Uncommon to fairly common migrant; uncommon to fairly common summer resident.

Spring: The arrival dates for the Black-billed Cuckoo vary widely from year to year, as also do the numbers seen. Most of the arrivals are in early May, but in some years migrants are still passing through in early June. It migrates through every county, but except at higher elevations it is never as common as the Yellow-billed. In some localities, it will not be encountered in every year.

First-seen Spring Dates: Kanawha County, 24

April; Cabell-Mason Counties, 1 May; Monongalia County, 15 May.

Summer: The Black-billed Cuckoo probably occurs, at least in small numbers, in all counties. However, some reports of June sightings probably refer to late migrants, and the bird may be less common in some lowland areas than is thought. There are definite nesting records from Berkeley, Jefferson, Pendleton, Pocahontas, Greenbrier, Hampshire, Preston, Webster, Nicholas, Barbour, Upshur, Summers, Hancock, Ohio, Wirt, Kanawha, and Cabell Counties. The lowest nesting record I have was at 430 m in Upshur, and in Hancock Counties, but it probably nests lower. The Black-billed Cuckoo is quite uncommon or absent below 300 m, but it will nest well above 1,200 m in the hardwood forests. It has been found in Northern Hardwoods, Cove Hardwoods, Oak-Hickory, and Oak-Chestnut forest types. It tolerates a somewhat denser forest than does the Yellow-bill and is much less frequently found in suburban areas.

Breeding Populations: The Breeding Bird Surveys have averaged 0.84 (3.0–0.2) birds per route. The Black-billed Cuckoo has contributed to the population of only six Singing Male Censuses, ranging from 1,200 m to 490 m, with five of these having populations of 17 males per 100 ha. Early June records at 180 m in Mason County probably are of migrants.

Fall: As with the previous species, the fall migration is inconspicuous and many people may fail to find the species during the season. The peak of migration is probably in early October, and some may remain until late October. At A.F.M.O., only 11 have been banded over the years, with four of these coming in one season.

Last-seen Fall Dates: Kanawha County, 25 September; Cabell-Mason Counties, 9 October.

Remarks: This species follows the tent caterpillars and varies widely in numbers from year to year. As mentioned in the next species, practically nothing is known about the interspecific relations of the two cuckoos.

Specimens: WVU, USNM, CM.

YELLOW-BILLED CUCKOO

Coccyzus americana (Linnaeus)

Status: Fairly common to common migrant; fairly common to common summer resident. Numbers may vary widely from year to year at a given location.

Spring: First arrival dates vary from year to year, but generally the Yellow-billed Cuckoo arrives in early May, with a few stragglers in late April. In some years, the migration is still taking place in early June and dates during the first half of June do not

necessarily mean the bird is breeding in that locality. The Yellow-billed Cuckoo migrates through every county, but is rare or absent at higher elevations.

First-seen Spring Dates: Kanawha County, 24 April; Cabell-Mason Counties, 1 May; Summers County, 5 May; Monongalia County, 6 May; Wood County, 18 May.

Summer: The Yellow-billed Cuckoo probably nests in every county, although definite records come only from Jefferson, Berkeley, Hampshire, Hardy, Pendleton, Randolph, Greenbrier, Monroe, Webster, Tucker, Preston, Monongalia, Hancock, Brooke, Ohio, Wood, Wirt, Gilmer, Fayette, Summers, Mason, Kanawha, Cabell, and Wayne Counties. This species becomes less numerous and eventually very scarce at higher elevations, and the highest nesting record I found was at 760 m in Pendleton County, although the birds occurred on census areas as high as 1,100 m in Pendleton County. The Yellow-billed Cuckoo is found in most wooded habitats, including suburban areas, although it is missing from the dense mature forest.

Breeding Populations: Breeding Bird Surveys have averaged 2.8 (8.5–0.3) per route. This species has been found to contribute to the population of 20 Singing Male Censuses in a wide variety of habitats. The greatest population was 50 males per 100 ha in an overgrown field in Ohio County, but 12 of the areas had populations of 7 males per 100 ha (one male per 15 acres).

Fall: In fall, migration of this species is very inconspicuous and most birds are gone by early October. A few remain almost until the end of October and there are a few November dates (as late as 25 November, Kanawha County). It is scarce at high elevations, although in one year five were banded at A.F.M.O. (but in 24 years of operation, only nine have been caught). There is a September specimen from Cheat Bridge at 1,160 m.

Last-seen Fall Dates: Kanawha County, 25 September; Cabell-Mason Counties, 3 October.

Remarks: Both of the cuckoo species are puzzling to work with and little is actually known about their ecology. Both species occur in a wide variety of forest types, although they are missing from the pure conifer forest, and they occur sympatrically over a wide area. Except for the tendency of the Yellow-bill to drop out at high elevations and the Black-bill to be missing at low elevations, I am unable to detect any differences in their ecology. Both species vary widely in numbers from year to year and from place to place. In particular, they follow the more or less cyclic populations of the tent caterpillar (*Malacasoma*). In years of heavy outbreaks those regions affected will have large cuckoo populations, but in years of few or no caterpillars there will be few (or even no) cuckoos.

Specimens: UMMZ, USNM, CM, MU.

Family Tytonidae   BARN-OWLS

COMMON BARN-OWL   *Tyto alba* (Scopoli)

Status: Uncommon permanent resident.

Distribution: The Barn-Owl probably occurs throughout the state except at the higher elevations, but recent records are few in number. Nests have been reported from Berkeley, Preston, Monongalia, Harrison, Tyler, Mercer, Brooke, Lincoln, Mason, and Cabell Counties. Additional reports come from Jefferson, Pendleton, Tucker, Randolph, Greenbrier, Monroe, Lewis, Hancock, Ohio, Wood, Nicholas, Fayette, McDowell, and Kanawha Counties. There may be some late-fall and winter influx into

the state, but so little is known of this species that no definite statements can be made.

Remarks: This bird is almost certainly more common than the few records would indicate, although in recent years it may have lost ground. Edeburn, et al. (1960), remarks that a decline occurred in the Huntington area in the decade of the 1950s. However, it was probably never extremely common, and in 1909 E. A. Brooks remarked that until that time he had never seen the bird in the state.

Specimens: WVU, OP, CU.

Family Strigidae   OWLS

EASTERN SCREECH-OWL   *Otus asio* (Linnaeus)

Status: Uncommon to common permanent resident. Probably more numerous than is evident.

Distribution: The Screech-Owl occurs throughout the state in wooded areas, including suburban areas, and at all elevations, although it is not usually found in the pure spruce forest. Actual nesting records come from Jefferson, Hampshire, Randolph, Greenbrier, Marion, Monongalia, Hancock, Brooke, Wood, Wirt, Summers, Lincoln, Kanawha, Mason, and Cabell Counties. This species is most evident on late-summer evenings when the birds, often young of the year, call and hunt along woodland edges.

Populations: Only seven Screech-Owls have been listed on the 155 Breeding Bird Survey Counts. Screech-Owls have been found on six Singing Male Censuses from 1,100 m to 300 m, but have not contributed to the numerical population of any of these. Only at Ona has the Screech-Owl been regularly reported on Christmas Counts, averaging two a year. As many as eight have been recorded in Hampshire County Christmas Counts. At Wheeling,

however, the use of the technique of playing recorded calls produced 17 owls on the 1973 count, 33 on the 1974 count, and 75 in 1975.

Remarks: As with other owls, this species deserves to be more thoroughly studied with the call-playback technique.

Specimens: WVU, WAL, UMMZ, MU, GMS, CU. All available specimens are referable to the northeastern subspecies *naevius* (Gmelin), but *asio* may occur in the southwestern part of the state.

GREAT HORNED OWL   *Bubo virginianus* (Gmelin)

Status: Rare to uncommon permanent resident.

Distribution: The Great Horned Owl probably occurs statewide and at all elevations but records are very few. Nesting records come from Berkeley, Hancock, Brooke, Wirt, Summers, Lincoln, Mason, and Kanawha Counties. Obviously more records should be available.

Populations: Great Horned Owls have been reported on Christmas Counts from Hampshire, Greenbrier, and Cabell Counties with five in one year in Greenbrier County being the maximum count.

Specimens: WVU, MU.

SNOWY OWL   *Nyctea scandiaca* (Linnaeus)

Status: Casual winter visitant.

Records: West Virginia lies too far south to see very much of the periodic southward influxes of the Snowy Owl, but in major invasion years a few may get into the state. Indeed, our records go back to Alexander Wilson (Wilson and Bonaparte, 1831) who saw one on the Ohio River near Long Reach, Tyler County, in late February or early March. There are records from Berkeley, Pendleton, Pocahontas, Hampshire, Monroe, Upshur, Monongalia, Brooke, Ohio, Tyler, Wood, Mason, Cabell, Kanawha, and Mercer Counties. The dates of observation range from 6 November to 13 April. Many of these birds have been shot, and some of them are mounted; consequently, mounted specimens are present in many odd places throughout the state.

Specimens: UMMZ; another is in the possession of Miss Marion Means of Parkersburg.

BARRED OWL   *Strix varia* Barton

Status: Uncommon permanent resident.

Distribution: The Barred Owl is present throughout the state and at all elevations. It is most characteristic of the mature deciduous forest, but also does occur in the mixed hardwoods-spruce forest, but only rarely is it found in the pure spruce forest. Numbers are probably less in the sparser oak-pine forests of the Ridge and Valley Regions.

Specimens: UMMZ, USNM, S, CU, MU, GMS.

LONG-EARED OWL   *Asio otus* (Linnaeus)

Status: Rare local permanent resident; may be more common in winter.

Distribution: This quite unobtrusive owl is almost unknown to the bird students of the state. Most of the records come from the Ohio River Counties, where according to Brooks (1944) they are found in the pine forests that occur just east of the river on the bluffs that define the flood plain. I can locate records from Brooke, Ohio, Wood, Mason, Cabell, and Wayne Counties. Away from the Ohio River, there are only a few scattered winter or migration period records from Morgan, Monongalia, Upshur, Webster, Summers, and possibly Grant Counties. The only nesting records known to me are from Oglebay Park, Ohio County (Breiding, 1955), and from Canaan Valley, Tucker County, in 1976 (C. Haverty). Haller (1940) had a report from Mason County of a nesting that was probably of this species. The nests in both Ohio and Mason Counties were in pine thickets while the Tucker County nest was in an alder swamp. In winter there may be an influx of birds from the north, particularly birds of the year, and these may occur in dense pine plantations in which the trees have grown to about 7 m high.

Specimens: WVU, BC, CU.

SHORT-EARED OWL   *Asio flammeus* (Pontoppidan)

Status: Rare or uncommon migrant or winter visitant.

Distribution: In recent years (1970s), the species has been a regular late-fall, winter, or early-spring visitant in small numbers near Lewisburg, Greenbrier County (C. O. Handley, pers. comm.). Other records at this season come from Jefferson, Berkeley, Tucker, Monongalia, Upshur, Lewis, Brooke, Ohio, Wood, Mason, Putnam, and Cabell Counties, but it must be classed as only accidental or casual at most of these places. There are relatively few suitable wintering habitats for this species in the state. To date there has been no suggestion that this species nests in the state, but it would not be surprising if it has nested (or will nest in the future) in such places as the Canaan Valley, the Cranberry Glades, or other extensive high mountain bog.

Specimens: WVU, GMS.

NORTHERN SAW-WHET OWL

Aegolius acadicus (Gmelin)

Status: Rare and very local permanent resident; rare to uncommon migrant and winter visitant.

Distribution: There is a small but apparently permanent breeding population of Saw-whet Owls in the higher Allegheny Mountains. The first breeding record for the state was established by the taking of a juvenile at Cranesville Swamp, Preston County, in 1932 (A. B. Brooks, 1933). Other juveniles have been taken at Cranberry Glades (Wetmore, 1938) and Kennison Mountain, Pocahontas County (Edeburn, 1950), and juveniles were seen at Alpena, Randolph County. Calling birds have been heard on Middle Mountain and Blister Pine Swamp in Randolph County (M. Brooks), on Gaudineer Knob, Pocahontas-Randolph Counties (Hall), and on Allegheny Front Mountain (E. Chandler) and Blackwater Falls State Park, Tucker County, as well as on Grassy Knob, Greenbrier County (R. Kletzley). All of these locations are either in the spruce forest or in the mixed spruce-hardwoods forest. Of the 22 Saw-whet Owls banded at A.F.M.O., most have been in September and these probably also represent the breeding population. Away from the mountains Edeburn (1968) collected two immatures on 21 May 1966 near Shoals, Wayne County. These probably were raised nearby, and thus the breeding range may be more extensive than we expect. There are some late-summer reports from Wheeling, a bird banded at Morgantown on 29 April 1969 is also suggestive of a breeding population near there, and since that time a report of young birds at Morgantown has been made (S. Grosscup).

Winter and Fall: The Saw-whet Owl may come into the state on most any winter and should be looked for while they are roosting, usually in dense pine plantations. At this time, they are very tame and sometimes permit capture by hand. Most of the winter records come from the Wayne-Cabell-Mason County area where there are frequent records on

Christmas Counts, but never more than one a count. October records from A.F.M.O. and bandings at Morgantown in November also probably represent

migrants. Periodically this species stages an influx south of its normal range.

Specimens: USNM, MU.

Family Caprimulgidae

Subfamily Chordeilinae   NIGHTHAWKS

COMMON NIGHTHAWK *Chordeiles minor* (Forster)

Status: Fairly common spring migrant; uncommon summer resident; abundant to very abundant fall migrant.

Spring: The Nighthawk arrives in late April or early May. There have been some March or early-April dates reported that are most unlikely for this insectivorous species. Frequently these reports result from the misidentification of the "peent" call of the American Woodcock. The Nighthawk probably migrates throughout the state, but in spring such movements are rather inconspicuous.

First-seen Spring Dates: Cabell-Mason Counties, 26 April; Kanawha County, 1 May; Monongalia County, 6 May.

Summer: The Nighthawk may breed in every county, but the distribution is very localized. In most areas, it nests only on the flat rooftops of buildings in the larger towns and is found only in such towns. In the mountainous region, it does nest on the ground and does occur in some of the wilder areas. Nests may be found almost any place where barren ground occurs, and it is possible that they nest more commonly than we know on fairly level strip-mined areas. Apparently, it has never been very common in the Northern Panhandle counties. In the late 1960s and 1970s, there is some indication that the city populations have declined. Despite the wide breeding range there are very few actual nesting records. I know of records from Jefferson, Berkeley, Grant, Hancock, Ohio, Wood, Summers, Kanawha, and Cabell Counties.

Populations: No attempt has been made to census Nighthawks, and only four birds appeared on the Breeding Bird Survey routes.

Fall: In the last half of August or the first part of September, large numbers of Common Nighthawks migrate through the state, being most evident in the evening hours. Flocks numbering in the hundreds are commonplace and counts of several thousand are not infrequent. C. O. Handley reported a flight of more than 200,000 birds over Charleston on 7 September 1947. While this flight occurs throughout the state, certain places seem to be particularly favored for concentrations. The mountain pass at A.F.M.O. is one of these, and nightly counts of several thousand are frequent there. However, some of these concentration points are not as obvious. I once saw a large flight pass over a stretch of highway in Upshur County in which the birds were concentrated along a flightline that was only about 200 yards wide. As far as one could tell, this flightline was no different from any of the nearby areas over which the birds did not fly. The large flights usually end in early September, although occasional stragglers are still present in October and there is a date for 2 November at Huntington, and a dead bird was found at Belle, Kanawha County on 12 November.

Last-seen Fall Dates: Cabell-Mason Counties, 28 August; Kanawha County, 1 September.

Specimens: WVU, UMMZ, CM, MU. All specimens examined have been the eastern subspecies, *minor,* but the autumn flight, particularly the late stragglers, may contain representatives of other subspecies.

Subfamily Caprimulginae   NIGHTJARS

CHUCK-WILL'S-WIDOW
           Caprimulgus carolinensis Gmelin

Status: Casual local summer resident.

Records: Until 1974, the Chuck-will's-widow was known only as an accidental visitant to the state. From 5 June to at least 7 July one, and possibly more, Chuck-will's-widows were heard near Harrisville, Ritchie County (Robbins, 1975). They also have been present at this location each year since

1974. It is not known if these birds have been present in Ritchie County for some time, but a local resident reported that he had not heard the song prior to 1974. On 3 June 1974, one was heard near Summersville, Nicholas County (Shearer and Shearer, 1975).

The only definite record prior to 1974 was of one collected near Lewisburg, Greenbrier County, on 23 April 1897 (Surber, 1898). Brooks (1944) had received a report of one at Alderson, Monroe County, and there was a report from Mercer County in 1953. While it had been expected that this bird might occur in the limestone outcrop areas of Monroe and Greenbrier County or along the Ohio River in the southwestern part of the state, the occurrence in Ritchie and Nicholas Counties was surprising.

In 1979 Chuck-will's-widow was present in western Berkeley County, in a Virginia pine plantation. This bird returned in 1980 and 1981 (R. Bartgis).

In 1982 the Brooks Bird Club Foray found several stations for the Chuck-will's-widow in Hampshire County.

Specimen: The present location of the Greenbrier County specimen is unknown. An excellent sound recording of the 1974 Ritchie County bird has been deposited in the Library of Natural Sounds of Cornell University.

WHIP-POOR-WILL *Caprimulgus vociferus* Wilson

Status: Fairly common to common summer resident.

Spring: Although a few Whip-poor-wills may arrive in late March or early April, the usual arrival is in the second half of April. Migrants are seldom reported from any but nesting areas, but it probably migrates throughout the state.

First-seen Spring Dates: Cabell-Mason Counties, 13 April; Kanawha County, 15 April; Wood County, 18 April; Summers County, 19 April; Randolph County, 25 April.

Summer: The Whip-poor-will is not common or is missing from areas of dense uninterrupted forest, and it may have been quite uncommon in presettlement days. After settlement and lumbering, the Whip-poor-will probably occurred in every county

and became extremely common in some. However, the numbers have generally decreased since the late 1950s, and it is now very rare or completely missing from areas where it was once common. Such an area is the slopes of Chestnut Ridge just east of Morgantown, where in the 1940s this species was quite numerous and now seems to be completely gone. Sutton (1933) reported it quite common in the Northern Panhandle, but now it is known there only as a migrant. It apparently was never very common along the Ohio River bottoms. It does not occur in the pure spruce forest but is present in the hardwoods-white pine or hardwoods-hemlock forest, and occurs sparingly in the northern hardwoods forest from 1,100 to 1,200 m. There are definite nesting records from Jefferson, Berkeley, Hampshire, Randolph, Greenbrier, Monroe, Preston, Monongalia, Hancock, Wetzel, Wirt, Upshur, Summers, Lincoln, Kanawha, and Cabell Counties.

Breeding Populations: The Whip-poor-will has been listed in 13 Singing Male Censuses, but has contributed to the numerical population of only two: Mixed deciduous woods, Hampshire County, 32 males per 100 ha, and upland oak-hickory forest, Kanawha County, 17 males per 100 ha. Breeding Bird Surveys have averaged 0.8 (2.1–0.2) birds per route, but this census method gives a very poor figure for this nocturnal species.

Fall: Departure of this species is very inconspicuous. It occurs in mid-September with almost all birds being gone from the state by early October. In 24 seasons, only 14 Whip-poor-wills have been banded at A.F.M.O.

Remarks: No immediate explanation for the major decline of the Whip-poor-will populations in some areas is apparent.

Specimens: WVU, MU, GMS.

Family Apodidae   SWIFTS

CHIMNEY SWIFT *Chaetura pelagica* (Linnaeus)

Status: Abundant migrant, particularly in the fall; fairly common to common summer resident.

Spring: The Chimney Swift arrives in mid-April in the south and in late April in the north. Occasionally, there are some very early "first seen" dates when a few birds are carried north on rapidly moving air masses associated with the passage of warm fronts. These birds disappear with the next cold spell. There have been instances of heavy Chimney Swift mortality when occasional freezing or wet-cold weather in early May has eliminated the flying insects.

First-seen Spring Dates: Kanawha County, 15

April; Summers County, 15 April; Wood County, 18 April; Cabell County, 20 April; Monongalia County, 21 April.

Summer: Although very few nests have been reported, the Chimney Swift nests throughout the state. It is most common in towns and cities where the nests are placed in chimneys, but in the mountainous areas they still nest in hollow trees, or perhaps on cliffs. E. A. Brooks told of finding nests on the eaves of buildings in lumber camps. Sutton (1928) tells of finding a nest in a hollow sycamore tree in Bethany in 1917. C. O. Handley (in litt.) has found nests in open manholes from which the tops had been removed at the McClintic Wildlife Station. Definite nesting records come from Berkeley, Jefferson, Hardy, Pocahontas, Randolph, Greenbrier, Monroe, Marion, Upshur, Barbour, Hancock, Wood, Wirt, Summers, Kanawha, Mason, and Cabell Counties.

Populations: The Breeding Bird Surveys have averaged 10.0 (29.4–0.3) birds per route.

Fall: In late summer and fall, large numbers of swifts congregate for roosting in certain favored chimneys. Counts may sometimes reach the thou-

sands. These aggregations take place throughout September and the numbers begin to decline late in the month. The latest departures take place in mid-October, but as with some other species this date is hard to pinpoint.

Last-seen Fall Date: Cabell-Mason Counties, 8 October.

Specimens: USNM, CM, GMS.

Family Trochilidae   HUMMINGBIRDS

RUBY-THROATED HUMMINGBIRD

Archilochus colubris (Linnaeus)

Status: Common migrant, particularly in the fall; fairly common summer resident.

Spring: The hummingbird migrates throughout the state, arriving in late April or early May.

First-seen Spring Dates: Kanawha County, 19 April; Cabell County, 22 April; Greenbrier County, 23 April; Randolph County, 25 April; Summers County, 30 April; Wood County, 5 May; Monongalia County, 7 May.

Summer: The hummingbird occurs throughout the state and almost certainly nests in every county, although there are records from only about half of them. The favored habitat is in lightly wooded areas containing much open land with blooming flowers. Therefore, it is common in suburban areas but rather scarce in densely wooded areas. The hummingbird is not common in the mountains and is absent from the spruce forest. However, a nest has been found at Cranberry Glades at an elevation of about 1,050 m.

In the late summer, large concentrations are likely to occur in areas where the jewelweeds (*Impatiens*) are in bloom. Altona Marsh in Jefferson County is such a place that supplies in addition to flowers a set of telegraph wires for perches. In August, sometimes large numbers are seen there.

Breeding Populations: Breeding Bird Surveys have averaged only 0.7 (3.0–0.1) birds per route. The hummingbird has contributed to the population of six of the 14 Singing Male Census areas it has been listed on (none of these above 1,000 m), with one area, virgin cove hardwoods, Greenbrier County, having 32 males per 100 ha, and five other areas having only 17.

Fall: Departure from this region and an influx of birds from the north begins in late August and continues through September. Stragglers may occur in October and occasionally a bird may remain until the end of that month. On warm days in early September, large numbers of hummingbirds migrate through the pass on the Allegheny Front at A.F.M.O. and at other mountain stations.

Specimens: WVU, CM, MU.

Family Alcedinidae   KINGFISHERS

BELTED KINGFISHER   *Ceryle alcyon* (Linnaeus)

Status: Fairly common migrant; uncommon summer resident; uncommon to fairly common winter resident.

Spring: Migrant kingfishers begin to appear in late March, but the presence of many wintering birds obscures this migration. In the northern part of the state, some birds appear as soon as there is open water on the ponds and lakes.

Summer: At one time, the kingfisher occurred in every county in moderately good numbers, but as more and more streams became too polluted to maintain aquatic life the kingfisher populations have

declined. Today, it is scarce or absent over wide areas of the state. It occurs in every forest type and at all elevations at which suitably sized streams occur. While it normally requires a steep bank for a nesting site, it may occasionally nest in hollow trees as described by Sutton (1928). The kingfisher has probably at some time nested in every county, but definite records come from only Jefferson, Berkeley, Pendleton, Tucker, Randolph, Greenbrier, Monroe, Hancock, Brooke, Ohio, Ritchie, Wirt, Braxton, Summers, Kanawha, and Cabell Counties.

Fall and Winter: The influx of birds from the north and the exit of the breeding birds take place in late September. In areas where open unpolluted water is present, some kingfishers remain all winter, but it is not known if these birds are the same ones that spend the summer there or whether they come from the north. Along the major streams, the winter population may exceed the summer population.

Populations: Breeding Bird Survey routes have averaged 0.6 (2.6–0.1) birds per route. Christmas Count averages are: Charles Town, 6; Inwood, 1; Hampshire County, 4; Pendleton County, 4; Wheeling, 6; Lewisburg, 1.5; Pipestem, 2.5; Mason County, 2; Kanawha County, 5; Ona, 5; and Huntington, 2. Most counts are of one or two birds, but a maximum count of 13 was listed at Charles Town.

Specimens: WVU, MU, GMS.

Family Picidae   WOODPECKERS

RED-HEADED WOODPECKER
Melanerpes erythrocephalus (Linnaeus)

Status: Uncommon, extremely local permanent resident; rare to uncommon migrant locally; uncommon winter visitant.

Summer: Most of the summer records of the Red-headed Woodpecker come from the periphery of the mountains. They are most common in the Ridge and Valley Region where the original oak-chestnut or oak-pine forest has been depleted, leaving scattered groves of oaks interspersed with grazing lands. Most of the recent nesting records come from Pendleton and Greenbrier Counties with other nesting records from Jefferson, Berkeley, and Monroe Counties and numerous sightings in Hardy, Hampshire, Pocahontas, and Randolph Counties. West of the mountains, the bird is not common but nesting records come from Marion, Barbour, Upshur, Lewis, Lincoln, Ohio (formerly), Wood, Kanawha, and Cabell (formerly) Counties. Grose (1945) listed them as "rather common" in Gilmer County. Elsewhere, the birds are seen from time to time and on occasion may even nest. However, even in those areas where they occur regularly they are extremely localized and occur in small pockets. The favorite habitat is a rather open grove of oak woods that lacks much understory cover.

Populations: Only four Red-headed Woodpeckers have been reported on the 155 Breeding Bird Surveys analyzed.

Fall: There is a considerable southward migration of Red-headed Woodpeckers along the eastern mountain ridges, and as many as 40 birds have been seen in one day at A.F.M.O. These often occur in flocks of five or six (family groups?). In most of the West Virginia range, migration is highly variable, the birds departing in falls in which there is a poor acorn crop and remaining for the winter in years in which the crop is good.

Winter: Most of the nesting birds do winter near the nesting area and their numbers may be augmented by migrants from the north. However, one should note the low Christmas Count figures in Pendleton County, an area of good summer populations. It is likely to be found almost anywhere in the oak woods, where shelter and food (acorns) are available, and sometimes occurs in sizeable numbers. Christmas Count averages (birds per party hour) are: statewide, 0.05 (0.08–0.02); Charleston, 0.08 (0.35–0.01); Charles Town, 0.06 (0.3–0); Ona, 0.03 (0.10–0); Pendleton County, 0.03 (0.13–0); Lewisburg, 0.25 (0.66–0.13); and Hampshire County, 0.01 (0.01–0).

Remarks: In the past, this species was more common and more widespread than it is today. Both Scott (1872) in Kanawha County and Brewster (1875) in Ritchie County reported them to be common. They still maintain some numbers in Kanawha County but were not located in Ritchie County in 1974. Elsewhere, the story is similar and they have disappeared completely from some areas. The peak populations were reached in the stands of dead and dying chestnut trees at the height of the chestnut blight. The European Starling is no doubt to blame for some of this disappearance, since it is able to appropriate nest cavities, but it seems likely that other factors, perhaps some changes in land use are also involved.

Specimens: USNM, MCZ.

RED-BELLIED WOODPECKER
Melanerpes carolinus (Linnaeus)

Status: Fairly common permanent resident.
Distribution: The Red-bellied Woodpecker is

most numerous in the Eastern Panhandle and in the south-central part of the Western Hills Region. It becomes less common in the region near the mountains; for example, it seems to be missing from the upper Tygart Valley near Elkins, and it is scarce or absent in the mountains. It is also uncommon in the Northern Panhandle but seems to be increasing there. It does not occur in the spruce forest or in the mixed spruce-hardwoods forest, but is sometimes seen in the northern hardwoods forest even as high as 1,200 m. The highest Singing Male Census area on which it has been reported was at 900 m in Greenbrier County. This is a southern species whose numbers have increased and whose range has been extended northward in the last 30 to 40 years.

There are definite nesting records for Jefferson, Berkeley, Greenbrier, Monroe, Monongalia, Pendleton, Upshur, Lewis, Nicholas, Brooke, Ohio, Wetzel, Wood, Wirt, Fayette, Lincoln, Kanawha, Wayne, and Cabell Counties.

Populations: Breeding Bird Surveys have averaged 1.7 (5.6–0.1) birds per route. The Red-bellied Woodpecker has occurred on 16 Singing Male counts but has contributed to only three of these, in each case only one male per study plot. Three winter population counts in Ohio County have had seven to ten birds per 100 ha. Christmas Count averages (birds per party hour) are: statewide, 0.29 (0.42–0.19); Charleston, 0.26 (0.56–0.03); Charles Town, 0.33 (0.60–0.10); Huntington, 0.35 (1.22–0.11); Inwood, 0.26 (0.44–0); Mason County, 0.18 (0.35–0); Ona, 0.25 (0.62–0.10); Pendleton County, 0.50 (0.6–0.4); Lewisburg, 0.25 (0.45–0.16); and Hampshire County, 0.53 (0.97–0.33).

Specimens: USNM, CM, MCZ. The specimens in USNM have been referred to the subspecies *carolinus* by Wetmore, but G. M. Bond considered them intermediate between that subspecies and the western *zebra*.

YELLOW-BELLIED SAPSUCKER

Sphyrapicus varius (Linnaeus)

Status: Uncommon to fairly common migrant; uncommon winter visitant; rare and local summer resident.

Spring: The Yellow-bellied Sapsucker migrates throughout the state and may occur in any wooded area at this time. Most of the arrivals will be in early April, with a few stragglers in March, and most birds will have departed by the first week in May.

First-seen Spring Date: Monongalia County, 5 April.

Last-seen Spring Dates: Cabell-Mason Counties, 29 April; Kanawha County, 1 May.

Summer: This species once nested in fair numbers in the mountainous region of the state with the greatest numbers being in the middle elevations, but it has been decreasing since the 1920s and now has become rare and local in summer. There are recent nesting records from Randolph County (Cheat Bridge, Shaver's Mountain) and Pocahontas County (Burner Mountain). Other summer sightings come from Cranberry Glades (Pocahontas County), Middle Mountain (Randolph County), Shenandoah Mountain (Pendleton County), Monroe County, and the Hampshire-Hardy County Line. Rives (1898) tells of collecting one near Davis, Tucker County, in June but there are no recent records from there.

Breeding Populations: The Yellow-bellied Sapsucker has been found on three Singing Male Census areas, all in Pocahontas County; upland black cherry forest, 1,160 m, 17 males per 100 ha; cutover mature hardwoods, 120 m, 17 males per 100 ha and present in a second census; virgin spruce-northern hardwoods, 7 males per 100 ha.

Fall: The sapsucker migrates throughout the state and is more common in fall than in spring. The earliest arrivals come in late September but the main flight is in October, with stragglers until mid-November. A total of 110 have been banded in 24 years at A.F.M.O.

First-seen Dates: A.F.M.O., 25 September; Cabell-Mason Counties, 27 September; Kanawha County, 5 October.

Winter: The sapsucker winters sparingly throughout the state, except at higher elevations. A favorite winter habitat is an orchard where they feed on frozen apples. Only the southern West Virginia Christmas Counts have consistently reported sapsuckers. Christmas Count averages (birds per party hour) are: statewide, 0.03 (0.05–0.01); Charleston, 0.07 (0.13–0.02); Charles Town 0.06 (0.1–0); Huntington, 0.07 (0.12–0); Ona, 0.04 (0.13–0); and Hampshire County, 0.04).

Remarks: This is one of the northern species (usually assigned to the so-called Alleghanian fauna) that once nested in the state but which have decreased markedly in the second half of the 20th century. The reasons for such a decline are not immediately apparent.

The Yellow-bellied Sapsucker may become an agricultural pest in orchard areas because of the habit of drilling for sap. Many trees, and apple trees are favorites, may be completely girdled by this activity.

Specimens: USNM, CM, AMNH, GMS. One specimen (AMNH) approaches the southern Appalachian subspecies, *appalachiensis* Ganier, which is doubtfully recognizable. All other specimens can be assigned to the subspecies *varius*.

DOWNY WOODPECKER

Picoides pubescens (Linnaeus)

Status: Fairly common to common permanent resident.

Distribution: The Downy Woodpecker is found throughout the state and nests in every county. It inhabits all wooded areas except the pure spruce forest, but it does occur sparingly in the mixed spruce-northern hardwoods forest. It occurs at all elevations, but becomes scarce above 1,000 m at which point the Hairy Woodpecker begins to surpass it in numbers. The Downy Woodpecker does not require very large trees and sometimes is found in habitats that would be considered non-forest. In winter they are often found in open fields searching for insects in dried ragweed stalks or, on occasion, dried cornstalks.

Populations: Breeding Bird Surveys have averaged 2.6 (5.1–0.3) birds per route with a maximum of 12. However, these surveys come too late in the year to properly census woodpeckers. The Downy Woodpecker has contributed to the numerical population of 37 of the 51 Singing Male Census areas on which it has been listed, and the average population has been 17 males per 100 ha. The highest populations were 32 males per 100 ha (two males per study plot) in oak-hickory forest, 400 m, Kanawha County; deciduous woodland, 300 m, Ohio County; park, 300 m, Ohio County; oak-hickory 280 m, Wetzel County; and oak-pine, 180 m, Berkeley County. The other areas had one male per study plot or less. The species did not contribute to the population on any study area above 600 m and occurred on only one area as high as 1,200 m.

Winter censuses gave populations as high as 57 birds per 100 ha in two Ohio County counts. Christmas Count averages (birds per party hour) are: statewide, 1.13 (2.65–0.60); Charleston, 0.98 (1.60–0.40); Charles Town, 1.74 (2.40–0.55); Huntington, 1.37 (3.56–0.52); Inwood, 1.45 (6.20–0.20); Mason County, 0.92 (1.23–0.45); Ona, 1.06 (3.0–0.37); Pendleton County, 1.10 (2.11–0.37); Lewisburg, 0.58 (0.88–0.18); and Hampshire County, 1.16 (1.72–0.82).

Specimens: USNM, CM, MCZ, GMS, MU. All specimens can be assigned to the subspecies *medianus* Swainson.

HAIRY WOODPECKER   *Picoides villosus* (Linnaeus)

Status: Fairly common permanent resident.
Distribution: The Hairy Woodpecker occurs throughout the state and undoubtedly nests in every county, although there are no actual records from some. It occurs in all forest types and all elevations. The only requirement seems to be a sufficiently large stand of more or less mature trees. At high elevations, the Hairy Woodpecker is usually more numerous than is the Downy, but elsewhere the numbers are always much less than those of the Downy.

Populations: Breeding Bird Surveys have averaged only 0.5 (3.0–0.1) bird per route with a maximum count of five, but as with the preceding species these surveys do not properly assess the population, and rather seldom do the routes pass through good Hairy Woodpecker habitat. The Hairy Woodpecker has contributed to the population of 19 of the 34 Singing Male Censuses that listed it. The largest populations were 25 males per 100 ha from virgin spruce-northern hardwoods, 1,200 m, Randolph County; mature deciduous forest, 1,200 m, Pocahontas County; hemlock-yellow poplar, 400 m, Fayette County; and mature northern hardwoods, 600 m, Pendleton County. Six areas had 17 males per 100 ha (one male per study plot) and the others had seven to ten males per 100 ha. Five winter-population studies averaged about 10 males per 100 ha. Christmas Count averages (birds per party hour) are: statewide, 0.16 (0.26–0.08); Charleston, 0.20 (0.36–0.03); Charles Town, 0.14 (0.35–0); Huntington, 0.21 (0.67–0.02); Inwood, 0.18 (0.40–0.01); Mason County, 0.24 (0.44–0); Ona, 0.10 (0.23–0.03); Pendleton County, 0.11 (0.22–0); Lewisburg, 0.15 (0.22–0.05); and Hampshire County, 0.27 (0.40–0.20).

Remarks: This species has been little studied in this state, as most observers are content to check it off on the list and go on. I suspect that there is a long-term population fluctuation of some sort. In the late 1950s, the Hairy Woodpecker had almost disappeared from the region around Morgantown, but in subsequent years it made a good recovery. In the mid-1970s, the populations again declined.

Specimens: USNM, MCZ, GMS. All specimens examined are referable to the nominate subspecies.

*BLACK-BACKED WOODPECKER   *Picoides arcticus* (Swainson)

Status: Hypothetical; accidental winter visitant.
Record: E. R. Chandler (1962) saw one at Arroyo, Hancock County, on 4 March 1962.

NORTHERN FLICKER   *Colaptes auratus* (Linnaeus)

Status: Fairly common to common migrant; fairly common to common summer resident; fairly common winter resident.
Spring: Migrant flickers will begin to arrive in mid-March and the peak of the migration will be in the first half of April. The presence of large numbers of wintering birds makes it difficult to establish arrival and departure dates. Early arrivals are quiet and may be overlooked, but on the first warm days of March flickers begin to call loudly and frequently.
Summer: The flicker occurs throughout the state

and at all elevations, nesting in every county. It is absent or in very low numbers in the pure spruce forest, but occurs in all other forest types. The greatest populations will be in areas where mature trees are interspersed with grassy areas. It is quite common in suburban garden and yard situations.

A possible limiting factor on the population of flickers is the local population of European Starlings. In some areas, the first nest cavity (and possibly the second) excavated by flickers is invariably appropriated by starlings.

Breeding Populations: Breeding Bird Surveys have averaged 7.4 (15.0–1.0) birds per route with a maximum count of 26. Flickers have been present in 26 Singing Male Census areas but have never contributed more than 17 males per 100 ha (one per study plot) and have usually not contributed to the numerical population figure.

Fall: There is a flight of migrating flickers through the fall starting in late September and lasting until the end of October or even early November. As in the spring, the exact dates of this migration are difficult to determine. Flickers are often seen flying southward along the mountain ridges, as at A.F.M.O., and the hawk-watching stations.

Winter: At least a few flickers are present throughout the state during the winter, except at the highest elevations. Wintering numbers are low in the eastern mountain valleys and in the Northern Panhandle, but in the southern part of the state and in the lower Ohio River Valley the flicker may sometimes be quite numerous. Christmas Count averages (birds per party hour) are: statewide, 0.35 (0.88–0.15); Charleston, 0.29 (0.81–0.01); Charles Town, 0.14 (0.45–0); Huntington, 0.44 (1.33–0.15); Inwood, 0.29 (0.8–0); Mason County, 0.65 (2.89–0.17); Ona, 0.36 (0.89–0.03); Pendleton County, 0.26 (0.2–0); Lewisburg, 0.034; and Hampshire County, 0.48 (0.51–0.41).

Remarks: The flickers of West Virginia belong to the group of subspecies once known as "Yellow-shafted Flickers." C. O. Handley, Sr., banded a bird at Lewisburg in the fall of 1969 that showed characters intermediate between "Yellow-shafted" and the western "Red-shafted" form. A few other such birds showing introgression of western genes have been reported and are to be looked for during the migration seasons.

Specimens: UNMZ, USNM, CM. All specimens examined have been assigned to the subspecies *luteus* Bangs, although Sutton (1933) remarked that his specimens were not quite typical of this race. Wetmore (1937) suggested that specimens from Huntington approached *auratus* and later (1940) he assigned three October specimens from Flat Top, Mercer County, to the northern race, *borealis* Ridgway.

PILEATED WOODPECKER
Dryocopus pileatus (Linnaeus)

Status: Uncommon to fairly common permanent resident.

Distribution: At present, the Pileated Woodpecker probably occurs in every county. It is present at all elevations and in all forest types where there are suitable numbers of mature trees for nesting and foraging. It is not very numerous in the spruce-northern hardwoods forest, but reaches the greatest numbers in the mixed hardwood forest. This species is now much more common than it was in the 1920s and 1930s when most of the state's forests were in a younger second-growth stage. With the abandonment of many farms and their reversion to woodland as well as the maturing of the forest in the cut-over lands, the Pileated Woodpecker has made a great comeback from the days when it was an event to see one. There are not many nesting records, despite the wide distribution, but these come from Jefferson, Berkeley, Hampshire, Hardy, Pendleton, Randolph, Monroe, Greenbrier, Preston, Monongalia, Barbour, Lewis, Summers, Gilmer, Hancock, Brooke, Ohio. Wetzel, Ritchie, Raleigh, Lincoln, Kanawha, and Cabell Counties.

This species is normally considered to be a permanent resident, but there is a small southward movement along the Allegheny Front. This may be simply a series of local movements, but almost all the birds seen are moving southwest.

Populations: The Pileated Woodpecker has been listed on 36 Singing Male Census areas, but in only one did it contribute to the population (7 males per 100 ha). Breeding Bird Survey counts have averaged 1.6 (3.7–0.1) birds per route with a maximum of 8 (Pendleton County). Christmas Count averages (birds per party hour) are: statewide, 0.19 (0.34–0.08); Charleston, 0.24 (0.41–0.03); Charles Town, 0.10 (0.50–0); Huntington, 0.13 (0.33–0.05); Inwood,

0.10 (0.50–0); Mason County, 0.11 (0.33–0); Ona, 0.13 (0.23–0); Pendleton County, 0.52 (1.22–0.45); Lewisburg, 0.25 (0.45–0.16); and Hampshire County, 0.78 (0.97–0.58).

Specimens: WVU, MCZ, MU. The number of specimens available is too few to make an accurate determination of the subspecies. The eastern subspecies of *pileatus* are a simple north-south cline and it is probable that West Virginia birds would be intermediate between the two extreme forms.

*IVORY-BILLED WOODPECKER
Campephilus principalis (Linnaeus)

Status: Hypothetical; extirpated; probably a former casual visitant.

Records: During the short time in which Alexander Wilson lived in Shepherdstown, Jefferson County, he collected an Ivory-billed Woodpecker someplace between Martinsburg and Winchester, Virginia, but it cannot be said on which side of the state line (which did not exist in his day) this collection was made. More concrete records come from archaeological specimens. Pieces of the bills of Ivory-billed Woodpeckers have been found in the Fairchance Indian burial mound in Marshall County (Parmalee, 1967). A portion of the skull with bill

missing was found in the Buffalo site, Putnam County (Guilday, 1971; Parmalee, pers. comm.). These bills were considered of high value by the pre-Columbian Indians and were passed from hand to hand over wide distances, so it can never be certain if these specimens actually originated on a living bird in West Virginia. The skull without a bill, however, does strongly suggest a local record.

Remarks: Haller (1940c) recounts a conversation with an elderly priest, Fr. C. Delaux, who told him of shooting (and eating) a woodpecker larger than an "Indian Hen" (*pileatus*), with a white bill, in Doddridge County in about 1900. Even today there occasionally comes a report of an Ivory-billed Woodpecker in some parts of the state, simply described as having a "white bill," although if what is known about the ecology of the species is correct, there is no possible habitat remaining here for this species.

It seems likely that the Ivory-billed Woodpecker did occasionally wander into the state in pre-Columbian times and possibly also in post-settlement times.

Specimens: The archaeological specimens are in the collection of P. W. Parmalee at the University of Tennessee.

Family Tyrannidae

Subfamily Fluvicolinae	Pewees and Allies

OLIVE-SIDED FLYCATCHER
Contopus borealis (Swainson)

Status: Casual to rare migrant; casual to rare local summer resident, but formerly more common.

Spring: The Olive-sided Flycatcher is silent during migration and is seldom observed. It may occur in any open wooded habitat throughout the state, but recent records come only from McClintic Wildlife Station, Mason County; Cranberry Glades, Pocahontas County; Beverly, Randolph County; and Shepherdstown, Jefferson County. All of these reports are in the last quarter of May.

Summer: At one time, this species was widely distributed in some numbers in the mountain counties. Brooks (1944) cited breeding records for Preston, Tucker, Grant, Randolph, Pocahontas, Pendleton, and Webster Counties. Since about 1950, however, the species has decreased over much of this range and it is now rarely reported. There are recent summer records from Canaan Mountain, Tucker County; Gaudineer Knob, Pocahontas-Randolph Counties; and Cranberry Glades, but I can

find only about half a dozen reports during the last 25 years. There seems to be no apparent reason for this decline. The preferred habitat of the Olive-sided Flycatcher is an opening in the spruce forest that contains a few trees for perches. Recently lumbered or recently burned-over areas with some still standing live trees are such places.

Fall: Fall records come from late August to early October and come from Preston, Monongalia, Marion, Grant, Greenbrier, and Kanawha Counties.

Specimens: DMNH, GMS.

EASTERN WOOD-PEWEE
Contopus virens (Linnaeus)

Status: Common summer resident.

Spring: The Wood-Pewee migrates throughout the state, usually arriving in early or mid-May.

First-seen Spring Dates: Cabell County, 30 April; Wood County, 29 April; Kanawha County, 5 May; Monongalia County, 8 May.

Summer: The Wood-Pewee occurs throughout the state, even at high elevations. It is not found in the spruce forest, although it may be present at the edges of clearings in this forest and in the mixed spruce-northern hardwoods forest. The favored habitats are fairly open mature mixed deciduous forest, or oak-hickory forest. It is less numerous in the denser forests, particularly those at high elevation. Nesting records come from throughout the state, and it undoubtedly nests in every county.

Breeding Populations: Breeding Bird Surveys have averaged 7.7 (16.0–0.7) birds per route. The pewee has occurred on 48 Singing Male Census areas averaging 13.5 males per 100 ha. Populations were: deciduous woodland, 300 m, Ohio County, 49 males per 100 ha; mixed park, 300 m, Ohio County, 49; brushy field, 360 m, Ohio County, 49; oak-hickory, 400 m, Kanawha County, 49; mature oak-hickory, 275 m, Wetzel County, 42; seven areas ranging from 1,220 to 300 m had 32 males per 100 ha.

Fall: As with the other flycatchers, the departure of this species is inconspicuous, but most birds are gone by mid-September; however, a few stragglers remain until early October. Now and then a bird may linger into early November.

Last-seen Fall dates: Kanawha County, 6 September; Cabell-Mason Counties, 15 September; A.F.M.O., 23 September.

Specimens: USNM, CM, GMS.

YELLOW-BELLIED FLYCATCHER
Empidonax flaviventris (Baird and Baird)

Status: Rare and local spring migrant; rare to uncommon local fall migrant.

Spring: The Yellow-bellied Flycatcher is seldom reported in the spring, but the few records available indicate that the migration is in late May and may even carry over into early June. It apparently is quite silent during spring migration and is probably overlooked. There are spring records from Jefferson County, Monongalia County, Preston County, Hancock County, Ohio County, Mason County, and Cabell County.

Summer: In June 1978, a singing male was found in a small wooded swamp near Glady, Randolph County. The bird remained for some time, and its songs were recorded, but it is not known if this bird had a mate. A singing male was heard at this place in 1979, 1980, and 1981 (E. Olliver and E. Hutton).

Fall: This species is more commonly observed in the fall, although misidentifications are extremely common in this genus. It is quite difficult to differentiate in the field between this species and some fall-plumaged Acadian Flycatchers. Most of the reliable records come from specimens and from banding operations. There are records from Grant, Monongalia, Mason, Brooke, Ohio, and Cabell

Counties. At A.F.M.O. a total of 60 have been captured over the years with a high count of eight in one year, although yearly totals of two or three are more usual. The migration begins in late August and continues until late September.

First-seen Fall Date: A.F.M.O., 4 September.
Last-seen Fall Date: A.F.M.O., 14 September.
Remarks: The nearest known nesting grounds of this species are in the Pocono Mountains of northeastern Pennsylvania, although there are summer records for north-central Pennsylvania. As with several other boreal species there seems to be no apparent explanation as to why the bird does not nest in some of the higher mountain bogs of West Virginia. Bibbee (1929) reported one from Cranesville Swamp on 26 May, but this was probably still a migrant. It would not be surprising if the species did eventually turn up as a breeding bird at Cranesville, Cranberry Glades, or Blister Run, Randolph County, or in a similar location.

Specimens: UMMZ, DNHM, GMS.

ACADIAN FLYCATCHER
Empidonax virescens (Vieillot)

Status: Common to abundant summer resident.

Spring: The Acadian Flycatcher arrives in early to mid-May, and the residents are conspicuous upon arrival. Birds of passage are little noted.

First-seen Spring Dates: Cabell-Mason Counties, 27 April; Kanawha County, 1 May; Wood County, 6 May; Monongalia County, 9 May.

Summer: The Acadian Flycatcher occurs throughout the state except in the spruce forest of the higher mountains. There are, however, a few records in the hardwoods forest at the edge of the spruce. It is most common below 900 m, and in certain moist mixed deciduous forests populations approach the abundant level. It usually will be found in streamside situations, and all the nests I have seen have been over water. Most nesting sites are in areas of rich lush growth. The Acadian Flycatcher is less common in the eastern part of the state, possibly because of the drier, more open forests there. It is not found in the pine forest nor in the oak-pine. It may nest in every county, but there are definite nesting records only from Jefferson, Berkeley, Morgan, Hampshire, Hardy, Pendleton, Preston, Monongalia, Tucker, Randolph, Pocahontas, Greenbrier, Upshur, Lewis, Gilmer, Nicholas, Hancock, Ohio, Wirt, Mason, Wetzel, Ritchie, Braxton, Summers, Webster, Lincoln, Kanawha, Cabell, and Wayne Counties.

Breeding Populations: Breeding Bird Surveys have averaged 5.6 (18–0.3) birds per route. The highest counts have been in the southwest. The Aca-

dian Flycatcher has contributed to the population of 29 of the 31 Singing Male Censuses that have recorded it with an average population of 53.5 males per 100 ha. Mature hardwoods, 300 m, Kanawha County, 180 males per 100 ha; mature hardwoods, 240 m, Wayne County, 138 males; bottomland hardwoods, 22 m, Wayne County, 138 males; mature northern hardwoods, 300 m, Brooke County, 101 males; mixed hardwoods, 580 m, Nicholas County, 99 males; mixed hardwoods, 370 m, Wetzel County, 91 males; hardwoods-hemlock, 760 m, Webster County, 81 males; park, 300 m, Ohio County, 64 males; brushy field, 370 m, Ohio County, 62 males; virgin cove hardwoods, 580 m, Greenbrier County, 32 males; upland oak-hardwoods, 400 m, Kanawha County, 32 males per 100 ha.

Fall: Departure is in mid- to late September and is most inconspicuous. As with the other species of *Empidonax,* identification in fall is difficult.

Last-seen Fall Dates: Kanawha County, 6 September; Cabell-Mason Counties, 15 September.

Specimens: UMMZ, USNM, CM, MCZ, MU.

TRAILL'S FLYCATCHER COMPLEX

Where the older literature recognized only one species, it is now considered that Traill's Flycatcher is a complex of two sibling species, the Alder Flycatcher, *Empidonax alnorum* Brewster, and the Willow Flycatcher, *E. traillii* (Audubon). In the field the two are separated only by song; *alnorum* is the bird which calls "way-be-o" and *traillii* which calls "fitzbew." It is not always possible to determine from the older literature which species is being referred to, so it seems better to discuss these two species under one heading and to attempt to list definite records only in those cases where no uncertainity exists.

Status: Both species are uncommon migrants; both are uncommon to fairly common local summer residents.

Spring: Both forms of this complex are relatively late migrants, usually not arriving in the state before the middle of May and often not appearing on the breeding grounds until the last week in May. They are often unnoticed, since they do not call much during migration. Both forms probably migrate throughout the state, but the Willow Flycatcher seems to be more common. While migrating, both species will frequent the same type of wet swampy habitat chosen for nesting.

Summer: The Alder Flycatcher (*E. alnorum*) is a fairly common to common summer resident in the mountain bogs and in areas flooded by beaver ponds, occurring usually above 900 m. It nests in the Canaan Valley, Tucker County, Cranberry Glades, Pocahontas County, and in numerous small bogs in Pocahontas and Randolph Counties. There are also summer reports from Preston, Nicholas, and Greenbrier Counties, in the latter county at low elevation near Lewisburg (C. O. Handley). The Alder Flycatcher apparently occurs also in Wood County where the Willow Flycatcher is more common. There are definite nesting records only from Tucker and Pocahontas Counties. The nesting habitat of the Alder Flycatchers is almost always a stand of low alder bushes in a wet situation. The Willow Flycatcher (*E. traillii*) is a relatively recent addition to the avifauna of the state, not having been known prior to the 1930s. It now nests in suitable habitat along the Ohio River counties, in the mountain valleys, and at other scattered locations throughout the northern and eastern parts of the state. It is not numerous at any place. There are summer records from Jefferson (Altona Marsh), Hampshire, Hardy, Pocahontas (Greenbrier Valley), Greenbrier, Monroe, Preston, Monongalia, Upshur, Lewis, Gilmer, Ritchie, Fayette, Raleigh, Mercer, Hancock, Brooke (Beech Bottom Swamp, formerly), Ohio, Wetzel, Braxton, Wood, Mason (Ashton, McClintic Wildlife Station), Putnam, and Cabell (Ona) Counties. There are definite nesting records from Jefferson, Greenbrier, Ohio, Gilmer, and Mason Counties. The Willow Flycatcher is commonly found nesting in willows or alders along streamsides or at the edge of marshes, but is not as strictly limited to this habitat as is the Alder Flycatcher. It sometimes nests in relatively dry upland situations in which the life form of the vegetation is similar to an alder swamp, such as a brushy meadow, and in Morgantown it has been found in suburban situations.

There are summer records from Pendleton County and from many of the other areas mentioned above that are not identifiable as to species at this time. The two forms apparently occur close together in Wood County, possibly in Greenbrier County, and in some of the mountain valleys.

Breeding Populations: Breeding Bird Surveys have averaged 0.6 (3.0–0.1) Willow Flycatchers per route (96 routes), and no Alder Flycatchers have occurred on these routes. One Singing Male Census in a wooded swamp, Tucker County, 3,200 m had a population of 67 males per 100 ha for Alder Flycatchers. Eight Singing Male Censuses averaged 37 males per 100 ha for Willow Flycatchers: overgrown ravine with multiflora hedge, 353 m, Ohio County, 64 males on two counts; other areas had only two males per census area.

Fall: The fall migration of "Traill's" Flycatcher is almost completely overlooked. Once the singing stops the birds are seldom noticed and most probably leave the state in late August and early September. At this season of the year, the two forms are not separable in the field. Over the 24-year period, eight "Traill's" Flycatchers have been banded at A.F.M.O.

Remarks: The Willow Flycatcher presumably entered the state from the west, although lacking suitable habitat it was not found first in the western part of the state. The earliest records were in Brooke and Monongalia Counties followed by Mason County. In the last 25 years, they have spread widely, and indeed may have driven the Alder Flycatcher out of some of its former habitats in the mountain valleys. If this is true and if the trend continues, the Alder Flycatcher may eventually be driven from the state.

Specimens: *E. traillii* WVU, CM, GMS, MU. E. A. Brooks (1914) reported taking a specimen at the Cranberry Glades, which was most probably *alnorum,* but the location of this specimen is unknown.

LEAST FLYCATCHER
Empidonax minimus (Baird and Baird)

Status: Uncommon to fairly common migrant; uncommon to fairly common local summer resident.

Spring: The Least Flycatcher migrates throughout the state, but the numbers vary widely. It is rare to uncommon in the Kanawha Valley and the Ohio Valley. It reaches the greatest numbers just west of the mountains, and in the breeding range. In Monongalia County it sometimes becomes quite common. East of the mountains it is uncommon. Migration occurs in the last week in April and lasts until the middle of May, with a few stragglers toward the end of the month.

First-seen Spring Dates: Monongalia County, 2 May; Wood County, 5 May; Cabell-Mason Counties, 7 May.

Last-seen Spring Date: Monongalia County, 20 May.

Summer: The principal breeding range of the Least Flycatcher is at middle elevations in the Allegheny Mountains and in the Ridge and Valley Regions from the ridges of western Berkeley County east to Preston County and south to Fayette and Mercer Counties. It is most numerous at elevations between 600 and 900 m. There are summer records from Berkeley, Hampshire, Hardy, Preston, Tucker, Pendleton, Randolph, Pocahontas, Webster, Nicholas, Fayette, and Greenbrier Counties. Away from the mountains there are scattered records from central Monongalia County, Ohio, Barbour, Upshur, Braxton, and Raleigh Counties. It nested in the 1950s in the lower parts of Monongalia County, but has since disappeared. It was reported as being common in Wetzel County, there were a few scattered records in Ritchie County, a nest was found in the 1930s in Pleasants County, and it was present in Ohio County in the summers of 1947 and 1948. Other nesting records come from Hampshire, Pendleton, Preston, Pocahontas, Randolph, Nicholas, and Fayette Counties.

Breeding Populations: Breeding Bird Surveys have averaged 1.0 (6.0–0.1) birds per route in 76 routes. Least Flycatchers have occurred on only four Singing Male studies: cut-over oak-hickory, 900 m, Greenbrier County, 82 males per 100 ha and 49 males per 100 ha; black cherry forest, 1,160 m, Pocahontas County, 17 males per 100 ha; and mixed hardwoods-spruce, 915 m, Pocahontas County, five males per 100 ha.

Fall: In the fall, Least Flycatchers migrate throughout the state, but without the singing of the spring they appear to be uncommon throughout. At A.F.M.O., 78 have been banded with a maximum of 17 in 1961. In the late 1960s and 1970s, the numbers handled there decreased from those of earlier years.

First-seen Fall Dates: A.F.M.O., 1 September; Cabell-Mason Counties, 12 September.

Last-seen Fall Date: A.F.M.O., 21 September.
Specimens: WVU, OP, WAL, GMS.

EASTERN PHOEBE   *Sayornis phoebe* (Latham)

Status: Common migrant in both spring and fall; fairly common summer resident; casual to rare winter visitant.

Spring: The earliest phoebes may arrive in early March, often before the advent of real spring weather and before adequate insect supplies are available. The peak of the migration is in late March and early April.

First-seen Spring Dates: Summers County, 5 March; Kanawha County, 7 March; Cabell-Mason Counties, 9 March; Monongalia County, 22 March.

Summer: The phoebe probably nests in every county and at all elevations providing suitable nesting sites are available. It does not occur in dense forest, but is limited to the forest edge, streamsides, and farms and rural habitations. The nests are placed under bridges, on barns and summer cabins, and in many places upon steep rock faces.

Breeding Populations: Breeding Bird Surveys have averaged 6.5 (13.2–1.0) birds per route with a maximum count of 18. The phoebe has contributed to the population of eight of the ten Singing Male Censuses upon which it was recorded. An oak-hickory plot in Fayette County had a population of 74 males per 100 ha, and a hemlock-yellow popular area in Fayette County had a population of 32 males per 100 ha. Pine-oak, Berkeley County, 17 males; virgin cove hardwoods, Greenbrier County, 17 males. Four other areas had populations of seven males per 100 ha.

Fall: Most phoebes leave in early October, but a few stragglers remain until early November. Only nine phoebes have been banded at A.F.M.O.

Last-seen Fall Dates: Cabell-Mason Counties, 20 September; Kanawha County, 1 October.

Winter: A few phoebes may winter in any part of the state except in the higher mountains, but they are regular only in the lower Ohio Valley. Christmas Counts seldom list more than two birds per count, and most counts will not list them at all. It is not known how many of the birds found in late December successfully winter in the state or how many retreat to a more southern location later in the winter.

Remarks: This species is subject to marked fluctuations in population, generally due to heavy mortality on the main wintering grounds during an occasional winter in which extremely cold weather penetrates far south. After one of these occurrences, phoebes may be hard to find, but the populations generally come back to normal within two or three years.

Specimens: UMMZ, USNM, MCZ.

*VERMILION FLYCATCHER
Pyrocephalus rubinus (Boddaert)

Status: Hypothetical; accidental visitant.
Record: A bird identified as being of this species was seen for several days before and after 12 May 1956 at Wellsburg, Brooke County, by W. Jennings and several others (Buckelew, 1976).

Subfamily Tyranninae | Kingbirds and Allies

GREAT CRESTED FLYCATCHER
Myiarchus crinitus (Linnaeus)

Status: Fairly common summer resident.
Spring: The Crested Flycatcher arrives in late April or in the first few days of May. Birds of passage are fairly inconspicuous and no great numbers are seen, but the loud call notes of the local residents are readily noticeable.

First-seen Spring Dates: Summers County, 25 April; Kanawha County, 26 April; Cabell-Mason Counties, 28 April; Monongalia County, 2 May; Wood County, 4 May.

Summer: The Crested Flycatcher probably nests in every county, although definite records are lacking for many. It occurs most commonly below 900 m, but in the oak forest it does occur as high as 1,100 to 1,200 m if the forest is not too dense. The favorite habitat is the mature oak-hickory forest or the mixed mesophytic forest. It will be found in the young forest, providing a few older trees are available to supply nesting cavities. The species is scarce in the heavy northern hardwoods forest and is absent from the spruce forest.

Breeding Populations: Breeding Bird Surveys have averaged 3.3 (10.2–0.2) birds per route. The Crested Flycatcher has contributed to the population of 19 of the 39 Singing Male Censuses in which it has occurred. The populations included: second-growth northern hardwoods, 700 m, Pendleton County, 40 males per 100 ha; cut-over oak-hickory forest, 710 m, Greenbrier County, 32 males; mature deciduous forest, 700 m, Webster County, 32 males; oak-hickory forest, 820 m, Greenbrier County, 25 males; 10 areas with 17 males per 100 ha; and seven areas with seven males per 100 ha.

Fall: The departure of this species is most inconspicuous, but most of the birds leave in the middle of September and all will be gone by the end of the month.

Last-seen Fall Dates: Kanawha County, 12 September; Cabell-Mason Counties, 16 September.

Specimens: UMMZ, USNM, WAL, GMS, MCZ. All specimens examined have been referable to the northern subspecies, *boreus* Bangs.

*WESTERN KINGBIRD *Tyrannus verticalis* Say

Status: Casual fall visitant.
Records: Brooks (1944) carried the Western Kingbird on the Hypothetical List on the basis of a report from Alderson, Greenbrier County, in the fall of 1943. According to Edeburn, et al. (1960), three records were for the Huntington area: 9 September 1955 (H. K. Land); and 5 October 1957 and 6 August 1960 (T. Igou). Igou also reported one from Crum, Wayne County, on 6 August 1966. R. Strosnider

and J. Walker saw one at Blacksville, Monongalia County, on 23 September 1973.

Remarks: This species qualifies for the Regular List under Rule 5. It may well be more common than the records indicate, since it is most likely to occur at a time when few birders are active and a casual or fleeting glance would misidentify it as a Great Crested Flycatcher.

EASTERN KINGBIRD *Tyrannus tyrannus* (Linnaeus)

Status: Fairly common summer resident; occasionally a very common migrant.

Spring: The kingbird migrates throughout the state, but occurs only in non-forested country. Arrival is in the last part of April, and at times large numbers may be seen in a day.

First-seen Spring Dates: Kanawha County, 22 April; Cabell-Mason Counties, 28 April; Wood County, 29 April; Summers County, 1 May; Monongalia County, 4 May.

Summer: The kingbird occurs throughout the state, except on the higher forested mountains and in heavily forested areas elsewhere. It does occur at least as high as 1,100 m in open situations; for example, one was collected at the Sinks of Gandy, Randolph County (Wetmore, 1937). In the higher mountain valleys, it becomes scarce, even in open country, and through much of central and southern West Virginia it is local and would be called uncommon. The optimum habitat consists of open areas with isolated trees or groves at least about 20 feet high. The orchards of the Eastern Panhandle are favorite places even though the trees are somewhat low, and the groves of sycamores along some of the larger rivers are also favored. Nests have been found throughout the state, and it probably nests in every county.

Populations: Breeding Bird Surveys have averaged 1.8 (9.0–0.1) birds per route. The kingbird has been recorded in six Singing Male Censuses with an average population of 17 males per 100 ha. Other populations were: overgrown field, Ohio County (three censuses), 25, 17, and 12 males per 100 ha; shallow pond-cattail marsh, Mason County, 17 males per 100 ha; and river bottom-wet meadow, Tucker County, seven males per 100 ha.

Fall: An influx from the north occurs in late August, and locally the species may be very common for a few days. Most of these birds, as well as the resident birds, will have left the state by mid-September, although a few stragglers may stay until the end of the month. No Eastern Kingbirds have been caught at A.F.M.O.and none have been seen flying along the Allegheny Front.

Last-seen Dates: Cabell-Mason Counties, 30 August; Kanawha County, 12 September.

Specimens: USNM, WAL.

*SCISSOR-TAILED FLYCATCHER
Tyrannus forficatus (Gmelin)

Status: Hypothetical; accidental visitant.

Records: One was seen in the Berry Hills section of Charleston on 21 May 1970 by several observers, none of whom had had previous experience with the species (A. Shreve, pers. comm.). There is little possibility for misidentification with such a distinctive species, but according to the rules this sighting does not qualify for the accepted list. It is noteworthy that there was a report of this western species from Westmoreland County, Pennsylvania, at about the same time. There is another, less certain, report from Barboursville, Cabell County, in the early 1950s (R. Estler, fide L. Kiff).

Family Alaudidae   LARKS

HORNED LARK   *Eremophila alpestris* (Linnaeus)

Status: Uncommon to fairly common permanent resident; fairly common to common winter resident and migrant.

Distribution: The Horned Lark occurs throughout the state wherever suitable large expanses of open fields with short grass are found. Pasture fields, airports, golf courses, old strip mines, and the grassy tops of mountains are common locations for this species. In some states, it is known to occur on the grassy median strips of superhighways in otherwise forested country, but as yet there are no records of this in West Virginia. It is found at all elevations,

but suitable habitat is not plentiful in the bottomlands.

As a breeding bird, it is not numerous any place but seems to be most common in the north, in the high mountains and the mountain valleys, becoming less so in the wooded hill country of the southwest. Indeed it may be absent from some counties. There are definite breeding records from Jefferson, Berkeley, Hampshire, Hardy, Tucker, Preston, Monongalia, Marion, Brooke, Ohio, Marshall, Upshur, Greenbrier, Nicholas, Summers, Kanawha, and Cabell Counties.

Populations: Breeding Bird Surveys have averaged only 0.6 (3.4–0.1) bird per route on 14 routes with counts seldom being over two. Horned Larks have occurred on one Singing Male Census (brushy field, 940 m, Tucker County), but did not contribute numerically to the population.

Winter: Large flocks may congregate to spend the winter in certain favored spots. These spots are often open fields in which manure is spread throughout the winter; for example, the fields of the University Dairy Farm at Morgantown. It is not known from how far these birds come. The flocks begin to break up in February and territorial singing is heard from that time. Nesting may start in March. Christmas Counts (birds per party hour) are: statewide, 0.93 (2.48–0.15); Charleston, 0.28 (1.19–0); Charles

Town, 0.68 (2.5–0); Huntington, 0.67 (0.48–0); Inwood, 1.13 (6.0–0); Mason County, 1.97 (11.11–0.05); Ona, 0.58 (1.44–0); Lewisburg, 4.15 (9.37–2.33); and Hampshire County, 0.77.

Specimens: USNM, WVU, CM, GMS. A single wintering specimen from Brooke County (GMS) is apparently of the subspecies *hoyti* Bishop, and this form may occur in winter more often than is known. All other specimens of both breeding and wintering birds are of the midwestern form *praticola* Henshaw. There are numerous sight records for the northern subspecies, *alpestris,* during the winter from as far south as Kanawha and Cabell Counties, but I know of no specimen of this form from the state.

Family Hirundinidae   SWALLOWS

PURPLE MARTIN   *Progne subis* (Linnaeus)

Status: Common spring migrant; locally common summer resident; very common to abundant fall migrant.

Spring: The Purple Martin migrates throughout the state, but is usually found most commonly in urban and suburban situations. It seldom occurs in the more heavily forested regions, and there are few reports from high elevations. Early arrivals reach the state in the last week in March, and the peak of migration is in early April.

First-seen Spring Dates: Cabell-Mason Counties, 24 March; Kanawha County, 25 March; Summers County, 10 April; Monongalia County, 19 April.

Summer: There are probably nesting colonies in every county, although the martin does not occur at high elevations. The highest occurrence that I have a record of was in the upper Greenbrier Valley at an elevation of about 850 m, and it was considered to be scarce there. Breeding colonies are often very local, and many persons put up nesting boxes that attract no birds. Most of the colonies are in fairly large nesting boxes, often of an elaborate nature, but in southwestern West Virginia it is common to see small one or two compartment houses in every house clearing. Sutton (1933) tells of nesting in hollow trees at Bethany in 1915 and Scott (1872) cited an instance of this in Kanawha County, but there are no recent records. Apparently, the species was once more common than it is today, since both Scott and Brewster (1875) found them to be quite numerous. It is likely that competition for nest holes from both House Sparrows and Starlings has had an important effect on the population of martins.

Populations: Breeding Bird Surveys have averaged 3.7 (9.0–0.2) birds per route on only 12 routes.

Fall: Starting in mid-July and reaching a peak in early August, the Purple Martin begins to assemble in large nighttime roosts. In the late evening, they frequently perch on TV antennas in large numbers. These nighttime roosts occur at certain favored localities, but are likely to be moved through short distances from year to year. The roost that has had the most attention is one that occurs annually someplace along the Kanawha River near Charleston, often within the city limits. This congregation begins to form in early July and usually peaks in early August with as many as 30,000 birds being present during the period of maximum abundance. In three years (1970–1972), some 1,300 of these birds were banded and recaptures have come from several other locations in nearby southwestern West Virginia and eastern Kentucky. Birds banded at Clarksville, Pennsylvania, have been captured there. The departure from this roost is sometimes quite abrupt; for example, in 1964 some 30,000 birds were present on 30 August and none on 3 September (Gluck, 1965). Most of the migrating martins will have left the state by early September.

First-seen Fall Date: Kanawha County, 4 July.

Last-seen Fall Date: Kanawha County, 5 September.

Remarks: This species is subject to occasional die-offs during periods of inclement weather in late May or June. The most carefully documented occasion was in late June 1972 when the aftermath of a tropical storm produced several days of cold, rainy weather. There were many reports of young birds dying in the nest as well as cases of extensive adult mortality. The population was virtually eliminated throughout the state. The following spring (1973) was cold and wet and the 1974 populations were even lower. Recovery from this has been slow, and by the early 1980s populations were still lower than in the early 1970s.

Specimens: WVU, MCZ, MU.

TREE SWALLOW   *Tachycineta bicolor* (Vieillot)

Status: Fairly common spring migrant, often locally very common; uncommon local summer resident; uncommon fall migrant.

Spring: The Tree Swallow probably migrates along every good-sized stream in the state but there are rather few records. There are reports from all parts of the state, but it seems to be common only in the northeast in Monongalia and Preston Counties. A few birds may arrive in late March, but the peak of the migration is the first half of April. Stragglers may remain in areas away from the breeding areas until early May.

First-seen Spring Dates: Kanawha County, 28 March; Randolph County, 1 April; Cabell-Mason Counties, 6 April; Greenbrier County, 15 April.

Last-seen Spring Dates: Kanawha County, 20 April; Cabell-Mason Counties, 10 May.

Summer: Most of the summer records come from the mountainous areas where nests have been found near beaver ponds and other flooded areas. Definite nesting records come from Hampshire, Preston, Tucker, Randolph, and Pocahontas Counties. Away from the mountains, we have nesting records only from the McClintic Wildlife Station in Mason County on several occasions, at Belle in Kanawha County in 1961, and in Raleigh County in 1975. Sightings in the summer come from Jefferson, Morgan, Pendleton, Greenbrier, Mercer, Wood, and Gilmer Counties. In all cases, these sightings involved only a very few birds, often only one or two.

Fall: Fall departure takes place in September and a few stragglers remain until late October or even early November. In most parts of the state, fewer birds are present than in the spring.

Last-seen Fall Date: Cabell-Mason Counties, 23 October.

Specimens: WVU, CM.

NORTHERN ROUGH-WINGED SWALLOW
        Stelgidopteryx serripennis (Audubon)

Status: Fairly common migrant (occasionally common to very common); fairly common summer resident.

Spring: The Rough-winged Swallow migrates throughout the state, but most commonly occurs over bodies of water and is rarely seen at any great distance from water. It arrives in early April in the south and late April in the north. The Rough-winged

Swallow rarely occurs in large flocks, although during inclement weather sizeable numbers may occur in the swallow concentrations over major streams.

First-seen Spring Dates: Cabell-Mason Counties, 7 April; Kanawha County, 15 April; Monongalia County, 2 May.

Summer: The Rough-winged Swallow occurs throughout the state during the summer and probably nests in every county. Nests are placed on bridge abutments, rocky banks, and cliffs. As more and more extensive highway cuts are being made, the Rough-winged Swallow is utilizing them for nesting sites. In these cases, the nests are not at the edges of streams but usually are not far from them. Swallows may be seen foraging over meadows and other upland sites. The Rough-winged Swallow occurs at all elevations, but I have found no nesting records above 900 m.

Breeding Populations: Breeding Bird Surveys have averaged 1.9 (8.1–0.2) birds per route.

Fall: Local residents depart in early August and will be gone by the middle of the month. Migrants from the north may be present until the first of September.

Last-seen Fall Date: Cabell-Mason Counties, 23 August.

Specimens: WVU, MCZ, WAL, GMS.

BANK SWALLOW   *Riparia riparia* (Linnaeus)

Status: Uncommon migrant, but locally on occasion it may be very common; very local uncommon summer resident.

Spring: The Bank Swallow arrives in mid-April to early May. It probably occurs throughout the state, but is much more common as a migrant east of the mountains than it is in the west. As a migrant it will rarely, if ever, be found away from a body of water, usually a large lake or major river. Under cool rainy conditions, large concentrations of Bank Swallows may collect at favored localities on major streams or large impoundments. At times, these same conditions will produce large concentrations of five swallow species together.

First-seen Spring Dates: Cabell-Mason Counties, 19 April; Kanawha County, 1 May; Monongalia County, 7 May.

Last-seen Spring Date: Cabell-Mason Counties, 10 May.

Summer: There are few nesting records. Scott (1872) collected fledglings at Coalburg, Kanawha County, in 1872 but it does not nest there today. Bibbee (1929) reported it nesting in Ritchie County but neither Brewster (1875) nor the 1974 Brooks Bird Club Foray recorded it in that county. Definite nesting records come from Jefferson, Berkeley, Hampshire, Mineral (Burlington), Pendleton (Ruddle), Pocahontas (Greenbank), Monongalia, Wirt, and Lewis Counties. There are summer records from Berkeley, Hardy, Randolph, Hancock, Wetzel, Jackson, Summers, Wood (considered common), Greenbrier, and Fayette Counties. In almost all of these cases, the recent records involved only a few birds. At the Mineral County site, about 50 nest holes were seen in 1967 but only five birds.

Populations: Bank Swallows have been reported on only four Breeding Bird Survey routes (three in the Eastern Panhandle) with counts of 1, 4, 33, and 20 birds.

Fall: The Bank Swallow has seldom been reported in autumn, but it begins to flock in early August and all are gone by late August.

Specimen: MCZ.

CLIFF SWALLOW   *Hirundo pyrrhonota* (Vieillot)

Status: Rare to uncommon spring migrant locally; rare to uncommon local summer resident; locally very common to abundant fall migrant.

Spring: The Cliff Swallow probably migrates throughout the state, but there are few spring reports. Arrival is usually in early April in the south and mid-April in the north. On occasion, concentrations of 40 to 50 will be seen, but more commonly there will be only one or two.

Summer: At present the Cliff Swallow seems to be largely limited to the Allegheny Mountains Region as a breeding bird. There are recent nesting records from Hampshire, Hardy, Pendleton, Tucker, Pocahontas, Greenbrier, Preston, and Summers Counties. Outside of the mountains, the only nesting reports come from western Berkeley County, east of the main mountain ridges, and from Upshur County in 1943. There are reports of summer birds from the Ohio River counties of Hancock and Wood, and from Fayette County. None of the nesting sites contain, at present, large colonies, although a colony of 90 nests was found at Cranesville, Preston County, in 1943. All nests have been placed on barns or other outbuildings and no cliff nests have been reported.

Breeding Populations: The Cliff Swallow has occurred on only four Breeding Bird Survey counts with high counts of 35 and 45 in Morgan County.

Fall: The Cliff Swallow begins to congregate in flocks in early August and the last birds are gone by mid-September. At some places, which are favored year after year, large concentrations of migrants build up in the fall, and in the late evening large flocks may be seen perched on electric wires along the highways. Such concentrations have been reported from Mason County (Edeburn et al., 1960), Nicholas County (Legg, 1944), Greenbrier County (C. O. Handley, in litt.), and from certain places in Poca-

hontas and Randolph Counties (Brooks, 1949). On several occasions, large numbers of Cliff Swallows have been seen crossing the Allegheny Front at A.F.M.O.

Remarks: This species was once more widespread and more numerous than at present. Scott (1872) in Kanawha County and Brewster (1875) in Ritchie County found them to be quite common as nesting birds, but they do not nest at these places now. The interruption of nesting and the appropriation of the nests by House Sparrows is probably a major factor in limiting the population. In Preston County, it has been observed that in two summers 36.6 percent of the Cliff Swallow nests under study were lost to House Sparrows (Samuel, 1969). A comparison of the breeding biology of the Cliff and Barn Swallows in Preston County has been published by Samuel (1971).

Specimens: CM, GMS.

BARN SWALLOW   *Hirundo rustica* Linnaeus

Status: Common to very common migrant; common to very common summer resident.

Spring: The Barn Swallow migrates throughout the state, and often during inclement weather large numbers may congregate at particular sites along major streams. Arrival is usual in early to mid-April but a late spring may defer arrival until late April.

First-seen Spring Dates: Summers County, 7 April; Cabell-Mason Counties, 8 April; Kanawha County, 11 April; Wood County, 20 April; Monongalia County, 21 April.

Summer: This is the most common swallow in the state, and it occurs in open farming country throughout the state, even at high elevations. It undoubtedly nests in every county. At the Sinks of Gandy Creek in Randolph County, Barn Swallows build their nests on the walls and ceilings of the entrance cave, and at a few other places in the state nests are placed on rock faces. However, most of the nests are placed on barns and other outbuildings, often in sizeable colonies.

Breeding Populations: Breeding Bird Surveys have averaged 17 (53.6–4.0) birds per route.

Fall: The Barn Swallow begins to flock in late July or early August and departure is usually from mid-August until early September. Stragglers will be present until mid-September, but after that they will be rare.

Last-seen Fall Dates: Cabell-Mason Counties, 7 September; Kanawha County, 20 September.

Remarks: As with other insectivores feeding on flying insects, this species is susceptible to mass die-offs on occasion when abnormally cold or wet weather reduces the insect supply in late May or June. Barn Swallows do not seem to be hit as hard as martins, but Barn Swallow populations may be low for several years after one of these occasions.

Specimens: USNM, GMS.

Family Corvidae   CROWS AND JAYS

BLUE JAY   *Cyanocitta cristata* (Linnaeus)

Status: Uncommon to fairly common permanent resident; very common to abundant (very abundant locally) spring and fall migrant.

Distribution: At present, the Blue Jay is found throughout the state, although populations are variable. It is numerous in the mountain areas, even at the highest elevations. In the upper Ohio Valley and in the Monongahelia drainage, it was once quite uncommon, being known only as a fall transient or winter visitant, but in the last 20 years it has increased markedly in these areas and has become fairly common to common. There was a nesting record from Hancock County in the 1880s (Hill, 1884). It nested in Ohio County for the first time in 1959, and for the first time in Monongalia County at about the same time. In the Eastern Panhandle and in the lower Ohio and Kanawha drainages, it was common and has been in these places for many years. However, populations in the Kanawha Valley have increased notably in the last 20 years. It is probable that it was once uncommon over a wide area of the state. Winter populations tend to vary with the availability of food, primarily acorns and beechnuts, and while some birds may migrate, some remain at all locations during the winter. There are nesting records from all over the state, and they may nest in every county at present.

Migration: Although the Blue Jay is considered to be a permanent resident, large numbers of jays migrate through the state, both in spring and fall. In the spring, loose flocks of jays are often seen moving north at a time when the local population is nesting. In the fall the numbers of southbound birds may be quite large. Flocks of jays totalling in the thousands per day are not uncommon along the Allegheny Ridges in the second half of September. At A.F.M.O. on several occasions, daily numbers of 3,000 to 4,000 have been estimated although no counts have been made. In 24 years 1,452 jays have been banded with a high year's count of 133. There

have been recoveries of these birds from Alabama and New York. The overwhelming majority of the southbound birds caught at A.F.M.O. have been birds of the year.

Populations: Breeding Bird Surveys have averaged 3.6 (13.0–0.1) birds per route. Most routes have only low numbers, but routes in Putnam and Morgan Counties have averaged 13.0 and 12.4 birds per route, respectively. Nine Singing Male Censuses have averaged 15 males per 100 ha. Young spruce forest, 1,350 m, Pocahontas and Randolph Counties, 32 males (but merely present in other years); young northern hardwoods, Tucker County, 1,140 m, 25 males. Christmas Count data (birds per party hour) are: statewide, 2.03 (4.46–1.12); Charleston, 2.14 (3.54–1.08); Charles Town, 0.72 (2.90–0.10); Huntington, 2.93 (8.22–1.54); Inwood, 1.31 (3.60–0.20); Mason County, 1.27 (2.78–0.33); Ona, 1.62 (2.64–0.15); Pendleton County, 1.42 (4.44–0.86); Lewisburg, 1.87 (3.83–0.33); and Hampshire County, 2.90.

Specimens: WVU, USNM, GMS, MU. Most breeding specimens and migrant specimens have been referable to the subspecies *bromia* Oberholser, but some specimens have approached the smaller subspecies *cristata* in size (Wetmore, 1937).

BLACK-BILLED MAGPIE   *Pica pica* (Linnaeus)

Status: Casual visitant; casual permanent resident (extirpated).

Records: Brooks (1944) included the magpie on his Hypothetical List on the basis that a bird seen by him in Huntington on 3 October 1938 may have been an escape. In early February 1951, eight magpies were seen for several days at Huntington and one was collected by R. M. Edeburn. It was later demonstrated that these birds were escapes. There was another sighting at Parkersburg in 1956. A magpie was collected near Morgantown on 5 May 1960 (Dickens, 1960).

In June of 1960, members of the Brooks Bird Club found a magpie and a nest containing infertile eggs in the Canaan Valley, Tucker County. Upon investigation they learned from the landowner, R. Beall, that several magpies had been present on his farm since about 1951, and starting in 1954 or 1955 they had nested successfully for several years. The total population had built up to 10 to 12, but gradually they had disappeared; some were known to have been shot by neighbors, and in 1960 it was thought that only the one bird was present. The details of this occurrence have been summarized by Burns (1961).

It is generally thought that this population has now been extirpated, but there have been a few nebulous reports of magpies in the Canaan Valley or at nearby Blackwater Falls State Park since 1960.

Remarks: The origin of the temporary population in Canaan Valley is unknown. Since the birds first appeared there shortly after the disappearance of the Huntington flock, it is tempting to conclude that the Huntington birds moved to Canaan Valley. In the mid-1950s, there was a wild breeding population near Pittsburgh, Pennsylvania, resulting from escapes from the local zoo. The Morgantown bird may have come from there, but this population was established after the birds were present in Canaan Valley. It is interesting to note that magpie bones have been found in Pleistocene deposits near Natural Chimneys, Virginia (Guilday, 1962), which is not far from the West Virginia border. It seems likely that the magpie was resident in West Virginia in glacial or early post-glacial times.

Specimen: WVU.

AMERICAN CROW   *Corvus brachyrhynchos* Brehm

Status: Common to abundant summer resident; abundant spring and fall migrant; locally abundant winter resident.

Distribution: The crow is found throughout the state and undoubtedly nests in all counties. It is not common as a summer bird in the spruce forest or in the northern hardwoods, and elsewhere in the mountains it is not as numerous as in the lowlands. In the Western Hills Region, it will be found in all rural areas, but is most common where woodland and open areas are mixed.

In mid-March, large numbers of crows migrate through the state, and groups aggregating 100 to 200 resting in open farmland are not unusual. These numbers are matched by large flocks moving south in October. At many places throughout the state, there are large winter roosts, often numbering in the many hundreds.

Populations: Breeding Bird Surveys have averaged 38 (62.4–5.0) per count. Crows have been recorded on many Singing Male Census areas, but the method does not give meaningful figures for this species. Six winter censuses, all in Ohio County, have averaged 27 birds per 100 ha. Christmas Count data (birds per party hour) are: statewide, 21.62 (81.32–5.39); Charleston, 1.26 (3.43–0.77); Charles Town, 137.91 (468–27); Huntington, 3.85 (10.28–0.76); Inwood, 10.4 (17.0–0.60); Mason County, 22.22 (59.09–0.89); Ona, 27.62 (169.5–2.92); Pendleton County, 6.64 (13.67–1.67); Lewisburg, 4.55 (10.56–2.06); and Hampshire County, 16.51.

Specimens: USNM, WAL. Wetmore (1937) has identified a breeding male from Calhoun County as *brachyrhynchos* and suggests that this is the breeding form in the northern and northwestern parts of the state. Birds from the Ohio River Valley and from Cranberry Glades, Pocahontas County, are closer to *paulus,* and he suggests that this may be the breeding form in southern and southeastern West Virginia. It would seem more likely that West Virginia lies in the overlap area between these two races, and that many specimens would be intermediate.

*FISH CROW   *Corvus ossifragus* Wilson

Status: Uncommon to common local permanent resident.

Distribution: The Fish Crow occurs only along the Shenandoah River in Jefferson County and along the Potomac at least as far up as Hampshire County. Eifrig (1904) found this species near Cumberland, Maryland, and at times it may occur up the Potomac as far as Mineral County. In 1982, the Brooks Bird Club found several in the South Branch Valley near Romney, Hampshire County. In Jefferson and Berkeley Counties, it may sometimes be heard or seen at some distance from the rivers, but most records are along the river courses. It has been recorded at Ridge, Morgan County. Since many observers fail to distinguish between this species and the Common Crow, very little is known about the actual numbers present. A flock of approximately 90 was seen in February 1979 (Bartgis), and it may be more common in winter than in summer, since Murray (1952) reported this to be the case in the upper Shenandoah Valley in Virginia.

The only positive nesting record was at Shepherdstown, Jefferson County, in 1981 (R. Bartgis), but it certainly has nested at other times.

Doan (1888) reported one in the Ohio Valley, but as with some other of his records this one must be placed in the "not proved" category.

Populations: The Fish Crow has occurred only on one Breeding Bird Census, Martinsburg, which averaged 1.6 birds in five counts (4–1).

Specimen: I am unable to locate any specimen for the state.

COMMON RAVEN   *Corvus corax* Linnaeus

Status: Uncommon to fairly common local permanent resident.

Distribution: The raven is a regular permanent resident in all the mountain counties from Morgan south along the Virginia border to Monroe and west to Preston, eastern Monongalia, Grant, Tucker, Randolph, Webster, and Nicholas Counties. There is a small population in the gorge region of Summers and Raleigh Counties. It probably nests on rock cliffs in every county within its range, but definite nestings are rather few. I know of nests in Monongalia-Preston (Cooper's Rock State Forest) (Conner and Pattison, 1938), Pendleton, Hardy, Monroe, and Summers Counties. Bowman (1956) listed some eight sites near Franklin, Pendleton County, where he had found nests in the period 1926–1941. S. S. Dickey had records of nests in Pocahontas, Grant, Mineral, Hardy, and Barbour Counties as well as from five locations in Randolph County. In 1981, a pair nested on a cliff on the Potomac River near Shepherdstown, Jefferson County, at an elevation of less than 100 m.

During the fall migration season, hawk watchers on the eastern ridges are often treated to good flights of ravens, with flocks of 20 to 30 birds occasionally seen. In the early 1950s, there was a winter roost of ravens somewhere along the rim of the north end of Canaan Valley, Tucker County, but its exact location was never determined, and it is not known if the roost is still in existence.

While the raven usually nests on cliff faces, it may forage throughout the forested area in its range, and it may also forage in open fields. In the Canaan Valley and near Davis, Tucker County, the raven is often more common than the crow in most seasons.

Occasionally, the raven may stray out of the normal range. It is seen regularly just west of the mountain ridges in Monongalia County. There are a few sight records from Ohio and Jackson Counties along the Ohio River, and from Cabwaylingo State Forest, Wayne County, and a Christmas Count record from Jefferson County.

Breeding Populations: The raven has been found on five Breeding Bird Survey Routes with an average of 0.48 bird per count. The population seems to have been steady for many years, or may even have shown a slight increase.

Specimens: WVU, USNM. These specimens are referable to the eastern race *principalis*.

Family Paridae   TITMICE

BLACK-CAPPED CHICKADEE

Parus atricapillus Linnaeus

Status: Common local permanent resident; occasionally a very common local late-fall migrant and winter visitant.

Breeding Distribution: As a breeding bird, the Black-capped Chickadee is confined to the Allegheny Mountain Region and some of the adjacent Ridge and Valley Region. The usual range extends from Hampshire County and the Virginia state line on the east, and west to the higher parts of Monongalia, Preston, Barbour, Upshur, Webster, Greenbrier, and Monroe Counties. It is apparently absent from the three easternmost counties. Along the edges of the range, it is generally confined to elevations above about 600 m in the west and slightly lower in the east. However, in the valleys within the main range, it has been found nesting as low as 290 m. Since about 1965, there have been a few summer records for the lowland portion of Monongalia County (down to about 430 m) and for Ohio County. It was reported in Raleigh County in June 1975 and in Jackson County in July 1972. There are recent nesting records from Preston, Tucker, Pendleton, Hardy, Randolph, Pocahontas, and Greenbrier Counties.

Within its breeding range, the Black-capped Chickadee may be found in almost any wooded area in which the trees have grown beyond the brush stage.

Populations: The Black-capped Chickadee has been recorded on 69 runs of 13 Breeding Bird Survey Routes with an average number of 1.1 (4.0–0.1) per route. It has not occurred in every year on some routes.

This species has contributed to the population of 30 out of 42 Singing Male Censuses. Some populations are: twenty-year-old pine forest, Hampshire County, 240 m, 74 males per 100 ha; young deciduous forest, Randolph County, 1,250 m, 49 males per 100 ha; and seven areas from 275 to 1,250 m had 33 males per 100 ha (two per study area).

Winter: A few Black-capped Chickadees from the north migrate into the state in almost every winter. In recent years, it has become quite common in Monongalia County, and occurs at least some winters in every county. In some years—for example, 1968 and particularly 1969—very large numbers may invade the state. In October and November of 1969, 75 were banded at one station at Morgantown. This influx extended to the south and 27 were listed on the Charleston Christmas Count that year. Christmas Count data (birds per party hour) are: statewide, 0.20 (0.65–0); Charleston, 0.10 (0.29–0); Charles Town, 0.11 (0.23–0); Huntington, 0; Inwood, 0.11 (0.27–0); Mason County, 0; Ona, 0.0 (0.08–0); Pendleton County, 1.25 (1.89–0.47); Lewisburg, 0.95 (3.11–0); and Hampshire County, 0.49 (0.86–0.34). In the southern part of the state, there is a tendency of birders to call all chickadees Carolinas; consequently, these figures may not be very accurate.

Remarks: The status of the two chickadee species appears to be undergoing a change at present. Previously, it had been considered (e.g., Brooks, 1944) that the Blackcap was the resident species in the highlands and the Carolina was the resident species in the other parts of the state. The two species approached one another on the lower slopes of the western ridges. In Monroe and Hampshire Counties (perhaps also in Mineral), they were sympatric. In winter, Blackcaps appeared only in the northern part of the state. However, in recent years the winter incursion has extended farther and farther south and at some places (e.g., Monongalia County) the Blackcaps have remained to breed at lower elevations than before. Thus, it is either driving out the Carolinas or is hybridizing with them. There is no direct evidence of hybridization, but an October specimen (CM 113610) from Bethany, Brooke County, is possibly a hybrid, and several birds netted and banded at Morgantown appear to be intermediates. The two species are known to hybridize in neighboring Giles County, Virginia (Johnston, 1971). Brewer (1963) and Tanner (1952) postulated a gap between the breeding ranges of the two species, and this may be present in eastern West Virginia, as indeed Brewer (loc. cit.) attempted to show. At present, the situation in Monroe and Hampshire Counties, two areas of sympatry, is unclear.

Specimens: USNM, CM, UMMZ, WAL. Breeding specimens have all been identified as *practicus* (Oberholser), but winter specimens from Brooke and Monongalia Counties are *atricapillus*.

CAROLINA CHICKADEE

Parus carolinensis Audubon

Status: Fairly common to common permanent resident; more evident, if not actually more numerous, in the winter.

Distribution: The Carolina Chickadee is the breeding chickadee in Jefferson, Berkeley, and Morgan Counties and in all parts of the state west of the foothills of the Allegheny Mountains. In Monroe and Hampshire Counties, it may be sympatric with

atricapillus. It is generally absent or rare from the eastern mountain valleys, even at low elevations, but there is a nesting record from Pendleton County. Where its range approaches that of the Blackcap in Monongalia, Taylor, Barbour, Upshur, Webster, and Nicholas Counties, it is usually found below 600 m, but away from the range of *atricapillus* it occurs to the tops of the highest mountains and has been found nesting as high as 914 m in Mercer County. There are definite nesting records from throughout the range, and it probably nests in every county within its range.

The Carolina Chickadee occurs in all deciduous forest habitats, once the trees have passed the brush stage, and it is also quite common in the pine and pine-oak forest.

Populations: Breeding Bird Survey Routes have averaged 4.5 (11.4–0.1) birds per route. Singing Male Censuses are not too reliable for this species since most of the counts have been made after the breeding season for this species is over. The Carolina Chickadee has occurred on 23 study areas and has contributed to the population of 16. The highest population was 49 males per 100 ha in a mixed park habitat in Ohio County, and 41 males per 100 ha in a pine-oak woods in Berkeley County. A pine-oak area in Berkeley County had 136 birds per 100 ha in a winter count. Other winter counts: park, Ohio County, 140 birds per 100 ha; overgrown field, Ohio County, 115; and mixed hardwoods, Ohio County, 107 birds per 100 ha. Christmas Count (birds per party hour) data are: statewide, 2.94 (3.83–1.61); Charleston, 3.83 (5.95–1.96); Charles Town, 1.97 (3.90–0.67); Huntington, 4.24 (11.11–1.77); Inwood, 2.62 (7.20–0.94); Mason County, 2.16 (3.88–1.18); Ona, 3.44 (9.50–1.41); Pendleton County, 0; Lewisburg, 0; and Hampshire County, 2.55 (3.61–1.78).

Remarks: There is no evidence for a fall movement southward in this species, but such a movement is possible. In recent years, the Carolina Chickadee appears to be retreating before an advancing Black-capped Chickadee population as described in the account of that species.

Specimens: USNM, UMMZ, CM, MCZ, AMNH. These specimens are all referable to the subspecies *extimus* Todd and Sutton, whose type locality is at Bethany, Brooke County.

*BOREAL CHICKADEE   *Parus hudsonicus* Forster

Status: Accidental fall visitant.

Records: One was netted and banded at Morgantown on 10 November 1969. The bird was photographed and shown to several other people. Two more were banded at the same place on 11 November (Hall and Hall, 1970).

Specimen: None. Photograph on file in the National Photoduplicate File. It was not possible to ascertain the subspecific identity of the banded birds from the measurements taken at the time.

TUFTED TITMOUSE   *Parus bicolor* Linnaeus

Status: Common permanent resident.

Distribution: The Tufted Titmouse occurs throughout the state and has been found at elevations as high as 1,340 m on occasion. It is not common, however, in the spruce forest or the mixed spruce-northern hardwoods forest. Titmice have probably nested in every county of the state.

Populations: Breeding Bird Surveys have averaged 12.4 (35.7–3.6) birds per route. Forty Singing Male Censuses averaged 26 males per 100 ha (82–3). Cutover hemlock and white pine, Pendleton County, 600 m, 82 males per 100 ha and deciduous woodland, Ohio County, 58 males per 100 ha. Eleven Winter bird censuses averaged 19 males per 100 ha (77–12). Christmas Count data (birds per party hour) are: statewide, 2.13 (3.33–1.71); Charleston, 3.43 (4.93–2.03); Charles Town, 1.11 (2.80–0.47); Huntington, 4.27 (11.11–1.67); Inwood, 0.94 (2.50–0.5); Mason County, 1.16 (2.22–0.27); Ona, 2.20 (4.87–1.10); Pendleton County, 1.11 (2.0–0.8); Lewisburg, 1.24 (1.94–0.27); and Hampshire County, 2.13.

Remarks: The Tufted Titmouse is usually considered to be a non-migratory species, but there is some evidence that in certain years there may be an autumn movement to the south. In the fall of 1969, 32 titmice were banded at A.F.M.O. The species does not normally nest at the A.F.M.O. station or elsewhere on the higher parts of the Allegheny Front, and since the birds behaved much as did normal migrants at that station, it is thought that they were performing a southward movement. For a time, by action of one House of the Legislature, the Tufted Titmouse was the official State Bird of West Virginia.

Specimens: USNM, MCZ.

Family Sittidae   **NUTHATCHES**

RED-BREASTED NUTHATCH
       Sitta canadensis Linnaeus

Status: Fairly common local summer resident; uncommon spring migrant; uncommon to fairly common fall migrant; uncommon (occasionally common) winter visitant.

Spring: The Red-breasted Nuthatch migrates through the state in late April and early May, with some birds remaining until late May. During this period it may be found in any forested habitat in all parts of the state.

First-seen Spring Dates: Kanawha County, 1 May; Ohio County, 4 May; Monongalia County, 30 April.

Last-seen Spring Date: Mason-Cabell Counties, 12 May.

Summer: As a summer resident, the Red-breasted Nuthatch is limited to the higher mountains and the mountain valleys, with very few records coming from below 900 m. It usually occurs in the mature spruce forest or the mixed spruce-hardwoods forest where the numbers fluctuate greatly. It is found only very sparingly in a pure northern hardwoods forest at the higher elevations, but the presence of even a small amount of spruce may be sufficient to produce a nesting population. There are summer records only from Tucker, Grant, Hampshire, Pendleton, Randolph, Pocahontas, Greenbrier, and Nicholas Counties. I know of definite nesting records only from Randolph County.

Populations: The Red-breasted Nuthatch has been found in 11 Singing Male Censuses, virgin spruce-northern hardwoods, 1,200 m, Randolph County, highest population, 40 males per 100 ha. In other years, this area had 15, 40, 25, 8, 20, +, and 8 males, respectively; young spruce forest, Randolph-Pocahontas Counties, 1,350 m, 32 males per 100 ha; spruce-fir swamp, Randolph County, 1,100 m, 32 males per 100 ha.

Fall: The Red-breasted Nuthatch migrates throughout the state in October and November, and at this time may be found in any forested habitat. There is a good movement along some of the mountain ridges. At A.F.M.O. 386 have been banded in 24 years (maximum count 101), and on some days large numbers are heard flying past the banding station. Away from the mountains it is not so numerous.

First-seen Fall Dates: A.F.M.O., 15 September; Mason-Cabell Counties, 26 September; Kanawha County, 6 October.

Winter: A few Red-breasted Nuthatches may winter at any point in the state. Christmas Counts have reported as many as 14. The statewide Christmas Count average is 0.10 bird per party hour with the highest count 1.11 per party hour. It is highly irregular and may not occur at all in some years. As with several other species that nest in the high mountains, very little is known about the winter populations in the breeding range.

Specimens: USNM, CM, OP, GMS, MU.

WHITE-BREASTED NUTHATCH
Sitta carolinensis Latham

Status: Uncommon to fairly common permanent resident.

Distribution: The White-breasted Nuthatch occurs throughout the state, even at the highest elevations where these are covered with a fairly mature hardwoods forest. Nuthatches do occur in the mixed spruce-hardwoods forest but are not found in the pure spruce forest. It occurs only sparingly in the mixed pine-hardwoods forest. White-breasted Nuthatches probably nest in every county in the state but definite records come only from Jefferson, Berkeley, Pendleton, Monongalia, Preston, Randolph, Pocahontas, Greenbrier, Monroe, Brooke, Ohio, Wood, Gilmer, Braxton, Kanawha, Lincoln, McDowell, and Cabell Counties.

Populations: As with the chickadees, most of the censusing has been done too late in the season to give good population estimates. The Breeding Bird Surveys have averaged 1.77 (6.7–0.2) birds per route. Twenty Singing Male Censuses showed an average of 19 males per 100 ha. The highest population was in a mature hardwood forest at 300 m in Kanawha County with 49 males per 100 ha. No other census area had more than two males on the study plot. Ten winter population counts averaged 19 birds per 100 ha. Christmas Count data (birds per party hour) are: statewide, 0.61 (0.90–0.17); Charleston, 0.99 (1.67–0.27); Charles Town, 0.45 (1.20–0.10); Huntington, 0.86 (2.44–0.31); Inwood, 0.42 (1.30–0.11); Mason County, 0.17 (0.44–0); Ona, 0.36 (0.61–0.07); Pendleton County, 1.18 (2.11–0.07); Lewisburg, 0.74 (1.38–0.20); and Hampshire County, 0.97.

Remarks: Although this species is generally considered to be nonmigratory, there is some southward movement in the fall, at least along the mountains. Forty-six have been banded at A.F.M.O. in 24 years. One of these birds was later recovered at Roanoke, Virginia, about 125 miles SSW of the station.

In some parts of the state, this species seems to undergo periodic fluctuations in population. In the early 1950s and again in the mid-1970s, White-breasted Nuthatches became extremely scarce in Monongalia County, and it was not unusual to fail to record them on field trips. Between these periods, the population built up to a more normal one, similar to those given above.

Specimens: USNM, MCZ, GMS, MU. All West Virginia specimens are referable to the northern subspecies, *cookei* Oberholser.

Family Certhiidae   CREEPERS

BROWN CREEPER   *Certhia americana* Bonaparte

Status: Fairly common local summer resident; fairly common spring and fall migrant; uncommon to fairly common winter visitant.

Spring: The Brown Creeper migrates in small numbers throughout the state and can be found in almost any forested habitat older than the scrub stage. The heaviest migration is in mid-April, but it is difficult to set early arrival dates since the wintering population is reasonably large. Migrants should be gone by early May. There are occasional mid- and late May records from the areas outside

of the expected breeding range, but as detailed below these may not be migrants.

First-seen Spring Dates: Cabell-Mason Counties, 21 March; Ohio County, 16 April; Monongalia County, 29 March.

Last-seen Spring Dates: Cabell-Mason Counties, 20 April; Kanawha County, 1 May.

Summer: Until the 1960s, the Brown Creeper was thought to be a summer resident only in the higher mountain areas. There were summer records from Preston, Tucker, Grant, Mineral, Pendleton, Randolph, Webster, and Pocahontas Counties, all from locations above 750 m. The only actual nesting records were in a virgin spruce-northern hardwoods forest at about 1,200 m in Randolph County in 1948 and at Terra Alta, Preston County, in 1975. Nesting was observed near Durbin, Pocahontas County, in 1978.

In 1963, a nest was found on the banks of the Shenandoah River in Jefferson County at an elevation of about 75 m (Hall and Laitsch, 1963). Since that time, nests have been found in Oglebay Park, Ohio County, in 1965 and 1966 (Vossler, 1967) and birds have been seen there in summer in recent years. Other nests have been found in Hancock County in 1969 and in Jefferson County in 1975. A pair nested at Bethany, Brooke County, in 1978 (Buckelew, 1978b). There are summer records from Hampshire, Upshur, Mason, Raleigh, and Kanawha Counties, but no nestings have been discovered there. It is very possible that the late-May records that have always been considered to be "late migrants" may indeed represent breeding records. It is not known whether these birds have been present at low elevation for some years and have been overlooked or whether this is a new development.

The primary requirement of this species seems to be dead or dying trees with loose bark to provide nesting sites. Thus, besides mature forests, favorite nesting sites may be around beaver ponds where flooding has killed trees, in park areas where certain rapid-growing but short-lived trees have been planted, or in areas with numerous disease-killed elms.

Populations: The Brown Creeper has occurred on only three Singing Male Census areas. The virgin spruce-northern hardwoods area at 1,200 m in Randolph County has had populations between 49 and 15 males per 100 ha; spruce-fir swamp, 868 m, Randolph County, 33 males per 100 ha.

Fall: The main migration of this species is largely in October. Away from the mountains they never occur in very large numbers but are widespread and may occur throughout the state. However, large numbers sometimes pass by along the mountain ridges. At A.F.M.O., 400 have been banded in 24 years with a maximum yearly total of 85.

First-seen Fall Dates: A.F.M.O., 23 September; Kanawha County, 6 October; Cabell-Mason Counties, 7 October.

Winter: The Brown Creeper may winter in small numbers throughout the state, even in the high spruce forests. It is irregular and may be missing at particular locations in some years. Six Winter Censuses averaged only 12 birds per 100 ha. Christmas Count data (birds per party hour) are: statewide, 0.14 (0.18–0.06); Charleston, 0.11 (0.22–0); Charles Town, 0.33 (0.90–0.19); Huntington, 0.10 (0.82–0); Inwood, 0.18 (0.44–0); Mason County, 0.07 (0.16–0); Ona, 0.12 (0.55–0); Pendleton County, 0.02 (0.13–0); Lewisburg, 0.05 (0.11–0); and Hampshire County, 0.16.

Remarks: The recent discoveries of nesting creepers at low elevations have been summarized by Hall (1969b).

Specimens: USNM, CM, UMMZ, WAL, GMS, MU. Breeding specimens from the mountain areas have been identified as the subspecies *nigrescens* Burleigh, while migrant and wintering specimens are mostly *americana*. In the absence of specimens, the subspecific identity of the birds that have nested at low elevations and of the birds that winter in the spruce forest is not known.

Family Troglodytidae   WRENS

CAROLINA WREN

Thryothorus ludovicianus (Latham)

Status: Fairly common to common permanent resident.

Distribution: The Carolina Wren occurs throughout the state, but becomes less numerous at higher elevations, and is not found in the spruce forest. Nests have been found as high as 900 m in Pocahontas County, but this species becomes uncommon above 750 m. It probably nests in every county. It occurs in a variety of habitats, but is most common in second-growth forest and wooded park situations. It is not usually numerous in dense mature forest.

Populations: Breeding Bird Surveys have averaged 7.5 (19.5–0.5) birds per route. Thirteen Singing Male Censuses averaged 24 males per 100 ha. Bottomland forest, Wayne County, 62 males per 100 ha; pine-oak woodland, Berkeley County, 67 males per 100 ha; and bottomland, Ohio County, 32 males per 100 ha. Seven winter bird counts averaged 13 birds per 100 ha. Christmas Count data (birds per party hour) are: statewide, 0.59 (0.90–0.41); Charleston, 0.94 (1.53–0.56); Charles Town, 0.24 (1.0–0.10); Huntington, 1.23 (3.11–0.46); Inwood, 0.12 (0.22–0); Mason County, 0.47 (0.78–0.27); Ona, 1.56 (1.92–0.72); Pendleton County, 0.16 (0.36–0); Lewisburg, 0.06 (0.11–0); and Hampshire County, 0.05.

Remarks: The Carolina Wren is particularly susceptible to winter mortality when snow covers the ground for long periods of time. This is most noticeable in the northern part of the state where the species is approaching the northern limits of its range. Typically a succession of mild winters will allow the population to build up to large numbers. Then a hard winter will come with prolonged snow cover, and large numbers will die. For a few years, the species will be scarce and then the cycle will repeat itself. In the southern part of the state, this die-off is less frequent. Such a situation occurred from 1976 on. In the fall of 1976, the population had built up to very large numbers, but two successive cold snowy winters almost eliminated the wren from the state even in the south. After 1978, the population began a slow recovery, which to this writing (summer 1981) has not yet reached normal.

Specimens: WVU, USNM, MCZ, GMS, MU. All specimens belong to the nominate subspecies.

BEWICK'S WREN *Thryomanes bewickii* (Audubon)

Status: Rare to uncommon, very local summer resident; rare winter visitant.

Spring: The Bewick's Wren arrives in late March or early April and is usually conspicuous by its song upon arrival. It may occur in all parts of the state, but is never numerous, and in any given year it may be absent from many places.

First-seen Spring Dates: Cabell-Mason Counties, 22 March; Monongalia County, 17 April; Kanawha County, 20 April.

Summer: At present, the Bewick's Wren is found regularly and in moderate numbers only in the dry open country of the valleys that lie just east of the main Allegheny Mountains. Most of these records come from Pendleton, Grant, Hampshire, and Hardy Counties. It occurs regularly in small numbers at high elevations in small clearings in the spruce forest. Elsewhere Bewick's Wren is very local and very irregular, but it may occur in every county. There are recent nesting records from Hampshire, Hardy, Pendleton, Pocahontas, Greenbrier, Monroe, Preston, Monongalia, Ohio, Wirt, Upshur, Summers, Braxton, Pleasants, and Kanawha Counties.

The favorite habitat is the open space around farmyards or on abandoned farmsteads. The nests are usually on the outbuildings of such farms, and it seems as if the more junk in the form of old rusting farm machinery, old automobile bodies, piles of fence wire, etc., there is in the farmyard the more likely there will be a Bewick's Wren nesting there.

Breeding Populations: Bewick's Wren has occurred on only 9 Breeding Bird Survey routes and has averaged 1 (2.5–0.2) bird per route. The two routes in Pendleton County have averaged 2.4

per route and others usually less than 1 per route. It had occurred on only one Singing Male Census, and did not have a numerical population on that one.

Fall and Winter: Most of the birds depart in the last half of September. At this season, they are generally inconspicuous, and fall departure may not be easily observed. There are frequent winter records from Nicholas, Mercer, and other southern counties. It may winter sparingly in most of the state, except for the higher mountains.

First-seen Fall Date: Kanawha County, 15 September.

Remarks: Bewick's Wren was once the common dooryard wren in most of West Virginia, although Scott (1872) did not find it in Kanawha County, nor did Brewster (1875) find it in Ritchie County. It was common and House Wrens were absent through the central part of the state. In the early part of this century, the House Wren invaded the state, and rapidly spread. Bewick's Wren is apparently unable to compete with the other species, and its numbers gradually declined. However, the House Wren may not be the sole cause of the decline of Bewick's Wren, since the latter has declined in population in areas where the House Wren is not especially numerous. Bibbee (1929) considered it to be still a common bird in central West Virginia, but this is no longer true. As mentioned above, its presence cannot be relied upon anywhere in the state except just east of the Allegheny divide. Smith (1980) has reviewed the decline of this species in the state.

Specimens: USNM, CU, DMNH. West Virginia breeding specimens have been identified as the subspecies *altus* Aldrich, whose type locality is near Philippi, Barbour County. It is of interest to note that the species no longer occurs at the type locality.

HOUSE WREN *Troglodytes aedon* Vieillot

Status: Uncommon to common summer resident.

Spring: The House Wren migrates throughout the state, arriving from the middle of April to the first few days of May. At this time, it is most likely to be found in dooryard or garden situations. As with some other species, the first conspicuous birds to be seen are the local residents and the birds migrating through an area on their way north will be seldom seen.

First-seen Spring Dates: Cabell County, 10 April; Ohio County, 17 April; Kanawha County, 18 April; Randolph County, 20 April; Monongalia County, 23 April; Wood County, 27 April.

Summer: At present, the House Wren probably occurs and nests in every county of the state, although this was not always the case. However, the distribution is spotty and the populations vary greatly from place to place. It is most common in the hill country of the western part of the state and in the major river valleys in the west. It is rare to uncommon in the Allegheny Mountain Region, and uncommon in the valleys of the Ridge and Valley Region in the east. The favored habitat is a greatly disturbed area such as is found near farms and suburban dwellings, but it also occurs in undisturbed areas including heavy forest. Brooks (1944) reported a nesting on Gaudineer Knob, Pocahontas-Randolph Counties, at 1,340 m in a young spruce forest.

Breeding Populations: Breeding Bird Surveys have averaged 3.9 (11.4–0.4) birds per route. Fifteen Singing Male Censuses have averaged 30 males per 100 ha; park habitat, Ohio County, 99 males per 100 ha; brushy field, Ohio County, 62; and deciduous woodland, Ohio County, 49. Only one count above 600 m listed House Wrens.

Fall: The fall migration of this species is unobtrusive, since once the singing period is over the bird is seldom seen except by banders. It does remain until late September, with stragglers present in the first half of October. There are numerous records from a variety of places of the House Wren being listed on Christmas Counts, but these birds probably do not successfully winter in our latitude.

Last-seen Fall Dates: Ohio County, 10 September; Kanawha County, 20 September; and Cabell-Mason Counties, 4 October.

Remarks: While it is quite common there at present, the House Wren is a relatively recent addition to the avifauna of the western part of the state. Although Brewster (1875) collected them in Ritchie County in 1874, the species was almost unknown a century ago except in the extreme east. E. A. Brooks (1908) stated that it was not to be found west of the summit of the Alleghenies.

Specimens: USNM, UMMZ, MCZ, GMS, MU. Specimens taken in most of the state have been identified as the subspecies *baldwini* Oberholser. A badly worn specimen (USNM 295617) collected in Charles Town, Jefferson County, in 1898 was identified by Oberholser (1934) as the nominate race *aedon* but specimens at the UMMZ from Leetown, Jefferson County, collected in the 1930s were identified by Oberholser as *baldwini*. The Eastern Panhandle may be in the area of intergradation between the two forms, or the status of the two races may have changed since the turn of the century. The collecting of specimens of this species in that area seems justified.

WINTER WREN *Troglodytes troglodytes* (Linnaeus)

Status: Uncommon to fairly common local summer resident; uncommon spring and fall migrant; fairly common winter resident.

Spring: The Winter Wren probably migrates throughout the state, but since it rarely sings during migration it is commonly overlooked. The presence of a few birds in the winter makes it difficult to establish arrival dates but most migration records are in the last third of April and the early part of May.

Last-seen Spring Dates: Cabell-Mason Counties, 23 April; Kanawha County, 1 May.

Summer: The Winter Wren occurs in summer in Preston, Tucker, Grant, Pendleton, Randolph, Webster, and Pocahontas Counties at elevations above 750 m, and most usually above 900 m. It is most common in the moist mixed spruce-hardwoods forest, for example, on the slopes of Shavers and Cheat Mountains in Randolph County, and in the canyon of the Blackwater River, Tucker County. It also occurs regularly in the pure spruce forest, such as on Gaudineer Knob. In such places as Burner Mountain and the higher parts of Webster County, they may nest in the pure northern hardwoods forest. On the east face of the Allegheny Front, they nest in rock-pile areas, but more usually nesting sites will be in forests with many stumps and windblown trees. E. A. Brooks reported nests at "The Pines," Randolph County, and M. Brooks (1944) reported a nesting in Webster County. The only other definite nesting record I find is of fledgling birds seen on Gaudineer Knob. A singing male was present near Jackson's Mill, Lewis County, in early June 1980.

Breeding Populations: Three Breeding Bird Survey runs have listed one Winter Wren each. Singing Male Censuses in the virgin spruce-northern hardwoods area at 1,200 m in Randolph County have ranged from 47 to 7 males per 100 ha; in the young spruce forest at 350 m on Gaudineer Knob, the count has been 32 males per 100 ha in three counts.

Fall: The Winter Wren is as inconspicuous in fall as in spring, but it is often found on streamsides overgrown with weeds or near brush piles throughout the state. In some years, a good flight occurs along the mountain ridges; for example, 32 were banded at A.F.M.O. in 1974. A total of 151 have been banded there in 24 years. The fall movement takes place largely in October.

First-seen Fall Dates: Kanawha County, 5 October; Cabell-Mason Counties, 14 October.

Winter: The Winter Wren is widespread in winter, but is generally found only in small numbers. The favorite habitat is usually a woodlot containing piles of brush or slash or along badly eroded banks of small streams. It is highly irregular in occurrence and winter numbers vary widely in any one place. The statewide Christmas Count average is only 0.03 bird per party hour with extremes of 0.17–0.

Specimens: USNM, UMMZ, GMS. Breeding

Plate 9.   Brown Creeper. Adult approaching nest under loose bark. *Hal H. Harrison.*

Plate 10.   Nest of Swainson's Thrush. Gaudineer Knob. *Hal H. Harrison.*

Plate 11.   Swainson's Thrush. Nest on Gaudineer Knob. *Hal H. Harrison.*

Plate 12.   Nashville Warbler. Canaan Mountain. First known West Virginia Nesting. *Hal H. Harrison.*

Plate 13.   Nest of Northern Parula in a piece of burlap lodged in a tree. Cabwaylingo State Forest. *Hal H. Harrison.*

Plate 14.   Chestnut-sided Warbler. Male. *Hal H. Harrison.*

Plate 15. Magnolia Warbler. Male. *Hal H. Harrison.*

Plate 16. Black-throated Blue Warbler. Male. *Hal H. Harrison.*

Plate 17.   Yellow-throated Warbler. Male. *Hal H. Harrison.*

Plate 18.   Mourning Warbler. Male. Gaudineer Knob. *Hal H. Harrison.*

Plate 19.   Swainson's Warbler. Kanawha County. *Hal H. Harrison.*

Plate 20.   Nest of Swainson's Warbler. Kanawha County. *Hal H. Harrison.*

Plate 21.   Summer Tanager. Female. *Hal H. Harrison.*

specimens from Randolph and Pendleton Counties have been identified as the southern subspecies *pullus* Burleigh. Wintering birds are *hiemalis* Vieillot, and the birds nesting in northern Preston County may be of this subspecies also, but no specimen is available from there.

SEDGE WREN   *Cistothorus platensis* (Latham)

Status: Uncommon, very local, summer resident; fairly common local fall migrant.

Spring: Outside of the limited breeding areas, there are spring records only from Monongalia, Ohio, and Wayne Counties, all in mid-May. The Monongalia County record was in a dense meadow, with dew-soaked grass, on a hilltop far from any marsh. Other records are usually from grassy marshes.

Summer: The Sedge Wren occurs in summer in many of the grass-sedge marshes in the Canaan Valley, Tucker County, at an elevation of about 900 m. It occurred, at least formerly, in sedge marshes at the head of Gandy Creek, Randolph County. In 1952, it was reported as being "common" in parts of Preston County (G. Breiding) and in 1964 there was a single record from Blister Pine Swamp, Randolph County (Foray Report). Poland (1938b) reported at least three pairs summering in Altona Marsh, Jefferson County, and he saw birds carrying nesting material there. It has not occurred in Altona Marsh in the summer in recent years. It has been reported in summer from Wood County (W. Armstrong), and Brooks (1944) reported it from Lorentz, Upshur County. In late July 1976, a pair was found in the Middle Ridge section of Charleston, and in August an empty nest was found there (Shreve, 1977). This is the only possible nesting record for the state. The nesting was in a hayfield rather than a marsh.

Fall: Haller (1940b) and the writer (in the 1950s) found large concentrations in the Altona Marsh in late August. Other fall records come from Mason County where Haller (1940b) found it to be common, Marion County (W. Lunk), Brooke County (Sutton, 1937), and Kanawha County. One was found in a TV tower kill in Kanawha County in October 1966. Migrants may be present from late August to late October, but as the Kanawha County record mentioned above demonstrates, nesting may take place very late in the summer.

Specimens: USNM, UMMZ, DMNH.

MARSH WREN   *Cistothorus palustris* (Wilson)

Status: Casual to rare summer resident; rare spring and fall migrant.

Spring: There are spring records for the Marsh Wren only from Greenbrier, Cabell, Mason, and Kanawha Counties. Most of these records are in late April or early May. They may occur elsewhere in the state in suitable marshy habitat.

First-seen Spring Date: Cabell-Mason Counties, 30 April.

Summer: There are recent summer records only from Jefferson, Tucker, Brooke, and Wood Counties. This species is almost exclusively limited to cattail marshes of which there are few in the state of large enough area to maintain a Marsh Wren population. They have probably nested, at least formerly, in the Altona Marsh near Charles Town, Jefferson County. Haller collected a juvenile bird there in August 1939 and young birds were seen there in 1953 (C. Miller). They have not occurred at this location since the 1950s. Sutton (1933) and Haller (specimen in UMMZ) collected specimens at the Beech Bottom Swamp, Brooke County, which were in heavy wing molt, indicating possible nesting there. This swamp is no longer in existence. In 1972, Marsh Wrens remained at the marsh near Boaz, Wood County, until the area was flooded in late June, at which time they disappeared. The 1960 Foray had one record near Hambleton, Tucker County, in June.

Fall: At the McClintic Wildlife Station and near Ashton, Mason County, the Marsh Wren is a moderately common fall migrant. Other fall records come from Jefferson, Greenbrier, Monroe, Monongalia, Nicholas, Mercer, Upshur, Brooke, Wood, Jackson, Mason, Kanawha, and Cabell Counties. Normally, the fall migrants will be found in marshes similar to the breeding ones, but as illustrated by a bird netted and banded on a hilltop in Monongalia County, they may sometimes occur away from water. Migrants will arrive in late August and may remain until early October. There is a December record from Ona, Cabell County (Christmas Count), and in 1979–80 one successfully wintered in Cabell County.

Last seen fall Date: Cabell-Mason Counties, 9 October.

Specimens: CM, UMMZ. In allocating West Virginia specimens, I have followed the revision by Parkes (1959) which seems more consistent with the facts than the treatment of the A.O.U. Check-list (1957). The juvenile from Jefferson County and the molting specimen from Brooke County mentioned above are closest to the eastern inland subspecies *dissaeptus* Bangs. Another September specimen from Brooke County is intermediate between this subspecies and *iliacus* but is closer to this one. All of the fall-migrant specimens from Mason County and two from Brooke County are closer to the midwestern subspecies *iliacus* (Ridgway), but would appear to come from the eastern portion of the range of this race.

Family Muscicapidae

Subfamily Sylviinae	OLD WORLD WARBLERS

GOLDEN-CROWNED KINGLET

Regulus satrapa Lichtenstein

Status: Fairly common to common spring and fall migrant; common to very common local summer resident; uncommon to common winter visitant.

Spring: The Golden-crowned Kinglet migrates throughout the state and occurs in almost any wooded habitat. Arrival dates are difficult to determine because of the fairly large wintering population, but migrants usually appear in late March or early April, and peak numbers are present in mid-April. By 1 May, almost all will have departed from the lowlands, but a few stragglers remain until the first third of May.

First-seen Spring Dates: Kanawha County, 23 March; Monongalia County, 10 April.

Last-seen Spring Dates: Cabell-Mason Counties, 27 April; Kanawha County, 1 May.

Summer: The Golden-crowned Kinglet is present in summer at high elevations, usually above 900 m, in Preston (Cranesville), Tucker, Grant (Allegheny Front), Randolph, Pocahontas (Cheat Mountains), Greenbrier (Fork Mountain), Pendleton (Spruce Knob), and Webster Counties. At Cranberry Glades, it nests as low as 975 m and at Cranesville down to 700 m. It is most numerous in the mature spruce forest and in the mixed spruce-northern hardwoods forest, but will occur also in pine plantations. In some other states, the Golden-crowned Kinglet has moved into pine plantations at fairly low elevations, and this is to be watched for in West Virginia. There are definite nesting records only for Tucker, Pendleton, and Randolph Counties.

Breeding Populations: The Golden-crowned Kinglet has occurred in only three Singing Male Census areas: virgin spruce-northern hardwoods, 1,250 m, Randolph County, 114 males per 100 ha, 99, 79, 54, 39, and 29 males per 100 ha; spruce-fir swamp, 1,100 m, Randolph County, 67 males per 100 ha; and young second-growth spruce forest, 1,350 m, Randolph-Pocahontas Counties, 32, 32, 17, and 3 males per 100 ha.

Fall: The kinglet migrates throughout the state in mid- and late October, and on occasion is seen in very large numbers. At A.F.M.O., 963 have been banded in 24 years with a maximum yearly count of 170, and as many as 44 caught in a single day.

First-seen Fall Dates: Cabell-Mason Counties, 4 October; Kanawha County, 6 October.

Winter: The Golden-crowned Kinglet winters throughout the state, even in the highest spruce forests, but the numbers will vary widely from place to place and year to year. A winter census in oak-pine woods in Berkeley County had 40 birds per 100 ha. Five winter censuses in Ohio County averaged 22 birds per 100 ha. Christmas Count data (birds per party hour) are: statewide, 0.46 (1.11–0.21); Charleston, 0.26 (0.62–0); Charles Town, 0.73 (2.20–0.14); Huntington, 0.37 (1.91–0); Inwood, 0.51 (0.80–0.19); Mason County, 0.49 (0.86–0.07); Ona, 0.31 (1.58–0); Pendleton County, 0.03 (0.13–0); Lewisburg, 0.20 (0.50–0); and Hampshire County, 0.46.

Specimens: WVU, USNM, GMS. All specimens are the eastern race, *satrapa*.

RUBY-CROWNED KINGLET

Regulus calendula (Linnaeus)

Status: Fairly common to common spring and fall migrant; rare to uncommon winter visitant.

Spring: The Ruby-crowned Kinglet migrates throughout the state, arriving usually in mid-April. Most will be gone by 1 May, but fair numbers remain until mid-May. At times it is exceptionally common, and those remaining into May are usually in full song at that time. During migration, it will occur in any sort of wooded habitat.

First-seen Spring Dates: Cabell-Mason Counties, 3 April; Kanawha County, 13 April; Ohio County, 16 April; Monongalia County, 17 April.

Last-seen Spring Dates: Cabell-Mason Counties, 27 April; Monongalia County, 3 May; Ohio County, 3 May; Kanawha County, 3 May.

Fall: A few Ruby-crowned Kinglets arrive in the last 10 days of September but the main migration is in mid- to late October, and stragglers are present in early November. In some seasons, they are extremely numerous. During migration, they are found in any wooded habitat. In 24 years, 1,002 have been banded at A.F.M.O. with a maximum year's count of 130 and as many as 30 in a day.

First-seen Fall Dates: A.F.M.O., 17 September; Kanawha County, 25 September; Cabell-Mason Counties, 4 October.

Last-seen Fall Dates: A.F.M.O., 14 October; Ohio County, 31 October; Monongalia County, 10 November; Cabell-Mason Counties, 11 November.

Winter: The Ruby-crowned Kinglet winters irregularly in small numbers throughout the state except in the high elevation forests, but is never as common as the Golden-crowned. Christmas Count data (birds per party hour) are: statewide, 0.06 (0.11–0.01); Charleston, 0.09 (0.35–0.02); Charles Town, 0.08 (0.30–0); Huntington, 0.10 (0.35–0); Inwood, 0.07 (0.20–0); Mason County, 0.03 (0.18–0); Ona, 0.05 (0.13–0); Pendleton County, 0; Lewisburg, 0; and Hampshire County, 0.06.

Remarks: There is no definite evidence that the Ruby-crowned Kinglet has ever nested in the state, but there is some suggestion that it might have. In 1955, a singing male was seen on 2 and 3 July in the Cheat Mountains by J. Terborgh (Brooks, 1955). On several occasions, Ruby-crowns have been netted at A.F.M.O. in early September before the migration should have started and on one occasion one was captured on 26 August. While these were most probably early migrants, the possibility exists that there may be a small nesting population on the Allegheny Front.

Specimens: USNM, GMS.

BLUE-GRAY GNATCATCHER
Polioptila caerulea (Linnaeus)

Status: Common spring migrant; fairly common summer resident.

Spring: The Blue-gray Gnatcatcher migrates throughout the state, except at higher elevations. Arrival is usually in the first half of April. At this time, it is quite conspicuous in the leafless trees, and is quite noisy. For a few days, every woodlot will seem to be full of gnatcatchers. Once the leaves come out, it is much less evident, and indeed it does not remain in some woodland types for the summer.

First-seen Spring Dates: Cabell-Mason Counties, 7 April; Kanawha County, 7 April; Summers County, 13 April; Monongalia County, 18 April; Ohio County, 20 April; Wood County, 21 April.

Summer: The Blue-gray Gnatcatcher is present in summer throughout the state at elevations below about 1,050 m. Sutton (1933) reported it to be uncommon in Hancock County, but the numbers there have increased in the intervening years and the population there today is about the same as elsewhere. Peak numbers are reached in the extensive oak-hickory-chestnut forests of the Western Hills Region with good numbers also in the oak-pine forests of the Ridge and Valley Region. It is not as common in the northern hardwoods, and gradually becomes scarce at increasing elevations. It has, however, nested at about 1,020 m at Cranberry Glades, Pocahontas County, at the very edge of the spruce forest. I know of no higher nesting record. It probably nests in every county, and definite nesting records are available for all counties in which extensive observations on birds are available.

Populations: Breeding Bird Survey Routes have averaged 4.0 (9.3–0.5) birds per route. Thirty-five Singing Male Censuses have averaged 32 males per 100 ha. Maturing oak-hickory forest, 800 m, Greenbrier County, 67 males per 100 ha; upland mixed woods, 250 m, Mason County, 67 males; cutover hemlock-white pine woods, 600 m, Pendleton County, 64 males; oak-pine forest, 180 m, Berkeley County, 59 males per 100 ha; mature deciduous forest, 700 m, Webster County, 49 males; and northern hardwoods, 700 m, Pendleton County, 49 males.

Fall: Gnatcatchers stop singing early in the nesting cycle, and in late summer they are very inconspicuous in the lush foliage. There are few reports of them at this time, and most of them depart in the middle of September. Twenty-eight have been banded at A.F.M.O. in 24 years.

Last-seen Fall Dates: Ohio County, 2 September; Kanawha County, 10 September; Cabell-Mason Counties, 10 September.

Specimens: WVU, USNM, MCZ, GMS.

Subfamily Turdinae   THRUSHES

EASTERN BLUEBIRD   *Sialia sialis* (Linnaeus)

Status: Uncommon to common migrant; uncommon to common summer resident; fairly common winter resident.

Spring: The bluebird that has been present all winter begins to sing in late February and an influx of migrants from the south occurs in early March. Exact arrival dates of the migrants are almost impossible to determine because of the large winter populations.

Summer: The bluebird occurs in summer throughout the state and probably nests (or did nest) in every county. It is uncommon in most of the Northern Panhandle and in the Eastern Panhandle.

It seems to be most numerous in the lower Ohio River Valley and in the Kanawha Valley below Charleston. It is not numerous at high elevations, but nests have been found in suitable habitat above 1,200 m.

The prime requisite for the bluebird would appear to be old or dying trees that supply nesting cavities. These must be present in areas surrounded by fairly open country, since the bird does not occur in densely forested locations. Thus, the prime nesting habitats are old or abandoned orchards or, at high elevations, the dead trees killed by the flooding of beaver ponds. Old snags on land that has been burned over often attract them. Old fence posts along country roads or in pastures also are commonly used for nesting sites. In recent years, people in many parts of the state have set out nesting boxes in attempts to improve the bluebird populations.

Breeding Populations: Breeding Bird Surveys have averaged 6.9 (29.7–0.3) birds per route. Eastern Bluebirds have occurred on only two Singing Male Censuses; apple orchard, 180 m, Berkeley County, 17 males per 100 ha, and shallow pond-cattail marsh, 180 m, Mason County, 17 males per 100 ha.

Fall: The Bluebird leaves the higher elevations in October. In the north, many of the summer birds appear to leave at this time but are replaced by birds from the north. In the southern part of the state, there is an influx of northern birds, but it is probable that only a part of the summer residents leaves those areas. As in the spring, no good migration dates are known. There is a small movement of bluebirds along the Allegheny Front in late October.

Winter: The Bluebird winters in highly variable numbers throughout the state at elevations below about 600 m. They are rare in the Northern Panhandle and become more numerous to the south. Two Winter Censuses in Ohio County had 22 and 16 birds per 100 ha. Christmas Count data (birds per party hour) are: statewide, 0.47 (0.88–0.25); Charleston, 0.70 (1.69–0.08); Charles Town, 0.05 (0.3–0); Huntington, 0.42 (0.58–0); Inwood, 0.04 (0.20–0); Mason County, 0.78 (1.78–0.09); Ona, 1.04 (2.26–0.34); Pendleton County, 0.03 (0.07–0); Lewisburg, 0.21 (0.38–0); and Hampshire County, 0.06.

Remarks: The Bluebird populations in the state are probably much lower than they were some years ago, and they tend to vary widely from time to time. The introduction of the European Starling had a disastrous effect on Bluebird populations in many parts of the state and changed the status of the latter from a common resident to a decidedly uncommon bird. Starlings compete for nest sites with Bluebirds and usually are dominant over them. Bluebirds are also subject to occasional catastrophic kills during hard winters, particularly those winters in which prolonged freezing weather extends far south into the wintering grounds. After one of these winters, populations in the north may be very low for a few years. Such major catastrophes occurred in the late winters of 1940 and 1955, for example, but none have occurred in recent years.

Specimens: USNM, MCZ, GMS.

VEERY   *Catharus fuscescens* (Stephens)

Status: Uncommon migrant; common local summer resident.

Spring: The Veery migrates throughout the state in spring, but does not seem to be numerous anyplace. As with the Hermit Thrush and the Black-throated Blue Warbler, it is particularly uncommon along the western foothills of the Allegheny Mountains, just a short distance from the breeding grounds. The early migrants may arrive in late April and indeed I have found them on the Preston County breeding grounds as early as 26 April but the main migration is in early May. A few birds may remain outside the breeding range as late as the last week in May. The early birds do little singing during migration, and thus they may be overlooked. However, I have heard them singing in late May along the Shenandoah River in Jefferson County at an elevation below 90 m.

First-seen Spring Dates: Wood County, 27 April; Kanawha County, 1 May; Cabell-Mason Counties, 2 May; Summers County, 1 May.

Last-seen Spring Dates: Kanawha County, 20 May; Cabell-Mason Counties, 24 May.

Summer: The Veery nests in the state in the hemlock forest or the mixed hemlock-hardwoods forest as low as 300 m in the north, but it is most common above 750 m and occurs on the highest peaks that have hardwoods forest on them. There are summer records from Pendleton, Monongalia, Preston, Tucker, Randolph, Webster, Pocahontas, and Greenbrier Counties. Definite nesting records come only from Preston, Pendleton, Randolph, and Pocahontas Counties. Over the years, it has been especially common in second-growth deciduous woods such as has been present along the shores of Lake Terra Alta in Preston County. In the Cheat Mountains, it probably reaches its peak populations and occurs in both pure deciduous forest and in the mixed spruce-northern hardwoods forest, often encroaching on the Hermit Thrush as mentioned beyond.

Breeding Populations: The Veery has contributed to the population of 19 Singing Male Censuses with an average of 47 males per 100 ha; young northern hardwoods, 1,250 m, Randolph County, 123, 81, and 67 males per 100 ha; mature northern hardwoods, 1,200 m, Pocahontas County, 84 and 49 males per 100 ha; same area, after being partially cutover, 25, 67, and 67 males per 100 ha; second-growth mixed hardwoods, 910 m, Pocahontas County, 57 males per 100 ha.

Fall: The Veery tends to depart quite early, in late August or early September. The records at A.F.M.O. are all in the first week of September, but only 137 birds have been banded there in 24 years. Almost all will be gone by mid-September, but there is a record of one killed at a TV tower in Kanawha County as late as 7 October. Except at banding stations, the bird is almost completely overlooked. It migrates at night and is seldom seen, although persons familiar with its distinctive callnote may notice its nocturnal flights. Fall arrival and departure dates are generally too few and too scattered to report reliable averages.

Specimens: USNM, CM, UMMZ, GMS. All specimens examined have been the eastern subspecies *fuscescens*. The western race *salicicola* Ridgway might be expected to migrate through the western part of the state, but no specimens have been collected.

GRAY-CHEEKED THRUSH
Catharus minimus (LaFresnaye)

Status: Rare spring migrant; uncommon fall migrant.

Spring: The Gray-cheeked Thrush is rarely reported in the spring. It very seldom, if ever, sings during migration; consequently, it passes through unnoticed. Some are probably also misidentified as Swainson's Thrushes, which are usually more common. This misidentification may work the other way also, and some reports of Gray-cheeks may be in error. At Morgantown, 17 years of spring banding have netted only 10 birds, and elsewhere the records are as scanty. Most Gray-cheeked Thrushes pass through during the third week in May and will be gone by the end of the month. April dates for arrival reported from Cabell-Mason Counties are undoubtedly in error, and there are no reliable average spring dates from any place.

Fall: The Gray-cheeked Thrush is much more common in fall than in spring, although except at banding stations it is seldom reported. Most of the birds arrive in the last third of September, although there are a few early September dates, and some remain until the middle of October. It probably migrates throughout the state. At A.F.M.O., 308 have been banded in 24 years, with a maximum count of 40 in one year, but in a few years none were netted.

First-seen Fall Dates: A.F.M.O., 23 September; Monongalia County, 23 September; Kanawha County, 20 September; Cabell-Mason Counties, 26 September.

Last-seen Fall Dates: Kanawha County, 3 October; A.F.M.O., 7 October; Monongalia County, 10 October; Cabell-Mason Counties, 12 October.

Remarks: Before the advent of widespread mist-netting, the Gray-cheeked Thrush was considered to be quite rare in the state, and indeed the first specimen was not taken until 1933 (M. Brooks, 1934d) and there had been only two previous records. As with several other species, the banding operations have shown this species to be much more abundant, particularly in the fall, than had been thought.

Specimens: CM, WVU, USNM, WAL. Most of the specimens in the state and most of the birds banded in the state have been the subspecies *minimus*. There are four records for the smaller subspecies *bicknelli* (Ridgway): Morgantown, 16 May 1940 (specimen—WAL) (Lunk, 1941); Charleston, 6 May 1961 (banded) (Ballentine and Ballentine, 1961); and Wheeling, 16 September 1961 (specimen—OP) (Breiding, 1962b). Of 188 birds banded at A.F.M.O. and 86 banded at Morgantown, only one has had the small size of *bicknelli*.

SWAINSON'S THRUSH　*Catharus ustulatus* (Nuttall)

Status: Common migrant both spring and fall, occasionally becoming very common; uncommon to very common local summer resident.

Spring: The Swainson's Thrush generally arrives in the second week of May, and it is quite numerous for perhaps about a week. Unlike some of the other thrushes, it sings during migration and is often very conspicuous. The amount of singing increases as the season progresses. Most of the migrants are gone by the end of May, but often a few will still be migrating in early June (e.g., the birds found in Raleigh County in June of 1975). It migrates throughout the state, and at this time is found in almost any wooded habitat, including parks and suburban houseyards.

First-seen Spring Dates: Cabell-Mason Counties, 17 April; Ohio County, 28 April; Kanawha County, 1 May; Summers County, 1 May; Wood County, 4 May; Monongalia County, 25 May.

Summer: The Swainson's Thrush remains to nest in the state at the very highest elevations and is almost exclusively confined to the spruce forest. Summer records come from Tucker, Grant, Pendleton, Randolph, Pocahontas, and Webster Counties. In the past, it also occurred in Preston County. In recent years, populations have declined somewhat, but in the spruce forest of the Cheat Mountains it still remains abundant. Oddly, it is absent in some years and present in low numbers only in other years in the spruce forest atop the Allegheny Front in Tucker County. The greatest numbers are in the pure spruce forest, even at a young age, but it also occurs in the mixed forest just below the spruce. Brooks (1944) reported them in good numbers in a pitch pine forest on the Allegheny Front in Grant County. The Cranberry Glades, Pocahontas County, seems to be the southernmost nesting station. Definite nesting records come only from Randolph and Pocahontas Counties.

Breeding Populations: The Swainson's Thrush has been listed in 13 Singing Male Censuses with an average number of males of 17 per 100 ha. Young spruce forest, 1,350 m, Pocahontas-Randolph Counties, 108, 99, 91, 57, 42 males per 100 ha;

virgin spruce-northern hardwoods, 1,200 m, Randolph County, 32, 32, 25, 25, 17 males per 100 ha.

Fall: The Swainson's Thrush migrates in September, but a few may arrive in late August and some may remain into early October. Along the mountain ridges, it may be abundant, and at most places it is common. It seems to be less numerous in the southwestern part of the state. At A.F.M.O., 6,026 birds have been banded in 24 years, with a maximum year's total of 592.

First-seen Fall Dates: A.F.M.O., 3 September; Cabell-Mason Counties, 16 September; Kanawha County, 20 September.

Last-seen Fall Dates: Kanawha County, 3 October; Cabell-Mason Counties, 5 October; A.F.M.O., 11 October.

Remarks: The populations of the "spotted thrushes" on Shavers and Cheat Mountains in Randolph and Pocahontas Counties show an oscillating zone of interspecific tension. In recent years, the Wood Thrush and Veery have been pushing up from the lower elevations and encroaching on the Hermit Thrush. The Hermit Thrush may then encroach on the Swainson's Thrush. In some years, the Veery and to a lesser extent the Wood Thrush may occur right to the spruce-clad summits, but in other years the two invaders are found only at lower elevations. Thus, the populations of the Hermit Thrush and the Swainson's Thrush oscillate somewhat. The Swainson's Thrush appears to hold its own fairly well, but in some years the Hermit Thrush may be nearly squeezed out.

Specimens: WVU, USNM, UMMZ, WAL, GMS. Most of these specimens are referable to the eastern subspecies *swainsoni* Tschudi but Wetmore (1939) has referred a migrant specimen from Enon, Summers County, to the western subspecies *almae* Oberholser.

HERMIT THRUSH *Catharus guttatus* (Pallas)

Status: Uncommon spring and fall migrant; fairly common local summer resident; rare to uncommon winter visitant.

Spring: The Hermit Thrush is the earliest of the "spotted thrushes" to arrive in the spring. The first migrants appear in the first week of April, and most of them are gone by the first of May. It may occur anywhere in the state during migration, but seldom exceeds the status of being fairly common. It is particularly scarce at low elevations just west of the main mountain chain even though these lowlands may be almost within sight of the nesting areas.

First-seen Spring Date: Ohio County, 17 April.

Last-seen Spring Dates: Kanawha County, 1 May; Cabell-Mason Counties, 6 May.

Summer: The Hermit Thrush is present, some-

times in good numbers, at higher elevations in Preston, Tucker, Grant, Pocahontas, and Randolph Counties. There are also summer records from Pendleton County (Spruce Knob) and northern Greenbrier County (Fork Mountain). It is most numerous in the mixed spruce-northern hardwoods forest, or at the edges of mountain bogs in the pure spruce forest. If the Swainson's Thrush is not present in the pure spruce forest, or at least is in low numbers (as the situation exists, for example, in the spruce forest on the Allegheny Front in Tucker County), the Hermit Thrush may then become numerous in the pure spruce, but generally it is not common in this forest. Most of the summer records come from above 1,050 m, and the species is most numerous above 1,200 m. There are definite nesting records only from Randolph and Pocahontas Counties, although extremely young, but independent, birds have been netted in September on Allegheny Front, Tucker County.

The Hermit Thrush has two zones of interspecific tension. At the lower edge of its range, it meets the Veery, and at the upper edge, the Swainson's Thrush. Both of these species seem to be dominant over the somewhat smaller Hermit Thrush and at times the latter species seems almost to be squeezed out.

Breeding Populations: No Hermit Thrushes have occurred on any of the Breeding Bird Survey routes. The Hermit Thrush has contributed to the population of only three Singing Male Census areas: young spruce plantation, 1,140 m, Tucker County, 25 males per 100 ha; young spruce forest, 1,350 m, Randolph-Pocahontas Counties, 25, 7, 7 males per 100 ha; and virgin spruce-northern hardwoods, 1,200 m, Randolph County, 10, 7 males per 100 ha.

Fall: The birds in the breeding areas begin to leave in late September, but migrant birds do not usually appear in the lowlands before 1 October. The main flight is over by the end of October, although some birds remain into the winter, particularly in the south and west. Only 193 Hermit Thrushes have been banded at A.F.M.O. in 24 years, but in many years operations there have ceased before the main Hermit Thrush flight.

First-seen Fall Dates: Cabell-Mason Counties, 17 September; Kanawha County, 6 October.

Last-seen Fall Dates: A.F.M.O., 11 October; Monongalia County, 31 October.

Winter: The Hermit Thrush winters in small numbers throughout the more southerly parts of the state at low elevations, and occasionally a few are seen in the northern part of the state. There are recent winter records from Jefferson, Berkeley, Hampshire, Monongalia, Ohio, Kanawha, Cabell, and Summers Counties. Christmas Count data have ranged as high as seven birds per count (Kanawha

County), but more usually only one or two are seen and the statewide average is only 0.01 bird per party hour.

Specimens: USNM, CM, GMS. All specimens are referable to the eastern subspecies, *faxoni* Bangs and Penard.

WOOD THRUSH *Hylocichla mustelina* (Gmelin)

Status: Common spring and fall migrant; common summer resident.

Spring: The first Wood Thrushes usually appear in mid-April, and the bulk of the migration will have passed through by the end of the first week in May. Transients usually are inconspicuous and most of the birds heard singing during this period are residents. This species migrates throughout the state and is found wherever there is a closed-cover hardwoods forest.

First-seen Spring Dates: Cabell-Mason Counties, 14 April; Kanawha County, 15 April; Monongalia County, 23 April; Ohio County, 25 April; Summers County, 29 April.

Summer: The Wood Thrush occurs throughout the state and undoubtedly nests in every county. It occurs primarily in dense mature deciduous forest and is found in this forest even at the highest elevations. It also occurs in the mixed spruce-northern hardwoods forest, but is absent from the pure spruce forest. Populations are not high in the oak-pine forests, which probably do not form a dense enough shade. The principal factor that is evident in prime habitat seems to be the completeness of the canopy so that the forest floor is in dense shade.

At the higher elevations, this species comes in contact with at least two and possibly three of the *Catharus* species. In some years, the Wood Thrush occurs at much higher elevations than it does in other years. At the same time, the Hermit Thrush and the Veery will be in lower than normal numbers. It is not possible to say whether the Wood Thrush advances into unoccupied territory when the other two species are in low numbers, or whether its presence produces the lower numbers of the other two.

Breeding Populations: Breeding Bird Surveys have averaged 20.4 (55.8–2.1) birds per route. This figure may not be very significant for this species, since many Wood Thrushes will have ceased singing before a Breeding Bird Survey count has been completed. The areas selected for the Singing Male Censuses over the years have been slightly biased toward good Wood Thrush habitat. Consequently, the species has occurred on 72 such counts, averaging 42 males per 100 ha. Young northern hardwoods, 1,140 m, Tucker County, 131 males per 100 ha; mixed hardwood forest, 580 m, Nicholas County, 131 males per 100 ha; mixed deciduous forest, 400 m, Hampshire County, 116 males; deciduous forest, 700 m, Webster County, 107 males; hardwoods-hemlock forest, 580 m, Tucker County, 104 males; oak-mixed hardwoods, 792 m, Webster County, 99 males; hemlock-yellow poplar forest, 400 m, Fayette County, 99 males; bottomland forest, 730 m, Wayne County, 84 males; mature hardwoods, 300 m, Kanawha County, 82 males; and mixed hardwoods, 360 m, Wetzel County, 74 males.

Fall: The fall migration of all the forest thrushes is rather inconspicuous except at banding stations where many may be caught. The birds stop their evening singing well before they leave, and then gradually disappear. Most Wood Thrushes will leave in the second half of September with stragglers remaining through the first third of October. Occasionally, one will be seen as late as 1 November. There does not seem to be any concentrated flight of Wood Thrushes along the mountain ridges since in 24 years only 576 have been banded at A.F.M.O. and in some years none were netted there.

Last-seen Fall Dates: Ohio County, 4 September; Kanawha County, 15 September; Cabell-Mason Counties, 26 September; A.F.M.O., 2 October.

Specimens: USNM, CM, CMZ, MU, GMS.

AMERICAN ROBIN *Turdus migratorius* Linnaeus

Status: Very common to abundant spring migrant; very common summer resident; very common fall migrant; common to very common local winter resident.

Spring: In the spring, the robin begins to appear in places where it has not wintered in late January or early February. By late February it will be present, at least in small numbers, almost throughout the state, but the peak of migration, both for transients and residents, is in March. On some days, large numbers may be encountered during the middle of March.

First-seen Spring Date: Kanawha County, 20 March.

Summer: The robin nests throughout the state, at all elevations, and in all habitats that contain at least a few trees. As is well-known, it is extremely common in suburban or even urban situations. Nests have been found in the spruce forest at the highest elevations. The favored habitats are areas of trees interrupted by grassy areas for feeding, but sometimes, as in the spruce forest, these last are missing.

Breeding Populations: Breeding Bird Surveys have averaged 44.2 (131.6–10.6) birds per route (highest count, 165), but these counts are biased toward getting large numbers of robins. The robin has occurred on 33 Singing Male Censuses averaging 22 males per 100 ha (84–8). Young spruce forest, 1,350 m, Randolph County, 84, 59, 49, 33 males per 100 ha; virgin spruce-northern hardwoods, 1,250 m, Randolph County, 49, 16, 8 males per 100 ha; and young northern hardwoods, 1,140 m, Tucker County, 42 males per 100 ha.

Fall: Except at certain vantage points, the fall migration of robins is rather inconspicuous. In the usual situation, the birds that have been present in yards and gardens during the summer disappear from these areas in early September. At this time, large flocks may be found locally in deeper woods. In October, these flocks begin to move south, but many remain in the state. Late in October, migrants from the north begin to appear. During late October and early November, large concentrations of robins are frequently seen migrating along the mountain ridges. At A.F.M.O., 405 robins have been banded in 24 years with a high year's count of 110.

Winter: There are flocks of robins, sometimes quite large, in most parts of the state during the winter. It is not known whether these flocks are the same birds that summer in the state or are migrants from farther north. The flocks usually frequent forested sites that offer some shelter and adequate food in the form of berries or other fruit. So localized are these flocks that casual observers may never be aware of their presence. Individual robins often winter in gardens or dooryards if food and shelter are available. Robins are not usually found in the spruce forest in winter but may occur at the edges of this formation.

Six winter bird censuses averaged 22 birds per 100 ha. The highest count was an overgrown ravine with multiflora rose hedge in Ohio County with 185 birds per 100 ha. Christmas Count data (birds per party hour) are: statewide, 0.67 (2.17–0.11); Charleston, 1.58 (9.57–0.22); Charles Town, 0.09 (0.31–0); Huntington, 1.36 (8.30–0.06); Inwood, 0.05 (0.20–0); Mason County, 0.19 (0.50–0.05); Ona, 0.90 (3.79–0.04); Pendleton County, 0; Lewisburg, 0.14 (0.27–0.02); and Hampshire County, 0.67.

Specimens: USNM, UMMZ, WVU, MU, GMS. Breeding specimens from the mountains have been identified as the nominate race *migratorius*. This subspecies migrates through the state, and may nest also in the Northern Panhandle and in Monongalia County. Specimens from the south and west of the state approach the southern form, *achrusterus* Batchelder. Wetmore (1937) identified as *achrusterus* specimens from Philippi, Barbour County, and Muddlety, Nicholas County. Haller (1951) collected *achrusterus* in Brooke County in April. Many specimens are intermediate, and in some areas the males approach *migratorius* and the females approach *achrusterus*. I collected a specimen in October on the Allegheny Front which approached the far northern subspecies *nigrideus* Aldrich and Nutt.

Family Mimidae   MOCKINGBIRDS AND THRASHERS

GRAY CATBIRD *Dumetella carolinensis* (Linnaeus)

Status: Common to very common summer resident; casual early winter visitant.

Spring: The Catbird migrates throughout the state, and is found at all elevations. Transients are difficult to detect in the presence of the summer resident population. The first arrivals are in the last third of April and the full nesting population is present by early May.

First-seen Spring Dates: Kanawha County, 18 April; Cabell-Mason Counties, 20 April; Summers County, 21 April; Ohio County, 24 April; Wood County, 27 April; Monongalia County, 30 April.

Summer: The Catbird occurs in numbers throughout the state and nests in all counties and at all elevations. The highest nesting record I find was at 1,150 m in Tucker County, but it probably nests higher. The Catbird is generally found in dense brushy areas or in second-growth forest containing a dense understory. It occurs in such situations in all forest types, but is uncommon in the pure spruce forest.

Breeding Populations: Breeding Bird Surveys have averaged 12.1 (23.8–2.5) birds per route. Twenty-five Singing Male Censuses have averaged 53 males per 100 ha. Overgrown field, 360 m, Ohio County, 185, 148, 148, 148 males per 100 ha; overgrown ravine, Ohio County, 101 males per 100 ha; hemlock-yellow poplar woodland, 400 m, Fayette County, 84 males; and park, Ohio County, 64 males per 100 ha.

Fall: In fall, the Catbird migrates throughout the state, but as with many species the departure is sometimes unnoticed. Sometimes, large concentrations have been present on the open huckleberry plains of the higher mountains such as the Allegheny Front at A.F.M.O. Most Catbirds depart in the first third of October, but a few stragglers may remain until mid-November.

Last-seen Fall Dates: Kanawha County, 20 September; A.F.M.O., 3 October; Cabell-Mason Counties, 8 October.

Winter: There are occasional Christmas Count records from Kanawha and Cabell Counties, as well as an earlier record from Braxton County. A few other reports of December birds are available, but it is doubtful if many of these birds spend the complete winter in the state. They will either die or depart during the coldest weather.

Specimens: USNM, MCZ, MU.

NORTHERN MOCKINGBIRD
Mimus polyglottos (Linnaeus)

Status: Uncommon to common permanent resident; in the north, more common in the winter.

Distribution: The Mockingbird occurs throughout the state, but in the recent past it has been uncommon in the Northern Panhandle and in Marion and Monongalia Counties as well as the counties of the Allegheny Mountain Region. It is most numerous in the Eastern Panhandle and in the valleys of the Ridge and Valley Region in the east. West of the mountains, it is most numerous in the lower Ohio Valley and in the central part of the Western Hills Region, becoming less common in the higher, more forested hills of the south. It does occur sparingly in the high mountain valleys and has been found nesting as high as 900 m at Bartow, Pocahontas County, and at 1,050 m near Osceola, Randolph County. The favored habitat is a brushy open situation such as may be found along fence rows, rural roadsides, and rural and suburban dwellings. Multiflora rose hedges are favorite wintering locations.

Except possibly in the eastern part of the state the Mockingbird appears to be a relatively recent addition to the state's avifauna. Neither Scott nor Brewster found it in the 1870s, and Johnston (1923) considered it rare in the Kanawha Valley. As late as the 1940s and 1950s, the Mockingbird was known in the northern part of the state primarily as a winter wanderer, although a nest was found in Marion County as early as 1909. Since the early 1960s, it has moved northward in numbers and nests have been found in Ohio and Brooke Counties. Other nesting records come from Jefferson, Berkeley, Hampshire, Pendleton, Grant, Randolph, Pocahontas, Greenbrier, Monroe, Hardy, Monongalia, Marion, Upshur, Lewis, Wood, Kanawha, and Cabell Counties, but it probably nests in all counties except possibly Hancock.

Populations: Breeding Bird Survey Routes have averaged 6.4 (28.7–0.2) birds per route on 23 routes with the highest average in Jefferson County. Mockingbirds have occurred on only two Singing Male Censuses with populations of 12 and 17 males per 100 ha. Two winter censuses in Ohio County had an average of 32 birds per 100 ha. Christmas Count data (birds per party hour) are: statewide, 1.07 (1.65–0.74); Charleston, 0.39 (1.02–0.06); Charles Town,

1.66 (3.40–0.57); Huntington, 1.35 (5.22–0.58); Inwood, 1.94 (4.50–0.94); Mason County, 0.63 (0.83–0.36); Ona, 0.48 (0.65–0.22); Lewisburg, 1.22 (1.81–0.86); Pendleton County, 0.92 (2.0–0.2); and Hampshire County, 1.07.

Specimens: WVU, UMMZ, MU.

BROWN THRASHER   *Toxostoma rufum* (Linnaeus)

Status: Fairly common summer resident; rare winter resident.

Spring: The Brown Thrasher migrates throughout the state. The earliest arrivals come in late March and the main migration occurs in early April. Arrival is very conspicuous, since the males sing constantly through the morning hours, usually from a high perch.

First-seen Spring Dates: Cabell-Mason Counties, 30 March; Kanawha County, 3 April; Summers County, 6 April; Monongalia County, 13 April; Ohio County, 18 April.

Summer: The thrasher occurs throughout the state and probably nests in every county, but is less numerous in the Northern Panhandle than elsewhere. Nests have been found on the highest mountains in suitable habitat. The favored habitat is open brush-filled land, often with an abundance of briars. If one drives slowly along a country road lined with weeds and brush, a thrasher will usually be flushed every hundred yards or so. It is not found in the spruce forest, but does nest on the edges of this formation.

Breeding Populations: Breeding Bird Surveys have averaged 5.1 (17.3–0.3) birds per route. These counts may take place too late in the year to correctly estimate thrasher populations, or they may be too concentrated on paved roads with "clean" roadsides. Thirteen Singing Male Censuses averaged 27 males per 100 ha (69–8). Overgrown ravine with multiflora rose hedge, Ohio County, 69 males per 100 ha; abandoned bottomland, Mason County, 33 males per 100 ha; overgrown pasture, Hardy County, 25 males; overgrown pasture, Ohio County, 25; and river bottom-wet meadow, Tucker County, 25.

Fall: Most thrashers depart in late September or the early part of October, but a few may remain until late October. At this time, it is inconspicuous and may be overlooked by observers. It migrates throughout the state.

Last-seen Fall Dates: Kanawha County, 25 September; A.F.M.O., 3 October; Cabell-Mason Counties, 9 October.

Winter: This species attempts to winter in the state more commonly than does its relative, the Gray Catbird. There are Christmas Count records from Kanawha (11 of 18 winters since 1954), Cabell (almost every year), Mason, Jefferson, Berkeley, and Greenbrier Counties. Many of these birds will fail to survive the winter in the state. Brooks (1944)

reported a January record from the Cranberry Glades, Pocahontas County, at 980 m.
Specimens: USNM, GMS, MU.

Family Motacillidae   WAGTAILS AND PIPITS

WATER PIPIT   *Anthus spinoletta* (Linnaeus)

Status: Uncommon to common spring migrant; common and occasionally very common fall migrant; uncommon local winter visitant.

Spring: The pipit probably migrates throughout the state, but the favored resting spots are very localized. Spring flocks may be seen year after year in certain fields, and may never be seen in nearby similar areas. Most of the migration takes place in mid-March, but a few stragglers remain well into April and occasionally some will be present in early May. It usually occurs only on broad open areas covered with short grass. Such areas may be the grassy hilltops so common in the central part of the state, the broader valleys in the east, or airports and golf courses throughout the state.

First-seen Spring Dates: Cabell-Mason Coun-

ties, 9 March; Kanawha County, 20 March; Monongalia County, 22 March.

Last-seen Spring Dates: Kanawha County, 5 April; Cabell-Mason Counties, 6 May.

Fall: A few pipits may be seen in late September, but the bulk of the migration comes in late October and early November. The habitats are the same as the spring ones, but on occasion flocks of one or two hundred may be seen.

First-seen Fall Dates: Cabell-Mason Counties, 2 October; Kanawha County, 30 October.

Last-seen Fall Dates: Kanawha County, 20 November; Cabell-Mason Counties, 1 December.

Winter: In recent years, small numbers have been wintering in Kanawha County. There are also a few scattered winter records from Berkeley, Jefferson, Monongalia, Upshur, Wood, Cabell, and Mason Counties.

Specimens: WVU, UMMZ.

Family Bombycillidae   WAXWINGS

*BOHEMIAN WAXWING
        Bombycilla garrulus (Linnaeus)

Status: Casual winter visitant.
Records: In February 1953, a small flock was seen in the University orchards at Morgantown by several observers (M. Brooks, C. Thomas, et al.) and another flock was present at Clarksburg at the same time (M. Seckman). All subsequent sightings have been at Morgantown, three of them at the home of Professor Brooks, which is only a short distance from the site of the first records. These records are 20 March 1960 and 26 March through 15 April 1962 (Wright, 1963); 17 November 1961, 15 and 16 January 1964, and 20 February 1972 (M. Brooks).
Specimens: None.

CEDAR WAXWING   *Bombycilla cedrorum* Vieillot

Status: An erratic species present someplace in the state throughout the year ranging from uncommon to very abundant.
Remarks: The Cedar Waxwing does not fit the formal pattern of presentation that has been adopted

here for the other species. It is essentially a nomadic species, wandering from place to place, presumably following a food supply. At any given location in the state, it may sometimes be present in large numbers, or it may be absent for long periods of time. It has probably nested in every county of the state, but in some summers it will be absent from particular places. The highest record of nesting I have was at the highway summit of Shavers Mountain on the border of Pocahontas and Randolph Counties at an elevation of 1,140 m.

On occasion, it may nest semicolonially, with several nests in a given tree. It is possible that given birds have no definite territory to which they return year after year, and they may nest at different places each year. Of the over 600 birds banded at Morgantown, none have ever been taken again at that station. A bird banded there in fall was recovered in Oaxaca, Mexico, later the same winter.

In the fall, movements follow the ripening of fruits, particularly the wild cherry and the pokeberry. Large numbers move past the banding station at A.F.M.O. annually, and on one occasion in September 1973 several thousand went by the station in a single day.

The waxwing may winter, sometimes in very large flocks, throughout the state except in the high mountain areas, and possibly the extreme north of the Northern Panhandle. During this season, they favor locations with planted trees such as *Crataegus* and *Pyracanthus,* which hold their fruit through the winter. Spring migration is not distinguishable from late winter wandering.

Populations: Breeding Bird Surveys have averaged 3.0 (8.5–0.1) birds per route. The waxwing has been present on 13 Singing Male Census areas but has never contributed more than one pair per study area, and more usually is indicated as being merely present. Christmas Count data vary greatly from place to place, and in one of the analyzed years none were reported in the state. The data (birds per party hour) are: statewide, 0.20; Charleston, 0.26 (0.52–0); Charles Town, 0.36 (0.70–0); Huntington, 0.18 (0.67–0); Inwood, 0.05 (0.20–0); Mason County, 0.56 (2.34–0); Ona, 0.15 (0.58–0); Pendleton County, 0.66; Lewisburg, 0; and Hampshire County, 0.30.

Specimens: WVU, USNM, GMS.

Family Laniidae   SHRIKES

NORTHERN SHRIKE   *Lanius excubitor* Linnaeus

Status: Accidental winter visitant.

Records: Surber (1888) reported that he collected a Northern Shrike at White Sulphur Springs, Greenbrier County, on 4 November 1887. The whereabouts of this specimen is unknown, but the American Museum of Natural History, New York, has a specimen taken by Surber at White Sulphur Springs with the date on the label of 7 December 1892. At this time, it cannot be resolved as to whether Surber had two records for Greenbrier County or if the date on the specimen label is in error (Hall, 1976a). Brooks (1944) mentioned possible sight records from Wood and Ohio Counties, but placed the species on the hypothetical list. In recent years, there have been two sight records: Newell, Hancock County, 3 January 1954 (E. R. Chandler) (Hall, 1954a) and McClintic Wildlife Station, Mason County, 20 March 1967 (G. F. Hurley) (Laitsch, 1967).

Remarks: In adult plumage, this species is difficult to distinguish from the much more common *ludovicianus*; consequently, a certain amount of reservation must be attached to all sight records other than those of immatures.

Specimen: AMNH.

LOGGERHEAD SHRIKE

                             Lanius ludovicianus Linnaeus

Status: Uncommon local summer resident; uncommon winter resident.

Spring: Wintering birds depart from early March until late April. There are very few spring reports that could be called migration, but the few are concentrated in late March and early April.

Last-seen Spring Date: Cabell-Mason Counties, 1 March.

Summer: The Loggerhead Shrike is most numerous in summer in the dry, open, eastern valleys such as the Shenandoah, the South Branch, and the North Fork of the South Branch. In the Eastern Panhandle, Hampshire, Grant, Pendleton, Greenbrier, and Monroe Counties, it may be found in almost any summer. Elsewhere it is a rare and local bird with summer records from Nicholas, Pocahontas, Tucker (Canaan Valley), and Hardy Counties. Definite nesting records are available from Berkeley, Hampshire, Hardy, Grant, Pendleton, Greenbrier, Monroe, and Barbour Counties.

The shrike prefers open farmland, usually perching on scattered trees or wires. Its favored nesting sites are in dense brush, most often with thorn trees of some sort, although it may sometimes nest in isolated trees on a roadside. In the midwest, Osage orange hedges are favorite spots but there are few of these in West Virginia. With the exception of the Canaan Valley record mentioned above, all records are from below 900 m.

Fall: In late October and early November, the Loggerhead Shrike begins to arrive in areas where it does not nest. At this time, it may occur throughout the state except at the higher elevations. They are most numerous in the southwestern part of the state.

First-seen Fall Date: Cabell-Mason Counties, 16 November.

Winter: The Loggerhead Shrike may winter in the lowlands throughout the state except perhaps in the Upper Ohio Valley, but will never be in large numbers. Most of the Christmas Count records come from the Ridge and Valley Region with a high year's count of 12 in Hampshire County.

Remarks: By the early 1980s, this shrike had almost completely disappeared from many of its usual locations. No reason is apparent for this unless

this species, which stands high in the food chain, has suffered from pesticide poisoning as have the large raptors.

Specimens: USNM, CM, UMMZ, GMS, MU, CU. Summer specimens from Monroe, Hardy, and Pocahontas Counties, as well as migrant specimens from Mason and Cabell Counties, have all been referred to the northern subspecies *migrans* Palmer. An October specimen (UMMZ) from Martinsburg, Berkeley County, has been identified as the subspecies *ludovicianus*.

Family Sturnidae   STARLINGS

EUROPEAN STARLING   *Sturnus vulgaris* Linnaeus

Status: Very common to abundant permanent resident.

Distribution: At present, the Starling is found throughout the state and probably nests in every county. It is most common in farmland-suburban situations, but in winter it occasionally becomes abundant in cities, roosting on bridges or in the eaves of large buildings. It becomes less common in heavily forested areas, but is found nesting in the cavities of old dead trees near beaver ponds or in old barns. It does occur in small numbers at the highest elevations and far from habitation.

The first record for the state was in 1914 at Morgantown, and after that they gradually spread throughout. Bibbee (1929) reported the first nesting of the species in the state as 1921 and gave the first records for Wood County as 1923 and Mercer County as 1926. Brooks (1944) reported that a resident of Cheat Bridge, Randolph County, at the edge of the spruce forest, had by that date seen starlings only twice at that location. In the years since then, it has invaded that area, although the numbers are still small.

There may be some migration of birds from the

north into the state during the winter but this is undocumented. In fall and winter, large flocks gather at favored sites. Television antennas are favored for fall congregations and it is probable that no moderate-sized city lacks one or more major winter roosts often numbering into the thousands.

Populations: Breeding Bird Surveys have averaged 83.7 (425–7.2) birds per route. Four Winter Censuses in Ohio County have averaged 42 birds per 100 ha. Christmas Count data (birds per party hour) are: statewide, 49.59 (90.16–17.61); Charleston, 168.14 (229.51–6.25); Charles Town, 41.53 (188.90–10.95); Huntington, 17.29 (38.89–6.41); Inwood, 39.02 (130.0–8.50); Mason County, 77.62 (160.87–7.27); Ona, 39.13 (121.21–5.90); Pendleton County, 13.47 (35.55–6.45); Lewisburg, 54.19 (111.11–15.63); and Hampshire County, 12.34.

Remarks: Most bird students totally ignore the Starling, except perhaps to castigate it. While it is true that its introduction has been of serious consequence to the Red-headed Woodpecker, and possibly also the Eastern Bluebird, the species today represents, in numbers, a very significant part of our total bird population, and as such it should attract more study and attention.

Specimens: WVU, MU.

Family Vireonidae   VIREOS

WHITE-EYED VIREO   *Vireo griseus* (Boddaert)

Status: Uncommon to common summer resident.

Spring: The White-eyed Vireo is the second member of the family to arrive in the spring, usually appearing in the third week of April. Most of the reports in spring migration come from the breeding range, but it is seen elsewhere, and it probably

migrates throughout the state except at high elevations.

First-seen Spring Dates: Cabell-Mason Counties, 17 April; Kanawha County, 18 April; Wood County, 21 April; Randolph County, 25 April; Brooke County, 30 April; Monongalia County, 1 May.

Summer: The White-eyed Vireo is most numerous, and can be called common, only in the

southwestern part of the state. Northward and eastward toward the mountains it becomes less numerous. Until recent years, it was not found in the
Northern Panhandle north of Marshall County, but
it now occurs in small numbers in all the Panhandle
counties. It does not occur in the high mountains,
but a few may be found in the mountain valleys.
East of the Allegheny Mountains, it becomes rare
and very local. In the mid-1970s, the White-eyed
Vireo expanded its range northward. In Monongalia
County, it is much more numerous than it was 25
years ago. In 1972 it was found to be common in
Upshur County where E. A. Brooks (1916) reported
that he had never found it. There are definite nesting
records from Jefferson, Berkeley, Preston, Monongalia, Tucker, Webster, Summers, Hancock, Brooke,
Ohio, Wetzel, Wirt, Wood, Ritchie, Upshur, Fayette, Lincoln, Kanawha, and Cabell Counties.

The White-eyed Vireo inhabits dense brushland
in all of the southern forest types. It is very scarce
or absent in the northern hardwoods, and is missing
from the spruce forest. There are records from the
Cranberry Glades region at about 1,100 m in the
mixed forest, and from the upper Greenbrier Valley
at about 900 m.

Breeding Populations: Breeding Bird Surveys
have averaged 4.2 (15.1–0.1) birds per route with
the largest numbers in Wayne, Lincoln, and Kanawha Counties. Eight Singing Male Censuses have
averaged 16 males per 100 ha, with a maximum
count of 32 males in an oak-hickory forest in Fayette
County.

Fall: The White-eyed Vireo departs in the second half of September, but a few stragglers remain
into early October. The fall migration may be overlooked by many observers since the birds are silent,
and almost invisible in their dense habitats. Only
10 have been banded at A.F.M.O. at 1,160 m.

Last-seen Fall Dates: Kanawha County, 15
September; Cabell-Mason Counties, 28 September.

Specimens: USNM, UMMZ, GMS. Five
USNM specimens have been identified as being the
northern subspecies *noveboracensis* Gmelin.

SOLITARY VIREO   *Vireo solitarius* (Wilson)

Status: Uncommon to fairly common spring
and fall migrant; rare to common local summer resident; accidental winter visitant.

Spring: The Solitary Vireo is the first of the
family to arrive in spring, with a few birds appearing
before the end of March. The main migration is in
full swing through most of April and as with some
other birds it is often present on the mountain breeding grounds while the migrants are still moving
through the lowlands. Most will have departed by
mid-May but a few may remain until late May.

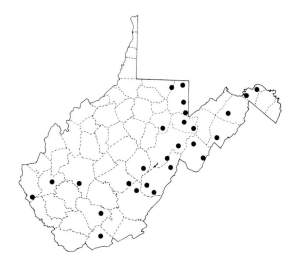
Fig. 3.   Breeding Season Records for the Solitary Vireo.

During migration, it may be found in any forest type,
and it probably migrates throughout the state. It is
strangely rare in Cabell County where Edeburn et
al. (1960) listed only a few records.

First-seen Spring Dates: Kanawha County, 17
April; Cabell-Mason Counties, 21 April; Monon-
galia County, 29 April; Wood County, 1 May; Ohio
County, 9 May.

Last-seen Spring Dates: Kanawha County, 3
May; Ohio County, 17 May.

Summer: The principal breeding range of the
Solitary Vireo in the state is along the Allegheny
Mountain axis, but it nests at lower elevations than
do some of the other mountain birds. Summer populations have been found as low as 300 m in Monongalia County. There are summer records from
Hampshire, Hardy, Pendleton, Tucker, Randolph,
Pocahontas, Greenbrier, Barbour, Webster, Nicholas, Preston, and Monongalia Counties. In these
areas, the species is found in the mixed northern
hardwoods-spruce forest, and in the pure northern
hardwoods, where competition with the Red-eyed
Vireo occurs. It will also be found in the hardwoods-
hemlock forest at lower elevations, and in the hardwoods-white pine forest. East of the mountains, it
has been found in hemlock woods in Spruce-Pine
Hollow, Morgan County. In the west away from the
main mountains, there is a population, usually in
hardwoods-hemlock, but often in pure hardwoods
extending from at least Raleigh County south to
Mercer County, and west to parts of Lincoln County
and Wayne County at Cabwaylingo State Forest. On
occasion, summer birds also have been found in
Kanawha State Forest, Kanawha County. Definite
nesting records, however, come only from Preston,
Randolph, Pocahontas, Greenbrier, Raleigh, and
Lincoln Counties.

Breeding Populations: The Solitary Vireo has
occurred on only six runs of four Breeding Bird

Surveys with an average of 0.27 bird per count. Twenty-two Singing Male Censuses averaged 25 males per 100 ha. Virgin spruce-northern hardwoods, 1,200 m, Randolph County, 64 males per 100 ha (this area also had counts of 47 males and later dropped off to 17 males per 100 ha); spruce-fir swamp, 1,100 m, Randolph County, 49 males per 100 ha; northern hardwood forest, 1,100 m, Pendleton County, 49 males; and oak-hickory forest, 800 m, Greenbrier County, 49 males.

Fall: A few Solitary Vireos may remain in the state until early November, but the main migration occurs in mid- to late October. It migrates throughout the state, but as in the spring seems to be rare in the southwest. Only 112 have been banded in 24 years at A.F.M.O., but operations there have usually ceased before the main flight comes in.

Occasionally, a Solitary Vireo will remain well into December, and in 1968 there was a record on 7 February from Marion County.

Specimens: USNM, CM, UMMZ. Specimens collected in the breeding season, including one from Wayne County, are all referable to the southern Appalachian race, *alticola* Brewster. The northeastern race, *solitarius,* has been collected throughout the state during migration. Summer specimens from Preston County seem to be intermediate between the two subspecies.

YELLOW-THROATED VIREO *Vireo flavifrons* Vieillot

Status: Uncommon to fairly common summer resident.

Spring: The Yellow-throated Vireo arrives in the third to fourth week in April, and the loud, distinctive song makes it quite evident as well as easily seen in the still leafless woods. It migrates throughout the state except at higher elevations.

First-seen Spring Dates: Kanawha County, 17 April; Cabell-Mason Counties, 20 April; Summers County, 25 April; Wood County, 30 April; Ohio County, 30 April; Monongalia County, 3 May.

Summer: The Yellow-throated Vireo may nest in every county in the state, but nowhere is it very numerous. The largest numbers are found in the mature mixed hardwoods, either of the southern type or the cove hardwoods. They are also numerous in the oak-hickory and oak-pine forests. Although it has been found in mature northern hardwoods at 1,200 m in Pocahontas County, it usually is found only below 900 m, and becomes less numerous at elevations below 300 m. There are definite nesting records from Hampshire, Pendleton, Hardy, Randolph, Webster, Greenbrier, Lewis, Summers, Monongalia, Harrison, Ohio, Wetzel, Wood, Kanawha, and Cabell Counties.

Breeding Populations: Breeding Bird Survey

Routes have averaged 2.4 (5.5–0.3) birds per route. Seventeen Singing Male Censuses have averaged 23 males per 100 ha. Mature mixed hardwoods, 240 m, Wayne County, 47 males per 100 ha; and maturing oak-hickory forest, 800 m, Greenbrier County, 42 males per 100 ha.

Fall: Most Yellow-throated Vireos depart in late September but fall records are very scarce. Only 24 have been banded in 24 years at A.F.M.O.

Last-seen Fall Dates: Kanawha County, 10 September; Ohio County, 14 September; Cabell-Mason Counties, 28 September.

Specimens: USNM, UMMZ, MCZ.

WARBLING VIREO *Vireo gilvus* (Vieillot)

Status: Uncommon to common summer resident.

Spring: The Warbling Vireo arrives in the nesting range during the last week in April or the first week in May. Although it is often difficult to see in the tree-top habitat, the loud characteristic song makes the arrival a conspicuous event. It migrates throughout the state except at high elevations, but is not common in heavily forested areas.

First-seen Spring Dates: Cabell-Mason Counties, 20 April; Kanawha County, 22 April; Ohio County, 27 April; Monongalia County, 1 May; Brooke County, 3 May; Summers County, 4 May.

Summer: The Warbling Vireo is present in summer, and presumably breeds throughout the state except at high elevations. The characteristic habitat is an area with widely spaced trees each with a broad, densely leafed crown. Usually the trees must be surrounded by open spaces, and once an area develops a closed-crown forest the Warbling Vireo will not be found except at the edges. Suitable habitat is most common on the banks of streams, in city parks, and in rural houseyards. The highest populations seem to be along the Ohio, Kanawha, and Big Sandy Rivers in the west. Eastward toward the mountains, it becomes less numerous and is often extremely local in occurrence. For example, at Morgantown in the 1950s I knew of only four or five places where it occurred. In the mountain areas, it may be found sparingly in the broader valleys, almost to an elevation of 900 m. East of the mountains, it is local in distribution except along the lower Potomac and Shenandoah Rivers, where it is common.

While it probably nests in every county, nests are hard to locate and there are definite nesting records only from Hampshire, Pendleton, Greenbrier, Upshur, Webster, Monongalia, Lewis, Brooke, Ohio, Wetzel, Gilmer, Mason, and Kanawha Counties.

Breeding Populations: Breeding Bird Surveys have averaged 2.1 (7.9–0.1) birds per route. The Warbling Vireo has contributed numerically to the population of only one Singing Male Census, 37 males per 100 ha in a brushy field, 360 m, Ohio County.

Fall: Once the singing stops in early August, the Warbling Vireo is almost unreported, since it is almost invisible in the dense treetops. Migration appears to take place in the last half of September, and all are gone by early October. In 24 years, none have been captured at A.F.M.O.

Last-seen Fall Dates: Ohio County, 6 August; Cabell-Mason Counties, 21 September.

Specimens: WVU, MCZ, GMS. All specimens belong to the eastern subspecies, *gilvus*.

PHILADELPHIA VIREO *Vireo philadelphicus* (Cassin)

Status: Rare spring migrant; uncommon fall migrant.

Spring: The Philadelphia Vireo probably migrates throughout the state except possibly at high elevations, but there are very few spring records. At Huntington, five of a total of seven records prior to 1960 were in the spring (Edeburn et al., 1960). Other spring records come from Berkeley, Hampshire, Monongalia, Marion, Upshur, Summers, Ohio, Mason, and Kanawha Counties. At Huntington most of the records were in the first half of May, but it is probable that most of the birds pass through in the latter half of May. In both appearance and song, this bird closely resembles the more common Red-eyed Vireo; as a result, it is probably overlooked, particularly by those people who "tune out" the ubiquitous Red-eye song.

Fall: There are more records in fall than in spring, but the species can never be considered to be common. Fall records come from Jefferson, Ohio, Brooke, Monongalia, Grant, Cabell, and Kanawha Counties. This is one of the several species that has been proven by banding operations to be more common than had previously been thought. At A.F.M.O., 319 birds have been banded in 24 years with a high yearly count of 33. Brooks (1944) remarked that the migration was in late August and early September and Edeburn et al. (1960), felt that it was in early September, but most of the A.F.M.O. dates are in the second half of September with a few October captures. The three records cited by Handley (1976) for Kanawha County were all in October. One was banded at Morgantown on 4 November 1973.

First-seen Fall Date: A.F.M.O., 14 September.
Last-seen Fall Date: A.F.M.O., 3 October.
Specimens: WVU, CM, UMMZ, GMS, CU.

RED-EYED VIREO *Vireo olivaceus* (Linnaeus)

Status: Common to abundant summer resident.

Spring: The Red-eyed Vireo migrates throughout the state, and during the spring it occurs in nearly any wooded area of the state. It arrives in the last week of April in the south and the first week of May in the north, but the peak of migration is probably in the first half of May.

First-seen Spring Dates: Cabell-Mason Counties, 20 April; Summers County, 20 April; Kanawha County, 22 April; Ohio County, 28 April; Wood County, 30 April; Monongalia County, 2 May; Brooke County, 8 May.

Summer: Except for a few colonial or semi-colonial nesters, the Red-eyed Vireo may be the most numerous breeding bird in West Virginia. It nests throughout the state in all forest types except the pure spruce forest. It is most numerous in the mixed deciduous forest, but populations are also high in the hardwoods-hemlock forest and the hardwoods-white pine forest. It is also numerous in the northern hardwoods forest at high elevations, but becomes much less common in the mixed hardwoods-spruce forest, where competition with the Solitary Vireo occurs. Numbers are not high in the scrub and pitch pine forest areas. It nests in every county.

Breeding Populations: Breeding Bird Surveys have averaged 22.2 (83.3–0.5) birds per route. Eighty Singing Male Censuses have averaged 69 males per 100 ha. Mature northern hardwoods, 1,200 m, Pocahontas County, 232 and 148 males per 100 ha (this area was then partially cutover and successive censuses at five-year intervals gave 67, 116, 49 males per 100 ha); northern hardwoods, 600 m, Pendleton County, 158 males per 100 ha; young oak-hickory, 330 m, Wayne County, 138 males per 100 ha; mature mixed hardwoods, 240 m, Wayne County, 121 males per 100 ha; bottomland deciduous forest, 230 m, Wayne County, 121 males; mature deciduous forest, 700 m, Webster County, 116 males; mature oak-hickory, 820 m, Greenbrier County, 116 males (on two counts); mixed deciduous forest, 580 m, Nicholas County, 116 males; northern hardwoods, 900 m, Pocahontas, 106 males; cove and northern hardwoods, 690 m, Tucker County, 106 males; hemlock-hardwoods, 640 m, Nicholas County, 106 males; white pine-hardwoods, 580 m, Greenbrier County, 106 males; oak-pine, 180 m, Berkeley County, 99 males; cove hardwoods, 550 m, Greenbrier County, 99 males; nine studies between 96 and 81 males per 100 ha; and 20 censuses between 72 and 49 males per 100 ha.

Fall: The Red-eyed Vireo migrates throughout the state in fall with the peak numbers coming in the second half of September. A few stragglers are present in early October. At A.F.M.O., a total of 843 have been banded in 24 years with a maximum yearly total of 101.

Last-seen Fall Dates: Ohio County, 5 December; Kanawha County, 14 September; Cabell-Mason Counties, 27 September; A.F.M.O., 6 October.

Specimens: USNM, MU.

Family Emberizidae

The families Parulidae (Wood Warblers), Icteridae (Blackbirds and Orioles), and Thraupidae (Tanagers) of the Fifth Edition of the A.O.U. Check-list have been reduced to subfamilies in the Sixth Edition. These subfamilies are combined with the subfamilies Cardinalinae (Cardinal Grosbeaks) and Emberizinae (New World Sparrows) of the family Fringillidae of the Fifth Edition into a new family Emberizidae.

Subfamily Parulinae   WOOD WARBLERS

The Wood Warblers have been designated on at least one occasion as West Virginia's most characteristic birds, and this is indeed true. Thirty-eight species (and the enigmatic Sutton's Warbler which may or may not be a species) have been recorded in the state and 29 species have been known to nest here. No woodland habitat in the state is without several nesting species. During the spring migration, the "waves" of these brightly colored little birds represent the height of birdwatching pleasure for countless persons. The fall migration is not usually so well studied, partly because of the difficulty in identification, but large numbers of many species migrate along the mountain ridges in the Allegheny Mountain Region and in the Ridge and Valley Region. This migration has been studied for many years at the banding station known as A.F.M.O. located on the Grant-Tucker County line.

BLUE-WINGED WARBLER

Vermivora pinus (Linnaeus)

Status: Uncommon spring migrant; fairly common to common local summer resident; rare fall migrant.

Spring: Except in the breeding range, the Blue-winged Warbler is a rare to uncommon bird during the spring. It probably occurs throughout the state, except at high elevations, during this period, but the numbers are very small. Arrival in the breeding range is in the last week of April, and presumed migrants may still be present in places outside of the breeding range in late May. At this time of the year, the Blue-winged Warbler frequents brushy woodlands, similar to the nesting territory, but it may also occur in open deciduous woodland.

First-seen Spring Dates: Kanawha County, 23 April; Cabell-Mason Counties, 25 April; Ohio County, 30 April; Wood County, 1 May; Brooke County, 2 May; Monongalia County, 2 May.

Summer: The principal breeding area of the Blue-winged Warbler in the state is the Ohio Valley. It occurs in summer in every county along the river from Hancock to Cabell and Wayne. In this region, it occurs on the ridges just back from the river, usually at elevations below 360 m. These forests are usually mixed hardwoods, oak-hickory, or oak-pine, and the Blue-wing occurs in all three types, the principal habitat requirement being a dense brushy undergrowth with some dead trees for singing perches. Blue-wings occur in numbers up the Kanawha Valley at least as far as Charleston, and in the Monongahela drainage in Marion and Monongalia Counties in lesser numbers. Elsewhere in the state, there are summer records from Berkeley, Morgan, Hardy, Hampshire, Greenbrier, Preston, Fayette, Summers, Nicholas, Lincoln, Lewis, Braxton, and Webster Counties. Most of these records are for single sightings or small pockets of birds, since in most of this area this species is replaced by the Golden-winged Warbler. There are definite nesting records from Hancock, Brooke, Ohio, Marshall, Ritchie, Summers, Kanawha, and Cabell Counties.

Breeding Populations: Breeding Bird Surveys have averaged 1.5 (7.3–0.2) birds per route on 85 runs of 14 routes. The largest number recorded was 11 in Marshall County. Singing Male Censuses averaged 30 males per 100 ha. Mixed hardwoods, 360 m, Ohio County, 49 males; deciduous woodland, 300 m, Ohio County, 42 males; bottomland, 185 m, Mason County, 17 males; and shallow pond-cattail marsh, 180 m, Mason County, 16 males per 100 ha.

Fall: The Blue-winged Warbler departs early. Singing stops in late June, and the species is seldom reported after that. There are September records for Monongalia and Kanawha Counties, and eight have been banded at A.F.M.O. in 24 years.

Remarks: Of the two members of the *Vermivora pinus* superspecies, *pinus* is the more southerly and western bird while *chrysoptera* is more northern and eastern. In the last century, *pinus* has been on the move, expanding its breeding range northward and eastward, perhaps in relation to the general amelioration of the climate, or perhaps to the subtle changes in habitat produced by man's activities. This expansion seems to come at the expense of *chrysoptera,* which seems to be disappearing in places. The change has been most dramatic in Kanawha County where in the last 15 years or so the Blue-winged has changed from an uncommon bird compared with the Golden-winged to a status where it is by far the more numerous of the two. The distribution of the species makes it obvious that *pinus* has invaded the state by way of the Ohio Valley, and is now in the process of expanding from that valley. However, the general decrease in suitable brushy habitat has caused some declines in population in recent years.

Specimens: WVU, OP, UMMZ, DMNH.

GOLDEN-WINGED WARBLER
Vermivora chrysoptera (Linnaeus)

Status: Uncommon spring and fall migrant; uncommon to fairly common summer resident.

Spring: The Golden-winged Warbler migrates in small numbers throughout the western part of the state. It is casual to uncommon in the Ohio Valley and rare east of the Alleghenies. Arrival is generally in the last week of April and migrants will have departed by the third week in May. During migration, it is found in second-growth deciduous woodland and in suburban situations.

First-seen Spring Dates: Kanawha County, 20 April; Cabell-Mason Counties, 27 April; Wood County, 30 April; Monongalia County, 3 May; Ohio County, 10 May; Randolph County, 5 May.

Last-seen Spring Date: Cabell County, 20 May.

Summer: The Golden-winged Warbler is absent as a breeding bird in the Ohio Valley where it is replaced by the Blue-winged, and it is rare in the Eastern Panhandle. Elsewhere it ranges from uncommon to fairly common throughout most of the western part of the state. There are summer records from Berkeley, Morgan, Hampshire, Hardy, Pendleton, Grant, Tucker, Pocahontas, Greenbrier, Preston, Monongalia, Lewis, Upshur, Tucker, Randolph, Hancock, Wetzel, Summers, Fayette, Pleasants, Webster, Braxton, Ritchie, Gilmer, Lincoln, Wayne, and Kanawha Counties. A nesting observed at Tomlinson Run State Park, Hancock County, in 1944 may actually have involved hybrid parents, since this area is well out of the normal range of this species and in the range of *V. pinus.*

Populations vary greatly from place to place, and it is most numerous in the oak-chestnut forest of the Allegheny Plateau above 450 m. In this region, it nests in brushy second growth and occasionally is quite common. The Golden-winged Warbler is one of the principal species inhabiting what Brooks (1940) has termed the "Chestnut-Sprout Association," the peculiar and characteristic brushy habitat that grew up after the American chestnut trees had died. With the passage of years, this formation has gradually decreased and the Golden-winged Warbler has decreased in numbers since the 1930s and 1940s. Brooks (1940) also noted the dependence of this species on the dead chestnut trees for singing perches, but by the mid-1970s the dead chestnut trees had almost entirely disappeared. Golden-wings occur in summer as high as 1,100 to 1,150 m in the Cheat Mountains and on the Allegheny Front but do not nest in the spruce forest.

Breeding Populations: Breeding Bird Surveys have averaged 1.5 (3.0–0.1) birds per route on 112 runs on 19 routes. Fourteen Singing Male Censuses have averaged 31 males per 100 ha. Oak-hickory, Fayette County, 84 males per 100 ha; brushy hilltop, 550 m, Nicholas County, 67 males; cutover hardwoods, 580 m, Nicholas County, 49 males; and cutover oak-hickory forest, 900 m, Greenbrier County, 49 males.

Fall: The Golden-winged Warbler ceases to sing in late June and early July, and most of them depart in the second half of August. Only a few stragglers will be left in early September. Only 14 have been banded at A.F.M.O. in 24 years, largely because operations there start after most of the Golden-wings have departed.

Last-seen Fall Date: Kanawha County, 8 September.

Specimens: USNM, CM, UMMZ, AMNH, MCZ, WAL, DMNH.

VERMIVORA HYBRIDS

Vermivora pinus and *V. chrysoptera* hybridize wherever their ranges meet. In West Virginia, this situation occurs in Kanawha County and along a line from there to eastern Wetzel, Marion, and Monongalia Counties, as well as in several isolated places in the state where *pinus* occurs in small numbers. The first-generation cross between these two species has been known as "Brewster's Warbler" (*V. leucobronchialis*). There are specimens of this form from Brooke County (CM) and Marion County (WAL). There are sight records from Preston, Monongalia, Hancock, Ohio, Ritchie, Greenbrier, Mercer, Upshur, and Kanawha Counties. Some of these sightings may not represent true "Brewster's" Warblers but may be back-crosses between the Brewster's and either of the pure parental types. Parkes (1951) and Short (1963) have discussed the characters of the several hybrid or introgressed forms. It seems likely that in this region of overlap many of the birds identified as one of the parental types by field observation may indeed be birds of impure genetic stock. For example, in the spring of 1975, I banded two birds at Morgantown that were superficially Blue-winged Warblers, but which clearly had a few Golden-winged genes.

The pure recessive form of this hybridization has been known as "Lawrence's Warbler" (*V. lawrencei*). No specimens of this form have been collected in the state, but there are sight records from Ohio, Monongalia, Preston, Upshur, Mercer, and Kanawha Counties.

In 1974 a nesting of a mixed *pinus-chrysoptera* pair was observed in Kanawha County by N. Gluck (1975).

TENNESSEE WARBLER

Vermivora peregrina (Wilson)

Status: Very common spring and fall migrant.

Spring: The Tennessee Warbler migrates throughout the state west of the Allegheny Mountains in extremely large numbers. Arrival is usually in early May but the peak of the flight comes in mid- to late May, and a few birds may be present in early June. In some years it may be abundant, but there is some evidence suggesting that the number of migrants passing through in the mid-1970s is not as large as it was 25 years ago. The drably colored bird is almost invisible in the tree-top foliage, but the loud characteristic song can be heard almost everywhere there are trees during the season. It occurs in any area, urban, suburban, as well as forest, where there are tall trees. East of the mountains, the Tennessee Warbler becomes uncommon and it is seldom reported from the Eastern Panhandle, although it is usually possible to find one or two there in a day in the field.

First-seen Spring Dates: Cabell-Mason Counties, 29 April; Wood County, 29 April; Kanawha County, 3 May; Monongalia County, 6 May; Ohio County, 8 May.

Last-seen Spring Dates: Kanawha County, 18 May; Cabell-Mason Counties, 25 May; Ohio County, 31 May.

Fall: The Tennessee Warbler is probably even more numerous in fall than in spring, but the silent birds moving through the lush vegetation of early autumn are quite inconspicuous. During this season, it migrates throughout the state except in the Eastern Panhandle. The earliest migrants arrive about the first of September and a few are still present in early October, with occasional stragglers into November. Tennessee Warblers have been the most abundant warbler banded at A.F.M.O. where 10,153 have been netted in 24 years. In 1981 a total of 1,848 were banded with a single day's count of 184.

First-seen Fall Dates: A.F.M.O., 2 September; Kanawha County, 6 September; Cabell-Mason Counties, 6 September.

Last-seen Fall Dates: Kanawha County, 16 September; A.F.M.O., 8 October; Cabell-Mason Counties, 13 October.

Remarks: A Tennessee Warbler banded at A.F.M.O. on 1 October 1974 was shot near Nueva Santa Rosa, Guatemala, on 8 November 1975.

Specimens: USNM, UMMZ, DMNH.

ORANGE-CROWNED WARBLER

Vermivora celata (Say)

Status: Casual to rare spring and fall migrant.

Spring: The principal route of the spring migration of the Orange-crowned Warbler lies to the west of West Virginia, and there are only a few scattered records for the spring. It may be more common than these records would indicate, since it may be overlooked among the abundant Tennessee Warblers. Definite records come only from Berkeley, Jefferson, Ohio, Monongalia, Mason, Kanawha, and Cabell Counties, but it probably occurs throughout the state west of the Alleghenies. The records are too few to give definite migration dates but most of them occur in early May.

Fall: The Orange-crowned Warbler is more numerous in fall than in spring, but even at this season it must be designated as rare. At A.F.M.O., only 13 have been banded in 24 years. An average of one a year is banded at Morgantown. Most of these records have been in early October. There are fall records from Ohio, Monongalia, Grant, Tucker, Marion, Wayne, and Kanawha Counties.

Specimen: DMNH. The eastern race *celata* is the one found in West Virginia.

NASHVILLE WARBLER

Vermivora ruficapilla (Wilson)

Status: Fairly common spring and fall migrant; uncommon local summer resident.

Spring: The Nashville Warbler arrives in late April, and generally is gone by the third week in May. During migration, it frequents areas of low brush or second-growth forest, often in wet or marshy situations. It is never as common as the Tennessee Warbler. It migrates throughout that part of the state west of the Allegheny Mountains, but as with the Tennessee Warbler it becomes uncommon to rare east of the mountains.

First-seen Spring Dates: Summers County, 25 April; Cabell-Mason Counties, 30 April; Kanawha,

Ohio, Monongalia Counties, 1 May; Brooke County, 3 May.

Last-seen Spring Dates: Cabell-Mason Counties, 19 May; Kanawha County, 18 May; Ohio County, 20 May.

Summer: From the late 1930s until at least the early 1960s, there was a large nesting colony of Nashville Warblers on Canaan Mountain, Tucker County. Here they were present in small openings that occurred throughout the then-young spruce plantation, and it was here in 1951 that the only definite nesting for the state was discovered. As the trees in this plantation grew, the Nashville Warbler decreased and in recent years the birds have been scarce at this station. Other summer records have come from Brown Mountain, Tucker County, and at the edge of some of the openings in the spruce forest on the Allegheny Front in Tucker and Grant Counties. At these stations, the habitat is usually a bog area, similar to that used farther north. In some years, at least, the Nashville Warbler has been present in Cranberry Glades, Pocahontas County, and it has probably nested on occasion in Cranesville Swamp, Preston County. Adult birds carrying food have been seen on the Maryland side of the Cranesville Swamp (Stewart and Robbins, 1958). It has been seen in June in Blister Pine Swamp and on Gaudineer Knob, Randolph County.

Breeding Populations: A Singing Male Census on Canaan Mountain, Tucker County, 1,140 m, had a population of 15 males per 100 ha.

Fall: Except at banding stations, the Nashville Warbler is not often reported in the fall, although it migrates in good numbers throughout the region west of the Alleghenies. At A.F.M.O., they are not very common and in 24 years only 826 have been banded (182 in 1981). Most of this movement comes in late September and early October. There is a record of a bird found dead (USNM) at Morgantown on 28 December 1951.

Specimens: USNM, UMMZ, AMNH, DMNH. These specimens represent the eastern race, *ruficapilla*.

NORTHERN PARULA *Parula americana* (Linnaeus)

Status: Uncommon to common summer resident.

Spring: The Northern Parula arrives in mid- to late April and reaches full numbers by early May, although as with several other warbler species it is difficult to distinguish migrants from summer residents. It probably migrates throughout the state, even at high elevations.

First-seen Spring Dates: Kanawha County, 17

April; Cabell-Mason Counties, 18 April; Randolph County, 20 April; Monongalia County, 28 April; Summers County, 30 April.

Summer: The Parula may nest in every county, at least locally, except those in the Northern Panhandle where it appears to be known only as a migrant. It is also considered a rare summer bird in Cabell County, although it is fairly common in the middle Ohio Valley. There are summer records from around 75 m along the Shenandoah River near Harper's Ferry to at least 1,250 m on the slopes of Shaver's Mountain in Randolph County. It breeds in a variety of habitats, but the highest populations are in the mixed hardwoods-hemlock forests. It also occurs commonly in the rich river bottom mesophytic forest (for example, along the Shenandoah and Potomac Rivers in the Eastern Panhandle), in the white pine-hardwoods forest in Greenbrier County, in the oak-pine forests, and in a variety of upland hardwoods forest types. It inhabits the edges of the spruce forest in reduced numbers. West Virginia lacks the Spanish moss used by this species in the south for nesting, and also has little *Usnea* lichen which is utilized by the species in the north. Nests are built in a variety of places that give a similar form to the nesting sites; thus nests have been found in tangles of debris left by floods in riverside trees, in the dense branches of hemlocks, in "witches broom" situations in hardwood trees, and in one case in an old burlap sack hanging over a branch. There are definite nesting records from Jefferson, Berkeley, Morgan, Hampshire, Hardy, Grant, Pendleton, Preston, Monongalia, Tucker, Randolph, Pocahontas, Greenbrier, Webster, Upshur, Doddridge, Mercer, Summers, Fayette, Kanawha, and Wayne Counties.

Breeding Populations: Breeding Bird Surveys have averaged 2.6 (10.8–0.1) birds per route, with the high average in Lincoln-Boone Counties. These data may not be truly representative of the populations in the state. Twenty-five Singing Male Censuses have averaged 40 males per 100 ha. Hemlock-yellow poplar forest, 400 m, Fayette County, 108 males per 100 ha; cove hardwoods, 550 m, Greenbrier County, 91 males; virgin hardwoods-white pine, 580 m, Greenbrier County, 91 males; mature mixed hardwoods, 240 m, Wayne County, 77 males; hardwoods-hemlock, 670 m, Tucker County, 67 males; mature deciduous forest, 700 m, Webster County, 67 males; deciduous-hemlock forest, 640 m, Nicholas County, 67 males; and second-growth hardwoods, 600 m, Nicholas County, 49 males per 100 ha.

Fall: The Northern Parula departs from the state in September but this movement is little noted. At A.F.M.O., only 67 birds have been banded in 24 years, with 12 in a single year.

Last-seen Fall Date: Kanawha County, 10 September.

Specimens: USNM, UMMZ, AMNH, MCZ, DMNH, CM. No subspecies are currently recognized for this species.

YELLOW WARBLER *Dendroica petechia* (Linnaeus)

Status: Common to very common summer resident.

Spring: The Yellow Warbler arrives in the state in mid-April and for a short time becomes the most conspicuous member of the family in the region. It is found throughout the state, and it sings profusely upon arrival. It is usually not possible to detect true migrants, but on occasion I have found far more than the normal breeding numbers to be present on suitable habitats for a few days.

First-seen Spring Dates: Cabell-Mason Counties, 13 April; Kanawha County, 16 April; Randolph County, 15 April; Brooke County, 22 April; Summers County, 23 April; Monongalia County, 25 April; Ohio County, 26 April; Wood County, 27 April.

Summer: The Yellow Warbler nests in every county in the state, and is the most widespread and common member of the family. The typical habitat is streamside forest, but numbers are usually large in city parks, cemeteries, college campuses, and large suburban garden areas, as well as abandoned fields growing back to brushy vegetation. It nests at the edges of almost all forest types, although it does not occur in the spruce forest. At high elevations in the spruce belt, they are sparingly found in streamside situations.

Breeding Populations: Breeding Bird Surveys commonly run through prime Yellow Warbler habitat and these have averaged 12.3 (38.0–1.5) birds per route. On the other hand, rather few of the Singing Male Censuses have been carried out in good habitat and the species has occurred on only 12 such counts, averaging 66 males per 100 ha. Overgrown field, 360 m, Ohio County, 185 males per 100 ha, 160 males, and 123 males; brushy bottom, 210 m, Wetzel County, 14 males; shallow pond-cattail marsh, 180 m, Mason County, 67 males; and bottomland, 185 m, Mason County, 67 males.

Fall: The main Yellow Warbler migration occurs in early August, and only a few are left by 1 September. These stragglers may remain into October, however, and there is a record of a bird at a feeder in Cabell County in February (Edeburn et al., 1960).

Specimens: USNM, CM, UMMZ, MCZ, MU, DMNH. All specimens available are referable to the eastern subspecies *aestiva* Gmelin. Any bird seen after 1 September may be the Newfoundland race,

amnicola Batchelder, or even the Alaskan race, *rubiginosa* Pallas, which has been found in Pennsylvania. Any birds caught by banders at this time should be carefully examined and it is suggested that specimens be saved if possible.

CHESTNUT-SIDED WARBLER
Dendroica pensylvanica (Linnaeus)

Status: Uncommon to common spring migrant; common to very common local summer resident; fairly common fall migrant.

Spring: The Chestnut-sided Warbler arrives in the last few days of April or the first week of May. It is common throughout the state except in the Northern Panhandle and in the Eastern Panhandle. At this time of the year, it is found in practically any brushy habitat. Unlike some other migrants, it sings well during migration and is quite conspicuous. Migrants will have departed from the nonbreeding areas by the last week in May, but a few stragglers may remain into June.

First-seen Spring Dates: Summers County, 30 April; Wood County, 1 May; Cabell-Mason Counties, 1 May; Kanawha County, 3 May; Monongalia County, 6 May; Brooke County, 11 May; Ohio County, 14 May.

Last-seen Spring Dates: Kanawha County, 15 May; Cabell-Mason Counties, 18 May; Ohio County, 23 May.

Summer: The Chestnut-sided Warbler nests along the Allegheny Mountain system from Preston County to northern Monroe County. The range then extends across the southern part of the Western Hills through Summers, Raleigh, Fayette, Wyoming, Mingo, and parts of Wayne Counties. In the Ridge and Valley Region, there are summer records from Hardy and Pendleton Counties. A July record from Ritchie County probably represents a straggler whose nesting was interrupted elsewhere. The Chestnut-sided Warbler is found from the tops of the highest mountains where there is suitable habitat, down to at least 450 or 350 m. It is found in the brush stage of cutover second-growth woodlands of any forest type and may be abundant in this habitat. The populations of this species have undergone profound changes. In the days before settlement when large forests dominated the whole area, it would have been uncommon. In the early part of this century, just after the peak of the lumbering industry, it would have been abundant throughout its range, but now in the latter part of the century, it probably is decreasing in numbers since brushy habitat is decreasing, as some forests grow and as other areas are eliminated by "development."

Breeding Populations: Breeding Bird Surveys have averaged 2.6 (8.7–0.2) birds per route on nine routes. Twenty Singing Male Censuses have averaged 68 males per 100 ha. Cutover oak-hickory, 900 m, Greenbrier County, 279 and 163 males per 100 ha; cutover northern hardwoods, 1,220 m, Pocahontas County, 148 males (on two counts); young northern hardwoods, 1,250 m, Randolph County, 84, 84, and 67 males; upland black cherry forest, 1,160 m, Pocahontas County, 99 males; wooded marsh, 975 m, Tucker County, 49 males; and second-growth hardwoods, 900 m, Pocahontas County, 49 males.

Fall: The Chestnut-sided Warbler departs from the breeding grounds in late August, but the main migration is in early September with stragglers remaining until 1 October. There is a late-November record from Morgantown. At A.F.M.O. where 480 have been banded in 24 years, most of the records fall in the first 10 days of September. It probably migrates throughout the state but is generally inconspicuous.

First-seen Fall Dates: A.F.M.O., 1 September; Cabell-Mason Counties, 17 September.

Last-seen Fall Dates: A.F.M.O., 22 September; Cabell-Mason Counties, 6 October.

Specimens: USNM, CM, UMMZ, DMNH.

MAGNOLIA WARBLER

Dendroica magnolia (Wilson)

Status: Fairly common spring and fall migrant; abundant to fairly common local summer resident.

Spring: The Magnolia Warbler migrates throughout the state. It generally arrives with the second wave of warblers around the first of May, but the peak of the flight is not usually until mid-May. Most birds are gone from the lowlands by 20 May, but a few may remain until the end of the month. During migration, it may be found in most wooded habitats containing shrubby or other low trees. It is not usually found in dense forest that lacks an understory or in a pure pine forest.

First-seen Spring Dates: Randolph County, 30 April; Cabell-Mason Counties, 24 April; Kanawha County, 5 May; Monongalia County, 9 May; Wood County, 12 May; Ohio County, 15 May.

Last-seen Spring Dates: Kanawha County, 10 May; Cabell-Mason Counties, 19 May; Ohio County, 25 May.

Summer: The Magnolia Warbler is restricted to the Allegheny Mountains as a breeding bird. There are summer records from Monongalia, Preston, Tucker, Upshur, Grant, Hardy, Pendleton, Pocahontas, Webster, Greenbrier, and Fayette Counties. It is most common above 900 m, but in Upshur County it has been found sparingly at 750 m and in Preston and Monongalia Counties as low as 550 m. It inhabits the brushy second-growth stages of

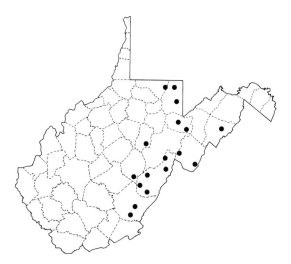

Fig. 4.   Breeding Season Records for the Magnolia Warbler. The distribution of many other typical Allegheny Mountains Region birds would be nearly the same as this.

almost all types of northern forest. Peak numbers have come in second-growth pure spruce forest, but it also occurs in the mixed hardwoods-spruce, the northern hardwoods, the oak-pine, and even in the oak-chestnut forest. There are definite nesting records only for Preston, Randolph, and Pocahontas Counties.

Breeding Populations: Nineteen Singing Male Censuses have averaged 116 males per 100 ha. Second-growth red spruce, 1,350 m, Randolph-Pocahontas Counties, has had populations of 247, 314, 314, 180, 146, 131 males per 100 ha on six counts over a 20-year period. Virgin spruce-northern hardwoods, 1,250 m, Randolph County, has had populations of 121, 131, 103, 17, 116, and 74 males per 100 ha; mixed spruce-hardwoods, 910 m, Pocahontas County, 103 males; spruce-fir swamp, 1,100 m, Randolph County, 74 males; and black cherry forest, 1,160 m, Pocahontas County, 49 males.

Fall: The Magnolia Warbler migrates through the state during most of September. A few may arrive in late August and a few stragglers are still present in early October. As in the spring, there seems to be no habitat preference except the avoidance of dense forest. As with several other boreal species, it is not commonly found in the spruce forest during migration. At A.F.M.O., 2,948 have been banded in 24 years, the eighth most abundant warbler species handled there. The largest number in one year was 148.

First-seen Fall Dates: A.F.M.O., 1 September; Cabell-Mason Counties, 15 September; Ohio County, 24 September.

Last-seen Fall Dates: Cabell-Mason Counties, 4 October; A.F.M.O., 6 October.

Specimens: USNM, UMMZ, CM, DMNH.

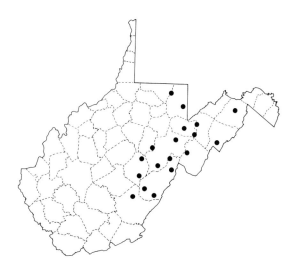

Fig. 5.   Breeding Season Records for the Black-throated Blue Warbler.

CAPE MAY WARBLER   *Dendroica tigrina* (Gmelin)

Status: Uncommon to common spring migrant; fairly common to very common or abundant fall migrant; casual winter visitant.

Spring: The Cape May Warbler arrives in the first week of May, but the peak of migration is in mid-month. It is inconspicuous if the trees have leafed out, and since the song is weak it may be overlooked. It probably migrates throughout the state, but in any given year only a few may occur at any one place. They occur in most wooded habitats, but at my home in Morgantown they are unusually common in a few ornamental Norway spruces, and are seldom seen elsewhere. A few stragglers may remain until the end of May.

First-seen Spring Dates: Cabell-Mason Counties, 30 April; Kanawha County, 4 May; Randolph County, 5 May; Monongalia County, 7 May; Brooke County, 7 May; Wood County, 8 May.

Last-seen Spring Dates: Kanawha County, 15 May; Cabell-Mason Counties, 17 May.

Fall: The Cape May Warbler is often abundant during fall migration. At such times, it commonly frequents suburban trees, often, as suggested by Brooks (1944), the insect-infested silver maples. It may also be found in numbers around grape arbors, and in places it has acquired a bad reputation of puncturing grapes to sip the juice. It probably occurs throughout the state, but as in the spring it may be absent from a given place in a given season. At A.F.M.O., a total of 7,337 has been banded in 24 years, with most of these coming in the years since 1969. The highest yearly total was 1,224 in 1974 and on one day, 16 September 1974, a total of 345 was banded.

First-seen Fall Dates: A.F.M.O., 31 August; Kanawha County, 8 September; Ohio County, 26 September.

Last-seen Fall Dates: Kanawha County, 14 September; Cabell-Mason Counties, 5 October; A.F.M.O., 6 October; Ohio County, 30 October.

Winter: There are more than a few scattered records of birds wintering in the state, usually at a feeding station. For example, Sutton (1933) reports one in Brooke County in December, and one spent the winter of 1966–67 at Romney, Hampshire County. A Cape May Warbler was present at a feeder in Vienna, Wood County, in the winters of 1980–81 and 1981–82 (T. Hurley). The early-March record in Cabell County (Edeburn et al., 1960) probably represents a successful wintering bird.

Specimens: USNM, UMMZ, AMNH, DMNH.

BLACK-THROATED BLUE WARBLER
Dendroica caerulescens (Gmelin)

Status: Rare to fairly common spring migrant; fairly common to common local summer resident; rare to fairly common fall migrant, but locally abundant.

Spring: The Black-throated Blue Warbler probably migrates throughout the state, but it is not very numerous anywhere. It is particularly rare at low elevations just west of the mountains where it nests, and at low elevations in the mountain valleys within the breeding range. This situation exists for several other species, e.g., the Hermit Thrush. The apparent rarity of this species as a migrant may be due in part to its being inconspicuous. During migration it does not sing much, and it generally will keep to its favored habitat of scrubby underbrush. Arrival is usually in the last few days of May, and migrants will have departed by the end of the third week in May.

First-seen Spring Dates: Cabell-Mason Counties, 28 April; Summers County, 28 April; Kanawha County, 6 May; Ohio County, 8 May; Wood County, 17 May.

Summer: The Black-throated Blue Warbler is another species that is essentially limited to the Allegheny Mountains as a breeding bird. It usually is found above 600 m but has been found as low as 450 m in some places. The main breeding range extends from eastern Monongalia County, and Preston County south through the higher elevations of Tucker, Grant, Pendleton, and Randolph Counties to a few of the higher ridges in northern Greenbrier County. There are also a few local summer records from Hampshire (Short Mountain), Hardy (Lost River State Park), Upshur (Hemlock), and Webster

(Dyer, Holly River State Park) Counties. Definite nesting records come only from Preston, Tucker, Pendleton, Randolph, and Pocahontas Counties.

The Black-throated Blue Warbler inhabits the denser stands of young spruce and the more mature spruce forests, either at the edges or in a dense understory. It occurs in the northern hardwoods forest that has a dense understory, often supplied by tangled stands of rhododendron. It occurs in the mixed hardwoods-spruce forest, the hardwoods-hemlock forest, and even in places in the oak-pine. Those birds found below 600 m most often are found in cool hemlock-covered ravines.

Breeding Populations: The Black-throated Blue Warbler has occurred on only 10 runs of six Breeding Bird Survey routes, where it averaged 0.6 bird per route. Twenty-nine Singing Male Censuses have averaged 40 males per 100 ha. Cutover mature hardwoods, 1,200 m, Pocahontas County, 99 males per 100 ha (this area had had 49 males and 42 males on other counts, and had 17 males per 100 ha before it was cut over); virgin spruce-northern hardwoods, 1,250 m, Randolph County, 89 males (this area had had 64, 49, 44, 39 males on other counts); upland black cherry forest, 1,160 m, Pocahontas County, 81 males; young deciduous forest, 1,250 m, Randolph County, 67 males; and cove hardwoods, 670 m, Preston County, 67 males.

Fall: The Black-throated Blue Warbler is seldom reported in the fall. It is silent at this time of year, and remains in the dense undergrowth. Departure is in early September and the flight continues until early October. Although seldom reported, there is no reason to doubt that it migrates throughout the state. Large numbers, however, can be seen flying along the Allegheny ridges in the early morning, the males being readily identifiable at a distance. This movement is reflected by the fact that at A.F.M.O. a total of 7,548 (third most-abundant warbler) has been banded in 24 years, with a high of 1,016 in one year.

First-seen Fall Date: Cabell-Mason Counties, 16 September.

Last-seen Fall Dates: Cabell-Mason Counties, 1 October; A.F.M.O., 9 October.

Specimens: USNM, CM, UMMZ, AMNH, MCZ, DMNH. Migrant specimens, particularly those from the western part of the state, are usually referable to the nominate subspecies. Most breeding specimens are assignable to the southern Appalachian race, *cairnsi* Coues, although Preston County specimens may be nearer *caerulescens*. It should be noted that *cairnsi* is at best a weakly distinct subspecies, and many specimens in collections have been assigned to it on purely geographical grounds. A thorough taxonomic examination of all West Vir-

ginia specimens, and possibly a careful study of the whole species, is in order.

YELLOW-RUMPED WARBLER
Dendroica coronata (Linnaeus)

Status: Common to very common spring and fall migrant; rare summer resident; rare to uncommon winter resident.

Spring: The Yellow-rumped Warbler migrates throughout the state, and often occurs in very large numbers. The presence of wintering individuals obscures the arrival of migrants that arrive in the middle of April. The peak of migration is in early May and most birds will have left before the last third of May. During the spring, it is found in a wide variety of wooded habitats ranging from mature forest to park and garden situations. It commonly sings, particularly late in the season, and is often the most numerous warbler to be seen. However, in some years they may not appear in any great numbers at particular locations.

First-seen Spring Dates: (migrants): Kanawha County, 31 March; Ohio County, 25 April; Summers County, 30 April; Brooke County, 18 April; Cabell-Mason Counties, 5 May.

Last-seen Spring Dates: Kanawha County, 1 May; Cabell-Mason Counties, 14 May; Ohio County, 15 May.

Summer: Some areas in the spruce forest at high elevations would appear to the human eye to be quite similar to the nesting habitat of Yellow-rumped Warblers in the north, but as far as is known they did not nest in West Virginia until recently.

Occasionally, there were sightings that indicated possible breeding; for example, one at Cranesville, Preston County, on 26 August 1914, and several late-August or early-September banding records at A.F.M.O. In 1975 a lone male was seen, acting as if defending a territory, on Gaudineer Knob, Randolph-Pocahontas Counties. In subsequent years, single males were seen there in late May or early June, and at least two males defended territories there in June 1978 (Hall, 1978). By 1981 at least three territories were present at that station, and in late June of that year a pair was seen apparently feeding young (G. Breiding). One was also seen on Spruce Knob, Pendleton County, in the summer of 1981 (R. Russell).

In 1982 a small population (41 males per 100 hectares) was censused in the stunted spruce trees on Spruce Mountain at Spruce Knob.

Fall: The Yellow-rumped Warbler may arrive in the state in late September but the main southbound flight occurs in mid- to late October and into early November. It migrates throughout the state, except possibly at high elevations. Very few birds have been caught at A.F.M.O., which is either a reflection of the fact that operations cease there before the main flight or else the birds do not use that route. It may also be that at the time of the Yellow-rumped flight the habitat on the Allegheny Front is not hospitable for this species. In the lowlands the birds often occur in great numbers. At the author's banding station at Morgantown, over 100 Yellow-rumps have been banded in a single day on occasion (peak day, 188 on 26 October 1975) and a season's totals have been as many as 200 to 400.

Winter: At least a few Yellow-rumped Warblers winter in various parts of the state. There are no records for the high mountains. On occasion, large numbers may be present in the lower Ohio and Kanawha Valleys. Christmas Count data (birds per party hour) are: statewide, 0.17 (0.47–0.03); Charleston, 0.25 (0.64–0.01); Huntington, 0.23 (1.35–0); and Ona, 0.56 (1.88–0). Other counts are less than 0.1.

Remarks: In all the literature prior to 1973, this species is known as the Myrtle Warbler.

Specimens: USNM, CM, UMMZ, AMNH, WVU, DMNH. All specimens referable to the eastern subspecies, *coronata.*

BLACK-THROATED GREEN WARBLER
Dendroica virens (Gmelin)

Status: Fairly common to common spring and fall migrant; common to abundant summer resident.

Spring: The Black-throated Green Warbler migrates throughout the state, although at high elevations the migrants who arrive after the local breeding population may be overlooked. During migration, it will be found in all forest types that contain nearly mature trees. It arrives well before the leaves are out and it commonly sings during migration, and is thus most conspicuous. Early arrivals reach the state by mid-April, the resident birds are on the breeding grounds by late April, but

in the lowlands the migration continues until the third week in May.

First-seen Spring Dates: Cabell-Mason Counties, 12 April; Kanawha County, 20 April; Summers County, 22 April; Monongalia County, 23 April; Brooke County, 27 April; Wood County, 28 April; Ohio County, 28 April.

Last-seen Spring Dates: Kanawha County, 15 May; Ohio County, 27 May.

Summer: The Black-throated Green Warbler may nest, at least sparingly, in every county except those along the Ohio River, and the two easternmost counties, Jefferson and Berkeley. Data are lacking from the extreme southern counties. The principal range is in the Allegheny Mountains from Monongalia and Preston south to Monroe, Greenbrier, and Fayette, and from Hardy west to the eastern parts of Nicholas, Webster, and Upshur Counties. It occurs commonly in some of the hill country in Wayne, Lincoln, and other southwestern counties, and there are summer records also from Kanawha, Clay, Ritchie, Barbour, and Morgan Counties. Definite nesting records come from Preston, Pocahontas, Randolph, Upshur, Monroe, Lincoln, and Wayne Counties. In Morgan County, it has occurred as low as 150 m and it occurs at the highest elevations.

At lower elevations and away from the mountains, the Black-throated Green Warbler is usually found in forests containing some conifers, most commonly hemlock, but often white pine or pitch pine. I have not found it in the eastern scrub pine forests. In Wayne County (Cabwaylingo State Forest), it occurs abundantly at 360 m in second growth central hardwoods. At the high elevations, it is rare in the pure spruce forest, common in the mixed spruce-northern hardwoods forest, but reaches its peak numbers in the northern hardwoods forest where conifers are lacking.

Breeding Populations: Breeding Bird Surveys have averaged 1.1 (3.7–0.1) birds per route for 10 routes. Thirty-two Singing Male Censuses have averaged 59 males per 100 ha. Mature northern hardwoods, 1,220 m, Pocahontas County, 247, and 232 males per 100 ha (this area was cutover, and successive counts at five-year intervals gave 7, 99, and 42 males); oak-hickory, 360 m, Wayne County, 148 males; mixed hardwoods-spruce, 900 m, Pocahontas County, 94 males; virgin spruce-northern hardwoods, 1,250 m, Randolph County, 74, 47, 20, 67, 86, 89 males; upland black cherry forest, 1,160 m, Pocahontas County, 82 males; and cove hardwoods, 670 m, Preston County, 67 males.

Fall: Early fall arrivals may be seen in late July or early August, but the main migration comes in September with the peak in the last week. Good numbers are still coming through in early October.

The Black-throated Green Warbler migrates throughout the state, and is usually quite conspicuous. Large numbers may be seen flying along the Appalachian Ridges on most fall days, and at A.F.M.O. it has been the fifth most abundant warbler with 4,662 banded in 24 years, and a high year's count of 1,089.

First-seen Fall Dates: Kanawha County, 5 September; Ohio County, 23 September.

Last-seen Fall Dates: Kanawha County, 20 September; A.F.M.O., 8 October; Cabell-Mason Counties, 13 October.

Remarks: In the northern part of the range this species is essentially limited to the coniferous forest and the mixed forest. As the data given above show, in West Virginia in the southern part of the range it not only occurs in the pure deciduous forest, but reaches extremely high populations there.

Specimens: CM, AMNH, UMMZ, DMNH.

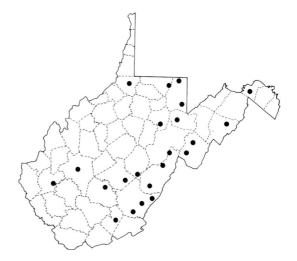

Fig. 6.   Breeding Season Records for the Blackburnian Warbler.

BLACKBURNIAN WARBLER

Dendroica fusca (Müller)

Status: Uncommon to common spring and fall migrant; common to very common local summer resident.

Spring: The Blackburnian Warbler migrates throughout the state, but is apparently uncommon in the upper Ohio Valley. Arrival is in late April or early May with a peak movement in mid-May. The last stragglers may remain until the first week in June. Resident birds in the mountain areas arrive well before the peak of migration in the lowlands, and indeed often are found defending territories before any migrants are seen in the lowlands. This early arrival of the mountain residents is characteristic of some other species.

First-seen Spring Dates: Cabell-Mason Counties, 23 April; Kanawha County, 24 April; Ohio County, 1 May; Summers County, 5 May; Monongalia County, 6 May; Wood County, 7 May; Brooke County, 11 May.

Last-seen Spring Dates: Kanawha County, 10 May; Cabell-Mason Counties, 12 May.

Summer: The principal breeding range of the Blackburnian Warbler in West Virginia is in the spruce forest, and the mixed spruce-northern hardwoods forest above 900 m. However, it also is common in the oak-hickory and the oak-pine forests at somewhat lower elevations, down to about 600 m. As a nesting bird, it occurs only in mature forest. There are summer records from Pendleton, Preston, Monongalia, Tucker, Randolph, Webster, Pocahontas, and Greenbrier Counties in these habitats. It does occur in small numbers in a few other places,

often as low as 450 m in Morgan, Hardy, Barbour, Wetzel, Fayette, Lincoln, and Summers Counties. There are early-June records from Ritchie and Wayne Counties but these are probably late migrants. Brooks (1940) suggested that they may breed in Hancock County, but there is no recent evidence of this. Definite nesting records are few and come from Pendleton, Pocahontas, Randolph, Greenbrier, and Lincoln Counties.

Breeding Populations: The Blackburnian Warbler has occurred on only three Breeding Bird Survey routes with an average of 0.4 bird per route. Twenty-one Singing Male Censuses have averaged 64 males per 100 ha. Virgin spruce-northern hardwoods, 1,250 m, Randolph County, 133, 163, 158, 99, 116, 131 males per 100 ha on six different counts; mature pine-oak, 760 m, Greenbrier County, 116 males; mature deciduous, 700 m, Webster County, 91 males; spruce-fir swamp, 1,100 m, Randolph County, 57 males; and upland black cherry forest, 1,160 m, Pocahontas County, 49 males per 100 ha.

Fall: The Blackburnian Warbler is one of the early group of warblers during fall migration, and the peak of the flight will be in the last two weeks in August and very early September. Stragglers are present throughout September, and even in early October. At A.F.M.O., 2,959 have been banded in 24 years with the largest year's count being 368.

First-seen Fall Dates: A.F.M.O., 30 August; Kanawha County, 1 September; Cabell-Mason Counties, 10 September; Ohio County, 29 September.

Last-seen Fall Dates: Kanawha County, 10 September; Cabell-Mason Counties, 27 September; A.F.M.O., 29 September.

Specimens: WVU, CM, UMMZ, USNM, MCZ, DMNH.

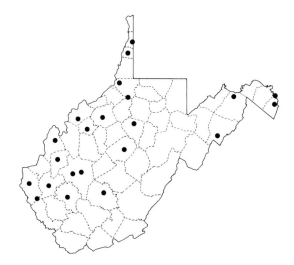

Fig. 7. Breeding Season Records for the Yellow-throated Warbler.

YELLOW-THROATED WARBLER

Dendroica dominica (Linnaeus)

Status: Uncommon to fairly common local summer resident; rare spring migrant away from nesting range.

Spring: The Yellow-throated Warbler is one of the earliest warblers to arrive on the nesting grounds, usually appearing in early April. There are a number of spring records in regions where it is not known to nest: from Preston, Monongalia, Marion, Monroe, Ohio, Brooke, Hancock, Upshur, and Nicholas Counties. These records all come in late April or early May, at which times nesting birds have already arrived on their breeding territories, but in all of these cases the bird was not present later in the season.

First-seen Spring Dates: Kanawha County, 9 April; Cabell-Mason Counties, 21 April; Wirt County, 22 April.

Summer: The nesting range of the Yellow-throated Warbler in West Virginia is pretty well limited to the Ohio River Valley from Wetzel County south, and in the tributary valleys of the Kanawha and the New Rivers. There are regular reports of summer birds from Wetzel, Wood, Wirt, Mason, Cabell, Putnam, Kanawha, Boone, Lincoln, Wyoming, Ritchie, Fayette, and Wayne Counties. There is also an isolated colony in the Shenandoah Valley and along the Potomac River in Jefferson County. Less regular summer reports come from Hampshire, Hardy, Webster, Lewis, and Braxton Counties. Definite nesting records come only from Lincoln, Kanawha, and Jefferson Counties. A nesting was observed in Ohio County in 1980 (Conrad, 1981). In most of this area, the bird is found in mature river bottom forest, typically where there are large sycamore trees.

However, near Charleston, where the largest population is, the birds are more common in the scrub pine woods.

Breeding Populations: The Yellow-throated Warbler has been recorded on only six Breeding Bird Survey routes with an average number of one bird per count.

Fall: The Yellow-throated Warbler departs from the nesting grounds in early September but little has been reported on the fall migration. There are fall records from Marion and Cabell Counties, as well as Kanawha County.

Last-seen Fall Date: Kanawha County, 10 September.

Remarks: Although Scott (1872) reported the taking of two specimens in Kanawha County, very little was known about the distribution of this species in the state for many years. Brooks (1944) could list only a few other scattered records. Most of the records outlined above were made in the last 15 years, but whether this represents a range expansion or more extensive field work is not known. It seems likely that the Shenandoah River population, first reported in 1962, has indeed moved into that location rather recently. In 1975 there were several birds present at Morgantown, suggesting a possible movement into that area, but apparently no permanent population has become established. In 1976 it was present in Hancock County.

In June 1975 a bird that was morphologically a Yellow-throated Warbler (probably *D. d. albilora*), which sang a "double Parula song," was seen, netted and banded, photographed, and song recorded. The behavior of this bird in response to playbacks of recorded songs, and the audiospectrographic analysis of its song, raised much speculation about the possible hybridization between *D. dominica* and *P. americana*.

Specimens: WVU, MU, CM. The WVU specimen is not subspecifically identifiable, but the MU specimen belongs to the western race, *albilora* Ridgway, and it is probable that all West Virginia birds are of that race.

SUTTON'S WARBLER   *Dendroica potomac* Haller

Records and Remarks: The first known specimen of Sutton's Warbler was collected by K. W. Haller and J. L. Poland at a site on the Opequon Creek, Berkeley County, on 30 May 1939. Two days later, they collected another specimen in Jefferson County, at an area known locally as Terrapin Neck, on the banks of the Potomac River (Haller, 1940d). M. Brooks and B. H. Christy (1942) reported seeing one near the Opequon Creek collecting site on 21 May 1942. H. Mitchell (1952) reported the sighting of still another one at the Opequon Creek site on

29 May 1950. L. Hicks and G. Breiding reported one from Morgan County in June 1944 (Hicks, 1945). Since these records, there have been numerous rumors, but only one authentic sighting [Kanawha County, 20 April 1970 (Eye, 1977)] of this form in the state, although several records have come from elsewhere. The Opequon Creek station in Berkeley County was subjected to annual surveys from 1951 to about 1962 without results.

This form has not been recognized as a valid species by the A.O.U. Check-list (1957) and is most commonly thought to be a hybrid between *D. dominica* and *Parula americana,* although this has not been proved. The original bird collected was said to have a song like that of the Northern Parula repeated twice and had other characters superficially like the Northern Parula while most closely resembling the Yellow-throated Warbler. At the time of the discovery, the Yellow-throated Warbler was not known for the eastern part of the state but has since appeared there in numbers.

At this time, I believe the safest course in considering this species (or hybrid) is to conclude that the final answer is not available. The relation of the strange Yellow-throated Warbler in Raleigh County in 1975 mentioned above to *D. potomac* is not clear.

The full details of the discovery of this enigmatic form have been outlined by Brooks (1945b).

Specimens: UMMZ.

PINE WARBLER   *Dendroica pinus* (Wilson)

Status: Uncommon to common, but very local summer resident; rare winter visitant.

Spring: The Pine Warbler is perhaps the earliest of the warblers to appear in the spring since migrants will arrive by the middle of March, and it will be well established on the nesting grounds by the end of the month. As with several other species, there are few records away from the nesting grounds, and the species is seldom or never seen in many parts of the state. In migration as in the nesting season, it is almost exclusively limited to pine forests. I have a single spring record for Morgantown (collected), which is the only Pine Warbler I have ever seen away from the pine woods.

First-seen Spring Dates: Kanawha County, 18 March; Cabell-Mason Counties, 8 April; Wirt County, 22 April.

Summer: The Pine Warbler nests in moderate numbers throughout the state, but it is strictly limited to forest stands containing large amounts of fairly mature pines. Along the Ohio and the Kanawha Rivers, they are found in scrub pine forests or in the oak-pine forest. In the Ridge and Valley Region, it also occurs in scrub pine or oak-pine forest. On the high eastern Alleghenies, it is found in pitch pine forests as high as 1,200 m. It does not occur in the spruce forest, and is rare in the white pine forests. In Wayne County, a pair was found inhabiting two or three yellow pines, the only conifers on the whole ridge. There are summer records from Jefferson, Berkeley, Hampshire, Hardy, Pendleton, Greenbrier, Preston, Grant, Morgan, Summers, Nicholas, Ritchie, Putnam, Lincoln, Kanawha, Cabell, and Wayne Counties. Definite nesting records come only from Berkeley, Grant, Hampshire, Ritchie, Lincoln, and Kanawha Counties.

Breeding Populations: The Pine Warbler has occurred on only one Breeding Bird Survey route with an average of 4.2 birds per count. Seven Singing Male Censuses have averaged 39 males per 100 ha. Oak-pine woods, 182 m, Berkeley County, 67 males; pine-oak-hickory, 275 m, Hampshire County, 67 males; northern hardwoods, 700 m, Pendleton County, 67 males; and young oak-pine, 490 m, Hardy County, 32 males per 100 ha.

Fall: The Pine Warbler leaves the nesting areas in September, but there are very few fall records. Only three have been captured at A.F.M.O. in 24 years.

Last-seen Fall Date: Cabell-Mason Counties, 7 October.

Winter: An occasional bird will winter in pine forest at lower elevations. There are winter records from Nicholas, Cabell, and Kanawha Counties. At the latter location, they are present in almost every winter, and six were listed on one Christmas Count.

Specimens: WVU, UMMZ, MCZ, DMNH, CM.

*KIRTLAND'S WARBLER

Dendroica kirtlandii (Baird)

Status: Hypothetical. Accidental spring migrant.

Records: There are four sight records for Kirtland's Warbler in the state, but since none of the observers had had previous experience with this species when they saw it, it seems best to include it on the hypothetical list. M. Brooks and I. Boggs (1937) saw one at Ice's Ferry, Monongalia County, on 19 May 1937; Boggs saw another at Morgantown on 16 May 1943; W. Wylie saw one at Wheeling in the early 1940s; and the writer saw one at Morgantown on 16 May 1954.

Remarks: This species must certainly migrate across the state, and only the very low total population is responsible for the scarcity of records.

PRAIRIE WARBLER   *Dendroica discolor* (Vieillot)

Status: Fairly common to common summer resident.

Spring: The Prairie Warbler arrives in the state

in the third week in April, and the loud characteristic song makes it conspicuous. It probably migrates throughout the state, except at high elevations, but is generally much more uncommon in the Northern Panhandle than elsewhere.

First-seen Spring Dates: Kanawha County, 15 April; Wood County, 21 April; Cabell-Mason Counties, 22 April; Monongalia County, 24 April; Summers County, 1 May; Brooke County, 2 May.

Summer: There are summer records for the Prairie Warbler from all parts of the state. It is most numerous in the central part of the Western Hills and in the Eastern Panhandle. It is missing from the spruce belt and most of the northern forest, but does occur in numbers in the brushy areas on the summit of the Allegheny Front, Tucker County, at about 1,160 m. It was unknown in the Northern Panhandle north of Marshall County 30 to 40 years ago, but in recent years it has moved into this area. There are definite nesting records from Jefferson, Berkeley, Hampshire, Hardy, Pendleton, Tucker, Preston, Monongalia, Randolph, Greenbrier, Webster, Upshur, Hancock, Marshall, Pleasants, Ritchie, Summers, Fayette, Lincoln, Kanawha, Wayne, and Cabell Counties.

The Prairie Warbler is found in dense brushy areas, either in overgrown abandoned pastures or in recently cutover areas. It is especially numerous in young pine plantations, and in places where pine or red cedar have invaded an old field, and can be considered a typical bird at the "shale barrens" of the Ridge and Valley Region. In Kanawha County, it is commonly found along power line cuts. Nests are frequently in blackberry tangles, or in the dense lower foliage of cedars or spruce.

Breeding Populations: Breeding Bird Surveys have averaged 4.7 (17.3–0.1) birds per route. Ten Singing Male Censuses have averaged 44 males per 100 ha. Overgrown pasture (red cedar), 290 m, Hardy County, 57 males per 100 ha; overgrown field (pine), 290 m, Morgan County, 91 males; brushy hilltop, 550 m, Nicholas County, 82 males; and briar patch, 600 m, Preston County, 57 males.

Fall: Once singing stops in July, the Prairie Warbler is quite inconspicuous. Most leave the state in late August or early September, but stragglers may remain until late September. Despite the fact that there is a breeding population at A.F.M.O., only 13 have been captured there. There is a record of one in Kanawha County on 2 January 1960 (G. Hurley).

Remarks: The Prairie Warbler has increased in numbers and has extended its range extensively in recent years, and it has become fairly common where it had not been known earlier. Neither Scott (1872) nor Brewster (1875) reported it, although they worked areas where it is now plentiful. E. A. Brooks

(1916) called it rare in the state, and at that time it occurred only in the Ridge and Valley Region.

The term "Prairie" is often considered inappropriate for this species, but when Wilson first used the name over 150 years ago the word "prairie" had a quite different meaning than it does today, and at that time was quite appropriate for a bird to be found only in forest openings.

Specimens: WVU, USNM, UMMZ, MU, DMNH.

PALM WARBLER   *Dendroica palmarum* (Gmelin)

Status: Uncommon spring migrant; uncommon to locally common fall migrant; casual or rare winter visitant.

Spring: The Palm Warbler is never very common in most parts of the state, and is seldom reported in the spring from the Northern Panhandle, the higher mountains, and the region just west of the mountains. It becomes more numerous in the western part of the state, especially in the open country of Mason County. Arrival is in late April and most are gone by mid-May. The Palm Warbler does not frequent the same habitat as other migrant warblers and since the song is inconspicuous, it may be overlooked by many people.

First-seen Spring Dates: Kanawha County, 13 April; Wood County, 5 May; Monongalia County, 7 May; Brooke County, 11 May.

Last-seen Spring Dates: Kanawha County, 5 May; Cabell-Mason Counties, 5 May.

Fall: The main migration of the Palm Warbler in the fall is in early October although early migrants will appear any time after 15 September and some remain well into November. At some places—for example, the McClintic Wildlife Station, Mason County, and the Canaan Valley, Tucker County—large numbers may be seen in open weed-choked fields and brushy fields. It is well distributed over the state in fall, but is absent from densely forested areas.

First-seen Fall Dates: Kanawha County, 18 September; Cabell-Mason Counties, 19 September; Ohio County, 23 September; Summers County, 10 October.

Last-seen Fall Dates: Kanawha County, 30 September; Cabell-Mason Counties, 25 October.

Winter: A few birds may be present until the end of December. There are recent records from Cabell, Kanawha, and Ohio Counties. It is not known whether any of these December birds survive the winter in the state.

Specimens: WVU, USNM, CM, UMMZ, MU, DMNH. All West Virginia specimens examined have been of the western subspecies *palmarum*. There are occasional sight records and numerous reports from banders of the eastern subspecies *hypochrysea* Ridgway, the "Yellow Palm Warbler." However, since some fall specimens of *palmarum* are very yellow, fall records for *hypochrysea* based on color alone should be considered doubtful in the absence of specimens. I have two records of birds banded in the spring at Morgantown, which were possibly *hypochrysea*.

BAY-BREASTED WARBLER
Dendroica castanea (Wilson)

Status: Rare to fairly common spring migrant; rare to common fall migrant.

Spring: The Bay-breasted Warbler migrates throughout the state, except at high elevations. It is rare to uncommon in the Northern Panhandle and also east of the Allegheny Mountains. Arrival is generally in mid-May, and the peak of migration is in the third week of May, with stragglers remaining until the last of the month. At this time of the year, it is found in the tops of mature trees, feeding on the insects gathered around the flowers of the trees, particularly the oaks. It seldom comes down low. The song is not very loud and may be overlooked, or sometimes may be misidentified as that of the Black-and-white Warbler.

A singing male was present for several days in Randolph County in June 1982.

First-seen Spring Dates: Kanawha County, 7 May; Cabell-Mason Counties, 8 May; Wood County, 5 May; Monongalia County, 10 May; Ohio County, 12 May.

Last-seen Spring Dates: Kanawha County, 20 May; Ohio County, 25 May; Cabell-Mason Counties, 27 May.

Fall: The Bay-breasted Warbler migrates throughout the state, but as in spring is rare east of the mountains and in the upper Ohio Valley. To the west and the south, it becomes more numerous and at Huntington it is the second most numerous warbler in the fall. At this time, it is found in most forest types, but oddly it is seldom found in the pure spruce forest, which resembles the nesting territory. At A.F.M.O. in the eastern part of the state, it has been the sixth most numerous warbler with 3,864 banded in 24 years and a maximum of 586 in one year. A Bay-breasted Warbler banded at A.F.M.O. in the fall of 1977 was recovered on an oil-drilling rig 40 miles offshore from Galveston, Texas, in May 1978.

First-seen Fall Dates: A.F.M.O., 5 September; Kanawha County, 5 September; Cabell-Mason Counties, 5 September; Ohio County, 10 September.

Last-seen Fall Dates: Ohio County, 20 September; A.F.M.O., 3 October; Cabell-Mason Counties, 14 October; Kanawha County, 15 October.

Specimens: WVU, USNM, UMMZ, DMNH.

BLACKPOLL WARBLER　　*Dendroica striata* (Forster)

Status: Uncommon to common spring migrant; fairly common to very common fall migrant.

Spring: The Blackpoll Warbler migrates throughout the state but is more numerous east of the Allegheny Mountains than in the west. It is uncommon in the Northern Panhandle, and, as with some other species, along the western slopes of the mountains. Although the literature implies that this is the last warbler to arrive in the spring, the early stragglers are present in early May. The bulk of the flight comes in the third week in May, and a few birds remain in early June, often until 10 June. At this season, it is found in almost any wooded area, including residential areas of the cities. After the leaves are on the trees, it is seldom seen, and its often abundant presence is evident only from its song.

First-seen Spring Dates: Cabell-Mason Counties, 2 May; Ohio County, 6 May; Randolph County, 10 May; Kanawha County, 10 May; Monongalia County, 11 May; Summers County, 12 May; Wood County, 13 May.

Last-seen Spring Dates: Kanawha County, 22 May; Ohio County, 25 May; Cabell-Mason Counties, 26 May.

Fall: The Blackpoll Warbler is probably the most abundant warbler in the fall in most of the state. It is found in almost any wooded habitat, but as with the preceding species it seems to avoid the pure spruce forest. The first arrivals appear in the first week of September, but the peak of migration does not come until the third week of September. It is still coming through in early October and may be present until the middle of the month. This has been the second most numerous species at A.F.M.O. with 9,877 banded in 24 years and a maximum year's count of 1,316. On several occasions, more than 100 have been banded in a single day. A Blackpoll Warbler banded at A.F.M.O. in the fall was recovered in the Dominican Republic, in the same fall and another in Montana the spring following banding.

First-seen Fall Dates: Kanawha County, 2 September; A.F.M.O., 4 September; Cabell-Mason Counties, 7 September; Ohio County, 19 September.

Last-seen Fall Dates: Kanawha County, 15 September; Cabell-Mason Counties, 3 October; A.F.M.O., 11 October.

Remarks: In fall plumage, the Blackpoll Warbler is difficult to distinguish from the Bay-breasted Warbler in the field, and some individuals may not be identifiable, even though the field guides indicate otherwise. Contrary to these guides, many Blackpoll Warblers have darkish tarsi and may be miscalled as Bay-breasts. The yellow feet (usually not visible in the field) and the white undertail coverts constitute the best field marks.

Specimens: USNM, UMMZ, DMNH.

Cerulean Warbler *Dendroica cerulea* (Wilson)

Status: Locally a very common summer resident; missing or rare in some areas.

Spring: The Cerulean Warbler arrives in the last week of April, and is conspicuous because of the song, even though it is difficult to see in the tree-top foliage. It probably migrates throughout the state, except at high elevations, but as with several other resident warblers true migrants are hard to detect.

First-seen Spring Dates: Kanawha County, 18 April; Cabell-Mason Counties, 24 April; Wood County, 28 April; Summers County, 30 April; Brooke County, 30 April; Ohio County, 2 May; Monongalia County, 5 May.

Summer: The Cerulean Warbler is common, and indeed is the most numerous breeding warbler, in the southern hardwoods forest and the oak-hickory forest in the counties along the Ohio, Monongahela, and Kanawha Rivers. It is quite common throughout the Western Hills Region, but eastward toward the Alleghenies it becomes uncommon and local. It is uncommon or missing in Randolph, Pocahontas, and possibly Monroe Counties. The greatest numbers are found below 600 m, but there is a nesting record for 900 m in Greenbrier County. East of the mountains, it occurs in a few localized places in the valleys, but is never as common as it is along the Ohio River. While it may nest in every county, definite nesting records come only from Preston, Hampshire, Lewis, Greenbrier, Doddridge, Wirt, Wetzel, Ohio, Brooke, Lincoln, Cabell, and Kanawha Counties.

Breeding Populations: Breeding Bird Surveys have averaged 2.6 (9.6–0.1) birds per route. Twenty-three Singing Male Censuses have averaged 62 males per 100 ha. Mature oak-hickory, 275 m, Wetzel County, 207 males per 100 ha; upland oak-hickory, 400 m, Kanawha County, 190 males; oak-hickory forest, 820 m, Greenbrier County, 131 males; oak-hickory, 820 m, Greenbrier County, 116 males; mixed hardwoods, 360 m, Wetzel County, 99 males; mixed upland forest, 250 m, Mason County, 99 males; oak-hickory, Fayette County, 59 males; and

northern hardwoods, 305 m, Brooke County, 57 males.

Fall: The Cerulean Warbler is almost unreported in the fall, being silent, and almost invisible in the tree-tops. The southward migration takes place mostly in August and most birds are gone by mid-September. Only 11 have been banded in 24 years at A.F.M.O.

Last-seen Fall Dates: Kanawha County, 15 September; Cabell-Mason Counties, 16 September.

Specimens: USNM, CM, MCZ, UMMZ, WVU, MU.

Black-and-white Warbler
Mniotilta varia (Linnaeus)

Status: Uncommon to common spring migrant; uncommon to common summer resident; uncommon fall migrant.

Spring: The Black-and-white Warbler belongs to the group of warblers that arrives in the state rather early, generally appearing in the leafless woodlands around the middle of April. As a rule, rather few are seen by an average observer in a given day. It migrates throughout the state, except at the higher elevations. Migrants inhabit the same mature forest habitat as do the breeding birds and are thus not easy to separate from the latter.

First-seen Spring Dates: Kanawha County, 10 April; Cabell-Mason Counties, 16 April; Summers County, 21 April; Wood County, 22 April; Monongalia County, 26 April; Ohio County, 28 April; Randolph County, 5 May; Brooke County, 6 May.

Summer: As a breeding bird, the Black-and-white Warbler probably occurs in every county, but its numbers vary greatly from place to place. It is most numerous at the middle elevations from about 300 to 900 m. It is quite uncommon below 300 m in the river valleys. It is uncommon in the northern hardwoods forest above 900 m, although it does occur sparingly at a few places above 1,200 m. It is absent from the spruce forest. The greatest populations seem to be in the oak-hickory forest and in the mixed deciduous-white pine forest. It occurs only in very mature forest having large trees with a closed canopy and usually rather sparse ground cover. A good ground cover of dead leaves, to be used in nest building, seems necessary.

There are nesting records from Morgan, Hampshire, Hardy, Pendleton, Pocahontas, Randolph, Greenbrier, Tucker, Preston, Monongalia, Marion, Upshur, Lewis, Brooke, Ohio, Wetzel, Wirt, Pleasants, Doddridge, Braxton, Webster, Nicholas, Fayette, Lincoln, Kanawha, and Wayne Counties. The highest elevation for a nesting that has been seen was at about 900 m.

Breeding Populations: Breeding Bird Surveys have averaged 2.5 (8.8–0.1) birds per route, but this species is not adequately sampled by this census method. Forty-eight Singing Male Censuses have averaged 36 males per 100 ha; cutover white pine-hemlock, 610 m, Pendleton County, 109 males per 100 ha; mature white pine-hemlock, 670 m, Pendleton County, 99 males; mature pine-oak, 760 m, Greenbrier County, 82 males; cutover oak-hickory, 900 m, Greenbrier County, 82 males; northern hardwoods, 610 m, Pendleton County, 74 males; cove hardwoods-hemlock, 610 m, Preston, 67 males; hemlock-deciduous, 640 m, Nicholas County, 67 males; and 10 areas with 49 males per 100 ha (three per census plot).

Fall: Migrant Black-and-White Warblers begin to appear in places where the species does not breed in mid-July and most of the migration occurs in August and early September, although a few stragglers are still migrating in early October. At A.F.M.O., only 316 have been banded in 24 years, with a maximum yearly count of 50.

First-seen Fall Date: A.F.M.O., 2 September.

Last-seen Fall Dates: Kanawha County, 13 September; Cabell-Mason Counties, 23 September; A.F.M.O., 28 September.

Remarks: It is possible that the Black-and-White Warbler is a declining species in this region, since populations appear to be lower today (early 1980s) than they were a quarter of a century ago.

Specimens: USNM, UMMZ, MCZ, MU, DMNH.

AMERICAN REDSTART

Setophaga ruticilla (Linnaeus)

Status: Common spring migrant; fairly common to abundant summer resident; uncommon fall migrant.

Spring: The Redstart arrives in the last week of April, and apparently migrates throughout the state. In the spring, it can be found in almost any middle-aged woodland stand in the state, often in large numbers.

First-seen Spring Dates: Kanawha County, 21 April; Cabell-Mason Counties, 22 April; Wirt County, 22 April; Summers County, 26 April; Randolph County, 25 April; Ohio County, 29 April; Monongalia County, 1 May.

Summer: The Redstart probably nests in every county of the state, and is often quite numerous. It does not breed in the spruce forest, and is, at present, uncommon in the northern hardwoods forest above 900 m. Below this elevation, it is found in the middle growth stages of every plant association type of the region, except possibly the oak-pine forest where it is again scarce. There are definite nesting records from Jefferson, Berkeley, Hampshire, Hardy, Pendleton, Preston, Randloph, Greenbrier, Monongalia, Marion, Ohio, Brooke, Wetzel, Wirt, Lewis, Gilmer, Doddridge, Pleasants, Nicholas, Fayette, Lincoln, Kanawha, Wayne, and Cabell Counties.

Breeding Populations: Breeding Bird Surveys have averaged 3.9 (10.3–0.1) birds per route. Nineteen Singing Male Censuses have averaged 55 males per 100 ha. Mature hardwood forest, 300 m, Kanawha County, 279 males; upland oak-hickory forest, 400 m, Kanawha County, 124 males; bottomland, 220 m, Wayne County, 114 males; oak-hickory, 365 m, Morgan County, 99 males; cutover oak-hickory, 900 m, Greenbrier County, 67 males; and mature deciduous forest, 700 m, Webster County, 49 males per 100 ha.

Fall: Most Redstarts leave in early September but a few stragglers remain until October. There are two very late records: one at a feeder in late December 1948 at Charleston and one banded at Elkins on 12 December 1974 (E. Olliver). Only 559 have been banded at A.F.M.O. in 24 years with a high yearly count of 104.

First-seen Fall Date: A.F.M.O., 3 September.

Last-seen Fall Dates: A.F.M.O., 23 September; Cabell-Mason Counties, 23 September.

Remarks: The peak populations of the Redstart in the state probably were reached in the 1930s and the 1940s. Since then much of the second-growth habitat has grown out of the stage favored by the Redstart and more recent clearings have not yet developed into good habitat. Since many of the recent forest clearing operations have involved more than timber removal, they may never reforest. It was the abundance of this species, in almost all parts of the state, that so impressed the early members of the Brooks Bird Club that they named their journal *The Redstart.*

Specimens: WVU, CM, UMMZ, MCZ, USNM, MU, DMNH.

PROTHONOTARY WARBLER
Protonotaria citrea (Boddaert)

Status: Uncommon to fairly common local summer resident; rare spring migrant outside of breeding range.

Spring: In the Eastern Panhandle, the Prothonotary Warbler is often on the nesting territories in the last third of April, but in the southwest its arrival is not usual until early May. There are very few records of migrant Prothonotaries away from the nesting range, but a few spring records come from Hancock, Ohio, Hampshire, Summers, Mercer, and Monongalia Counties. Most of these records are in late May. Unlike some other warbler species, this one is rarely found in habitats other than the wooded swamps similar to its breeding areas. A rare exception is of a bird picked up dead after colliding with a window at Blackwater Falls State Park, Tucker County.

First-seen Spring Dates: Wood County, 5 May; Cabell-Mason Counties, 9 May.

Summer: There are definite nesting records from Jefferson, Wood (Shields and Shields, 1948), Mason, Kanawha, and Cabell Counties. Most of these nests have been found in early to mid-May, so the late May records mentioned under spring migration may represent birds not far from their nesting habitat. There are other summer records from Hampshire, Pendleton, Pocahontas (Cranberry Glades), Summers, Nicholas, Gilmer, and Wayne Counties, but most of these are of isolated birds. There are two June records for Ritchie County.

The Prothonotary Warbler nests in hollow trees, almost always over, or at least near, a pool of stagnant water. The greatest population in the state is found along the Shenandoah River in Jefferson County where the spring floods leave pools of standing water along the banks. The nests have been in wooded swamps in Wood and Mason Counties. One nest in Jefferson County, however, was on a hillside some distance from the water (Hall, 1967).

Fall: This species is almost unknown during fall migration. However, there are two rather late records: Clay County, 29 November, and Marion County, 10 October.

Specimen: MU. The dead bird found in Tucker County was examined by several ornithologists, including the author, but this specimen was later inadvertently destroyed. Doan (1888) claimed to have collected one in fall in Upshur County, but as with his other records this one must be considered uncertain.

WORM-EATING WARBLER
Helmitheros vermivorus (Gmelin)

Status: Uncommon to common summer resident.

Spring: As with some other of our resident warblers, the Worm-eating Warbler is little known as a migrant. It may not sing much during migration, so most of the spring records are from the breeding areas. Arrival is generally in the last week of April.

First-seen Spring Dates: Kanawha County, 21 April; Cabell-Mason Counties, 24 April; Monongalia County, 3 May; Ohio County, 11 May; Wood County, 16 May.

Summer: The Worm-eating Warbler may nest in every county of the state, at least sparingly. It is not common below 300 m and is present in greatest numbers in the middle elevations between 300 and 750 m. It has nested as high as 1,100 m in the Cranberry Glades region, and has been seen in summer at close to 1,200 m on Shaver's Mountain, Randolph County, at the edge of the spruce forest. There are definite nesting records from Berkeley, Hampshire, Hardy, Preston, Monongalia, Marion, Pendleton, Pocahontas, Greenbrier, Lewis, Upshur, Braxton, Gilmer, Doddridge, Hancock, Ohio, Wirt, Summers, Fayette, Pleasants, Kanawha, and Wayne Counties.

The Worm-eating Warbler occurs in all types of mature deciduous forest, but is most common in the beech-maple forest. It also occurs in numbers in the oak-chestnut and the oak-pine forest on rather dry hillsides.

Breeding Populations: Breeding Bird Survey Routes have averaged 0.9 (2.9–0.1) birds per route on 17 routes. Twenty-seven Singing Male Censuses have averaged 30 males per 100 ha. Mature northern hardwoods, 610 m, Pendleton County, 99 males per 100 ha and 74 males per 100 ha; cove hardwoods-hemlock, 610 m, Preston County, 67 males; oak-hickory, 900 m, Greenbrier County, 49 males; and pole-sized oak woods, 900 m, Greenbrier County, 49 males.

Fall: As in the spring, little is known about the migration of the Worm-eating Warbler. After it stops singing in August it is seldom reported. The main migration seems to be in early September. In 24 years, 43 have been banded at A.F.M.O.

Last-seen Fall Dates: Cabell-Mason Counties, 13 September; Kanawha County, 16 September.

Specimens: CM, UMMZ, MCZ, DMNH.

SWAINSON'S WARBLER
Limnothlypis swainsonii (Audubon)

Status: Uncommon to fairly common, very local summer resident.

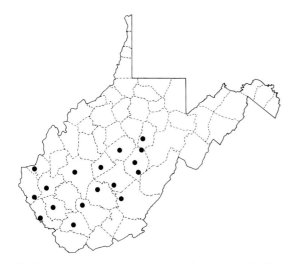

Fig. 8.   Breeding Season Records for Swainson's Warbler.

Spring: Swainson's Warbler is almost unknown as a migrant except in its breeding range where it generally arrives about the third week in April. It has been reported as a casual migrant in Summers County, and two were banded at Morgantown on 13 May 1972 and 4 May 1977 (but see below).

First-seen Spring Date: Kanawha County, 20 April.

Summer: The Swainson's Warbler nests in small pockets over a broad range in central and south-western West Virginia. This distribution has been discussed in detail by Hurley (1972). There are summer records from Upshur, Webster, Braxton, Nicholas, Greenbrier (near Rainelle), Fayette, Raleigh, Wyoming, Clay, Kanawha, Lincoln, Logan, Mingo, Wayne, and Mason Counties. Definite nesting records come only from Kanawha and Nicholas Counties.

The first record for the state was of one collected by Bibbee in 1924 at Cooper's Rock State Forest, Monongalia County, far from what is now considered to be its breeding range. It was not known from that area again for 48 years when the banding record mentioned above was made. However, in 1973 a reliable sight record (R. Strosnider) was made again at Cooper's Rock State Forest. It may be that there is a small unknown population there. Brooks (1944) had predicted that it might turn up in all counties west of the Alleghenies.

In the central part of the state, the favored habitat is dense rhododendron or mountain laurel thickets in the mixed hemlock-hardwoods forest (Legg, 1942). Such a thicket gives a dense habitat not unlike the canebrakes of the coastal plain where the bird is common. Rhododendron does not occur in the Kanawha County area and the surrounding counties. Here, the birds occupy steep ravines where the cover is cove hardwoods with dense understory of

spicebush (*Lindera benzoin*) and greenbrier (Sims and DeGarmo, 1948). Meanley (1971) has likened this habitat to a Coastal Plain floodplain forest on the side of a hill.

Populations: No formal population studies have been made of this species in the state, but Brooks and Legg (1942) reported 10 or 11 singing males within 1.5 miles in Nicholas County and Meanley (1971) counted seven males in a mile in Donnally Hollow, Kanawha County, but Hurley (op. cit.) says that an average of four pairs nest there.

Fall: Song ceases in late summer and the birds are essentially missing after this. Fall departure dates are few, but most birds must leave in mid-September. However, several were found in a TV tower kill at St. Albans, Kanawha County, on 7 October. If these were not local birds, it is difficult to say where they have come from.

Last-seen Fall Date: Kanawha County, 10 September.

Remarks: In the 1950s, the several steep ravines more or less perpendicular to the Kanawha River across from Charleston were prime Swainson's Warbler habitat, and bird students came from many places to see them there. Through the years, these ravines ("hollows") have gradually been built up with houses, and the birds have been forced out.

Specimens: WVUM, USNM, UMMZ. All of these specimens are referable to the Appalachian subspecies, *altus* Meanley and Bond.

OVENBIRD   *Seiurus aurocapillus* (Linnaeus)

Status: Fairly common to very common summer resident.

Spring: The Ovenbird migrates throughout the state, arriving in the last week of April. Its ringing song makes it immediately conspicuous on arrival.

First-seen Spring Dates: Kanawha County, 18 April; Cabell-Mason Counties, 18 April; Wirt County, 22 April; Summers County, 28 April; Brooke County, 30 April; Monongalia County, 2 May; Randolph County, 5 May; Ohio County, 6 May.

Summer: The Ovenbird nests in every county in the state. It is rare in those areas that have little mature hardwoods forest, but in regions of extensive mature forest it is often abundant. It is absent from the pure spruce forest and is found in reduced numbers in the spruce-northern hardwoods mixed forest, but in the pure northern hardwoods they are numerous even at elevations above 1,200 m. The requirements for a satisfactory nesting territory seem to be only a mature forest with rather open understory, and a good accumulation of dead leaves on the ground. There are definite nesting records from Jefferson, Berkeley, Hampshire, Hardy, Pendleton,

Preston, Monongalia, Tucker, Barbour, Randolph, Pocahontas, Greenbrier, Monroe, Nicholas, Upshur, Hancock, Ohio, Brooke, Wetzel, Wirt, Wood, Raleigh, Lincoln, and Kanawha Counties.

Breeding Populations: Breeding Bird Surveys have averaged 2.4 (7.0–0.10) birds per route. Fifty-eight Singing Male Censuses have averaged 67 males per 100 ha. Mature northern hardwoods, 1,200 m, Pocahontas County, 232 males per 100 ha, 166 males (this area was cutover and the population dropped to 42 males); mature hemlock-white pine, 670 m, Pendleton County, 148 males; virgin hardwoods-white pine, 580 m, Greenbrier County, 146 males; northern hardwoods, 1,100 m, Pendleton County, 131 males; mature pine-oak, 760 m, Greenbrier County, 123 males, 99 males; mixed hardwoods, 580 m, Nicholas County, 116 males; pole-sized oak woods, 710 m, Greenbrier County, 116, 106 males; mature deciduous forest, 700 m, Webster County, 116 males; young northern hardwoods, 1,140 m, Tucker County, 99 males; cutover hardwoods, 580 m, Nicholas County, 99 males; northern hardwoods, 1,100 m, Pendleton County, 99 males; and 27 other areas with more than 32 males per 100 ha (two males per study area).

Fall: The ovenbird migrates throughout the state during the fall, but is not often reported except by banders. Most of the records are through the month of September, although a few stragglers remain into early October. At A.F.M.O., 1,425 have been banded in 24 years, with a maximum year's count of 243.

Last-seen Fall Dates: A.F.M.O., 3 October; Cabell-Mason Counties, 28 September; Kanawha County, 10 September.

Remarks: Since about 1960, I have noticed a steady decrease in the number of Ovenbirds in Monongalia County. I do not know the cause, nor am I aware if a similar situation exists elsewhere. Increased parasitism by the cowbird may be a factor.

Specimens: WVU, USNM, MCZ, MU, DMNH.

NORTHERN WATERTHRUSH
Seiurus noveboracensis (Gmelin)

Status: Uncommon spring migrant; common local summer resident; uncommon fall migrant.

Spring: The Northern Waterthrush probably occurs in every county in the state during migration, but at most places it is uncommon. It migrates later than does the Louisiana Waterthrush and the peak of the migration is usually in mid-May, with the latest records coming in the last few days of May. It is seldom found away from water, and is most commonly found in the heavily wooded bottomlands of the larger streams.

First-seen Spring Dates: Kanawha County, 3 May; Wood County, 5 May.

Summer: In summer the Northern Waterthrush is found in numbers only in Preston, Tucker, Randolph, and Pocahontas Counties, mostly at elevations above 1,000 m, but occasionally as low as 750 m. There are single records from Webster County (Camp Caesar) and Greenbrier County (North Fork of the Cherry). The southernmost records are from the Cranberry Glades. Definite nesting records come only from Preston, Tucker, Pocahontas, and Randolph Counties.

The favorite habitat is the edge of mountain bogs or beside beaver ponds. It does occur along flowing streams, but is not limited to that habitat as is the Louisiana Waterthrush. The two waterthrushes often occur at the same locations, usually at about 900 m elevation. In these situations, the Louisiana is found along the smaller, faster streams, and the Northern along the larger streams and beside ponds. However, there is a population of Northern Waterthrushes that occurs in the young spruce forest, well away from any streams or ponds. One is led to surmise that it is wet vegetation—and in the nesting season the spruce forest is often quite wet from rains—that is the requirement for this species, and not streams or bogs as such.

Breeding Populations: Six Singing Male Censuses have averaged 36 males per 100 ha. Spruce-fir swamp, 1,110 m, Randolph County, 56 males; mixed spruce-deciduous, 910 m, Pocahontas, 52 males; young spruce forest, 1,350 m, Randolph-Pocahontas Counties, 49 males, 25 males, 25 males.

Fall: Both waterthrushes leave the state in late August and any bird found after 10 September is a straggler. There are a few records as late as the last of September. As in the spring, almost all of these records come from streamside locations, but I have a number of banding records from a dry hilltop in Monongalia County, and 34 have been banded at A.F.M.O.

Specimens: USNM, CM, MCZ, DMNH. Brooks (1944) listed two subspecies as occurring in the state, but more recent taxonomic opinions are in agreement that no subspecies should be recognized for this species.

LOUISIANA WATERTHRUSH
Seiurus motacilla (Vieillot)

Status: Fairly common summer resident.

Spring: The Louisiana Waterthrush is the earliest of the warblers to arrive, often appearing before the end of March and usually being at full numbers at most places by mid-April. It migrates throughout the state, except possibly at elevations above 900 m, but I have seen it as high as 1,000 m. During migration, it is found almost exclusively along wooded stream-bottoms in all forest types.

First-seen Spring Dates: Kanawha County, 29 March; Summers County, 29 March; Cabell-Mason Counties, 1 April; Ohio County, 10 April; Brooke County, 17 April; Monongalia County, 18 April; Randolph County, 20 April.

Summer: The Louisiana Waterthrush probably breeds in every county in the state, although definite nesting records come from only Jefferson, Berkeley, Hampshire, Hardy, Pendleton, Preston, Tucker, Randolph, Nicholas, Pocahontas, Greenbrier, Monroe, Monongalia, Hancock, Brooke, Ohio, Wetzel, Wirt, Ritchie, Gilmer, Doddridge, Upshur, Fayette, Raleigh, Kanawha, Lincoln, and Wayne Counties. It is common in all types of deciduous forest, but is strictly limited to streamside situations. It is not numerous in the lower river valleys, but at mid-elevations it sometimes is extremely common with densely packed more-or-less linear territories along suitable streams. The highest populations appear to be in the cool forests that contain some hemlock. It does occur in the northern hardwoods forest and at the very edge of the spruce forest at least as high as 1,050 m, and commonly to 900 m. In several places in the state, the two waterthrushes nest almost side by side.

Breeding Populations: Breeding Bird Surveys have averaged 1.7 (5.6–0.2) birds per route. Nineteen Singing Male Censuses have averaged 23 males per 100 ha. Mixed hardwoods-hemlock, 670 m, Tucker County, 81 males; hemlock-yellow poplar, 400 m, Fayette County, 67 males per 100 ha. All other areas had usually one or less male per study area.

Fall: The Louisiana Waterthrush leaves the state soon after the young are fledged, and this may be in late July. It is seldom seen at this time, and by mid-September nearly all have left the state. Only one has ever been netted at A.F.M.O.

Last-seen Fall Dates: Ohio County, 13 August; Cabell-Mason Counties, 15 September.

Specimens: USNM, MCZ, DMNH.

Kentucky Warbler *Oporornis formosus* (Wilson)

Status: Fairly common to common summer resident; uncommon fall migrant.

Spring: The Kentucky Warbler usually arrives in the last week of April, although in a retarded season it may not appear until early May. Its presence usually is made known by the loud ringing song, since like the other members of this genus it keeps to the denser underbrush and is seldom seen. It migrates throughout the western part of the state except at higher elevations, although birds of passage are not commonly seen.

First-seen Spring Dates: Kanawha County, 24 April; Cabell-Mason Counties, 25 April; Wood County, 30 April; Summers County, 30 April; Monongalia County, 2 May; Ohio County, 3 May; Brooke County, 4 May.

Summer: The Kentucky Warbler is one of the most characteristic breeding birds of the Western Hills Avifaunal Region. It probably nests in every county west of the mountains, but definite breeding records come only from Preston, Monongalia, Tucker, Randolph, Upshur, Lewis, Webster, Hancock, Brooke, Wetzel, Pleasants, Tyler, Gilmer, Braxton, Fayette, Summers, Lincoln, Kanawha, Wayne, and Cabell Counties. The preferred habitat is a densely wooded ravine, with ample ground cover and underbrush. It is perhaps most common in the southern or central hardwoods forest, but it also occurs in the oak-hickory and the oak-pine. It occasionally enters the northern hardwoods forest and in places is found at the edge of the mixed spruce-hardwoods forest up to about 1,100 m.

East of the mountains it is quite uncommon, although there are scattered records from Jefferson (nesting); Morgan (nesting); Hampshire (nesting); Hardy; and Pendleton Counties.

Breeding Populations: Breeding Bird Surveys have averaged 2.3 (7.6–0.2) birds per route. Twenty-four Singing Male Censuses have averaged 19 males per 100 ha. Mixed hardwoods, 580 m, Nicholas County, 82 males; mature hardwood forest, 300 m, Kanawha County, 67 males; mixed hardwoods, 350 m, Wetzel County, 49 males; cove hardwoods, 670 m, Preston County, 49 males; mixed hardwoods, 250 m, Wayne County, 47 males; and upland oak-hickory forest, 400 m, Kanawha County, 43 males per 100 ha.

Fall: The Kentucky Warbler is often not reported in fall. It is silent and keeps well hidden in the dense foliage of autumn. Most birds will depart in early September, and all will be gone by the last week of the month.

Last-seen Fall Dates: Cabell-Mason Counties, 6 September; Kanawha County, 10 September.

Specimens: USNM, UMMZ, AMNH, MCZ, DMNH.

Connecticut Warbler *Oporornis agilis* (Wilson)

Status: Casual spring migrant; rare to uncommon fall migrant.

Spring: The Connecticut Warbler migrates fairly late, usually after mid-May, and is rarely seen in the open. The main migration route in the spring is up the Mississippi Valley, and there seem to be more records for the western part of West Virginia than the eastern. There are spring records from Jefferson (specimen), Monongalia (banded), Upshur,

Ritchie, Mason, Cabell, and Kanawha Counties. Both Bibbee (1929) and Brooks (1944) attribute three Ritchie County records to Brewster, but these are not mentioned in his account of the Ritchie County trip (1875). The species may well be more common than the few records would indicate, but there are so few dates that average first-seen dates are not meaningful.

Fall: In the fall, the Connecticut Warbler migrates south along the Atlantic Coast; consequently, West Virginia lies on the western edge of the flight path. Although at this time it is hard to locate—being silent and seldom leaving the dense undergrowth—it is not uncommon in some places. In recent years, banders have found them to be more common than had been thought earlier. In 24 years, 135 have been banded at A.F.M.O. and an average of two to three are banded each fall at Morgantown. There are other fall records from Cabell, Wood, and Kanawha Counties. A few arrive in late August, but they are most common through the last half of September with the latest departures in early October.

First-seen Fall Date: A.F.M.O., 11 September.
Last-seen Fall Date: A.F.M.O., 24 September.

Remarks: West Virginia lies outside of the normal migration path of this species, being too far east for the northbound flight and too far west for the southbound flight, so the species can only be considered a straggler. However, it probably is more common than most observers realize. Sight records in the spring must be taken with some reservation, since despite what the field guides indicate some female Mourning Warblers in the spring do have eye-rings, and may be misidentified as Connecticuts. Valid spring records should depend on the song or on birds carefully examined by banders, the wing-tail ratio and the wing formula being the only reliable characters.

Specimens: WVU, DMNH.

MOURNING WARBLER
Oporornis philadelphia (Wilson)

Status: Rare spring and fall migrant; locally common summer resident.

Spring: The Mourning Warbler is one of the late-arriving group of warblers and usually does not appear in the state before mid-May, with the peak of migration in the third week in May. As with other members of this genus, it usually stays well hidden in the dense underbrush, and seldom presents a decent view to the bird-watcher. This species, too, may be more common than is generally realized. As the spring season progresses, the males sing more and more, becoming more conspicuous. The Mourning Warbler probably occurs in every county in the spring.

First-seen Spring Dates: Kanawha County, 5 May; Cabell-Mason Counties, 7 May; Monongalia County, 19 May.
Last-seen Spring Date: Cabell-Mason Counties, 16 May.

Summer: The Mourning Warbler breeds in the mountain counties above 900 m. There are summer records from Preston (very spotty in distribution), Mineral, Grant, Tucker, Pocahontas, Randolph, Webster, and Greenbrier Counties (northern only). It is not common in the northern portion of this range, and oddly is very scarce on the Allegheny Front in Tucker County. The peak populations seem to be in the Cheat Mountain uplift in Randolph and Pocahontas Counties and there are definite nesting records only for those counties. In these places, Mourning Warblers occur in the openings of the spruce forest and the northern hardwoods forest. The favorite habitat seems to be a dense tangle of briars that have a few trees for singing perches. Once the trees grow so as to shade the area completely, the warbler may leave. It can be found on dry hillsides as well as on the edges of the mountain bogs such as Cranberry Glades if a suitable thick vegetation is present. It is often abundant along some of the U.S. Forest Service roads in the mountain areas.

Breeding Populations: Seven Singing Male Censuses have averaged 29 males per 100 ha. Young deciduous forest, 1,250 m, Randolph County, 42, 42 males; cutover mature northern hardwoods, 1,220 m, Pocahontas County, 42, 32 males per 100 ha.

Fall: The Mourning Warbler is almost unnoticed in the fall. It generally leaves the breeding ground in August although there are records on 20 September in Cabell County and 26 October in Monongalia County (banded).

Specimens: USNM, UMMZ, AMNH, OP, CM, DMNH.

COMMON YELLOWTHROAT
Geothlypis trichas (Linnaeus)

Status: Common spring and fall migrant; common summer resident.

Spring: The Yellowthroat arrives in the state in the last week of April and the migration continues until about mid-May. It occurs throughout the state at this time and is found in habitats typical of the nesting season.

First-seen Spring Dates: Kanawha County, 21 April; Wood County, 21 April; Cabell-Mason Counties, 22 April; Summers County, 23 April; Ohio County, 29 April; Monongalia County, 30 April; Brooke County, 3 May.

Summer: The Yellowthroat is one of the more numerous summer warblers, and it breeds throughout the state and at all elevations, right up to the highest mountains that offer suitable habitat. Definite nesting records come from Jefferson, Berkeley, Hampshire, Preston, Monongalia, Tucker, Randolph, Pocahontas, Greenbrier, Monroe, Nicholas, Webster, Hancock, Brooke, Ohio, Wetzel, Wirt, Wood, Gilmer, Braxton, Pleasants, Fayette, Mason, Lincoln, Kanawha, and Cabell Counties.

In many parts of its range, the Yellowthroat is characteristically found in marshlands, but in West Virginia it is more versatile. It does occur in the marshes and at the edges of mountain bogs, but it also commonly nests in old weedy fields, in weed-covered hillsides where the forest has been cut, and in many small clearings in the higher mountains. It is a common and a characteristic bird of the acres of "huckleberry" plants on the Allegheny Front. The Yellowthroat inhabitats all forest types in the state if they have suitable brushy-weedy fields present.

Breeding Populations: Breeding Bird Surveys have averaged 12.9 (28.3–2.0) birds per route. Twenty-five Singing Male Censuses have averaged 36 males per 100 ha. Wooded marsh, 975 m, Tucker County, 116 males; abandoned bottomland, 185 m, Mason County, 116 males; overgrown ravine with multiflora hedge, 350 m, Ohio County, 101 and 52 males; overgrown pasture, 360 m, Ohio County, 74 males (nine years later the species was barely present on this area); river bottom-wet meadow, 470 m, Tucker County, 67 males; brushy hilltop, 550 m, Nicholas County, 67 males; and brushy bottom, 210 m, Wetzel County, 49 males per 100 ha.

Fall: The fall migration of the Yellowthroat is rather inconspicuous, but occasionally very large numbers pass through the state. Most of this movement takes place throughout September, but a few stragglers are present in October. At A.F.M.O., 1,549 have been banded in 24 years with a peak year of 194.

Last-seen Fall Dates: Ohio County, 2 September; Kanawha County, 10 September; Cabell-Mason Counties, 27 September; A.F.M.O., 30 September.

Specimens: USNM, UMMZ, DMNH. Specimens collected in most of the state, including all the western part, as well as from Laneville, Tucker County, and Cheat Bridge, Randolph County, have been identified as the subspecies *brachydactylus* Swainson, while specimens from Charles Town and Leetown, Jefferson County, Baker and Lost City, Hardy County, and from Mineral County have been identified as *trichas.* Intermediate specimens have come from Lost City and from Cranesville, Preston County. These two subspecies should probably be synonymized (Lowery and Monroe, 1968).

HOODED WARBLER   *Wilsonia citrina* (Boddaert)

Status: Fairly common to common summer resident.

Spring: The Hooded Warbler arrives in the last third of April. It migrates throughout the state, except at high elevations. As a migrant, it is uncommon in the mountain valleys. It occurs in any mature wooded habitat at low elevations.

First-seen Spring Dates: Kanawha County, 19 April; Cabell-Mason Counties, 21 April; Wood County, 22 April; Summers County, 24 April; Monongalia County, 28 April; Randolph County, 1 May; Ohio County, 4 May.

Summer: The distribution of the Hooded Warbler in the state in many ways parallels that of the Kentucky Warbler. It is a common breeding bird of the mature deciduous forest in the Western Hills Avifaunal Region below 750 m. As with the Kentucky Warbler, it is partial to densely wooded ravines, and it occurs in all forest types. Populations are generally highest in oak-hickory or in oak-pine forest providing there is enough ground cover and understory. In the mountains it does occur, in lesser numbers, in the northern hardwoods forest at least as high as 1,100 m on Cheat Mountain in Randolph County, and perhaps to 1,200 m in the extreme south. However, it is missing from the mixed spruce-hardwoods and the pure spruce forest, and does not occur on the highest summits. East of the mountain system, it becomes uncommon and quite local in distribution. In this region, it is most common in the oak-pine forest. Definite nesting records come from Berkeley, Hampshire, Hardy, Pendleton, Randolph, Pocahontas, Tucker, Nicholas, Preston, Upshur, Braxton, Hancock, Wirt, Lincoln, and Kanawha Counties.

Breeding Populations: Breeding Bird Surveys have averaged 2.0 (7.0–0.1) birds per route. Forty Singing Male Censuses have averaged 43 males per 100 ha. Oak-pine, 180 m, Berkeley County, 116 males; mixed hemlock-hardwoods, 640 m, Nicholas County, 116 males; oak-hickory, 330 m, Wayne County, 106 males; oak-hickory, 900 m, Greenbrier County, 82 males, 67 males; upland oak-hickory, 400 m, Kanawha County, 84 males; cove hardwoods, 670 m, Preston County, 67 males; mature deciduous forest, 700 m, Webster County, 67 males; and cove and northern hardwoods, 690 m, Tucker County, 67 males.

Fall: As with most of the other warblers whose niche is largely in the lower story of the woodlands, Hooded Warblers are not commonly reported in the fall. Migration occurs mostly in late September and a few may remain until late October. In 24 years, 104 have been banded at A.F.M.O.

Last-seen Fall Dates: Kanawha County, 12 September; Cabell-Mason Counties, 22 September; A.F.M.O., 24 September.

Specimens: USNM, UMMZ, MCZ, DMNH.

WILSON'S WARBLER *Wilsonia pusilla* (Wilson)

Status: Rare to uncommon spring migrant; uncommon fall migrant.

Spring: The Wilson's Warbler probably migrates throughout the state, except possibly in the spruce forest. It is usually found in dense brush, either the undergrowth of an open, uncrowded, mature forest or a brushy cutover area. It seldom makes itself visible to the observer, and the song is very faint and inconspicuous. However, once an observer learns the song, he will find that the bird is more common than had been previously thought. Most records are in the second half of May, and stragglers may occur as late as the end of May.

First-seen Spring Dates: Kanawha County, 1 May; Cabell-Mason Counties, 2 May; Ohio County, 10 May; Monongalia County, 13 May; Wood County, 13 May.

Last-seen Spring Dates: Cabell-Mason Counties, 25 May; Ohio County, 27 May.

Fall: The Wilson's Warbler migrates through the state in larger numbers in fall than in spring, but it is silent at this time of the year and is seldom reported. It inhabits the dense vegetation and is seldom seen, but banding stations find them to be fairly numerous. At A.F.M.O., 590 have been banded over the years, with a peak number of 62 in one year. It generally passes through throughout September with a peak in the middle third of the month.

First-seen Fall Dates: A.F.M.O., 31 August; Cabell-Mason Counties, 18 September.

Last-seen Fall Dates: A.F.M.O., 28 September; Cabell-Mason Counties, 28 September.

Specimens: WVU, DMNH.

CANADA WARBLER *Wilsonia canadensis* (Linnaeus)

Status: Rare to fairly common spring migrant; common local summer resident; rare to uncommon fall migrant.

Spring: The Canada Warbler is one of the late migrants, not generally arriving until mid-May, although as with some other northern species the breeding birds may be on their nesting territories at high elevations before the migrants arrive in the lowlands. The peak of the migration is in the third and fourth week of May with a few stragglers present in early June. It migrates throughout the state, but is rare to uncommon throughout most of the western region. It appears to be most common just west of the main mountain system. At this time, they are found in almost any habitat that contains dense brush and a few taller trees.

First-seen Spring Dates: Summers County, 1 May; Cabell-Mason Counties, 2 May; Kanawha County, 5 May; Wood County, 13 May; Brooke County, 18 May; Ohio County, 23 May.

Last-seen Spring Dates: Kanawha County, 10 May; Cabell-Mason Counties, 22 May.

Summer: As a nesting bird in the state, the Canada Warbler is limited to the Allegheny Mountains Region. It is normally found in Preston, Tucker, Randolph, Pocahontas, and northern Greenbrier Counties, with definite nesting records from Preston, Randolph, Pocahontas, and Greenbrier Counties. There are also summer records from Hampshire (one report—no data given), Hardy (Lost River State Park), Monongalia (Cooper's Rock State Forest), Upshur (Hemlock and Adolph), and Fayette Counties. The breeding habitat is in brushy undergrowth particularly in openings, along roads, or under power lines. Good populations have also been found in the understory of the virgin spruce-northern hardwoods area in Randolph County. It occurs in the spruce forest and in the northern hardwoods. In Preston and Monongalia Counties, it penetrates the lower hardwoods forests, particularly in ravines choked with hemlock and rhododendron, and here is commonly found as low as 600 m; I have found them as low as 450 m in Monongalia County.

Breeding Populations: Thirteen Singing Male Censuses have averaged 31 males per 100 ha. Virgin northern hardwoods-red spruce, 1,250 m, Randolph County, 84, 59, 40, 32, 32, 32 males per 100 ha. Other areas had one male or less per study area.

Fall: The Canada Warbler is an early-fall migrant often appearing in the lowlands in late August and most are gone by mid-September. As with other warblers that live in the undergrowth, they are quite inconspicuous in fall. At A.F.M.O., only 187 have been banded in 24 years.

First-seen Fall Date: Cabell-Mason Counties, 11 September.

Last-seen Fall Date: A.F.M.O., 13 September.

Specimens: USNM, UMMZ, CM, DMNH.

YELLOW-BREASTED CHAT *Icteria virens* (Linnaeus)

Status: Common to very common spring migrant; common to very common summer resident; uncommon fall migrant.

Spring: The Yellow-breasted Chat usually arrives in the state in the last half of April and the peak of the migration is in early May. At this time, it is found in habitats similar to its breeding habitat throughout the state, even at the highest elevations.

First-seen Spring Dates: Cabell-Mason Counties, 15 April; Kanawha County, 24 April; Wood County, 27 April; Monongalia County, 1 May; Summers County, 1 May; Ohio County, 2 May; Brooke County, 2 May.

Summer: The Yellow-breasted Chat probably nests in every county in the state, but definite nesting records come only from Jefferson, Berkeley, Hampshire, Hardy, Pendleton, Preston, Monongalia, Tucker, Randolph, Greenbrier, Monroe, Marion, Upshur, Lewis, Braxton, Nicholas, Ohio, Marshall, Brooke, Hancock, Wetzel, Wirt, Wood, Ritchie, Pleasants, Raleigh, Fayette, Kanawha, Wayne, and Cabell Counties. It occurs in openings in the forest, particularly ones containing heavy growths of blackberries, in all forest types, even to the tops of the highest peaks in the spruce forest. At lower elevations, it occurs in abandoned fields, also favoring those with dense growths of *Rubus,* and almost any other bushy situation. It requires a few taller trees for singing perches, and favors open locust groves with dense understory, but the chats leave an area as soon as the canopy closes. While they do occur at the highest elevations, they are not numerous there and the largest populations occur below 600 m.

In the late 1970s, a marked population decline occurred throughout much of northern West Virginia.

Breeding Populations: Breeding Bird Surveys have averaged 15.6 (33.0–1.3) birds per route. Twenty-six Singing Male Censuses have averaged 47 males per 100 ha. Abandoned bottomland, 190 m, Mason County, 148, 131 males; overgrown pasture, 360 m, Ohio County, 123, 99, 62 males; oak-hickory forest, Fayette County, 99 males; brushy hilltop, 550 m, Nicholas County, 99 males; pine-oak woods, 180 m, Berkeley County, 67 males; brushy bottom, 210 m, Wetzel County, 49 males; and "Briar Patch," 600 m, Preston County, 49 males per 100 ha.

Fall: The chat leaves the breeding areas in mid-August, and it is most secretive and difficult to find during fall migration. It may well be more common than the few records indicate. Most birds are gone by mid-September.

Last-seen Fall Dates: Kanawha County, 12 September; Cabell-Mason Counties, 27 September.

Specimens: USNM, UMMZ, MCZ, DMNH.

Subfamily Thraupinae   TANAGERS

SUMMER TANAGER   *Piranga rubra* (Linnaeus)

Status: Fairly common to common local summer resident.

Spring: In the southern part of the state, which is in the main breeding range, the Summer Tanager arrives in the last week in April, but arrival is not usually until the first week in May at the northern edge of the range. In mid- to late May, a few wanderers may be found north of the breeding range, but usually these areas will have no records of this species.

First-seen Spring Dates: Cabell-Mason Counties, 22 April; Kanawha County, 24 April; Monongalia County, 7 May; Wood County, 8 May.

Summer: The Summer Tanager is common only in the southern portion of the Western Hills Region, particularly in the southern Ohio Valley. At Huntington it is more common than the Scarlet Tanager and at Charleston the two species are about equal in number. Farther north and east the Summer Tanager population decreases, and in the Ohio Valley it is rare north of Marshall County. It occurs in low numbers locally in Upshur, Barbour, Marion, and Monongalia Counties. I know of no records above 600 m. It is absent from the high mountain areas and from the mountain valleys, but it reappears in some numbers in the lower Potomac (as far up as Romney) and Shenandoah Valleys. There are definite nesting records from Jefferson, Berkeley, Upshur, Lewis, Wetzel, Ritchie, Wirt, Wood, Pleasants, Fayette, Lincoln, Kanawha, Wayne, and Cabell Counties.

The Summer Tanager occurs most commonly in oak-hickory woods, particularly those woodlots that are slightly open, perhaps lightly grazed, but it also is common in other aspects of the southern forests. Except in the lower Ohio Valley, the Summer Tanager is always less numerous than the Scarlet Tanager (see below), although it is not clear at this time what the habitat separation between the two species is, nor how much interspecific competition there is.

Populations: Breeding Bird Surveys have averaged 2.2 (10–0.2) birds per route on only 21 routes. Six Singing Male Censuses have averaged 29 males per 100 ha. Pine-oak, 180 m, Berkeley County, 32 males; oak-hickory, 330 m, Wayne County, 29 males; and oak-hickory, Fayette County, 25 males.

The ratio of *olivacea* to *rubra* in the Berkeley County study area was 42/32; in the Wayne County area it was 15/30; and in two other Wayne County studies it was 37/7 and 22/+. Breeding Bird Survey Counts gave ratios of *olivacea* to *rubra* of: Wayne County, 0.11; Putnam County, 0.60; Mason County (Arlee), 0.85; Kanawha County, 1.3; Jackson County, 1.36; Lincoln County, 1.40; Roane County, 1.5; and Mason County (Point Pleasant), 2.0. All other counts to the north and to the northeast had ratios exceeding 10.0 and in many cases the Summer Tanager was absent.

Fall: Most Summer Tanagers depart in late September or very early October, but there are some records as late as 15 October at Morgantown, 19 October at Huntington, and 26 November at South Charleston.

Last-seen Fall Dates: Kanawha County, 20 September; Cabell-Mason Counties, 12 October.

Remarks: In the northern part of the range, as in Monongalia County, most of the Summer Tanagers seen are second-year males usually in mottled red and green plumage, but occasionally one with a bright golden yellow plumage is found. This latter variety results from some failure in the normal hormone cycle that controls the feather color.

Specimens: WVU, OP, USNM, MCZ.

SCARLET TANAGER   *Piranga olivacea* (Gmelin)

Status: Fairly common to common summer resident.

Spring: The Scarlet Tanager migrates throughout the state and is found in any wooded habitat. It sings readily, even while migrating, and so is easily located, although it is more invisible in the treetops than the bright colors would lead one to believe. The first arrivals are in the last week of April, but the peak of migration is perhaps in the second week of May. During migration season, it often is very common, and on some days the woods seem to be full of tanagers. On occasion, it may be quite tame and is easily approached, often seeming to be exhausted after a long night's flight.

First-seen Spring Dates: Kanawha County, 20 April; Cabell-Mason Counties, 26 April; Ohio County, 26 April; Monongalia County, 30 April; Wood County, 30 April; Randolph County, 5 May; Summers County, 2 May; Brooke County, 3 May.

Summer: The Scarlet Tanager is found during the summer throughout the state in forested areas. It is uncommon in the southwestern part of the state near Huntington, but farther east the numbers increase. The greatest numbers occur in the oak-hickory forest, but it is found in all types of forest, except the pure spruce forest, although numbers in the pine forest are low. There are small populations in the mixed spruce-northern hardwoods forest above 1,200 m, but populations may be good on those mountains on which northern hardwoods occur at the summit. There are definite nesting records from Berkeley, Jefferson, Hampshire, Hardy, Pendleton, Preston, Monongalia, Randolph, Webster, Pocahontas, Greenbrier, Monroe, Mercer, Hancock, Brooke, Ohio, Wirt, Fayette, Lincoln, Kanawha, and Cabell Counties, although it probably nests in all counties.

Breeding Populations: Breeding Bird Surveys have averaged 5.0 (8.0–0.3) birds per route. Sixty-one Singing Male Censuses have averaged 24 males per 100 ha. Mature oak-hickory woods, 275 m, Wetzel County, 59 males; mature northern hardwoods, 610 m, Pendleton County, 57 males; upland oak-hickory forest, 395 m, Kanawha County, 57 males; virgin cove hardwoods, 550 m, Greenbrier County, 49 males; mature deciduous forest, 1,200 m, Pocahontas County, 49 males, 32 males; other areas had only two males per census plot.

Fall: The fall migration of the Scarlet Tanager occurs throughout September, with a few birds still present in early October. At this time of the year, the males have donned their dull winter plumage, and most observers will fail to find the species. At A.F.M.O., 274 have been banded in 24 years.

Remarks: The Scarlet Tanager is generally more common than the Summer Tanager, but see the remarks under that species.

Specimens: WVU, USNM, MCZ, GMS.

*WESTERN TANAGER   *Piranga ludoviciana* (Wilson)

Status: Hypothetical; accidental summer visitant.

Record: A Western Tanager was reported on 5 June 1944 near the junction of the Holly River with the Elk River in Braxton County by James Monroe (Monroe, 1945).

Specimen: None.

Subfamily Cardinalinae   CARDINAL GROSBEAKS

NORTHERN CARDINAL
        Cardinalis cardinalis (Linnaeus)

Status: Common to very common permanent resident.

Distribution: The Cardinal occurs throughout the state except at the highest elevations. It is not common in heavily forested areas, but is found in town residential areas, along roadsides, in rural farm areas, and in other greatly disturbed habitats having thick brush cover. In the Allegheny Mountains, it occurs in the valleys of the upper Greenbrier and other streams to at least 900 m, although they are not numerous there. I have found it in summer at

Cheat Bridge, Randolph County, at about 1,080 m, and in winter along U.S. Highway 250 east of Bartow on the ascent of Allegheny Mountain well above 900 m. In late fall and winter, large congregations sometimes occur and at some winter feeding stations groups of 20 to 30 at one time are not uncommon, and occasionally more are seen.

The Cardinal undoubtedly nests in every county.

Populations: Breeding Bird Surveys have averaged 23.5 (45.5–2.5) birds per count, but these counts are biased toward listing large numbers of Cardinals and other roadside birds. Thirty-eight Singing Male Censuses have averaged 29 males per 100 ha. Mixed upland habitat, 250 m, Mason County, 82 males; brushy field, 690 m, Ohio County, 62 males; deciduous woodland, 305 m, Ohio County, 49 males; mixed hardwoods, 690 m, Ohio County, 49 males; pine-oak, 180 m, Berkeley County, 49 males; hemlock-yellow poplar, 400 m, Fayette County, 49 males; second-growth pine, 240 m, Hampshire County, 49 males; and overgrown field, 690 m, Ohio County, 49 males. Ten winter population counts, all but one in Ohio County, have averaged 42 males per 100 ha (131–7). Christmas Count data (birds per party hour) are: statewide, 6.02 (11.10–3.85); Charleston, 5.25 (9.13–1.64); Charles Town, 3.96 (7.80–2.15); Huntington, 8.85 (26.67–4.35); Inwood, 4.09 (6.90–1.40); Mason County, 9.76 (23.33–2.78); Ona, 6.47 (25.0–2.48); Pendleton County, 2.96 (4.89–1.20); Lewisburg, 4.04 (5.17–1.40); and Hampshire County, 5.10.

Remarks: The Cardinal is the official State Bird of West Virginia.

Specimens: USNM, MCZ, GMS, MU.

ROSE-BREASTED GROSBEAK
Pheucticus ludovicianus (Linnaeus)

Status: Fairly common spring and fall migrant; fairly common to common local summer resident.

Spring: The Rose-breasted Grosbeak arrives in the last week of April and is usually quite conspicuous. It sings during migration, and its call note is distinctive. At this season, it may be found in any mature woodland, often in fair numbers. Outside of the breeding range, the grosbeak departs in mid-May and all are gone by the last week in May. It occurs throughout the state, but seems to be uncommon east of the mountains.

First-seen Spring Dates: Cabell-Mason Counties, 19 April; Ohio County, 26 April; Kanawha County, 27 April; Wood County, 1 May; Monongalia County, 2 May; Brooke County, 10 May.

Last-seen Spring Dates: Cabell-Mason Counties, 13 May; Kanawha County, 20 May.

Summer: The Rose-breasted Grosbeak is another of the species whose breeding range in the

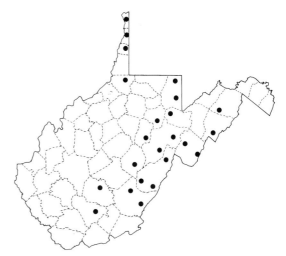

Fig. 9. Breeding Season Records for the Rose-breasted Grosbeak.

state is almost entirely confined to the Allegheny Mountains, except that it does nest in the Northern Panhandle from Wheeling north. There is also a summer report from Hundred, Wetzel County. It also occurs at some of the higher elevations in Raleigh County. In the mountain areas, it is found above 600 m and occurs to the highest summits if these are covered with hardwoods forest. While it occurs in small numbers in the mixed spruce-hardwoods forest, the prime habitat is pure northern hardwoods, but it occurs in other deciduous forests. It enters in a wooded area when the trees are quite young, and remains until the climax stage is reached. There are summer records from Hancock, Brooke, and Ohio Counties in the Northern Panhandle and Hampshire (rare), Pendleton, Preston, Monongalia, Hardy (rare), Tucker, Randolph, Barbour, Webster, Pocahontas, Greenbrier (north only), Fayette, and Raleigh Counties, with nesting records only from Hancock, Ohio, Pendleton, Preston, Randolph, and Pocahontas Counties.

Populations: Breeding Bird Surveys have averaged 0.5 (1.0–0.2) birds per count on 10 routes. Fifteen Singing Male Censuses have averaged 22 males per 100 ha. Young northern hardwoods, 1,100 m, Tucker County, 74 males; young deciduous forest, 1,250 m, Randolph County, 49 males.

Fall: The fall migration of the Rose-breasted Grosbeak occurs throughout September with the peak in the last two weeks. At A.F.M.O., large numbers cross the mountain; on some days hundreds pass by, although relatively few are netted. In 24 years, 872 have been banded with a peak year's count of 120. Elsewhere it is common, but often not conspicuous.

First-seen Fall Dates: Kanawha County, 5 September; A.F.M.O., 10 September; Cabell-Mason Counties, 26 September.

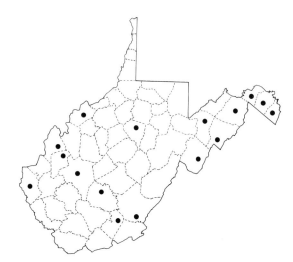

Fig. 10.   Breeding Season Records for the Blue Grosbeak.

Last-seen Fall Dates: Kanawha County, 10 September; A.F.M.O., 6 October.
Specimens: USNM, CM, MU.

*BLACK-HEADED GROSBEAK

Pheucticus melanocephalus (Swainson)

Status: Casual winter visitant.
Records: First recorded in the state in 1971 when one was present at a feeder in South Charleston from 6 March to early April (Koch, 1971). Another was seen at St. Albans from 14 April to 21 April 1971. One was present at the same location in St. Albans from 15 to 17 January 1972 (G. Hurley). One and possibly two birds were present for a short time in January 1974 at South Charleston. One came to a feeder in Triadelphia 9 December 1979 (Conrad and Conrad, 1980).
Remarks: Some systematists would consider this species to be conspecific with the Rose-breasted Grosbeak, and indeed the two interbreed in the Great Plains states. A hybrid has been found in western Pennsylvania (Parkes, 1968) and birds in this area should be carefully examined for this possibility. Color paintings of hybrids were published as a frontispiece to volume 84 (1974) of *The Wilson Bulletin.*
Specimen: No specimen has been collected, but a photograph is on file at the National Photoduplicate File at Laurel, Maryland.

BLUE GROSBEAK   *Guiraca caerulea* (Linnaeus)

Status: Rare to uncommon, local summer resident; casual to rare wanderer in spring.
Spring: There are a few spring records, mostly in late May, from Monongalia, Barbour, Kanawha, Putnam, and Cabell Counties. There are too few data to make any statements about the spring migration in the state.

Summer: The distribution of the Blue Grosbeak, primarily a southern species, presents a picture that is not easily summarized. It occurs sparsely and in scattered localities in the valleys of the Shenandoah River, Back Creek, and the Great Cacapon River in the Eastern Panhandle. It also occurs locally in the South Branch Valley in Hampshire County, near Moorefield, Hardy County, and at a few places in Pendleton and Grant Counties.

In recent years, one or more Blue Grosbeaks have spent the summer in the Middle Ridge area of Kanawha County. There are also June records from Lewis County (Jackson's Mill), Greenbrier County (one present at Lewisburg all summer in 1972), Fayette County, Braxton County, Summers County, Wood County, and Wayne County. In the summer of 1976, there was a notable influx of grosbeaks in Putnam and Mason Counties (Kiff et al., 1977).

The favored habitat in the eastern part of the state is in orchards or in the low brushy trees (e.g., *Crataegus*) that line the country roads. In Kanawha County, they frequent old fields that are growing back to a mixture of brush and scrubby young trees.

Nests have been found in Jefferson, Berkeley, Morgan, Mineral, Hampshire, Mason, Kanawha, and Putnam Counties, and fledged young birds have been reported from Grant and Kanawha Counties.
Fall: There are a number of late-July and August records that probably represent post-breeding wandering. These come from Brooke, Ohio, Lewis, Cabell, and Kanawha Counties. The bird that summered in Greenbrier County departed on 12 August.
Remarks: Persons unfamiliar with this species occasionally misidentify Indigo Buntings that seem to look as large as Blue Grosbeaks. In my experience, the two are quite distinctive in appearance and one would "know" when he was seeing a Grosbeak.
Specimens: CM, OSM.

INDIGO BUNTING   *Passerina cyanea* (Linnaeus)

Status: Common to very common summer resident.
Spring: The Indigo Bunting arrives in the last week of April or the first week of May, with a peak of migration in the second week of May. At this time, it occurs throughout the state, except possibly in the pure spruce forest.
First-seen Spring Dates: Cabell-Mason Counties, 14 April; Wood County, 21 April; Ohio County, 27 April; Kanawha County, 28 April; Summers County, 1 May; Monongalia County, 4 May; Randolph County, 5 May; Brooke County, 7 May.
Summer: The Indigo Bunting probably nests in every county of the state, although definite nesting records come only from 24 counties representing all parts of the state. The Indigo Bunting is a bird of

"edge" situations and it nests either at the edges of woodlands, particularly along road rights-of-way or in abandoned fields that are growing up to widely scattered brush or trees. Because of the affinity of buntings for roadside situations, a roadside count through the state would probably list the Indigo Bunting as the most abundant bird in the state. Given the right stage in plant succession, the Indigo Bunting occurs in all forest types except the pure spruce. A cutover pure northern hardwoods area in Pocahontas County at 1,220 m supported a good population for a few years.

Populations: Breeding Bird Surveys have averaged 35.2 (70.0–12.6) birds per count, showing the relationship between this species and roadsides. Forty-seven Singing Male Censuses have averaged 38 males per 100 ha. Cutover oak-hickory, 900 m, Greenbrier County, 131 males; apple orchard, 180 m, Berkeley County, 109 males; oak-hickory, Fayette County, 84 males; river bottom-wet meadow, 470 m, Tucker County, 82 males; pine-oak, 180 m, Berkeley County, 74 males; second-growth hardwoods, 900 m, Pocahontas County, 57 males; deciduous woodland, 300 m, Ohio County, 57 males; cutover white pine-hemlock, 610 m, Pendleton County, 57 males; mixed hardwoods, 360 m, Ohio County, 57 males; and 10 studies with 49 males per 100 ha ranging from 210 to 1,100 m.

Fall: Most Indigo Buntings depart in late September with stragglers into mid-October. Some evidence from banding data at Morgantown suggests that the local birds leave much earlier and the October birds may be migrants from the north. Only 24 Indigo Buntings have been banded in the 24 years of operation at A.F.M.O. Since the bunting is abundant on the lower slopes of the Allegheny Front, they apparently do not migrate along the ridge. In Greenbrier County, very heavy flights have been noted from 15 August to 15 September.

Last-seen Fall Dates: Kanawha County, 30 September; Monongalia County, 5 October; Cabell-Mason Counties, 6 October.

Specimens: USNM, MCZ, GMS.

*PAINTED BUNTING   *Passerina ciris* (Linnaeus)

Status: Hypothetical.

Record: One was seen at Blue Jay, Raleigh County, on 27 April 1979 (James, 1980).

Remarks: The male of this species is so distinctively marked that misidentification is very unlikely. Brooks (1944) mentions that John Burroughs reported seeing one on the Cheat River in Tucker County, but he relegated this record to the hypothetical list.

Specimen: None.

DICKCISSEL   *Spiza americana* (Gmelin)

Status: Irregular but occasionally fairly common spring migrant; uncommon local summer resident; rare winter visitant.

Spring: The Dickcissel is usually a late migrant, and may not arrive until the last third of May. Records from early June may also represent migrants. At this time of the year, they may be found in almost any kind of open field except closely grazed pasture. Brushy intrusions or nearby electric lines are needed for singing perches. There are spring records from Jefferson, Berkeley, Morgan, Grant, Monongalia, Wood, Jackson, Hancock, and Kanawha Counties. Early April records from Morgantown probably are of wintering birds, and a 3 June 1936 record from Cranesville, Preston County (M. Brooks), may be a belated migrant.

Summer: The Dickcissel breeds, or has bred, sparingly in open fields in several parts of the state, but they may not be present at any one place in every year, and indeed may not nest in the state in every year. There are summer records over the years from Jefferson, Berkeley, Mineral, Hampshire, Pendleton, Randolph, Monroe, Brooke, Ohio, Monongalia, Upshur, Pleasants, Jackson, Putnam, and Mason Counties. To my knowledge, no actual nesting has been established. The favorite habitat of the Dickcissel is an alfalfa field, particularly if there are a few singing perches nearby, but they also are found sparingly in weed-grown fields.

Breeding Populations: A Breeding Bird Survey Route in Jefferson County has averaged 1.8 birds per count, listing the species on eight of nine years.

Fall: Fall records come mostly in late August and September, with a few into October. The Dickcissel has been reported in fall from Mason, Greenbrier, and Kanawha Counties.

Winter: The Dickcissel occasionally winters in small numbers, particularly where feeders are available, and often in the company of flocks of House Sparrows. There are November records from Mason County and winter records from Randolph, Greenbrier, Monongalia, and Kanawha Counties.

Remarks: It is not certain that the Dickcissel is closely related to the Cardinaline finches, and it is thought by some authorities to belong to the subfamily Icterinae.

Specimens: UMMZ, S, CM.

*Green-tailed Towhee

Pipilo chlorurus (Audubon)

Status: Accidental winter visitant.

Record: A Green-tailed Towhee came to the feeding station at the home of the B. Kiffs of Ona, Cabell County, from 19 December 1957 to 17 April 1958. During this time it was seen by many observers and its identity fully confirmed (Edeburn et al., 1960).

Rufous-sided Towhee

Pipilo erythrophthalmus (Linnaeus)

Status: Very common summer resident; uncommon to very common winter resident.

Spring: In areas where they do not winter, the towhee first appears in early March, but the arrival varies widely from year to year depending on the season's weather. The peak of migration occurs in late March and early April. During this time, it occurs throughout the state in almost any brushy habitat.

First-seen Spring Dates: Ohio County, 3 March; Brooke County, 11 March; Summers County, 14 March; Monongalia County, 22 March; Wood County, 27 March.

Summer: In summer, the towhee occurs throughout the state at all elevations. There are definite nesting records from only about half of the counties, but it undoubtedly nests in all 55 counties. The favored habitat is the brushy second-growth stage of all forest types. Overgrown fields, partially cutover woodlots, and rural roadsides are favorite nesting sites. The towhee was abundant in the second-growth red spruce on Gaudineer Knob when the trees were about 30 years old, but had disappeared from the area when the trees were 50 years old.

Breeding Populations: Breeding Bird Surveys have averaged 15.4 (36.3–4.3) birds per route. Sixty-nine Singing Male Censuses averaged 37 males per 100 ha. Brushy hilltop, 550 m, Nicholas County, 148 males; abandoned bottomland, 185 m, Mason County, 116 males; oak-hickory, Fayette County, 116 males; cutover white pine-hemlock, 600 m, Pendleton County, 108 males; young red spruce, 1,350 m, Randolph-Pocahontas Counties, 91 males, 82 males, 67 males; overgrown field, Ohio County, 86 males; cutover mature hardwoods, 1,200 m, Pocahontas County, 82 males, 57 males; overgrown field, 290 m, Morgan County, 82 males; northern hardwoods, 1,100 m, Pendleton County, 82 males,

57 males; overgrown pasture, 365 m, Ohio County, 74 males; pine-oak, 180 m, Berkeley County, 74 males; abandoned bottomland, 185 m, Mason County, 67 males; cutover hardwoods, 580 m, Nicholas County, 67 males; and cutover oak-hickory, 900 m, Greenbrier County, 67 males.

Fall: The towhee leaves the nesting grounds in the north and in the mountains in the last week of September or the first week of October. As in the spring, the exact dates vary from year to year with the weather. Throughout October there is some influx of birds from the north.

Winter: In southern and southwestern West Virginia, the towhee is a common to very common winter resident, and in this region it probably is better classified as a permanent resident. The numbers present fluctuate from winter to winter. They are common in the valleys east of the mountains, but in the mountains and in the north they become quite uncommon. In some winters they may be present in good numbers in Monongalia County, but they become absent or rare in the Northern Panhandle counties. Christmas Count data (birds per party hour) are: statewide, 0.77 (1.44–0.13); Charleston, 2.98 (5.08–0.54); Charles Town, 0.02 (0.11–0); Huntington, 1.74 (5.33–0.38); Inwood, 0.15 (0.75–0); Mason County, 0.51 (0.91–0); Ona, 1.11 (3.31–0); Pendleton County, 0; Lewisburg, 0.14 (0.62–0); and Hampshire County, 0.02.

Specimens: USNM, WVU, CM, MU. All breeding specimens are referable to the eastern subspecies *erythrophthalmus.* An individual of the subspecies *arcticus* Swainson, the "Spotted Towhee," was present at a feeder and then banded at Charleston in the winter of 1968–69.

*Brown Towhee   *Pipilo fuscus* (Swainson)

Status: Hypothetical; accidental fall visitant.

Record: In October 1969, R. and M. Brooks saw a Brown Towhee at their home in Morgantown, but such a single sighting does not qualify for the accepted list.

Specimen: None.

Bachman's Sparrow

Aimophila aestivalis (Lichtenstein)

Status: Rare migrant; rare local summer resident; accidental winter visitant. Formerly more widespread and more numerous.

Spring: In the last 20 to 30 years, there have been very few spring records of Bachman's Sparrow in the state, but records have come from Berkeley, Monongalia, Nicholas, Kanawha, Mason, and Cabell Counties. Most of these reports are in late April to mid-May.

Summer: The Bachman's Sparrow was first recorded in West Virginia in Wood County in 1903 (E. A. Brooks, 1912), and soon thereafter it spread and became common in much of central West Virginia. M. Brooks (1938a) summarized the range as being practically all of the territory northeast of the Kanawha River and west of the Alleghenies. Outside of this area there were a few records from Berkeley, Hardy, Ohio, Kanawha, Cabell, and Wayne Counties. Other than one record from Ohio County, there were no records in the Ohio Valley north of Wood County. The species reached its maximum abundance in the period between 1915 and 1922, and then began to decline and withdraw from parts of its range. In 1944, Brooks wrote that "it . . . now seems definitely on the increase." From the late 1930s to the early 1950s, this seemed to be true, since there were many reports from the old range in central West Virginia and now there were numerous reports from the Eastern Panhandle. However, at no time during this period did it reach its former abundance. In the late 1950s, another decline started and by the 1960s and early 1970s it had almost disappeared, at least from those areas covered by bird students. In 1961, there was a report from Preston County and one from Berkeley County. In the 1960s, there were three reports during the breeding season from Charleston and one from Mason County. In 1972, one pair was present at Charleston all summer and young birds were seen (A. Shreve). However, at the present time, there is no place known in the state at which one can confidently expect to find this species.

In its years of abundance, Bachman's Sparrow occurred as high as 900 m in Randolph County, but its usual range was from about 300 to 600 m. The most common habitat was in abandoned fields, beginning to grow up in brush, and containing a few shrubs and small trees. Almost invariably it occurred on steep hillsides, and usually an erosion gully was present in the territory.

Fall and Winter: Fall records have been mostly in late October and early November and have come largely from Cabell, Mason, and Kanawha Counties. There are December records from Huntington in 1948 and 1953.

Remarks: There is no apparent reason for the disappearance of this species from its former range. Suitable habitat would seem to exist in abundance in the area where it was once numerous.

Specimens: WAL, DMNH.

AMERICAN TREE SPARROW

Spizella arborea (Wilson)

Status: Fairly common winter visitant.

Spring: Migrant Tree Sparrows from the south appear in early March to augment the wintering flocks. Most of the tree sparrows have departed from the state by the end of March, although a few may remain into the first week of April.

Last-seen Spring Dates: Monongalia County, 21 March; Cabell-Mason Counties, 4 April.

Fall: The first Tree Sparrows of the season usually appear about the first of November, although an unusually early severe cold wave in late October may bring them to the state. During November, they are quite numerous, but populations decline in December as migrants leave for the south.

First-seen Fall Dates: Cabell-Mason Counties, 30 October; Kanawha County, 1 November; Monongalia County, 12 November.

Winter: The Tree Sparrow winters throughout the state except at the very high elevations. They avoid the heavily forested areas, and are usually found in open brush-covered areas, weed-filled abandoned fields, and suburban gardens and yards. At any one place, the numbers from year to year are highly variable and in some years it may be quite scarce, but in others large numbers will occur. It may be that in some winters only a small portion of the normal wintering population comes as far south as West Virginia. Banding data do indicate, however, that many birds return to the same site winter after winter.

Winter Populations: Seven Winter Bird Counts averaged 140 birds per 100 ha. An overgrown pasture in Ohio County had 417 birds per 100 ha and 382 birds per 100 ha on two different counts. Two other Ohio County counts had 77 and 69 birds per 100 ha. Christmas Count data (birds per party hour) are: statewide, 2.19 (6.11–0.95); Charleston, 0.34 (0.56–0); Charles Town, 3.41 (10.89–0.86); Huntington, 0.64 (2.02–0); Inwood, 3.89 (28.0–0.20); Mason County, 3.36 (6.67–0.57); Ona, 1.15 (3.75–0); Pendleton County, 0; Lewisburg, 1.10 (2.22–0); and Hampshire County, 4.04.

Specimens: WVU, USNM, GMS.

CHIPPING SPARROW *Spizella passerina* (Bechstein)

Status: Common summer resident; casual winter visitant.

Spring: The Chipping Sparrow arrives in the second half of March in the southern part of the state and during this period is found almost anywhere except in the heavily forested areas. At times, large flocks are seen working their way along fence rows or woodland edges.

First-seen Spring Dates: Cabell-Mason Counties, 19 March; Kanawha County, 29 March; Brooke County, 1 April; Ohio County, 6 April; Monongalia County, 8 April.

Summer: The Chipping Sparrow nests throughout the state at all elevations. The favored habitats include suburban yards and gardens, orchards, abandoned fields containing scattered small trees, and roadsides. The Chipping Sparrow also occurs in mature deciduous woodlands if the trees are well spaced and the ground cover is sparse, as in a grazed woods. They are common in the fields growing up to red cedar that occur in the eastern part of the state, and also in the pine forest, but I have not found them in the spruce forest.

Breeding Populations: Breeding Bird Surveys have averaged 21.3 (60.1–3.0) birds per route. Nine Singing Male Censuses averaged 23 males per 100 ha. Apple orchard, 180 m, Berkeley County, 49 males; overgrown pasture, 365 m, Ohio County, 49 males; and mixed park habitat, Ohio County, 25 males.

Fall: The Chipping Sparrow begins to migrate in late September and the peak of migration continues through October, with some still present in early November. As in the spring, large flocks sometimes occur during this period. Apparently it does not migrate along the mountains since only seven have been caught at A.F.M.O. in 24 years.

Winter: There are scattered winter records from Kanawha, Cabell, and Summers Counties, but the species must be classified as casual at this season.

Specimens: WVU, USNM, GMS.

*CLAY-COLORED SPARROW

Spizella pallida (Swainson)

Status: Accidental.

Record: A Clay-colored Sparrow was present near Green Spring, Hampshire County, on 28 and 29 April 1977, and was seen by several people, some of whom had had previous experience with the species, and was photographed. Attempts to net the bird were in vain (Lanham, 1977).

Specimen: None. Photographs taken of this bird were later lost.

FIELD SPARROW

Spizella pusilla (Wilson)

Status: Common summer resident; fairly common to common local winter visitant.

Spring: The Field Sparrow begins to arrive in the state in late March, but the main migration is in early April. At this time the numbers moving through the state must be very large, although the

average observer will not notice many of the migrants. Occasionally, sizeable flocks are seen, but the real numbers present are evident only from banding operations. It migrates throughout the state.

First-seen Spring Dates: Cabell-Mason Counties, 14 March; Monongalia County, 22 March; Summers County, 22 March; Kanawha County, 1 April; Brooke County, 1 April; Ohio County, 3 April.

Summer: The Field Sparrow is present during the summer throughout the state and probably nests in every county. It occurs at all elevations where there is suitable habitat and in all forest types. Brushy fields, overgrown pastures, and woodland edges are the favored locations. As one drives along the roads in the state, one will seldom be out of earshot of singing Field Sparrows, except in the heavily forested regions. The preferred nesting areas will have trees 4–6 m high, widely spaced, and interspersed with grass and weeds.

Breeding Populations: Breeding Bird Surveys have averaged 14.4 (36.3–3.0) birds per route. Twenty-three Singing Male Censuses averaged 46 males per 100 ha. Overgrown pasture, 365 m, Ohio County, 124 males; overgrown pasture, 290 m, Hardy County, 99 males; abandoned bottomland, 186 m, Mason County, 99 males; overgrown field, 290 m, Morgan County, 92 males; brushy hilltop, 550 m, Nicholas County, 82 males; and apple orchard, Berkeley County, 67 males.

Fall: The Field Sparrow migrates in October and, as in spring, large numbers sometimes pass through the state. These flocks are found in situations similar to the breeding habitat, but the birds are often inconspicuous. At A.F.M.O., 114 have been banded in 24 years.

Last-seen Fall Dates: Cabell-Mason Counties, 22 October; Monongalia County, 13 November.

Winter: At least a few Field Sparrows may winter in any part of the state except in the higher mountains. In the north the numbers are low, but in southwestern West Virginia the Field Sparrow is as common in winter as in summer. Christmas Count data (birds per party hour) are: statewide, 0.62 (1.47–0.27); Charleston, 0.94 (2.61–0.29); Charles Town, 0.04 (0.10–0); Huntington, 0.44 (1.11–0); Inwood, 0.05 (0.36–0); Mason County, 1.22 (2.91–0); Ona, 1.52 (5.08–0.15); Pendleton County, 0.03 (0.11–0); Lewisburg, 0.04 (0.06–0); and Hampshire County, 0.54.

Specimens: WVU, USNM, GMS, MU.

VESPER SPARROW

Pooecetes gramineus (Gmelin)

Status: Fairly common migrant; uncommon to fairly common summer resident; uncommon local winter resident.

Spring: Migrating Vesper Sparrows appear in

small flocks during the last half of March or early April, depending on the general weather conditions. It migrates throughout the state, but is found only in open grassy situations that have a few small trees nearby. Such habitat is uncommon through much of the state. Migrating flocks commonly work along brushy fence rows.

First-seen Spring Dates: Kanawha County, 23 March; Cabell-Mason Counties, 7 April; Monongalia County, 4 April; Ohio County, 4 April; Randolph County, 6 April.

Last-seen Spring Date: Kanawha County, 1 May.

Summer: The Vesper Sparrow is present in summer, at least sparingly, in all parts of the state except the extreme southwest. It does summer in Mason and Cabell Counties, is rare in Lincoln County, and seems to be known only as a migrant in Kanawha County. The habitat consists of open grassy areas of considerable extent, so it becomes very uncommon in the heavily forested areas since small clearings are inadequate. It does occur at high elevations in those places where the mountains are topped by grassy fields, but east of the mountains it is scarce and hard to find. The greatest numbers seem to be in the Northern Panhandle and a band down through Monongalia and Marion Counties south to the center of the state. In this area there are many hilly, grassy pastures containing scattered trees that make a prime habitat for the Vesper Sparrow. It is also fairly common in recently planted orchards where the trees are still too small to bear fruit. There are definite nesting records from Jefferson, Berkeley, Hardy, Pendleton, Pocahontas, Greenbrier, Monroe, Preston, Marion, Upshur, Wirt, Hancock, and Ohio Counties, but it may nest in all of the northern counties.

Breeding Populations: The Vesper Sparrow has appeared on only 15 Breeding Bird Survey routes where the average has been 1.1 (4.7–0.2) birds per route. A Singing Male Census in a commercial apple orchard in Hampshire County had 32 males per 100 ha. A brushy field in Ohio County had 12 males and a grass-sown strip-mined area in Raleigh County had 17 males per 100 ha. Thirteen censuses on recovered strip mines in Preston County (approx. 580 m) averaged 27.8 males per 100 ha (91.5–4.8). One mine over five years had 4.8, 16.9, 50.6, 45.8, 48.2 males per 100 ha, respectively.

Fall: During late October and early November, the Vesper Sparrow migrates throughout the state where there is suitable habitat. At times, it may become quite numerous. The principal habitat in fall is weed-grown fields and brushy fence rows. Fourteen have been banded at A.F.M.O. in 24 years.

Last-seen Fall Date: Cabell-Mason Counties, 1 November.

Winter: The Vesper Sparrow winters in small numbers in Cabell, Mason, and Kanawha Counties in almost every year. North and east of this area numbers are usually less and they are more irregular, but a few winter as far north as Upshur County.

Specimens: USNM, GMS.

LARK SPARROW   *Chondestes grammacus* (Say)

Status: Rare and very local summer resident; casual migrant. Formerly much more numerous and more widely distributed.

Spring: There are only a few scattered records of the Lark Sparrow in the last 25 years: Ashton, Mason County, on 7 May 1950 and 4 May 1952 (H. Land); Ohio County, 12 May 1957; Charleston, May 1953 (G. Hurley); Valley Chapel, Lewis County, 17 April 1966 (N. Gluck); Putnam County, spring 1968 (L. Kiff); and one banded at Lewisburg, Greenbrier County, on 25 April 1969 (C. O. Handley). Brooks (1938b) gives arrival dates in Upshur County in the last days of April during the second and third decades of this century when they were much more common.

Summer: At present, the Lark Sparrow apparently can be found in only two widely separated localities in the state. There is a small but regular population in the North Fork Valley and the South Branch Valley in Pendleton County, which probably extends sparingly through Hampshire County into parts of Mineral County. There is also a small population in Jackson County, which may extend to neighboring areas. There was a July record for Kanawha County in 1972. A nest has been found in Pendleton County and a nest was found in Hampshire County in 1982. Young birds recently out of the nest have been seen in Pendleton, Mineral, Hardy, and Jackson Counties within the last few years. The Lark Sparrow frequents hillside pasture fields, particularly overgrazed ones, and abandoned fields with grassy-weedy growth. Rocky outcrops or other similar areas seem necessary for display purposes.

Fall: In recent years there are scattered fall records from Tucker, Kanawha, Mason, and Cabell Counties. Most of these records come in the last half of September to mid-October.

Past Distribution: Brooks (1938b) summarized the distribution and other information about the Lark Sparrow in the central Appalachians up to the time of writing. The Lark Sparrow was first discovered in the state in 1900 in Upshur County. In the next few years, it increased in numbers and spread to most parts of the western half of the state. By the 1930s, it had been found in most of the counties west of the Allegheny Mountains except those along the Ohio River. The greatest numbers were reached in the Monongahela drainage system. There were only two records from east of the mountains and they apparently did not occur above about 900 m in the mountains. From about 1910 to 1925, they were abundant throughout this area. After 1925, the populations began to decline and the summer range in the state contracted. By 1944 (Brooks, 1944), there had been reported recent records from Berkeley, Jefferson (specimen), Hampshire, Mineral, Barbour, Upshur, Brooke (specimen), Ohio, Marshall, and Gilmer Counties. The decline continued through the 1940s and 1950s, but during this time there were reports from Jackson, Braxton, Barbour, Kanawha, Cabell, and Mason Counties. In the years of abundance, Brooks reported many nests from Upshur County, but the latest nest west of the mountains that I have a record of was in Preston County in 1946 (Parsons, 1946).

Specimens: USNM, CM.

Lark Bunting

Calamospiza melanocorys Stejneger

Status: Casual winter visitant.

Records: The Lark Bunting was first reported in the state by W. R. DeGarmo at Kanawha City, Kanawha County, on 1 January 1949. This bird was later collected by C. O. Handley, Sr., on 3 January. A Lark Bunting was present at a feeder at the home of M. Brooks at Morgantown in December 1966 and January 1967. Handley banded one at Lewisburg, Greenbrier County, on 9 May 1967 and another there on 31 October 1969. The latter bird remained at Lewisburg until 7 May 1970.

Remarks: In winter plumage, Lark Buntings look amazingly like House Sparrows with too many white feathers; consequently, they may be overlooked.

Specimen: USNM.

Savannah Sparrow

Passerculus sandwichensis (Gmelin)

Status: Fairly common migrant; fairly common local summer resident; casual winter visitant.

Spring: A few Savannah Sparrows may arrive in mid-March, but the peak of migration is in the early part of April. It is apparently more common as a migrant in the lower Ohio and Kanawha Valleys than elsewhere. The normal habitat is in broad, open, grassy areas such as meadows, lightly grazed pastures, airports, or golf courses, but in migration the flocks may follow along fence rows with light brush or appear at the edges of marshes.

First-seen Spring Dates: Cabell-Mason Counties, 7 March; Kanawha County, 1 April; Monongalia County, 6 April; Wood County, 20 April; Ohio County, 23 April.

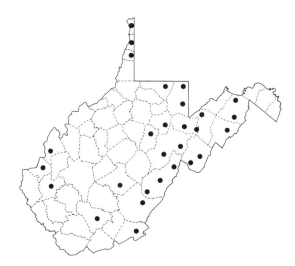

Fig. 11.   Breeding Season Records for the Savannah Sparrow.

Last-seen Spring Dates: Kanawha County, 1 May; Cabell-Mason Counties, 4 May.

Summer: The main summer range of the Savannah Sparrow is along the axis of the Alleghenies from Preston County in the north, south to northern Greenbrier County and occasionally Monroe County. In this area, it inhabits grassy mountaintops up to the highest elevations, and the meadowlands in the intermountain valleys as well. There are summer records from Preston, Hampshire (two locations), Pendleton (Franklin, Germany Valley), Hardy, Tucker, Grant, Pocahontas, Randolph, Greenbrier, and Monroe Counties. This mountain range extends some distance from the main mountains to the lowlands of Hardy County, where it is uncommon, to Monongalia County, where it is common on grassy hilltops and to the valley of the Buckhannon River in Upshur and Lewis Counties; Belington, Barbour County; Mt. Nebo, Nicholas County; County Airstrip, Braxton County; and Beckley, Raleigh County. There is also a breeding population of the Savannah Sparrow in the Northern Panhandle from Hancock to Ohio Counties and here, too, it occupies grassy hilltops. Summer birds have also been found near Ashton, Mason County; Mercer's Bottom, Cabell County; and in Lincoln County. There are definite nesting records from Ohio, Monongalia, Preston, Upshur, Tucker, Pocahontas, Raleigh, and Cabell Counties.

Breeding Populations: Only eight Breeding Bird Survey routes have reported the Savannah Sparrow with an average of 0.8 (1.63–0.2) bird per route. The only Foray Singing Male Census to record a population of Savannah Sparrows was a brushy field in Tucker County at 945 m with a population of 10 males per 100 ha. Seventeen censuses on recovered strip mines in Preston County (approx. 580 m) averaged 32.0 males per 100 ha (105.2–6.1). Ungrazed mine—105.2, adjoining grazed area—15.0. One mine over five years had 19.3, 21.7, 57.8, 57.8, 33.7 males per 100 ha, respectively.

Fall: There is a good migration of Savannah Sparrows through the state in late September and early October. At some places, it becomes quite common in weed-filled fields. A few are caught each year in September at A.F.M.O. with the 24-year total being 44.

First-seen Fall Dates: Cabell-Mason Counties, 11 September; Kanawha County, 15 September.

Last-seen Fall Dates: Kanawha County, 1 October; Cabell-Mason Counties, 23 October.

Winter: The Savannah Sparrow is occasionally reported on the Christmas Counts from Cabell and Kanawha Counties, and a few winter in those areas from time to time. One was banded at Elkins on 7 February 1975 (E. Olliver).

Specimens: WVU, CM, USNM, UMMZ, GMS. The breeding subspecies in the state has been identified as *mediogriseus* Aldrich by J. Aldrich. The subspecies *savanna* may migrate through the state, but all West Virginia specimens need a careful re-evaluation. The northeastern subspecies *labradorius* Howe has been taken in Cabell and Monongalia Counties during migration.

GRASSHOPPER SPARROW

Ammodramus savannarum (Gmelin)

Status: Uncommon to fairly common migrant and summer resident.

Spring: The Grasshopper Sparrow arrives in the last week of April or the first week in May. It migrates throughout the state but is never found away from grasslands, usually areas of taller grass, or fields with more weeds than the areas frequented by Savannah Sparrows. If the Grasshopper Sparrow did not sing, it would be completely overlooked. As it is, the weak high-pitched song is out of the hearing range of many people.

First-seen Spring Dates: Greenbrier County, 17 April; Cabell-Mason Counties, 19 April; Kanawha County, 25 April; Ohio County, 27 April; Brooke County, 1 May; Monongalia County, 3 May.

Summer: The Grasshopper Sparrow may nest in any suitable grassland in every part of the state. In most places it is uncommon, partly because of the lack of suitable habitat. They become common in a few places, such as the broad valleys of the eastern part of the state and on many of the recovered strip mines. The highest record I have is at the Sinks of Gandy, Randolph County, at about 1,200 m, and Brooks (1944) reported them as high as 1,300 m in Pocahontas County. There are definite nesting records from Jefferson, Berkeley, Preston, Upshur, Greenbrier, Brooke, Ohio, and Cabell Counties.

Breeding Populations: Breeding Bird Surveys have averaged 4.4 (24.9–0.3) birds per route on 22 routes. Seven Singing Male Censuses on Forays averaged 22 males per 100 ha. Overgrown ravine, Ohio County, 40 males, 12 males; another Overgrown ravine, Ohio County, 35 males, 17 males; and commercial apple orchard, Hampshire County, 35 males. Twenty censuses on recovered strip mines in Preston County (approx. 580 m) averaged 54.9 males per 100 ha (203.6–15.0). One mine over five years had 21.7, 28.9, 79.5, 74.7, and 60.2 males per 100 ha, respectively.

Fall: Because of its retiring nature and the dense habitat, the Grasshopper Sparrow is almost unreported in the fall. The migration takes place in late September or early October. Dead birds have been picked up at a TV tower in Kanawha County on 7 October, and at a fire tower in Monongalia County on 19 October. There are some November records but no reports of wintering.

Remarks: Since the mid-1960s, the Grasshopper Sparrow populations in the eastern United States, including West Virginia, have been declining. The two Singing Male studies from Ohio County cited above may illustrate this, since in each case the first figure given was the population in 1962 and the second in 1965. The cause of this decline is not known.

Specimens: USNM, CM, GMS.

HENSLOW'S SPARROW

Ammodramus henslowii (Audubon)

Status: Rare to uncommon migrant; erratic uncommon summer resident.

Spring: The Henslow's Sparrow arrives in the last half of April, but the distribution is so erratic and the bird is so inconspicuous that it may be overlooked. Nowhere is it very common.

First-seen Spring Dates: Ohio County, 28 April; Monongalia County, 2 May.

Summer: The Henslow's Sparrow was not known from the state until 1935 when one was collected near Masontown, Preston County, in October of that year. An earlier record (Hicks, 1938) from Mason County is unacceptable in light of present knowledge. In the next few years, a few scattered nesting colonies were located: Mineral County (Brooks and Haller, 1936); Grant County (Stony River Dam) (M. Brooks, 1937); and specimens were taken in Monroe County. Since the 1930s, summer records have come from Jefferson, Berkeley, Hampshire, Preston, Monongalia, Tucker, Morgan, Randolph, Pocahontas, Greenbrier, Marion, Barbour, Upshur, Hancock, Ohio, Wetzel, Wood, Ritchie, Putnam, Jackson, and Mason Counties. Definite nesting records come only from Mineral, Grant, Preston, and Ohio Counties.

In some years, the Henslow's Sparrow is quite common locally, and then vanishes within a year or two. They prefer fields with growths of orchard grass or a rank weedy growth. Such fields usually are suitable for the sparrow for only a few years; then they usually are plowed or developed a brushy growth. In either case, the Henslow's Sparrow leaves.

The Henslow's Sparrow has been most numerous in the northern part of the state, and in the 1950s and early 1960s it reached a high level of population, but in the 1970s it declined greatly.

Breeding Populations: Five Breeding Bird Surveys have averaged 0.4 bird per route with a maximum count of four. An overgrown ravine in Ohio County had a population of 12 males per 100 ha.

Fall: Fall migration probably occurs in early October but there are very few records.

Specimens: WVU, UMMZ, GMS. Specimens from Ohio and Preston Counties have been identified as being the nominate subspecies while specimens from Mineral and Monroe Counties are nearest the eastern subspecies *susurrans,* but are clearly intermediate between the two subspecies (Haller, Hall).

LE CONTE'S SPARROW

Ammodromus leconteii (Audubon)

Status: Accidental fall visitant.

Records: Sutton and Haller saw one in the Beech Bottom Swamp, Brooke County, on 8 September 1936 and Sutton collected one there on 19 September 1936 (Sutton, 1937).

Specimen: CM.

SHARP-TAILED SPARROW

Ammodromus caudacutus (Gmelin)

Status: Accidental fall visitant.

Records: Haller collected two on 20 September 1948 and one on 1 October 1948 at Beech Bottom Swamp, Brooke County (Haller, 1949). Since that time, there have been three additional sight records: Silver Lake, Preston County, 26 September 1953; Kingwood, Preston County, fall 1953 (L. Schwab) (Brooks, 1953); and McClintic Wildlife Station, Mason County, 10 November 1965 (Shreve, 1966).

Specimens: CM. All three specimens are referable to the inland subspecies *nelsoni* Allen.

FOX SPARROW

Passerella iliaca (Merrem)

Status: Uncommon to common spring and fall migrant; rare to fairly common local winter visitant.

Spring: The Fox Sparrow is one of the earliest migrant sparrows to arrive, usually appearing in late March or early April, and practically all are gone by mid-April. It is highly variable in numbers, and may be missing at any given locality in any one year. It migrates throughout the state, but is most common in the southwest while in the north it becomes rather rare. As with other sparrows, it most commonly occurs in weed-filled fields, brushy fields, and along fence rows.

In 1964, there were three reports in mid-June from Pocahontas County (Cass, Wanless, and Cranberry Glades), but there is no evidence that these were any other than stragglers.

First-seen Spring Dates: Brooke County, 23 March; Summers County, 25 March; Kanawha County, 27 March.

Fall: The Fox Sparrow arrives in late October or early November, and is much more common than in spring. I have encountered flocks of 30 to 50 at 1,160 m on the Allegheny Front, and such flocks occasionally are seen elsewhere. It migrates throughout the state, but as in spring it may be missing from a given location in any one year. Only 28 have been banded at A.F.M.O., but operations there usually cease before the main movement of the Fox Sparrow.

First-seen Fall Dates: Cabell-Mason Counties, 12 October; Monongalia County, 26 October; Kanawha County, 1 November.

Last-seen Fall Date: Monongalia County, 16 November.

Winter: The Fox Sparrow is a regular wintering bird in small numbers in the southwestern part of the state where it frequents similar situations to the other sparrows. Elsewhere it may occur irregularly in small numbers except at the higher elevations. The Huntington Christmas Count has averaged 0.11 (0.26–0) bird per party hour, but all other counts have averaged less than 0.1.

Specimens: WVU, USNM, MU.

SONG SPARROW

Melospiza melodia

Status: Common permanent resident; more numerous during migration season.

Spring: There are very heavy movements of migrating Song Sparrows through the state in early and mid-April. At this time, the wintering birds are augmented by those summer residents that do move south. The real intensity of the spring migration is evident only at banding stations where large numers are caught. The presence of wintering birds makes it impossible to assign migration dates.

Summer: The Song Sparrow nests in every county, and at all elevations, although it is not very common above 900 m. It is found in a variety of habitats, but favorite sites are brushy fields, particularly near streams, lightly wooded streamsides, and suburban situations.

Populations: Breeding Bird Surveys averaged 27.5 (43.5–5.0) birds per route. Sixteen Singing Male Censuses averaged 48 males per 100 ha. Overgrown ravine with multiflora hedge, 353 m, Ohio County, 101, 87 males; overgrown pasture, 365 m, Ohio County, 99 males; abandoned bottomland, Mason County, 81 males, 67 males; brushy field, 365 m, Ohio County, 25 males; and shallow pond-cattail marsh, 185 m, Mason County, 49 males.

Fall: As in spring, large numbers of Song Sparrows arrive from the north in mid-October. This flight continues until early November. When these transients leave, a few of the nesting birds, particularly in the north, leave with them.

Winter: The Song Sparrow winters in some numbers throughout the state, except at the highest elevations. Some of these may be winter visitants from the north, but a great many of them, as shown by banding, are the same birds present in summer. They occur in the same habitats as in summer: suburban yards and gardens, weed-filled fields, particularly those with water nearby, and the edges of woodlands if water is near. In the north, perhaps most of the wintering birds are associated with farms or suburban dwellings. Christmas County data (birds per party hour) are: statewide, 3.02 (4.72–1.64); Charleston, 3.15 (6.62–1.64); Charles Town, 2.06 (4.89–0.57); Huntington, 3.76 (10.33–1.19); Inwood, 2.84 (7.08–1.72); Mason County, 4.15 (10.25–1.39); Pendleton County, 0.24 (0.44–0); Lewisburg, 0.95 (1.83–0.20); and Hampshire County, 0.21.

Specimens: USNM, CM, MCZ, UMMZ, GMS. The breeding subspecies throughout most of the state is *euphonia* Wetmore, the type locality of which is Cranberry Glades, Pocahontas County. A specimen taken in Halltown, Jefferson County, in 1898 has been identified as the subspecies *melodia*. This subspecies may breed in the extreme eastern part of the state, but the population there may be intermediate. Migrant *melodia* was taken at Arnett, Raleigh County, and intermediates were taken in Nicholas and Barbour Counties in May (Wetmore, 1937). It is entirely possible that *euphonia* is not separable from *melodia*.

LINCOLN'S SPARROW

Melospiza lincolnii (Audubon)

Status: Uncommon spring and fall migrant; accidental winter visitant.

Spring: The Lincoln's Sparrow is generally an inconspicuous bird during migration, since it does not sing and remains concealed in the underbrush. Prior to the use of banding techniques, Lincoln's Sparrow was considered to be quite rare, and the average bird watcher usually finds it to be so. However, at banding stations it is found to be somewhat more common than previously thought. It seems to be more numerous in the northern part of the state, on the western slope of the mountains, but nothing is known of the migration in the mountains themselves. The northward movement usually peaks in the first week in May, but a few may be present until the last week of May.

First-seen Spring Dates: Kanawha County, 1 May; Monongalia County, 4 May.

Last-seen Spring Dates: Kanawha County, 8 May; Monongalia County, 21 May.

Fall: The Lincoln's Sparrow probably is more common in fall than in spring, but it is even more inconspicuous at this season, and most of our records come from banding stations. The only mention of large numbers is by Sutton (1937) who found them from 10 to 100 daily from 18 to 23 September at Bethany, Brooke County. The migration starts in mid-September and continues to mid-October. At A.F.M.O., a total of 97 have been banded in 24 years with a maximum count of 15 in one year. Several were found among the dead birds killed on the Chestnut Ridge Fire Tower, Monongalia County, on 18 October 1975.

First-seen Fall Dates: Monongalia County, 26 September; Cabell-Mason Counties, 1 November; A.F.M.O., 18 September.

Winter: There are two winter records: Ona, Cabell County, on 1973 Christmas Count (L. Kiff) and Wheeling on 18 January 1972 (N. Laitsch).

Specimens: WVU, USNM, UMMZ, GMS.

SWAMP SPARROW   *Melospiza georgiana* (Latham)

Status: Fairly common spring and fall migrant; common to very common local summer resident; fairly common to common local winter resident.

Spring: The Swamp Sparrow begins to migrate in mid-April and the movement is generally finished by early May, although a few stragglers may remain until late May. As a migrant, it is almost exclusively confined to wooded swamps similar to the nesting areas, but occasionally it is found away from water. I have banded several at my hilltop banding station in Monongalia County. The Swamp Sparrow probably migrates throughout the state, but suitable habitat is very localized.

First-seen Spring Dates: Cabell-Mason Counties, 11 March; Kanawha County, 5 April; Preston County, 17 April.

Last-seen Spring Dates: Kanawha County, 1 May; Cabell-Mason Counties, 8 May.

Summer: The Swamp Sparrow breeds in the mountain swamps, near beaver ponds, and along some of the mountain streams in the Allegheny

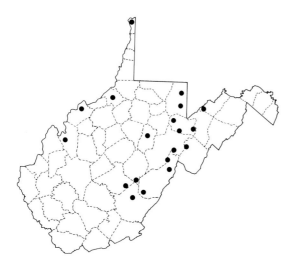

Fig. 12.   Breeding Season Records for the Swamp Sparrow.

Mountains Region, Preston County (Cranesville, Lake Terra Alta), and south through Mineral, Tucker, Grant, Pendleton, Pocahontas, Randolph, Nicholas, Webster, Greenbrier, and Fayette Counties. Most of these records are from above 700 m. Away from the mountains, there are summer records from near Buckhannon, Upshur County, near Middlebourne, Tyler County, Jackson County, Wood County, and Hancock County. Nests have been found in Preston, Tucker, Randolph, Pocahontas, and Jackson Counties. As a nesting bird, the Swamp Sparrow usually is limited to swampland, usually alder swampland, which may or may not contain some cattails, but the Jackson County site was a wet grassy area.

Fall: A few Swamp Sparrows are caught flying along the Allegheny Front at A.F.M.O. in September, but these may a part of the local nesting population. A total of 175 have been banded there, but most of these were caught on the plateau in moist woods. The main movement in fall takes place in October with a few present in November. As in spring, it is almost always found only in swampy situations, but a few (more than in spring) may be found in upland situations.

First-seen Fall Date: Cabell-Mason Counties, 10 October.

Last-seen Fall Date: Cabell-Mason Counties, 11 October.

Breeding Populations: The Swamp Sparrow has occurred on only one Singing Male Census, a wooded swamp at 975 m in Tucker County where the population was 148 males per 100 ha.

Winter: A few Swamp Sparrows may winter from about Upshur County south, as well as in the South Branch Valley in Hampshire County. The greatest wintering populations are in Mason County, particularly at the McClintic Wildlife station, and near Ona, Cabell County. Christmas Count data

(birds per party hour) are: statewide, 0.23 (0.58–0.04); Charleston, 0.02 (0.05–0); Charles Town, 0; Huntington, 0.22 (1.26–0); Inwood, 0; Mason County, 0.73 (2.22–0.09); Ona, 0.58 (1.32–0.03); Pendleton County, 0; Lewisburg, 0.03 (0.11–0); and Hampshire County, 0.01.

Specimens: USNM. Breeding specimens have been identified as the eastern subspecies *georgiana,* and this subspecies migrates through the eastern part of the state. The only migrant specimens from Cabell, Mason, and Mercer Counties are the western subspecies *ericrypta* Oberholser, but *georgiana* may also migrate through there.

WHITE-THROATED SPARROW
Zonotrichia albicollis (Gmelin)

Status: Common to very common spring and fall migrant; common to very common winter visitant; accidental summer resident.

Spring: With the first warm days of March, the winter-resident White-throated Sparrow begins to sing, and it is conspicuous for the rest of the spring. The wintering numbers are augmented by migrants from the south in the last few days of March, and from then until mid-April very large numbers of White-throats are present throughout the state. Numbers decrease in late April and stragglers may be present until mid-May. The long, drawn-out migration of this species contrasts with the brief movement of the White-crowns.

First-seen Spring Date: Ohio County, 22 March.

Last-seen Spring Dates: Kanawha County, 1 May; Wood County, 4 May; Monongalia County, 7 May; Ohio County, 8 May; Cabell-Mason Counties, 9 May.

Summer: Brooks (1944) reported that he and Haller had seen White-throats at Cranesville, Preston County, on 3 June 1936, but no definite nesting was established in the state until Ganier and Buchanan (1953) found two nests in two different bogs near Terra Alta, Preston County, in June of 1952. In subsequent years, these bogs were flooded by beaver activity and no more summer records of White-throated Sparrows came from there. On 1 August 1970, G. Breiding and B. Vossler saw juveniles at what is now the Alpine Lake Resort, also near Terra Alta. In June 1973, A. Shreve and C. Katholi saw a singing male near Spruce Knob Lake, Pendleton County. A bird that was almost certainly simply a late straggler was found near Beckley, Raleigh County, in June 1975 by D. Conrad.

Fall: The vanguard of the White-throated Sparrow migration often arrives in the last week of September, but more usually they appear in early October. The principal migration occurs after the first strong cold front in October, and from then until early November White-throated Sparrows, together with juncos, perhaps are the most common passerine birds seen in the state. They occur in brushy fields and along fencerows as well as in open woodlands throughout the state. I have found large numbers in the brushy areas atop the Allegheny Front at A.F.M.O., but rather few have been banded there (548 in 24 years) indicating that they use a different path than the warblers.

First-seen Fall Dates: A.F.M.O., 26 September; Monongalia County, 3 October; Cabell-Mason Counties, 3 October; Kanawha County, 6 October.

Winter: The White-throated Sparrow winters at low elevations in all parts of the state. In the Eastern Panhandle and in the central and southern parts of the state, it is very numerous, and may be one of the two most common species. In the north— for example, Monongalia County—it was formerly quite rare in winter, but since the late 1960s the wintering numbers there have increased greatly. The White-throated Sparrow commonly occurs in second-growth woodlands, brushy fields, suburban yards, and gardens. A good place to look for them is in a tangle of grapevines in an open woodlot.

Winter Populations: Four winter surveys, all in Ohio County, averaged nine birds per 100 ha. Christmas Count data (birds per party hour) are: statewide, 2.41 (5.05–0.89); Charleston, 3.65 (12.00–1.54); Charles Town, 2.19 (8.00–0.33); Huntington, 3.47 (7.78–2.00); Inwood, 1.98 (4.20–0.70); Mason County, 3.48 (10.41–0.11); Ona, 2.84 (8.00–0.59); Pendleton County, 0; Lewisburg, 0.55 (1.88–0); and Hampshire County, 0.13.

Specimens: WVU, USNM, MCZ, GMS.

WHITE-CROWNED SPARROW

Zonotrichia leucophrys (Forster)

Status: Uncommon to very common spring and fall migrant; fairly common to common local winter visitant.

Spring: In areas where it does not winter, the White-crowned Sparrow makes its appearance in the last week in April and the main migration is in early May. The migration period often is very short with the sparrows being present at a given location for only a few days. During the peak of migration, they commonly may be heard singing and are often in good numbers. Good-sized flocks move through, even at high elevations. While it migrates throughout the state, the movement often is quite localized and none appear in some places. By the third week in May, almost all are gone from the state.

First-seen Spring Dates: Summers County, 20 April; Brooke County, 25 April; Monongalia County, 3 May.

Last-seen Spring Dates: Cabell-Mason Coun-

ties, 7 May; Kanawha County, 8 May; Ohio County, 8 May; Monongalia County, 14 May.

Fall: The White-crowned Sparrow does not appear in the fall until about the second week in October. As in the spring, the migration period may be short; for example, at Morgantown I have sometimes found them present for only one or two days. The fall migration routes are also rather localized and the bird is rare to uncommon at many places. The Ohio and Kanawha Valleys seem to be particularly favored migration routes and numbers are often high there. At A.F.M.O., only 66 have been banded in 24 years, but most of them pass through after operations at A.F.M.O. have ceased.

First-seen Fall Dates: Cabell-Mason Counties, 13 October; Monongalia County, 21 October.

Last-seen Fall Date: Monongalia County, 22 October.

Winter: The White-crowned Sparrow is quite common in winter in the Eastern Panhandle and in some areas in southwestern West Virginia, the most noteworthy place being the McClintic Wildlife Station in Mason County. In winter, there apparently is a strong relation between the occurrence of White-crowns in numbers and the presence of multiflora rose hedges. Good numbers also winter in Greenbrier County and lesser numbers in Kanawha and Cabell Counties as well as the other southern counties. They are rarely found in winter in the central and northern parts of the state.

Winter Populations: A pine-oak woods in Berkeley County had seven birds per 100 ha, and two Ohio County areas had only four birds per 100 ha. Christmas Count data (birds per party hour) are: statewide, 2.22 (3.76–0.33); Charleston, 0.22 (0.46–0); Charles Town, 2.07 (10.00–0.20); Huntington, 0.29 (0.72–0.07); Inwood, 2.52 (9.44–0.13); Mason County, 7.12 (27.78–1.96); Ona, 0.71 (1.80–0.20); Pendleton County, 0; Lewisburg, 2.88 (6.11–0); and Hampshire County, 0.

Specimens: WVU, USNM, MU. The common subspecies found in the state is *leucophrys,* but there are banding records for the western subspecies *gambelii* Nuttall from Monongalia, Mason, and Greenbrier Counties. These last were identified largely by the color of the lores only, and since no other characters were reported and no specimens exist the subspecies *gambelii* is of uncertain occurrence in the state.

HARRIS' SPARROW   *Zonotrichia querula* (Nuttall)

Status: Casual winter visitant.

Records: A Harris' Sparrow was present at a feeder at the home of M. Brooks in Morgantown from January to May 1965, during which time it was observed by most of the bird students in the area. One was present at a feeder in Charleston from 25 March to 8 April 1967, during which time it was trapped and banded (Shreve, 1968). Other records are: Mason County, May 1949; Cabell County, 30 November 1966 and 28 December 1970 (collected); Berkeley County, 1967; Brooke County, 26 February 1971; Kanawha County, 9 November 1967 and winter of 1968-69; and Lewis County, 10 February 1973.

Remarks: The Harris' Sparrow is to be watched for at winter feeding stations as well as in wintering flocks of White-throated and White-crowned Sparrows.

Specimen: WFVZ.

DARK-EYED JUNCO   *Junco hyemalis* (Linnaeus)

Status: Very common to abundant spring and fall migrant; common to very common local summer resident; very common to abundant winter visitant.

Spring: In the last part of March, new juncos arrive from the south to join the already large flocks that have been present all winter. At this time of the year, they are found throughout the state usually in the brushy-weedy fields, scrubby woodland, and in small numbers in mature woodland if there is undergrowth. By the third week in April, almost all of these birds are gone and the latest stragglers are seen around the first of May.

Last-seen Spring Dates: Monongalia County, 21 April; Cabell-Mason Counties, 30 April; Kanawha County, 1 May.

Summer: The Dark-eyed Junco is a common to very common breeding bird throughout the Allegheny Mountains above about 700 m in the north and 900 m in the south. It occurs in summer from Preston County (Cranesville) through Mineral (Allegheny Front), Grant, Tucker, Pendleton, Pocahontas, Randolph, Nicholas, Webster, Greenbrier, and sparingly in Upshur (Hemlock, Adolph), Monroe, and Mercer Counties. Nests have been found in all these counties except Monroe and Mercer. At

these high elevations, it occurs in all forest types, and while the numbers are highest in the brushy "edge" situations, it also occurs in good numbers in more mature forest. The hiker on the high country trails will find juncos to be the most conspicuous bird along the entire route.

Populations: Twenty-seven Singing Male Censuses averaged 73 males per 100 ha. Virgin spruce-northern hardwoods, 1,250 m, Randolph County, 227, 82, 32, 89, 54, 54 males on six counts; young spruce forest, 1,350 m, Pocahontas-Randolph Counties, 131, 165, 131, 74, 99, 165 males; spruce-fir swamp, 1,110 m, Randolph County, 66 males; and young deciduous forest, 1,250 m, Randolph County, 84 males.

Fall: The breeding juncos are non-migratory, although many may withdraw to sheltered places in the valleys during the worst weather. Migrant juncos from the north usually arrive with the first strong cold front that occurs after 1 October, although a few stragglers may come in late September. The migration continues through October and most of November and very large numbers of juncos pass through all parts of the state.

First-seen Fall Dates: Kanawha County, 5 October; Monongalia County, 13 October.

Winter: The junco winters throughout the state, even at the highest elevations. Small flocks collect in weed-filled fields or in brushy woodlots and often contain 30 or more birds per flock. There is some evidence from banding that, although most birds return faithfully to the same wintering grounds year after year, the wintering flocks do roam over a wide area during this time. Christmas Count data (birds per party hour) are: statewide, 6.87 (15.65–3.01); Charleston, 6.14 (9.01–2.69); Charles Town, 3.70 (17.78–0.50); Huntington, 6.17 (10.33–4.44); Inwood, 8.70 (10.00–0.36); Mason County, 3.69 (7.27–0.41); Ona, 6.19 (14.10–1.74); Pendleton County, 5.81 (11.11–1.18); Lewisburg, 8.04 (12.02–3.5); and Hampshire County, 14.95.

Specimens: USNM, CM, AMNH, UMMZ. The breeding subspecies, at least as far north as Tucker County, is the southern Appalachian race *carolinensis* Brewster. This race is essentially non-migratory although the birds do move to lower elevations in the winter. The breeding birds in Preston County may be intermediate between *hyemalis* and *carolinensis,* while *hyemalis* is the common wintering form except in the Allegheny Mountains. Each winter there are reports of "Oregon" Juncos in various parts of the state, and the western subspecies do occasionally wander this far east. An individual of the *oreganus* group of subspecies was collected in Charleston in 1955. The evidence from birds banded at Morgantown indicate that the northwestern subspecies *cismontanus* Dwight is of frequent occurrence, and that the subspecies *montanus* Ridgway occurs infrequently.

LAPLAND LONGSPUR

Calcarius lapponicus (Linnaeus)

Status: Casual late winter visitant.

Records: The Lapland Longspur was added to the state list when M. Brooks saw two near Redhouse, Putnam County, on 7 March 1936 (Brooks, 1936b). Wetmore and Perrygo collected two from a flock of 25 near Moorefield, Hardy County, on 1 January 1937 (Wetmore, 1937). All but one of the other few scattered records come from Morgantown. It was seen there in February 1940 (Brooks and Peck, 1940); 1 March 1952 (W. Davis and Hall); 15 March 1952 (Hundley); 14 March 1958 (Brooks); and 17 February 1960 (G. Knight and Hall). In the spring of 1974, a West Virginia University ornithology class saw one at McClintic Wildlife Station, Mason County.

Remarks: This species is to be looked for on golf courses, airports, or in wintering flocks of Horned

Larks. Two of the Morgantown records above were the result of careful examination of the flocks of Horned Larks on the University farms.

Specimen: USNM.

*SNOW BUNTING *Plectrophenax nivalis* (Linnaeus)

Status: Casual local winter visitant.

Records: West Virginia lies too far south to get the migration of the Snow Bunting every winter, but in some winters it does appear, usually in small flocks. The dates of occurrence range from 23 October to early March. They are of almost regular occurrence in the Eastern Panhandle Counties of Jefferson and Berkeley. There are also winter records from Monongalia, Preston, Pocahontas, Hancock, Ohio, Harrison, Gilmer, Upshur, Mercer, and Kanawha, and a lone sighting from Jackson County.

Specimen: One with insufficient data at WVU but presumably collected locally. Bibbee reported collecting one in Mercer County, but the location of this specimen is unknown to me.

Subfamily Icterinae	BLACKBIRDS AND ORIOLES

BOBOLINK   *Dolichonyx orizivorus (Linnaeus)*

Status: Fairly common to common local spring migrant; uncommon local summer resident; common to very common and occasionally abundant local fall migrant.

Spring: The Bobolink migrates throughout the state, but is rarely seen in the heavily forested regions, and in many parts of the state it is rare and unusual. In the open meadows of Jefferson and Berkeley Counties, the open fields of Mason County, and on the grassy hilltops of Monongalia and Preston Counties, it is often quite common, but in Ohio, Kanawha, and Cabell Counties it is rare and may not be

reported in every year. The Bobolink arrives in the fourth week of April, and flocks may remain in certain favored spots for as long as three weeks. Some birds are still migrating in late May.

First-seen Spring Dates: Greenbrier County, 25 April; Cabell-Mason Counties, 29 April; Monongalia County, 2 May; Kanawha County, 11 May.

Last-seen Spring Dates: Greenbrier County, 10 May; Cabell-Mason Counties, 10 May; Kanawha County, 20 May.

Summer: The Bobolink nests in numbers only in the highlands of Preston County where it occupies meadows and to a lesser extent pastures at elevations above 600 m. It also nests in some numbers in Hancock County and less numerously in Brooke County; in scattered places in Tucker County (Canaan Valley, Camp Kidd); and in the grassy areas at high elevations along the borders of Pocahontas and Randolph Counties (Sinks of Gandy). There also are a few scattered summer records from Berkeley, Kanawha, Summers, Marion, Lewis, Raleigh, and Greenbrier Counties. Nests have been found only in Hancock, Preston, and Greenbrier Counties and young birds were reported on one occasion in Nicholas County (Brooks, 1934a).

Fall: In fall, large flocks of Bobolinks often congregate in favored spots, that usually are the same places favored in spring. They begin to flock in the nesting areas in late July and arrive in other areas in early September or late August. Flocks may remain until almost mid-October. An aggregation of about 2,000 was reported in Mason County on 12 October.

First-seen Fall Dates: Kanawha County, 10 September; Cabell-Mason Counties, 11 September.

Last-seen Fall Date: Cabell-Mason County, 6 October.

Specimens: WVU, GMS.

RED-WINGED BLACKBIRD

Agelaius phoeniceus (Linnaeus)

Status: Very common summer resident; uncommon (but locally abundant) winter resident.

Spring: Migrant Red-winged Blackbirds arrive in the last week of February or the first week in March, depending upon the weather of the season. They are conspicuous on arrival and occur throughout the state in open country.

First-seen Spring Dates: Cabell-Mason Counties, 27 February; Brooke County, 4 March; Ohio County, 5 March; Monongalia County, 8 March; Kanawha County, 13 March.

Summer: The Redwing nests throughout the state wherever it finds suitable habitat, and has undoubtedly nested in all counties, although data are lacking for many. It is missing from the forested country, but I have found single males in small isolated cattail bogs surrounded by forest at elevations above 1,000 m. They occur at the edges of beaver ponds at 1,200 m on the Allegheny Front. The prime habitat is cattail marsh, and where these occur there may be large numbers of Redwings. However, cattail marshes are not abundant in the state and other habitats are utilized. Wet meadows, wooded marshes, hayfields, and unused pastures, even those well away from any water, all support good populations. In many parts of the state, the Redwing is found only on grassy hilltops, providing the grass is long enough for their needs.

Populations: As with the meadowlark, the Breeding Bird Surveys are ideally adapted to sampling Redwing populations, and these have averaged 59.3 (230–4.0) birds per route. The Redwing has occurred on only nine Singing Male Censuses and these have averaged 43 males per 100 ha. Overgrown ravine, with multiflora hedge, 353 m, Ohio County, 96, 40 males; and overgrown ravine, 360 m, Ohio County, 59 males on two counts. Not included in these averages was a shallow pond-cattail marsh in Mason County, which had 5,400 males per 100 ha.

Fall: Once nesting is finished, the Redwing leaves the nesting marshes or meadows and collects in large flocks that may be encountered in any open areas in all parts of the state. These flocks often join with other icterine species or with Common Star-lings. At this time of the year the Redwing may constitute an agricultural pest, since it will feed on the ripening corn. Fortunately in most places in West Virginia, neither the number of blackbirds nor the amount of corn is large enough to make this a serious problem, but in some of the Ohio River areas severe economic damage may be done. Most of these birds leave in October.

Last-seen Fall Date: Cabell-Mason Counties, 15 November.

Winter: In the lower Ohio and Kanawha Valleys, some large mixed flocks of blackbirds occur almost annually. In recent years, one such winter roost has been near Hurricane, Putnam County. These congregations usually number in the tens of thousands but on occasion have exceeded a million. Christmas Count data seldom show these winter roosts, except by accident. The State-wide Christmas Count average (birds per party hour) is 1.17 (2.76–0.09), but the only Counts exceeding 0.5 bird per party hour are Mason County, 1.60 (4.45–0.06) and Ona, 5.16 (12.82–0.03). (One notes the wide range of values quoted here.)

Specimens: WVU, UMMZ, USNM, MCZ, GMS. Breeding specimens are all of the subspecies *phoeniceus,* but several fall specimens from Mason County (UMMZ) and one spring specimen from Nicholas County (USNM) have been identified as the northern subspecies *arctolegus* Oberholser. It is possible that other subspecies may occur in the fall and winter flocks.

EASTERN MEADOWLARK

Sturnella magna (Linnaeus)

Status: Common to very common summer resident; uncommon to very common winter resident. In some parts of the state, it may be a permanent resident.

Spring: While at least a few meadowlarks may be present all winter, the numbers are greatly augmented by the arrivals of migrants in the last few days of February and the first week of March. Wintering birds also begin to sing at this time. It is found in suitable habitat throughout the state.

First-seen Spring Dates: Kanawha County, 20 February; Monongalia County, 3 March; Summers County, 28 February; Ohio and Brooke Counties, 16 March.

Summer: The meadowlark is present in summer throughout the state wherever open grassy areas occur. It favors meadows, pasture fields, and golf courses, but also inhabits abandoned fields for a few years until the scrub growth becomes apparent. The Meadowlark almost certainly nests in every county, but definite records are lacking for many.

Breeding Populations: Breeding Bird Surveys

are well adapted to sampling meadowlark populations and have averaged 18.5 (90.9–0.33) birds per route. The Meadowlark has occurred on only nine Singing Male Censuses, averaging 29 males per 100 ha. Pasture field, 670 m, Greenbrier County, 49 males, 32 males; overgrown ravine with multiflora hedge, 350 m, Ohio County, 40 males on two censuses.

Fall: Once the meadowlark quits singing in the late summer, it is difficult to determine its presence; as a result, migration dates are seldom recorded accurately. On occasion in late September, I have encountered large numbers of meadowlarks perched in fields and on fence posts. These may represent migrants from the north.

Winter: In the southwestern part of the state, meadowlarks winter in sizeable numbers wherever open grassy fields occur. It is not known how many of these are migrants from the north, and how many are the birds that nested in these locations. Elsewhere in the state, the wintering numbers are smaller, but at least a few winter throughout the state, even in the Canaan Valley at 900 m. In the north, many are attracted to winter at places where barn manure is spread on the fields at almost daily intervals. Christmas Count data (birds per party hour) are: statewide, 1.14 (2.49–0.36); Charleston, 0.24 (1.02–0.08); Charles Town, 1.52 (6.25–0); Huntington, 0.23 (0.58–0); Inwood, 0.52 (2.70–0); Mason County, 1.85 (9.57–1.61); Ona, 2.35 (10.75–0.25); Pendleton County, 0.43 (1.67–0); Lewisburg, 1.81 (3.80–0.05); and Hampshire County, 0.82.

Specimens: WVU, USNM, MU.

*WESTERN MEADOWLARK

Sturnella neglecta (Audubon)

Status: Accidental visitant.

Records: On 21 May 1961, a group of observers from the Brooks Bird Club, five of whom had had previous experience with this species, studied a Western Meadowlark for some time on the side of the Blue Ridge in Jefferson County (Hall, 1963). The bird sang well and some of the distinguishing field marks were observed. There are some other possible "song" records: Marshall County, prior to 1961 (R. Brooks); Tucker County, June 1960 (J. Grom); Lincoln County, June 1961 (N. Laitsch); and Inwood, Berkeley County, October 1965 (C. Miller).

Specimen: None.

*YELLOW-HEADED BLACKBIRD

Xanthocephalus xanthocephalus (Bonaparte)

Status: Accidental visitant.

Records: Sutton (1933) saw one near Bethany, Brooke County, 16 July 1914. R. S. Slack photo-graphed one at his home in Huntington in June 1960. One was seen at the McClintic Wildlife Station, Mason County, 30 October 1962 (T. Shields), one at Scary, Putnam County, 8 March 1964 (B. Greenlee, G. Hurley, and G. Koch), and one in Lincoln County a number of years ago (fide M. Thacker). There was a report of one at Princeton, Mercer County, 15 October 1975 (J. Phillips, 1977). In 1977, two were seen on 3 October and one on 14 October at Keenan, Monroe County (Flouer). Doan (1888) claimed that one was collected at Buckhannon in 1886, but this record is largely discredited, although Doan's report is probably responsible for the "Spring, 1888" record mentioned by Taylor (1926). The late R. C. Dustman described for me one that he saw along the Cheat River sometime prior to 1951.

Specimen: None. Photo on file with National Photoduplicate File.

RUSTY BLACKBIRD   *Euphagus carolinus* (Müller)

Status: Locally a common and often abundant spring and fall migrant; locally a fairly common to common winter visitant; rare to uncommon at most places in the state.

Spring: The Rusty Blackbird arrives in the latter half of March, and migrates throughout the state. Most depart by mid-April, but a few stragglers remain until the last of April. At this time of the year, it is almost exclusively found in wooded marshes that have standing water and at least low bushes for cover. Those regions that have little of this habitat attract very few Rusty Blackbirds.

First-seen Spring Dates: Ohio County, 16 March; Monongalia County, 21 March; Kanawha County, 1 April.

Last-seen Spring Dates: Kanawha County, 25 April; Cabell-Mason Counties, 11 May.

Fall: Fall migrant Rusty Blackbirds arrive in mid-October, and except for the wintering birds they are gone by mid-November. At this season of the year, they are not so strictly limited to wetlands, and on occasion they may be mixed with other icterids in the large flocks so prevalent in autumn. On one occasion, I witnessed a heavy migration of Rusties (and Grackles) crossing the Allegheny Front at A.F.M.O. in mid-October. The blackbirds were using the same route as the migrating warblers do, but were flying too high to be captured.

First-seen Fall Dates: Cabell-Mason Counties, 2 October; Kanawha County, 6 October.

Last-seen Fall Date: Kanawha County, 6 November.

Winter: Rusty Blackbirds winter in fairly good numbers in the Eastern Panhandle and in the lower Ohio and Kanawha Valleys, which are also the areas that have the largest numbers during migration.

Christmas Count data (birds per party hour) are: statewide, 0.73 (2.55–0.05); Charleston, 0.04 (0.26–0); Charles Town, 1.45 (3.87–0); Huntington, .05 (0.15–0); Inwood, 0.65 (5.30–0); Mason County, 0.57 (4.16–0); and Ona, 3.08 (16.0–0). The other counts reported none during the the period under analysis. They also have been recorded at least once on a Christmas Count in Summers County, and there is a record for Cranberry Glades at 1,060 m on 21 January 1955 (R. W. Bailey).

Specimens: USNM, CM, UMMZ, GMS.

*BREWER'S BLACKBIRD
Euphagus cyanocephalus (Wagler)

Status: Casual spring and fall visitant.

Records: There are a number of good sight records for this species: 1 November 1951, Cabell County (E. Seeber and D. Pilkenton); 9 April 1953, Mason County (H. K. Land); 14 May 1958, Monongalia County (M. Brooks); late September 1965, Marion County (P. Davisson); Fall 1961, Kanawha County (E. Bowers); 26 November 1966, Kanawha County (A. Shreve); March 1970, Monongalia County (M. Brooks); 14 March 1971, South Charleston (K. Anderson, 1976), and 26 October 1980, Lewisburg, Greenbrier County (C. O. Handley, Jr.) (Handley, 1981). Most of these records were of singles or pairs, and on some occasions the Brewer's Blackbirds were with Rusty Blackbirds. On the 1980 Christmas Bird Counts, 20 were listed at Lewisburg, 20 December, and one at Wheeling, Ohio County, 21 December.

Remarks: This species might better be listed as Hypothetical, but under Rule 5 for acceptance it qualifies for the accepted list. Brewer's Blackbirds have been expanding their range eastward for a number of years, and more records are to be expected in the future.

Specimen: None.

COMMON GRACKLE *Quiscalus quiscula* (Linnaeus)

Status: Common to abundant summer resident; locally abundant winter resident, but an uncommon winter resident at most places.

Spring: The grackle arrives in late February or early March, and populations build up rapidly. It migrates throughout the state and is found in practically any non-forested area.

First-seen Spring Dates: Berkeley County, 2 March; Kanawha County, 9 March; Wood County, 10 March; Cabell-Mason Counties, 11 March; Ohio County, 12 March; Monongalia County, 13 March; Summers County, 15 March; Randolph County, 15 March.

Summer: At present, the Common Grackle is found in large numbers throughout the state except in the heavily forested areas, at high elevations, and in the mountain valleys. The largest populations appear to be in the Shenandoah Valley, but the other eastern valleys of the Ridge and Valley Region have lesser numbers, and it becomes uncommon in the Allegheny Mountains Region. West of the mountains, it again becomes quite common with the highest populations in the lower Ohio Valley. It probably nests in every county, but definite nesting records are available only from Jefferson, Berkeley, Morgan, Hampshire, Hardy, Preston, Monongalia, Tucker, Randolph, Pocahontas, Greenbrier, Monroe, Hancock, Brooke, Ohio, Wirt, Wood, Gilmer, Upshur, Braxton, Lewis, Kanawha, and Cabell Counties.

Until the early 1960s, grackles were quite uncommon over much of western West Virginia from Monongalia County, just west of the main mountains, to Kanawha County. In the late 1950s, the population began to increase, and at present the grackle is very common to abundant in most agricultural areas west of the mountains, but it is still uncommon in the higher mountains, although I have found them nesting at about 1,050 m in the Upper Greenbrier Valley in Pocahontas County. It is almost strictly limited to agricultural land or suburban areas, and where ornamental conifers have been planted it becomes almost colonial in its nesting.

Breeding Populations: Breeding Bird Surveys have averaged 89.2 (720–2) birds per route. Grackles have been listed on only two Singing Male Censuses with populations of only 17 and 5 males per 100 ha. Normal breeding populations may be much higher than this.

Fall: In late July and August, grackles begin to congregate into large flocks, which may number into the thousands. At this time, as with other blackbirds, they can become serious agricultural pests. These flocks generally depart by late October.

Last-seen Fall Date: Cabell-Mason Counties, 31 October.

Winter: A few grackles remain to winter throughout the state, except at high elevations. On occasion in the lower Ohio Valley, some very large numbers are present, often gathered with the large flocks of Starlings and Red-winged Blackbirds. Christmas Count data (birds per party hour) are: statewide, 1.92 (10.99–0.01); Charleston, 0.59 (2.81–0); Charles Town, 0.50 (2.44–0); Huntington, 0.89 (8.33–0); Inwood, 0.95 (8.70–0); Mason County, 10.96 (83.30–0); Ona, 2.20 (9.09–0); Pendleton County, 0; Lewisburg, 0; and Hampshire County, 0.01.

Specimens: WVU, CM, USNM, AMNH, UMMZ, MCZ, GMS. Breeding specimens from Jefferson County have been identified as the subspecies *stonei* Chapman, as have some specimens from

Greenbrier County (AMNH). Specimens from the western part of the state taken in the 1930s or before have all been identified as the subspecies *versicolor* Vieillot. There are specimens in the AMNH from Greenbrier, Berkeley, Monroe, and Pendleton Counties that were identified by Frank Chapman as the subspecies *ridgwayi*. This subspecies is now considered to be merely an intermediate between the other two races. At present, it is not clear which race inhabits the higher elevations nor which race has staged the range expansion into western West Virginia. Handley (1976) remarks that *stonei* is found in the upper Kanawha Valley and *versicolor* in the lower Kanawha Valley. If this is true, it would indicate an influx of grackles from east of the mountains along the Greenbrier and the New Rivers meeting another influx coming from the west. This is a case where further collecting of specimens is fully justified and should be done.

BROWN-HEADED COWBIRD

Molothrus ater (Boddaert)

Status: Common summer resident; locally uncommon to fairly common winter resident.

Spring: The cowbird generally arrives in mid-March and by mid-April the numbers will have decreased to the breeding populations. They are most common in open agricultural land but will also be found in lightly forested areas.

First-seen Spring Dates: Ohio County, 5 March; Cabell-Mason Counties, 13 March; Monongalia County, 17 March; Kanawha County, 20 March; Brooke County, 23 March.

Summer: The cowbird probably breeds in every county of the state, reaching the maximum numbers in the open agricultural lands of the Eastern Panhandle and the lower Ohio Valley. However, they also are common in forested areas and in the highlands. They are found in summer in the northern hardwoods and in the mixed spruce-northern hardwoods forest at elevations as high as 1,280 m. I have not seen them in the pure spruce forest.

Breeding Populations: Breeding Bird Surveys have averaged 16.2 (76.2–3) birds per route. The cowbird has occurred on 37 Singing Male Census areas but has contributed to the population numerically on only two of these. These census areas have been in all forest types, except the pure spruce, and at all elevations from 180 to 1,250 m.

Fall: In August, the cowbird begins to congregate, either in flocks of cowbirds alone or in mixed flocks with Starlings and Redwings, and these flocks are often very large. A flock of 10,000 (mixed with Starlings) was seen in Mason County in August. These flocks tend to disappear by mid-October. In late October, good numbers of cowbirds have been seen crossing the Allegheny Front at A.F.M.O.

Last-seen Fall Dates: Kanawha County, 6 October; Cabell-Mason Counties, 24 October.

Winter: The cowbird winters sparingly in the north and probably does not occur at higher elevations. In some years, sizeable numbers winter in the lower Ohio and Kanawha Valleys, but in other years there are few. Christmas Count data (birds per party hour) are: statewide, 1.13 (2.77–0.22); Charleston, 0.70 (3.21–0.02); Charles Town, 0.14 (1.50–0); Huntington, 0.10 (1.14–0); Inwood, 0.10 (2.50–0); Mason County, 0.54 (1.67–0); Ona, 5.05 (21.21–0); Pendleton County, 0.34 (1.34–0); Lewisburg, 1.22 (6.88–0); and Hampshire County, 0.07.

Remarks: The Brown-headed Cowbird has probably entered this state only since settlement, although the earliest ornithologists reported it as being common. No assessment can be made of the effect of cowbird nest-parasitism on the populations of small passerines. Certain of the warbler species, for example the Ovenbird, may have been greatly affected by this parasitism.

Specimens: USNM, WVU, GMS.

ORCHARD ORIOLE   *Icterus spurius* (Linnaeus)

Status: Uncommon to fairly common summer resident.

Spring: The Orchard Oriole arrives on the breeding grounds in the last week of April. Although it is not as conspicuous as the Northern Oriole, it is in good song and is quite evident. It migrates throughout the state except in the heavily forested areas and at high elevations. Birds of passage are present for about a week, after which the numbers recorded drop off.

First-seen Spring Dates: Cabell-Mason Counties, 24 April; Kanawha County, 27 April; Brooke County, 29 April; Summers County, 30 April; Monongalia County, 30 April.

Summer: Neither the Orchard nor the Northern Orioles are numerous in heavily forested country; consequently, in much of the south-central and eastern parts of the state, these species are found only in towns or in farmyards. Elsewhere in the state, the Orchard Oriole is a bird of the open farmland, and it is present throughout the state at elevations below 600 m. Above this elevation, it becomes quite local. There are a few records from the upper Greenbrier Valley at elevations of about 900 m. In most areas, the Orchard Oriole is much less numerous than are Northern Orioles, but in Cabell County the reverse is true. The Orchard Oriole becomes uncommon in the Northern Panhandle. There are nesting records from Jefferson, Berkeley, Hampshire, Pendleton, Preston, Monongalia, Marion,

Tucker, Randolph, Nicholas, Webster, Pocahontas, Greenbrier, Lewis, Upshur, Braxton, Brooke, Ohio, Marshall, Wetzel, Wirt, Wood, Ritchie, Mason, Gilmer, Fayette, Lincoln, Kanawha, and Cabell Counties.

The Orchard Oriole requires open fields interspersed with large trees with broad spreading canopies for nesting sites.

Breeding Populations: Breeding Bird Surveys have averaged only 1.4 (5.0–0.2) birds per route. The Orchard Oriole has appeared on only two Singing Male Census counts, both in Ohio County. Overgrown pasture, 37 males per 100 ha; brushy field, 25 males per 100 ha.

Fall: The Orchard Oriole quits singing in late June, and after that time it is almost unreported. Most of them probably leave the state by mid-August although migrants from the north may pass through in early September, but no hard data exist.

Specimens: WVU, MU.

NORTHERN ORIOLE   *Icterus galbula* (Linnaeus)

Status: Fairly common to common a summer resident; casual winter resident.

Spring: The Northern Oriole arrives in the last week of April, or the first few days in May, and is remarkably consistent in arrival date at a given location. The loud cheerful songs and the spirited aerial chases of the males combine to make the arrival an easily observed event. In about the second week of May, there is a good flight of migrants and by the third week in May the residents start to nest. It occurs throughout the state except in heavily forested areas, and is rather uncommon at high elevations.

First-seen Spring Dates: Kanawha County, 24 April; Randolph County, 25 April; Ohio County, 28 April; Cabell-Mason Counties, 29 April; Monongalia County, 30 April; Summers County, 30 April.

Summer: The Northern Oriole occurs in every county of the state, but is scarce in heavily forested areas. At high elevations near the spruce forest, it is rare or missing, and I know of no records from

above about 1,000 m. It seems to be rare in the lower Ohio Valley (Edeburn et al., 1960) and is uncommon to rare in the low valleys in the heart of the Allegheny Mountains. This oriole reaches its greatest numbers in open farmland or residential areas that are interspersed with tall, old trees. There are definite nesting records from Jefferson, Berkeley, Hampshire, Hardy, Pendleton, Preston, Monongalia, Tucker, Randolph, Webster, Pocahontas, Greenbrier, Monroe, Upshur, Braxton, Lewis, Hancock, Ohio, Brooke, Wetzel, Wirt, Wood, Ritchie, Gilmer, Fayette, Raleigh, Cabell, Lincoln, and Kanawha Counties.

Breeding Populations: Breeding Bird Surveys have averaged 4.0 (9.7–0.3) birds per route. The Northern Oriole has occurred on only six Singing Male Censuses with an average of 37 males per 100 ha. Overgrown field, 365 m, Ohio County, 62 males per 100 ha on two counts; brushy field, 365 m, Ohio County, 49 males.

Fall: As with the Orchard Oriole, the Northern Oriole becomes quite inconspicuous after the singing season ends. The fall migration is seldom observed, but most birds are gone by mid-September. In 24 years, only 18 Northern Orioles have been banded at A.F.M.O.

Winter: Each year a few Northern Orioles attempt to winter in our area, even as far north as Ohio County. Most of these are reported on Christmas Counts taken in late December, and after that they either die or disappear from the region. A few, particularly those coming to feeding stations, manage to survive through the winter.

Remarks: This species is more familiar to most people under the time-honored name of the "Baltimore Oriole." The great weight of evidence indicates that this form and the western "Bullock's Oriole" are conspecific, and the new name applies to the combined species. It is not incorrect, however, to use the old name when referring to the eastern form alone.

Specimens: WVU, USNM, MCZ, GMS. All West Virginia specimens are referable to the eastern subspecies *galbula*.

Family Fringillidae   FINCHES

PINE GROSBEAK   *Pinicola enucleator* (Linnaeus)

Status: Casual winter visitant.

Records: The Pine Grosbeak comes as far south as West Virginia only rarely, and prior to the 1950s there were only a few records. In the winter of 1933–34, several small groups were seen in Upshur County (M. Brooks) (Handlan, 1934). In December 1938,

one was found at Bethany, Brooke County (Montagna, 1939), and in October 1948 one was seen near Cheat Lake, Monongalia County (Conn, 1948). Eifrig saw a flock of 50 in Mineral County 10 February 1900. In the winter of 1951–52, there was a moderate flight with records from Ohio County in December 1951 and Tucker County in March 1952. A very heavy flight occurred in the winter of 1955–

56 with reports from Middle Mountain, Randolph County; Canaan Valley, Tucker County; and Cooper's Rock State Forest in both Monongalia and Preston Counties. A few were seen in Tucker and Monongalia Counties in December 1955. A good-sized flock remained at Oglebay Park, Ohio County, from late November 1961 to February 1962. They were reported on both the Morgantown and Charleston Christmas Counts in December 1959. Since 1962, there have been only a few scattered records: Morgantown, 1963–64 (M. Brooks); Canaan Valley, 12 December 1965 (M. Brooks); Cheat Mountain, Randolph County, 2 March 1973 (G. Hall); Charleston, 4 April 1982 (Williams, Hurley).

Specimens: OP. There was reported in 1893 (E. A. Brooks, 1938) that a specimen from West Virginia with no further data was in the collection of the Illinois Wesleyan University. The Oglebay Park specimen is the subspecies *eschatosus* Oberholser.

PURPLE FINCH   *Carpodacus purpureus* (Gmelin)

Status: Common to very common spring and fall migrant; fairly common local summer resident; irregular common to very common winter resident.

Spring: In those areas where it has not wintered, the Purple Finch arrives anytime after early March, but in some years it does not appear until early May. The numbers present at any given place vary widely from year to year between being uncommon to very common. It sings well during migration and usually is quite conspicuous. As with the goldfinch, it tends to swarm into certain tree species when these are in bloom to eat the flowers. In the south, wintering birds and migrants depart in early May, but in the north they remain until the third week in May.

First-seen Spring Date: Monongalia County, 14 April.

Last-seen Spring Dates: Kanawha County, 3 May; Cabell-Mason Counties, 5 May; Wood County, 8 May.

Summer: The Purple Finch nests, often in good numbers, in the spruce forest, at its edges, and near the mountain swamps. There are summer records from Preston (Cranesville), Mineral, Grant, Tucker (Canaan Valley, Allegheny Front, Davis), Pendleton (Circleville), Randolph (Cheat Bridge, Helvetia, Gaudineer Knob), Pocahontas (Briery Knob, Cranberry Glades, Thornwood), and Greenbrier Counties. There is also a summer record from Camp Caesar, Nicholas County, and a July record from Huntington. Nests have been found only at Cheat Bridge, Randolph County; Davis, Tucker County; and Camp Pocahontas, Pocahontas County. A juvenile was collected in Canaan Valley, Tucker County. The Purple Finch has nested in spruce plantations

at East Liverpool, Ohio, across the river from Hancock County, and at a few places at low elevations in western Pennsylvania, but the first nesting at low elevation in West Virginia was in Brooke County in 1976 (W. Jennings). A female with a broad patch was netted at Morgantown in May 1982 indicating probable nesting there.

Populations: Three Breeding Bird Surveys have averaged 0.14 bird per route (never more than one listed). Eleven Singing Male Censuses have averaged 14 males per 100 ha. Virgin spruce-northern hardwoods, 1,290 m, Randolph County, 27, 17, 10, 10 males; second-growth spruce, 1,350 m, Randolph-Pocahontas Counties, 17 males on three counts.

Fall: The Purple Finch begins to migrate through the state in early October, and occasionally reach the very common or even abundant status. However, in the fall as in the spring it is irregular and may be missing or nearly so in some years. The migrants are gone by late October, leaving the wintering flocks.

First-seen Fall Dates: Cabell-Mason Counties, 7 October; Kanawha County, 15 November.

Winter: In southern West Virginia near Charleston and Huntington, Purple Finches are regular in winter and usually are common, but occasionally have a year of unusually low or unusually high numbers. Farther north and east, they become more irregular and may be absent in some winters. In the north, the winter numbers in the 1970s were greater than they were in the 1950s and 1960s. Christmas Count data (birds per party hour) are: statewide, 0.30 (0.81–0.03); Charleston, 0.44 (4.19–0.03); Charles Town, 0.13 (0.67–0); Huntington, 1.07 (11.11–0.07); Inwood, 0.09 (0.40–0); Mason County, 0.07 (0.21–0); Ona, 0.33 (1.21 -0); Pendleton County, 0; Lewisburg, 0.12, (0.39–0); and Hampshire County, 0.28.

Specimens: WVU, USNM.

HOUSE FINCH   *Carpodacus mexicanus* (Müller)

Status: Uncommon to common local permanent resident; uncommon winter visitant where not resident.

History: The first House Finches in the state were reported from Charles Town, Jefferson County, where they appeared at feeders in the winter of 1971–72 (C. Miller and D. Caperton). In December 1973, House Finches occurred at feeders in Buckhannon, Upshur County (M. Thacker), and Blacksville, Monongalia County (R. Strosnider). On 5 February 1974, they were first reported from Huntington, Cabell County (J. Musser), and on 27 April 1974 from St. Albans, Kanawha County (G. Hurley and F. Johnstone). The first record at Wheeling, Ohio

County, was 12 March 1975 (A. Dunnell), and the first at Morgantown, Monongalia County, was 31 March 1975 (G. Hall). In the late 1970s, it spread throughout the state, being first recorded from Athens, Mercer County, on 23 January 1978, and being listed from the Upper Greenbrier Valley in Pocahontas County in the summer of 1978 (B.B.C. Foray).

Distribution: The House Finch now occurs throughout the state, being most common in suburban areas, small towns, and parklike areas such as the University campus at Morgantown. It is much less common in rural areas, although it does frequent feeding stations in such places.

The first known nesting in the state was at Morgantown in the spring of 1975, although they had presumably nested in Jefferson County before this. There are now nesting records from Ohio, Cabell, and Mercer Counties but they probably have nested in every county in which they occur.

Numbers: The following are data from the 1978 and 1979 Christmas Counts: Charles Town, 37, 95; Hampshire County, 0, 6; Huntington, 0, 103; Inwood, 17, 41; Lewisburg, 0, 12; Ona, 0, 4; Pendleton County, 1, 18; Wheeling, 8, 1; Oak Hill, −, 31; and Parkersburg, −, 67.

Remarks: A further increase of this attractive species throughout the state may be expected.

Specimens: CM, WVU.

RED CROSSBILL   *Loxia curvirostra* Linnaeus

Status: Irregular fall and winter visitant, sometimes very common; uncommon local summer resident.

Summer: Flocks of Red Crossbills, often of 30 to 40 birds, are seen during almost every summer in the spruce forest areas of the Allegheny Mountains. Such flocks are most commonly reported from Gaudineer Knob and surrounding Shaver's Mountain in Randolph County, but reports also come from Barton Knob on Cheat Mountain, Randolph County, Spruce Knob and Reddish Knob, Pendleton County, and the Allegheny Front, Grant-Tucker

Counties. Flocks also have been found in the upper Greenbrier Valley and the valleys of the various forks of the Cheat River, all above 900 m. Crossbills have been seen at these locations from April through September, but there is no direct evidence that they have nested in the state, although a nest was found in 1980 just over the border in Rockingham County, Virginia. Birds in dull, first-year plumage, but able to fly well, have been seen being fed by adults. A bird-of-the-year was collected on Gaudineer Knob in July. There is a June report from Lake Sherwood, Greenbrier County, at well below 900 m.

Fall and Winter: Periodically, Red Crossbills from some part of North America invade the east in late summer, fall, or winter. One such invasion occurred in 1941, when supposedly western birds were collected at Gaudineer Knob (Brooks and Lunk, 1942). Another such invasion occurred in the late summer of 1972, when crossbills arrived in Randolph, Hampshire, and Tucker Counties in August and stayed some weeks. No specimens were taken but it is likely that these were western birds. In many other winters, smaller numbers of crossbills invade the state, particularly in those areas where scrub and pitch pines are common. There are more records from Kanawha County than anywhere else, but this may simply reflect the greater birding activity there. The origin of these birds is not known, but the occurrence in the pine forests suggests that a different race is involved than the small-billed race (or races) that feed in the spruce forest.

Remarks: The Red Crossbill does not behave in the way we normally think a "well-behaved" bird does. It is nomadic to the extreme, as illustrated by the presence of birds from the far west in West Virginia in the summer. The species may nest at any time of the year, and "western" races have been known to nest far east of their "normal" range.

Specimens: UMMZ, USNM, AMNH, WVU. The taxonomy of *L. curvirostra* as given by the A.O.U. Check-list (1957) apparently is not correct and in the following discussion I have relied on the as-yet unpublished treatment of Dr. A. R. Phillips, who has identified the specimens listed and who has offered much instructive comment (in litt.). There are two specimens in the National Museum of Natural History collected at Morgantown in March 1888 by E. F. Jacobs, which can be identified as the small subspecies *minor* Brehm [not *minor* as misapplied by the AOU (1957), which includes the true *minor* under *sitkensis* Grinnell]. Two specimens in the American Museum of Natural History collected by T. Surber in Greenbrier County on 13 March 1889 also are identifiable as *minor*. It may be remarked that these specimens were erroneously stated by Griscom (1937) to have been collected in Ritchie County and on his authority have been attributed to Ritchie County in the later literature. Three specimens (UMMZ) collected by M. Brooks and W. Lunk on 11 June 1941 on Gaudineer Knob also were small birds like *minor* but represent the dull-colored extreme of the small-size class. Such birds are included in *minor* by Griscom (1937) and in *sitkensis* by the A.O.U. (1957), but they may represent an undescribed eastern or northern Appalachian race. A somewhat larger bird collected by Brooks and Lunk on Gaudineer Knob on 15 June 1940 (UMMZ) was once identified as *bendirei* Ridgway, a race resident in the northern Rocky Mountains but Phillips now prefers to allocate this specimen to a medium-sized group of birds, which may represent another eastern population. A bird-of-the-year collected in July 1952 on Gaudineer Knob by W. Davis and myself was assigned by me to the northeastern subspecies *neogaea* Griscom, a name incorrectly synonymized with *minor* by the A.O.U. Phillips believes that this specimen should not be more closely identified than to put it in the medium-size class. The birds that invaded the state in the late summer of 1972 may have been still larger-sized birds such as were collected elsewhere in the east in that year. These were mainly the western race *benti* Griscom. The situation remains confused, however, and additional collecting, particularly of birds in fresh plumage, is both justified and desirable.

WHITE-WINGED CROSSBILL
Loxia leucoptera Gmelin

Status: Casual winter visitant, sometimes very common; casual summer visitant.

Summer: Brooks and Lunk (1942) found a flock of more than 100 at the Dolly Sods Fire Tower on the Allegheny Front on 9 June 1941, and they found them numerous on Gaudineer Knob, Randolph-Pocahontas Counties, on 9, 10, and 11 June 1941. J. L. Smith saw two on Briery Knob, southern Pocahontas County, on 16 June 1969. There was a report from Charleston on 27 May 1973 (Shreve).

Winter: There was a great invasion throughout the state in the winters of 1920 and 1921 (Brooks, 1944). For many years after that, the White-winged Crossbill was not reported in the state, but in recent years occurrences have been more frequent. They were seen in Ohio County in December 1948. In November 1954, they were present at Oglebay Park, Ohio County, and in December 1954 there were some at Cooper's Rock State Forest. One was taken in Cabell County on 18 January 1963. There was a major invasion in 1963–64 with reports from Charleston and Wheeling, and in 1965–66 a more widespread invasion produced reports from Pendleton, Pocahontas, Monongalia, Marion, and Ohio Counties. There was a single record from Charleston

in March 1969 and another at Morgantown in November 1969. Another major flight took place in the winter of 1969–70. Since 1970, White-winged Crossbills have been almost yearly visitors to the Charleston area. A flock was seen at Wheeling in October 1977. During the winter of 1981–82, flocks appeared at Morgantown, Monongalia County, Bruceton Mills, Preston County, and Jackson's Mill, Lewis County.

White-winged Crossbills are especially partial to hemlock cones and the winter flocks are most commonly seen in hemlock groves.
Specimen: OP, MU, WFVZ.

COMMON REDPOLL *Carduelis flammea* (Linnaeus)

Status: Irregular casual winter visitant, sometimes very common.

Records: Brooks (1944) reported only three records for the state, all in the north: Morgantown, 1934–35 (H. Howell); Morgantown, February 1940 (Peck); and Terra Alta, Preston County, January 1937 (Brooks and A. Margolin). There was also a record from Nicholas County in 1939 (A. McClung). There are two earlier records: 6 December 1901, Mineral County (near Cumberland) (W. Eifrig), and 1 May 1911, Adrian, Upshur County (F.E. Brooks). Until the 1960s, this constituted the state record. A few were seen in Charleston in the winter of 1961–62 (R. Yunick) and they were present at Inwood, Berkeley County, in February 1962 (C. Miller) and at St. Albans, Kanawha County, in February 1963 (A. Shreve). Sixty-five were seen on the Ona, Cabell County, Christmas Count in 1965–66. In the late winter of 1969–70, a major invasion took place with large flocks reported from Morgantown, Bethany, Weirton, and Charleston. In the spring of 1972, there were reports from Kearneysville, Jefferson County (C. Miller), Morgantown (Hall), and Vienna, Wood County. A few were seen in the late fall of 1972 in the Eastern Panhandle (C. Miller). Nine were seen on the Charleston Christmas Count in 1980.

Remarks: It is entirely possible that the large flocks of the 1969–70 and the 1971–72 invasions may have contained a few individuals of the Hoary Redpoll (*Carduelis hornemanni* Holboell).
Specimens: None.

PINE SISKIN   *Carduelis pinus* (Wilson)

Status: Irregular spring and fall migrant; irregular winter visitant, uncommon to very common; casual summer resident locally, often common.

Summer: A few Pine Siskins may be found in the spruce forest in the high mountains in some summers. On rare occasions, they have been quite numerous. There are summer records from Grant,

Pendleton, Tucker, Randolph, and Pocahontas Counties, all above 1,000 m. In late May 1982, a female with a well-developed broodpatch was netted at Morgantown, Monongalia County. This bird had been present there since at least February, so nesting undoubtedly occurred. There is also an uncertain report of a nest found near the Cranberry Glades, Pocahontas County.

Fall, Winter, and Spring: The Pine Siskin is present in at least small numbers almost every year, but in some years extremely large numbers are present. Arrival is highly variable. Sometimes, large flocks come in early October (for example, the fall of 1969), but usually arrival is not until November. Many of these birds are passage birds that pass through on their way farther south. During the winter, flocks still move from place to place, and the siskin does not return to the same places winter after winter. In the spring, large flocks may again be seen, and these remain until late April or even early May. Often there are sizeable numbers present in mid-May, usually to be seen feeding on the seed-heads of dandelions so common at that time. During the migration and winter season, the Pine Siskin may be found in almost any wooded or semi-wooded area, and they do not seem to be limited to conifers.

Winter Numbers: The Charleston Christmas Count has recorded the siskin on six of eight counts, with an average number of 12.5 birds. Other counts have seldom reported more than one bird and most have not reported any.

Specimens: WVU, USNM, GMS, MU.

AMERICAN GOLDFINCH *Carduelis tristis* (Linnaeus)

Status: Common to very common spring and fall migrant; fairly common to common summer resident; uncommon to very common winter resident. May be a permanent resident at some places.

Spring: Migrant goldfinches arrive from the south in late April or early May, and for a short period of time they may be the most abundant bird in a given area. This time of abundance coincides with the flowering of elms and silver maples in city parks and along streamsides and in residential areas. Goldfinches and Purple Finches swarm in these flowering trees feeding on the flowers. This also is the time of the seeding of the dandelions, which, too, is a favorite food. By the last week in May, the numbers have decreased, and goldfinches are not so conspicuous except at higher elevations where the flowering is later. The presence of large numbers of wintering birds makes it difficult to arrive at normal migration dates.

Summer: The goldfinch nests in every county of the state and at all elevations. It occurs at the edge of the spruce forest as well as in all deciduous forest types. It is a bird of the semi-open brushy country and most often is seen feeding in open grassy or weed-filled land. Nesting takes place in a variety of small trees, usually in an edge situation. Since nesting occurs very late, in July and August, rather few nesting records are available, since many bird students have retired from the field at this season. There are definite nesting records from Jefferson, Berkeley, Hampshire, Randolph, Greenbrier, Brooke, Ohio, Wood, Kanawha, and Cabell Counties and young birds are still in the nest in October in Mason County.

Populations: Breeding Bird Surveys have averaged 16.9 (34.3–5.2) birds per route. Since the Singing Male Counts usually are made in early June, it is doubtful if this method adequately samples the Goldfinch nesting population. Four such counts have averaged 22 males per 100 ha. Apple orchard, Berkeley County, 32 males; and overgrown ravine, Ohio County, 25 males.

Fall: By mid-September, large flocks of goldfinches may be seen moving south. This migration continues well into late October or even early November. At A.F.M.O. in late September or early October flock after flock, totalling many hundreds in some days, are seen flying across the Allegheny Front, but only 599 have been banded in 24 years.

Winter: In southern West Virginia, the goldfinch is as common in winter as in summer in non-forested areas. It is not known whether or not these wintering birds are the same ones that nest there. Farther north, the numbers are fewer and in Monongalia and Ohio Counties, for example, it is regular but uncommon. The goldfinch is missing from the high mountains in the winter, but reappears in moderate numbers in the eastern valleys.

Winter Populations: Six winter population counts, five in Ohio and one in Berkeley Counties have averaged 11 birds per 100 ha. Christmas Count data (birds per party hour) are: statewide, 2.62 (8.38–1.03); Charleston, 2.13 (3.21–0.20); Charles Town, 1.47 (6.50–0.01); Huntington, 2.54 (5.11–0.31); Inwood, 4.46 (32.00–0.08); Mason County, 2.83 (2.93–0.68); Ona, 2.63 (6.50–0.75); Pendleton County, 0.44 (0.78–0.06); Lewisburg, 2.87 (7.33–0.22); and Hampshire County, 1.80.

Remarks: In northern West Virginia, banding evidence suggests that the permanent resident population is very small. Only 12 birds out of 1,100 banded at Morgantown have been retrapped there after an interval greater than a few days.

Specimens: WVU, USNM, MCZ, GMS.

EVENING GROSBEAK

Coccothraustes vespertina (Cooper)

Status: Formerly a casual winter visitant; presently a regular winter visitant often very common to abundant.

Distribution: In 1944, Brooks (1944) could list only three definite records of Evening Grosbeaks for West Virginia (from Pocahontas, Barbour, and Marshall Counties) and one uncertain record for the species. This was a reflection of the rarity of the species in the eastern United States up to that time. The massive invasion into the northeast that occurred in 1945–46 reached at least as far south as Marion County where W. Lunk collected the first specimen for the state (Lunk, 1945). The next heavy invasion was in 1949–50 when they were reported in numbers in Elkins (W. DeGarmo). Subsequent influxes came in almost alternate years, and grosbeaks were found in Monongalia and Randolph Counties and southward along the mountains in these years. A particularly heavy invasion came in 1955–56. Each invasion produced more birds which appeared over a wider area. These invasions came in alternate years until the late 1960s when they became annual affairs. Eventually the Evening Grosbeak was reported from throughout the state, being first seen in Kanawha County in February 1954 (D. Shearer) and in Cabell County in the winter of 1954–55 (G. Gunnoe).

At present, it may be found anywhere in the state during the winter months in greatly varying numbers. The largest numbers apparently are still to be found along both sides of the main Allegheny Mountains system, and in the mountains themselves. It seems to be usually in rather low numbers in the upper Ohio Valley. The Evening Grosbeak generally arrives in late November, although at some places it does not appear until after the first of January. However, a few early birds have been seen flying along the Allegheny Front in mid-September, and a few may pass through in October. As a rule, these early birds go on farther south and do not stop here. In some years, the grosbeak may disappear or decrease in numbers in mid-winter and then increase in early spring as it returns from farther south. It may remain until the middle of May before departing, and there are records up to 1 June. In the lowlands, it frequents feeding stations offering sunflower seeds, and also feeds commonly on the seeds of the box elder (*Acer negundo*), but it occurs commonly in the mountains where neither of these foods is available.

First-seen Fall Dates: Kanawha County, 15 December; Monongalia County, 21 December.

Last-seen Spring Dates: Monongalia County, 24 April; Cabell County, 26 April.

Populations: Individual flocks may vary from a dozen to a hundred, but a given region may contain many flocks. Christmas Count totals have ranged from as high as 1,200 to as low as one or two. Christmas Count data (birds per party hour) are: statewide, 0.55 (2.60–0); Charleston, 0.48 (2.00–0); Charles Town, 0.48 (3.00–0); Huntington, 0.10 (3.61–0); Inwood, 0.89 (2.73–0); Mason County, 0.13 (2.22–0); Ona, 0.02 (6.06–0); Pendleton County, 0.77 (3.90–0); Lewisburg, 0.09 (0.33–0); and Hampshire County, 0.80.

Specimens: WVU, WAL, MU, CU.

Family Ploceidae   WEAVER FINCHES

HOUSE SPARROW   *Passer domesticus* (Linnaeus)

Status: Very common to abundant permanent resident.

Distribution: The House Sparrow is present and nests in every county, although nesting records are seldom reported. It is not found in the spruce forest and is more or less uncommon in the mountain areas. It was abundant in all cities and all towns prior to the advent of the automobile, but now it reaches peak numbers only in certain suburban areas and in farmyard situations where a reliable food supply is present. The House Sparrow is an important member of many ecosystems of the state, but it is largely ignored by bird students; consequently, little is known of the populations or the nesting habits in the state.

Populations: Breeding Bird Surveys have averaged 44.1 (323 - 1.5) birds per count. A recent urban census at Morgantown averaged 396 birds seen per 100 ha and 516 heard per 100 ha (Goetz, 1975). Christmas Count data (birds per party hour) are: statewide, 9.66 (20.70–4.78); Charleston, 2.82 (4.64–1.82); Charles Town, 21.14 (66.67–11.05); Huntington, 3.48 (6.56–1.11); Inwood, 21.45 (67.00–6.87); Mason County, 6.01 (12.27–1.61); Ona, 1.58 (3.00–0.83); Pendleton County, 9.74 (20.00–5.09); Lewisburg, 6.79 (12.50–1.30); and Hampshire County, 2.27.

History: According to Barrows (1889), the earliest report of the House Sparrow in West Virginia came from Shepherdstown, Jefferson County, in 1866. Most places in the state did not report them until the late 1870s and the early 1880s. By 1889, when Barrows wrote, they were reported throughout the state, although it had not yet been present at Ansted, Fayette County; Clifton Mills, Preston County; Ronceverte, Greenbrier County; Wayne C. H., Wayne County; West Union, Doddridge County; and several other places. No liberations and introductions are known to have been made in West Virginia, but liberations were made in Marietta, Ohio, in 1870 and Steubenville, Ohio, in 1880.

Specimens: WVU, USNM.

Exotic Species

At various times, the state agency formerly known as the Conservation Commission or various private sportsmen's groups have liberated certain gallinaceous species in the hope of establishing them as game species. Perhaps the most commonly introduced species was the Gray Partridge (*Perdix perdix*) of Europe, which was liberated in the 1920s and 1930s at various places. In some cases, they nested and survived for several years (Brooks, 1944) but eventually all of them died out. The Chukar Partridge (*Alectoris chukar*) also has been liberated at a number of places, with rather recent records from Kanawha and Preston Counties, but these also have never become established. In 1944, the Conservation Commission liberated a number of Sharp-tailed Grouse (*Tympanuchus phasianellus*) in some of the mountain counties but these also did not become established.

With the increased popularity in recent years of exotic birds as caged pets, it was inevitable that some of these would escape and would be found some distance from the original site. Those species found free flying and living in the wild in West Virginia include the Monk Parakeet (*Myiopsitta monachus*) reported to have been caught in Kanawha County (Handley, 1976), an Amazon parrot (*Amazona* sp. ?) seen near Morgantown by the writer, a Red-crested Cardinal (*Paroraria coronata*) trapped in Jefferson County by C. Miller, a whydah (*Vidua* sp. ?) trapped in Randolph County by W. Wylie, and two Ringed Turtle-Doves (*Streptopelia risoria*), seen by B. Bennett at a feeder in Kanawha County.

It is to be expected that other of the popular avicultural species may be found as escapes in the future.

GAZETTEER

Adolph, southeastern Randolph County.

Albemarle Marsh, eastern Jefferson County near Charles Town.

Alderson, southern Greenbrier County.

Allegheny Front, a mountain and escarpment from Potomac River in Mineral County to northeastern Pendleton County.

Allegheny Front Migration Observatory (A.F.M.O.), banding station on the Allegheny Front on boundary between Grant and Tucker Counties.

Alpena, northern Randolph County.

Alpine Lake Resort, private resort development near Terra Alta, eastern Preston County.

Alton, southern Upshur County.

Altona Marsh, a large marsh west of Charles Town, Jefferson County.

Anthony Creek, tributary of the Greenbrier River draining extreme Pocahontas and eastern Greenbrier Counties.

Arroyo, Hancock County.

Arthurdale, west central Preston County.

Athens, Mercer County.

Ashton, southern Mason County.

Back Allegheny Mountain, Pocahontas County. A continuation of Shaver's Mountain, south of U.S. Route 250.

Backbone Mountain, Preston and Tucker Counties.

Back Creek, tributary of the Potomac River draining western Berkeley County.

Baker, northeastern Hardy County.

Bartow, northern Pocahontas County.

Bear Rocks, rock formation on Allegheny Front Mountain used as a hawk lookout. Tucker-Grant Counties.

Bear Rock Lakes, western Ohio County.

Beaver Lake, small impoundment near Beckley, Raleigh County.

Beckley, county seat, Raleigh County.

Beech Bottom, formerly a wooded swamp and marsh in Brooke County. Now completely filled-in and occupied by industrial site.

Belle, central Kanawha County.

Benwood, northeastern Marshall County.

Berkeley Springs, county seat, Morgan County.

Berry Hills, suburban section of Charleston, Kanawha County.

Bethany, southeastern Brooke County.

Beverly, central Randolph County.

Big Sandy River, boundary between West Virginia and Kentucky in Wayne County.

Blacksville, western Monongalia County.

Blackwater Falls State Park, Tucker County.

Blackwater River, tributary of Cheat River draining eastern Tucker County.

Blister Pine Swamp, boreal wooded swamp, on Blister Run, a tributary of Shaver's Fork, Randolph County.

Bloomery, Hampshire County.

Bluefield, county seat of Mercer County.

Blue Jay, Raleigh County.

Blue Ridge, mountain forming boundary between Virginia and Jefferson County.

Bluestone Reservoir, artificial impoundment on the New River in Summers County.

Boaz, town, but usually refers to small marsh in western Wood County.

Briery Knob, elevation 1,377 m, southwestern Pocahontas County.

Brown Mountain, northern Tucker County, western boundary of Canaan Valley.

Buckhannon, county seat of Upshur County.

Buffalo, northern Putnam County.

Cabwaylingo State Forest, southern Wayne County.

Cacapon State Park, Morgan County.

Cacapon River, see Great Cacapon River.

Caldwell, southern Greenbrier County.

Camp Caesar, 4-H camp in central Webster County.

Camp Kidd, 4-H camp in eastern Tucker County.

Camp Pocahontas, 4-H camp in northern Pocahontas County.

Canaan Mountain, central Tucker County, western boundary of Canaan Valley.

Canaan Valley (pronounced to rhyme with inane), anticlinal valley in Tucker County.

Cass, northern Pocahontas County.

Charleston, county seat of Kanawha County, and state capital.

Charles Town, county seat of Jefferson County.

Cheat Bridge, former lumber town in eastern Randolph County, a frequently cited specimen locality.

Cheat Lake (also Lake Lynn), artificial impoundment on the Cheat River in Monongalia County.

Cheat Mountain, mountain ridge extending from central Preston County to southern Pocahontas County.

Cheat River, major tributary of the Monongahela River, formed in Tucker County by the union of several forks, draining Preston and Monongalia Counties.

Cherry River, tributary of the Gauley River, Nicholas and Greenbrier Counties.

Chestnut Ridge, westernmost Applachian Ridge in Monongalia and Preston Counties.

Circleville, southwestern Pendleton County.

Clifton Mills, northern Preston County.

Clinton, Ohio County.

Coalburg, Kanawha County.

Coal River, tributary of the Kanawha River, draining Kanawha, Lincoln, and Boone Counties.

Coonskin Park, city park, Charleston, Kanawha County.

Cooper's Rock State Forest, Monogalia and Preston Counties.

Cranberry Glades, boreal bogs in southern Pocahontas County.

Cranesville, central Preston County.

Cranesville Bog, boreal bog on the Maryland border, Preston County.

Crum, southern Wayne County.

Dailey, central Randolph County.

Davis, central Tucker County.

Deep Creek Lake, artificial impoundment in western Garrett County, Maryland.

Dunlow, southern Wayne County.

Dyer, Webster County.

Eastern Panhandle, informal name for the easternmost counties, Jefferson, Berkeley, and Morgan, but sometimes also including Hampshire, Hardy, Mineral, and Grant.

East Lynn Reservoir, artificial impoundment of the East Fork of Twelvepole Creek, Wayne County.

Elk River, tributary of the Kanawha River draining Pocahontas, Randolph, Webster, Braxton, Clay, and Kanawha Counties.

Elkins, county seat of Randolph County.

Eureka, Cabell County.

Eureka Dam, dam on Ohio River, Cabell County.

Fields Park, city reservoir and former park near Morgantown, Monongalia County.

Fork Mountain, Greenbrier County.

Flattop Lake, private lake and development, northern Mercer County.

Fort Seybert, northeastern Pendleton County.

French Creek, southern Upshur County.

Gallipolis Dam, dam on Ohio River near Point Pleasant, Mason County.

Gandy Creek, a major tributary of the Cheat River, Randolph County.

Gap Mills, southeastern Monroe County.

Gaudineer Knob, high point (1,355 m) on Shaver's Mountain, Randolph-Pocahontas Counties.

Germany Valley, eastern Pendleton County.

Great Cacapon River, tributary of the Potomac River draining Hampshire and Morgan Counties, known as the Lost River before the underground portion.

Great Kanawha River, usually called Kanawha River, tributary of the Ohio formed by the union of the Gauley and the New Rivers in Kanawha County and draining Kanawha, Putnam, and Mason Counties.

Greenbrier River, major tributary of the New River, Pocahontas, Greenbrier, and Monroe Counties.

Great North Mountain, mountain forming Virginia border in Hampshire and Hardy Counties.

Greenbank, central Pocahontas County.

Halltown, eastern Jefferson County.

Harper's Ferry, eastern Jefferson County.

Harrisville, county seat, Ritchie County.

Helvetia, west-central Randolph County.

Hemlock, eastern Upshur County.

Hinton, county seat, Summers County.

Holly River, tributary of the Elk River in Braxton and Webster Counties.

Holly River State Park, Webster County.

Huntington, county seat, Cabell County.

Ice's Ferry, site of the highway bridge across Cheat River near Morgantown, Monongalia County.

Inwood, central Berkeley County.

Jackson's Mill, State 4-H camp near Weston, Lewis County.

Kanawha City, suburb of Charleston, Kanawha County.

Kearneysville, northwestern Jefferson County.

Kennison Mountain, Pocahontas and Greenbrier Counties.

Lake Avalon, Ohio County.

Lake Louise, small pond in western Jefferson County.

Lake Lynn, Monongalia County, formerly official name of Cheat Lake.

Lake Terra Alta, artificial impoundment on Snowy Creek, north of Terra Alta, Preston County.

Lake of the Woods, artificial impoundment and private establishment on Chestnut Ridge in Preston County.

Laneville, former lumber town on Red Creek, Tucker County.

Lavalette, Cabell County.

Leachtown, Wood County.

Leetown, Jefferson County, site of Federal Fish Hatchery.

Letart Island, island in Ohio River, Mason County.

Lewisburg, county seat, Greenbrier County.

Linside, Monroe County.

Long Reach, community in Tyler County, refers to a long straight stretch of Ohio River.

Lost City, eastern Hardy County.

Lost River, stream in Hardy County, which becomes the Great Cacapon River after disappearing underground and re-emerging some distance away.

Lost River State Park, Hardy County.

Martinsburg, county seat, Berkeley County.

McClintic Wildlife Station, Mason County, an abandoned munitions plant—site managed by the Department of Natural Resources for upland game and waterfowl.

Middle Mountain, major mountain, Pocahontas and Randolph Counties.

Middle Ridge, suburban area of Charleston, Kanawha County.

Mercer's Bottom, Mason County.

Mill Hill, Greenbrier County.

Moncove Lake, artificial impoundment in Monroe County.

Moorefield, county seat, Hardy County.

Mt. Lookout, community in southern Nicholas County.

Mt. Nebo, community in southern Nicholas County.

Muddlety, northwest Nicholas County.

New Cumberland, county seat, Hancock County.

New Martinsville, county seat, Wetzel County.

Newell, northern Hancock County.

Nitro, western Kanawha County.

North Fork (River), tributary of the South Branch of the Potomac, Pendleton and Grant Counties. There are numerous lesser streams known as North Fork.

North Fork Mountain, Pendleton and Grant Counties.

North Mountain, Berkeley County.

North River Mountain, eastern Hampshire County.

Northern Panhandle, unofficial name for Marshall, Ohio, Brooke, and Hancock Counties.

Oglebay Park, city park at Wheeling, Ohio County.

Ona, Cabell County.

Opequon Creek, tributary of Potomac River forming boundary between Jefferson and Berkeley Counties.

Parsons, county seat, Tucker County.

Petersburg, county seat, Grant County.

Peters Mountain, eastern Monroe County, forming the Virginia border.

Pickaway, northern Monroe County.

Pickens, Randolph County.

Philippi, county seat, Barbour County.

Pipestem State Resort, Summers County.

Poca, southern Putnam County.

Point Pleasant, county seat, Mason County.

Reddish Knob, high point on Shenandoah Mountain (1,340 m) on Virginia-Pendleton County border.

Redhouse, Putnam County.

Ridge, Morgan County, site of a State Fish Hatchery.

Ronceverte, southern Greenbrier County.

Ruddle, Pendleton County.

Rupert, central Greenbrier County.

St. Albans, western Kanawha County.

St. Marys, county seat, Pleasants County.

Scary, Putnam County.

Seneca Rocks, spectacular rock formation in Pendleton County.

Seneca Creek, tributary of North Fork River, Pendleton County.

Shaver's Fork, a principal fork of the Cheat River in Randolph and Tucker Counties.

Shaver's Mountain, major mountain extending from Preston to Randolph and Pocahontas Counties, known as Back Allegheny Mountain south of U.S. Route 250.

Shenandoah Mountain, major mountain on the Virginia border in Pendleton County.

Shenandoah River, major tributary of the Potomac River, Jefferson County.

Shepherdstown, eastern Jefferson County.

Shoals, Wayne County.

Short Mountain, Hardy-Hampshire Counties.

Silver Lake, artificial impoundment near Maryland border in southern Preston County.

Sinks of Gandy, Randolph County. Gandy Creek disappears underground and emerges a mile away on the other side of the mountain.

South Branch of the Potomac (South Branch Valley), main branch of the Potomac from Hampshire County south into Hardy County.

South Charleston, Kanawha County.

Speedway, Mercer County.

Spruce Knob, highest point in the state (1,481 m) on Spruce Mountain, Pendleton County.

Spruce Knob Lake, artificial impoundment on a tributary of Gandy Creek, Randolph County.

Spruce Pine Hollow, a narrow valley on Sleepy Creek, Morgan County.

Stony River Reservoir, artificial impoundments on Stony River, Grant County. The older, upstream impoundment has been abandoned with the construction of a much larger one downstream.

Sugar Grove, southeastern Pendleton County.

Sugar Ridge, Greenbrier County.

Summersville, county seat, Nicholas County.

Summersville Reservoir, large artificial impoundment in Nicholas County.

Sutton, county seat, Braxton County.

Sutton Reservoir, impoundment on Elk River, Braxton County.

Thornwood, northern Pocahontas County.

Tomlinson's Run State Park, Hancock County.

Troy, Gilmer County.

Twelvepole Creek, tributary of the Ohio River, Wayne County.

Tygart Reservoir, artificial impoundment on Tygart's Valley River, Taylor County.

Tygart's Valley River, principal tributary of the Monogahela River draining Randolph, Barbour, Taylor, and Marion Counties.

Vienna, Wood County.

Volga, Barbour County.

Wanless, Pocahontas County.

Walkersville, Lewis County.

Warwood, a subdivision of Wheeling, Ohio County.

Waverly, Wood County.

Wayne Court House, Wayne County.

Weirton, Hancock County.

Wellsburg, county seat, Brooke County.

West Union, county seat, Doddridge County.

Wheeling, county seat, Ohio County.

White Sulphur Springs, Greenbrier County.

Williams River, tributary of the Gauley River, draining Pocahontas and Webster Counties.

Willow Island, Pleasants County.

UNCITED LITERATURE

FORAY AND SORTIE REPORTS

The lists of birds found on each of the Forays of the Brooks Bird Club and the Sorties of the Handlan Chapter have not been cited individually for each county record for each species in the text. These reports are listed below in abbreviated citation arranged by counties. Most of these reports are accompanied by a list of nests found, usually by a different author. The earlier reports often were only simple lists, but the recent ones have detailed annotations. Since some Forays covered more than one county, the appropriate reports are cited in both places.

Berkeley
    Banks, C. S., Redstart, 25:30–53 (1958)
    DeGarmo, W. R., Redstart, 17:29–30 (1950)

Braxton
    Bell, R. K., Redstart, 44:55–64 (1977)

Fayette
    Conrad, C., Redstart, 21:68–73 (1954)

Gilmer
    Koch, G., Redstart, 39:54–60 (1972)

Greenbrier
    Bell, R. K., Redstart, 34:11–18 (1967)
    Bell, R. K., Redstart, 39:2–12 (1972)
    Breiding, G. H., Redstart, 17:44–53A (1950)
    Phillips, J. D., Redstart, 49:4–13 (1982)

Hampshire
    Bell, R. K., Redstart, 35:44–50 (1968)

Hancock
    Breiding, G. H., Brooks Bird Club 1944 Foray Report, pp. 15–21 (mimeo).

Hardy (see also Hampshire)
    Bell, R. K., Redstart, 45:2–11 (1978)
    Olsen, H., Redstart, 7:68–75 (1940)
    Handlan, P., and C. Conrad, Redstart, 8:80–84 (1941)
    Phillips, G., Redstart, 22:57–64 (1955)

Jefferson
    Banks, C. S., Redstart, 25:30–53 (1958)
    DeGarmo, W. R., Redstart, 17:29–38 (1950)

Kanawha
    Hurley, G., Redstart, 35:66–75 (1968)
    Koch, G., Redstart, 44:107–110 (1977)

Lewis (see Upshur)
    Phillips, J. D., Redstart, 48:4–8 (1981)

Lincoln
    Koch, G., Redstart, 42:70–80 (1975)

Mason
    Koch, G., Redstart, 38:90–99 (1971)
    Koch, G., Redstart, 41:94–100 (1974)

Mineral (see Hampshire)

Monroe
    Koch, G., Redstart, 46:72–81 (1979)

Morgan
    Banks, C. S., Redstart, 25:30–53 (1958)
    DeGarmo, W. R., Redstart, 17:29–38 (1950)

Nicholas
    Olsen, V. B., Redstart, 38:31–37 (1971)

Pendleton (see also Pocahontas and Randolph)
    Rudy, C., Redstart, 37:2–12 (1970)
    Smith, J., Redstart, 31:5–11 (1964)

Pocahontas
    Anderson, K. H., Redstart, 26:30–38 (1959)
    Bell, R. K., Redstart, 32:39–50 (1965)
    Bell, R. K., Redstart, 36:2–13 (1969)
    Bell, R. K., Redstart, 41:2–12 (1974)
    Brooks, S. T., Redstart, 46:2–16 (1979)
    DeGarmo, W. R., Redstart, 14:50 -53 (1947)
    Hall, G. A., Redstart, 21:5–16 (1953)
    Handlan, J. W., Redstart, 16:46–55 (1949)

Preston
    Brooks, S. T., Redstart, 47:66–77 (1980)
    Handlan, J. W., Report of the Brooks Bird Club Foray (1943) (mimeo) (unpaged)
    Shields, T. E., Redstart, 30:4–12 (1963)

Raleigh
    Bell, R. K., Redstart, 43:11–21 (1976)

Randolph
    Anderson, K. H., 26:30–38 (1959)
    Bell, R. K., Redstart, 32:39–50 (1965)
    Bell, R. K., Redstart, 36:2–13 (1969)
    Bell, R. K., Redstart, 41:2–12 (1974)
    Brooks, S. T., Redstart, 46:2–16 (1979)
    Hall, G. A., Redstart, 21:5–16 (1953)
    Handlan, J. W., Redstart, 12:67–72 (1945)
    Handlan, J. W., Redstart, 16:46–55 (1949)

Ritchie
    Koch, G., Redstart, 42:8–14 (1975)
    Koch, G., Redstart, 42:14–18 (1975)

Tucker
    Hall, G. A., Redstart, 18:32–46 (1951)
    Laitsch, N., Redstart, 28:29–36 (1961)

Upshur
    Bell, R. K., Redstart, 40:3–12 (1973)

Wayne
    Heimerdinger, H., Redstart, 19:74–90 (1953)
    Koch, G. and G. Hurley, Redstart, 39:94–101 (1972)

Webster
    DeGarmo, W. R., Redstart, 15:47–55 (1948)
    Dressel, E. C., Redstart, 24:13–20 (1956)
    Handlan, J. and T. Frankenberger, Report of the Brooks Bird Club Foray (1942) (mimeo) (unpaged)

Wetzel
    Dressel, E. C., Redstart, 29:37–43 (1962)

REGIONAL LISTS

These annotated lists from various parts of the state have not been cited individually.

Breiding, G. H., 1949. Notes on the birds of Jackson and Webster Counties, West Virginia. Redstart, 16:69–71.

Brooks, M. G., 1942. Birds of the Cooper's Rock Region, West Virginia Conservation, 6: (3) 6 (and many following).

Chandler, E. R., 1942. A preliminary list of the birds of Tomlinson Run State Park. Redstart, 10:1–8.

Flouer, G. F., 1943. Winter birds of Lost River State Park—A preliminary list. Redstart, 10:35–37.

Green, N. B., 1944. Winter birds in the region of Huntington, West Virginia. Redstart, 11:29–32.

Kiff, L. F., 1978. The West Virginia oological collection of Charles Van Alstine. Redstart, 45:72–83.

Phillips, J. D., 1979. An ornithological study of southern West Virginia. Redstart, 46:137–147.

Pattison, J., 1937. Some birds of the Terra Alta, West Virginia Region. Redstart, 4:62–63.

Randle, W. R., 1945. Winter birds of the Cranberry Glades, Pocahontas County, West Virginia. Redstart, 12:26–28.

Shields, T. E., 1939. Some birds of Pleasants County, West Virginia. Redstart, 6:23–29.

Skaggs, M. and M. Skaggs, 1968. Birds of Holly River, 1942–1966. Redstart, 35:106–107.

Trott, J. and W. Wiggins, 1968. Summer bird population studies in the Cacapon Valley, Hampshire County, West Virginia. Redstart, 35:86–96.

SEASONAL SUMMARIES

Much information has been extracted from the seasonal summaries published four times a year in *The Redstart* and *Audubon Field Notes/American Birds* but in most cases these sources have not been cited in the species accounts.

American Birds (1971–   ) The Appalachian Region. Compiled by G. A. Hall.

Audubon Field Notes (1948–1970) The Appalachian Region. Compiled by M. Brooks (1948–1958) and G. A. Hall (1959–1970).

The Redstart (1952–   ) Field Notes. Compiled by G. A. Hall (1952–1956), G. H. Breiding (1956–1957), G. F. Hurley (1958–1963), N. Laitsch (1964–1976), G. Phillips (1977–1980), G. Eddy (1981–1982).

LITERATURE CITED

AMERICAN ORNITHOLOGISTS UNION
1957. Check-list of North American Birds. 5th Ed., Baltimore.
1982. Thirty-fourth supplement to the American Ornithologist's Union Check-list of North American birds. Auk (Supplement), 99:1cc–16cc.
1983. Check-list of North American birds. 6th Ed. (in press)

ANDERSON, K. H.
1976. Brewer's Blackbird at South Charleston, West Virginia. Redstart, 43:72.

ANDERSON, K. H., AND G. F. HURLEY
1974. White-fronted Geese at Kyger Creek, Ohio, Redstart, 41:125–126.

ANON. (= A. Shreve)
1967. Cattle Egret in West Virginia. Redstart, 34:74.

APPEL, J. C.
1957. Waterfowl development, McClintic Wildlife Station, Point Pleasant, West Virginia, 1953–June 30, 1957. Redstart, 24:70–77.

ASHWORTH, J., AND R. ASHWORTH
1977. Red Phalarope at Charleston, Redstart, 44:68–70.

AUDUBON, J. J.
1831. Ornithological Biographies. Vol. 1. Adam and Charles Black, Edinburgh.

BAILEY, R. W., AND K. T. RINNELL
1968. History and management of the Wild Turkey in West Virginia. W. Va. Dept. Nat. Res., Div. Game and Fish, Bull. No. 6.

BALLENTINE, R., AND G. BALLENTINE
1961. Confusing spring thrushes. Redstart, 28:101.

BARROWS, W. B.
1889. The English Sparrow in North America, especially in its relation to agriculture. U. S. Dept. Agri., Div. Econ. Ornithol. and Mammal., Bull. 1.

BELL, R. K.
1973. The 1972 Foray bird list. Redstart, 40:3–12.

BELLROSE, F. C.
1968. Waterfowl migration corridors east of the Rocky Mountains in the United States. Biol. Notes 61, Illinois Nat. Hist. Surv.

BIBBEE, P. C.
1929. Birds of West Virginia. Unpubl. M. S. Thesis, West Virginia Univ.
1934. Birds of West Virginia: A Check-list. Bull. 258, W. Va. Agri. Exp. Sta., Morgantown.

BOWMAN, H. M.
1956. Locations of nests of Ravens. Redstart, 23:73–74.

BRAUN, E. L.
1950. Deciduous forests of eastern North America. The Blakiston Co., Philadelphia.

BREIDING, G. H.
1944. Ornithology. Brooks Bird Club 1944 Foray Report, pp. 15–44.
1955. A nesting record for the Long-eared Owl in West Virginia. Redstart, 22:36–37.
1962a. Evidence of Blue-winged Teal (recent) and Mallard (old) nesting in Ohio County. Redstart, 29:17.
1962b. Some comments on the occurrence of some of the "brown" thrushes in the Wheeling area. Redstart, 29:50–51.
1962c. Red Phalarope in West Virginia. Wilson Bull., 74:288.
1971. A record of the American Bittern nesting in West Virginia. Redstart, 38:119.

BREWER, R.
1963. Ecological and reproductive relationships of Black-capped and Carolina Chickadees. Auk, 80:9–47.

BREWSTER, W.
1875. Some observations on the birds of Ritchie County, West Virginia. Annals. Lyceum Nat. Hist. of New York, 11:129–154.

BROOKS, A. B.
1933. West Virginia breeding record for Saw-whet Owl. Auk, 50:361–362.
1930. Yellow-crowned Night Heron taken at Wheeling, West Virginia. Auk, 47:75.

BROOKS, E. A.
1909. List of birds found in West Virginia. Report of W. Va. State Board of Agr., No. 12.
1912. Notes from West Virginia. Auk, 29:111–112.
1914. West Virginia notes. Auk, 31:544–546.
1916. The game birds of West Virginia. Fourth Biennial Rept. Forest, Game and Fish Warden, Charleston, W. Va.
1929. Birds of West Virginia. West Virginia Encyclopedia. Charleston.
1934. Notes on West Virginia waterbirds. Auk, 51:248–249.
1939. A descriptive bibliography of West Virginia ornithology. Privately printed.

BROOKS, C. L., A. B. BROOKS, AND M. BROOKS
1926. Hudsonian Curlew of West Virginia. Auk, 43:541.

BROOKS, M.
1934a. Notes on Bobolink in West Virginia. Auk, 51:90–91.
1934b. First West Virginia record for Sanderling. Auk, 51:232–233.
1934c. Virginia Rail at Jackson's Mill, Lewis County, West Virginia. Redstart, 1:6–7.
1934d. Gray-cheeked Thrush in West Virginia. Auk, 51:241.
1936a. Unusual birds in central West Virginia. Auk, 53:96–98.
1936b. Lapland Longspurs noted in West Virginia. Auk, 53:454.
1936c. Recent West Virginia additions to the 1931 AOU Checklist. Redstart, 4:21–23.
1937. Observations at Stony River Dam. Redstart, 4:68–69.
1938a. Bachman's Sparrow in the north-central portion of its range. Wilson Bull., 50:86–109.
1938b. The Eastern Lark Sparrow in the upper Ohio valley. Cardinal, 4:181–200.
1938c. Snowy Egret in West Virginia. Auk, 55:122.
1940. The breeding warblers of the central Allegheny Mountain region. Wilson Bull., 52:249–266.
1944. A check-list of West Virginia birds. Bull. 316, W. Va. Agri. Exp. Sta. Morgantown.
1945a. Great Black-backed Gull in Monongalia County, West Virginia. Auk, 62:634.
1945b. George Sutton and his warbler. Audubon Mag., 47:145–150.
1949. Fall aggregations of Cliff Swallows in the Allegheny Mountains. Auk, 66:288–298.
1952. The Allegheny Mountains as a barrier to bird movement. Auk, 69:192–198.
1953. The ornithological year in West Virginia—1953. Redstart, 21:1–3.
1955. Nesting season, Appalachian Region. Audubon Field Notes, 9:379.

BROOKS, M., AND I. B. BOGGS
1937. Sight record for Kirtland's Warbler in West Virginia. Redstart, 4:61.
1938. Scoters on Lake Lynn, West Virginia. Auk, 55:122–123.

BROOKS, M., AND B. H. CHRISTY
1942. Sutton's Warbler again. Cardinal, 5:187–189.

BROOKS, M., AND K. W. HALLER
  1936. Eastern Henslow's Sparrow breeding in West Virginia. Auk, 53:453.
BROOKS, M., AND W. C. LEGG
  1942. Swainson's Warbler in Nicholas County, West Virginia, Auk, 59:76–86.
BROOKS, M., AND W. A. LUNK
  1942. White-winged Crossbills and Sitka Crossbills summering in West Virginia. Auk, 59:118–119.
BROOKS, M., AND C. K. PECK
  1940. Northern Fringillidae in West Virginia. Cardinal, 5:96.
BUCKELEW, A. R., JR.
  1976. Birds of the West Virginia Northern Panhandle. Redstart, 43:90–107.
  1978a. American Avocet in West Virginia. Redstart, 45:86.
  1978b. Brown Creeper nesting in the Ohio Valley. Redstart, 45:128–129.
BURNS, R. K.
  1961. Nesting of the Black-billed Magpie in Tucker County, West Virginia and a consideration of its status in northeastern United States. Redstart, 28:62–68.
CABOT, S., JR.
  1839. Observations on the plumage of red and mottled owls (*Strix asio*). Boston J. Nat. Hist., 2:127.
CHANDLER, E. R.
  1962. Sight record for Black-backed Three-toed Woodpecker in West Virginia. Redstart, 29:97.
CHANDLER, E. R. AND E. CHANDLER
  1980. Canada Geese winter in the B.B.C. Wild Bird Sanctuary in Chester City Park. Redstart, 47:119.
CONN, R. C.
  1948. Pine Grosbeaks at Cheat Lake, Monongalia County. Redstart. 16:14.
CONNER, F. AND J. PATTISON
  1938. Nest and eggs of Northern Raven in Monongalia County, West Virginia. Redstart, 5:78–79.
CONRAD, C. L.
  1968. Hudsonian Godwit is a West Virginia record. Redstart, 35:59.
  1981. Breeding record for Yellow-throated Warbler in Ohio County, W. Va. Redstart, 48:115.
CONRAD, C. AND H. CONRAD
  1980. A Black-headed Grosbeak visits Ohio County. Redstart, 47:83–84.
DAWSON, W. L.
  1903. The birds of Ohio. Wheaton Publ. Co., Columbus.
DEGARMO, W. R.
  1950. Ornithological results of the 1949 Foray in the Eastern Panhandle of West Virginia. Redstart, 17:29–38.
  1953. A five-year study of hawk migration. Redstart, 20:39–54.
DICKENS, B.
  1960. Magpie collected at Morgantown. Redstart, 27:64.
DOAN, W. D.
  1888. Birds of West Virginia. Bull. No. 3, W. Va. Agri. Exp. Sta., Morgantown.
EDEBURN, R. M.
  1950. Saw-whet Owl (*Aegolius a. acadicus*) in West Virginia. Auk, 67:386–387.
  1954. King Eider in West Virginia. Wilson Bull., 66:141.
  1964. Black-legged Kittiwake in West Virginia. Wilson Bull., 76:214–215.
  1968. Breeding range extension of Saw-whet Owls in West Virginia. Wilson Bull., 80:232.
EDEBURN, R. M., E. L. SEEBER, H. LAND, H. LAND, AND L. KIFF.
  1960. Birds of the lower Ohio Valley in West Virginia. Marshall Univ., Huntington (mimeo).

EIFRIG, C. W. G.
  1902. Northern Phalarope and Black Tern at Cumberland, Maryland. Auk, 19:76–77.
  1904. Birds of Alleghany and Garrett Counties, western Maryland. Auk, 21:234–250.
ENVIRONMENTAL DATA SERVICE
  1968. Climatic atlas of the United States. Environmental Sci. Adm., U. S. Dept. Commerce, Washington.
EYE, O. L.
  1977. Sighting of Sutton's Warbler. Redstart, 44:67–68.
FENNEMAN, N. M.
  1938. Physiography of Eastern United States. McGraw-Hill Book Co., New York.
FLOUER, G.
  1938. Waterbirds in Morgan County, West Virginia. Redstart, 6:18.
  1940. Yellow Rail in West Virginia. Auk, 57:413–414.
FRAZIER, H. H.
  1948. Holboell's Grebes at Lake Lynn, Monongalia County. Redstart, 16:16.
FRYE, W. M.
  1967. Passenger Pigeon note. Redstart, 34:77.
GANIER, A. F., AND F. W. BUCHANAN
  1953. Nesting of White-throated Sparrow in West Virginia. Wilson Bull., 65:277–279.
GLUCK, N.
  1965. Purple Martin roost in South Charleston. Redstart, 32:86–90.
  1975. Blue-wing mates with Golden-wing in Coonskin. Redstart, 42:104–105.
GLUCK, N., AND C. O. HANDLEY, SR.
  1973. Birds of the upper Kanawha Valley, 1872 and 1972. Redstart, 40:66–69.
GOETZ, E. J.
  1975. Habitat variables and urban songbird populations. Unpubl. M. S. Thesis, West Virginia Univ.
GREEN, N. B.
  1949. King Rail nesting in Wayne County, West Virginia. Redstart, 16:35.
GRISCOM, L.
  1937. A monographic study of the Red Crossbill. Proc. Boston Soc. Nat. Hist., 41:77–210.
GROSE, E. R.
  1945. Birds of the Glenville section. Redstart, 12:32–40.
GUILDAY, J. E.
  1962. The Pleistocene local fauna at Natural Chimneys, Augusta County, Virginia. Ann. Carnegie Mus., 36:87–122.
  1971. Biological and archeological analysis of bones from a 17th century Indian Village (46 PU 31), Putnam County, West Virginia. W. Va. Geol. and Econ. Survey, Report of Arch. Invest. No. 4.
HAHN, P.
  1963. Where is that vanished bird? Royal Ontario Museum.
HALL, G. A.
  1954a. Field Notes: The winter season. Redstart, 21:40–44.
  1954b. Surf Scoters in Monongalia County, West Virginia. Redstart, 21:62.
  1959. A late record for Northern Phalarope in West Virginia. Wilson Bull., 71:194.
  1960. West Virginia records for the three species of scoter. Redstart, 27:43–44.
  1963. Western Meadowlark in West Virginia. Wilson Bull., 75:279.
  1967. Yellow-throated Warbler and Prothonotary Warbler nests in Jefferson County, West Virginia. Redstart, 34:77.

1969a. The present status of the West Virginia bird list. Redstart, 36:62–65.

1969b. Breeding range expansion of the Brown Creeper in the Middle Atlantic States. Redstart, 36:98–103.

1971. The list of West Virginia Birds. Redstart, 38:2–18.

1973. Supplement to "The List of West Virginia Birds." Redstart, 40:102–104.

1974. The Appalachian Region. Amer. Birds, 28:52–56.

1976a. An addition to the West Virginia list—Northern Shrike. Redstart, 43:114–115.

1976b. Buff-breasted Sandpiper in West Virginia. Redstart, 43:123–124.

1978. Yellow-rumped Warbler summers in West Virginia. Redstart, 45:127–128.

1982. Supplement II to "The list of West Virginia Birds". Redstart, 49:62–64.

HALL, G. A., AND T. HALL
1970. Boreal Chickadees at Morgantown, a new species for West Virginia. Redstart, 37:61.

HALL, G. A., AND N. LAITSCH
1963. Brown Creeper nesting in West Virginia. Wilson Bull., 75:278.

HALLER, K. W.
1940a. List of birds of Mason, Cabell, Jackson and Putnam Counties, West Virginia. Redstart, 7:37–52.

1940b. Observations in the Eastern Panhandle of West Virginia. Redstart, 7:57.

1940c. Untitled communication. Redstart, 7:65–66.

1940d. A new Wood Warbler from West Virginia. Cardinal, 5:49–52.

1949. Nelson Sharp-tailed Sparrow in West Virginia. Auk, 66:369.

1951. *Turdus migratorius achrusterus* and *Passerculus sandwichensis mediogriseus* in the Northern Panhandle of West Virginia. Wilson Bull., 63:45.

HANDLAN, J. T., JR.
1938. Heavy flight of waterfowl on Lake Lynn, West Virginia. Auk, 55:129–130.

HANDLAN, J. W.
1934. Other observations of interest, Canadian Pine Grosbeak. Redstart, 1:4.

1941. Loon and Least Tern in the Kanawha Valley. Redstart, 9:20.

1944. White Pelican in Kanawha County, West Virginia. Redstart, 10:61.

HANDLEY, C. O., (SR.)
1931. The Black Vulture in Greenbrier County, West Virginia. Auk, 48:598–599.

1976. Birds of the Great Kanawha Valley. McClain Publishing Co., Parsons, W. Va.

HANDLEY, C. O., JR.
1979. Avocet in West Virginia. Redstart, 46:148.

1981. Brewer's Blackbird in eastern West Virginia. Redstart, 48:62–63.

HARWOOD, P. D.
1974. Green-winged Teal nests in West Virginia. Redstart, 41:86.

HEIMERDINGER, H. O.
1974. 1971 hawk watch on Allegheny Front Mountain at Bear Rocks. Redstart, 41:119–120.

HICKS, L. E.
1935. A migration of Mute Swans. Auk, 52:301–302.

1938. Western Henslow's Sparrow taken in West Virginia. Wilson Bull., 50:291.

1945. Some West Virginia breeding season records. Wilson Bull., 57:129–131.

HILL, W. E.
1884. Birds of the "Panhandle" of West Virginia. Ornithologist and Oologist. 9:3–9.

HONIG, R. A.
1981. Birds Observed at the National Fisheries Center, Leetown, W.Va. April 1980–September 1981. Redstart, 48:118–126.

HURLEY, G. F.
1970. Fall hawk migration along Peters Mountain in Monroe County, W.Va. Redstart, 37:81–86.

1972. Swainson's Warbler distribution in West Virginia. Redstart, 39:110–112.

1975. Fall hawk migration along Peters Mountain, Part 2. Redstart, 42:114–117.

JAMES, B. E.
1980. A Painted Bunting in Blue Jay, West Virginia. Redstart, 47:122.

JOHNSTON, D. W.
1971. Ecological aspects of hybridizing chickadees (*Parus*) in Virginia. Amer. Midland Naturalist, 85:124–134.

JOHNSTON, I. H.
1923. Birds of West Virginia. State Dept. Agri., Charleston.

1926. Sooty Tern (*Sterna fuscata*) in West Virginia. Auk, 43:535–536.

KEHRER, V.
1936. Baird's and Least Sandpipers at Wheeling, West Virginia. Redstart, 4:11.

KIFF, L. F.
1965. White Pelican at Huntington, West Virginia. Redstart, 32:107.

KIFF, L. F., M. C. KIFF, AND L. P. WILSON
1977. Further notes on the status of the Blue Grosbeak in southwestern West Virginia. Redstart, 44:104–107.

KOCH, G.
1971. The Black-headed Grosbeak in South Charleston and St. Albans, West Virginia, March and April 1971. Redstart, 38:127.

1975. The 1974 Sortie. Redstart, 42:8–14.

KOEPPE, C. E., AND G. C. DELONG
1958. Weather and Climate. McGraw-Hill Book Co., New York.

LAITSCH, N.
1967. Field Notes, The spring season. Redstart, 34:99–104.

LANHAM, C.
1977. Clay-colored Sparrow: A new accidental species for West Virginia. Redstart, 45:101–102.

LEGG, W. C.
1942. Swainson's Warbler in Webster County, West Virginia. Wilson Bull., 54:252.

1944. A preliminary list of the birds of western Nicholas County. Redstart, 11:37–44.

1947. Water birds at a Nicholas County pond. Redstart, 12:56–57.

LESSER, W.
1960. Brant in Doddridge County, West Virginia. Redstart, 27:45.

LOWERY, G. H., JR., AND B. L. MONROE, JR.
1968. Family Parulidae, Wood Warblers. A Check-list of birds of the world. Vol. 14 (R. A. Paynter, Jr. (ed.), Mus. Comp. Zool., Cambridge, Mass. p. 39.

LUNK, W. A.
1941. Bicknell's Thrush in West Virginia. Auk, 58:264.

MACARTHUR, R. H., AND E. O. WILSON
1967. The theory of island biogeography. Princeton Univ. Press, Princeton, N. J.

MEANLEY, B.
1971. Natural History of Swainson's Warbler. N. Amer. Fauna, 69.

MENGEL, R. M.
   1965. The Birds of Kentucky. Ornithol. Monogr. #3 Amer. Ornithol. Union.

MILLER, C.
   1969. Common Snipe wintering in Berkeley and Jefferson Counties of West Virginia. Redstart, 36:82–83.

MITCHELL, H. D.
   1952. Sutton's Warbler (*Dendroica potomac*) again observed in West Virginia. Wilson Bull., 64:47–48.

MONROE, J.
   1945. Western Tanager. Redstart, 12:46.

MONTAGNA, W.
   1939. Pine Grosbeak in northern West Virginia Panhandle. Auk, 56:342.
   1940. King Rail in West Virginia Panhandle. Cardinal, 5:70.

MURRAY, J. J.
   1952. A check-list of the birds of Virginia. Virginia Soc. Ornithol.

OBERHOLSER, H. C.
   1934. A revision of the North American House Wrens. Ohio J. Sci., 34:90–96.

PARKES, K. C.
   1951. The genetics of the Golden-winged × Blue-winged Warbler complex. Wilson Bull., 63:5–15.
   1959. Systematic notes on North American birds. 3. The northeastern races of the Long-billed Marsh Wren (*Telmatodytes palustris*). Ann. Carnegie Mus., 35:275–281.
   1968. Some bird records from western Pennsylvania. Wilson Bull., 80:100–102.

PARMALEE, P. W.
   1967. Additional noteworthy records of birds from archaeological sites. Wilson Bull., 79:155–162.

PARSONS, D. W.
   1946. Field Notes, Lark Sparrow. Redstart, 13:58.

PAULEY, T. K.
   1974. An unusual date for a Sandhill Crane in West Virginia. Redstart, 41:109.

PHILLIPS, G.
   1961. Foray records of the Brooks Bird Club. Redstart, 28:102–110.

PHILLIPS, J.
   1977. A Yellow-headed Blackbird near Princeton, West Virginia. Redstart, 44:82.
   1980. American Avocet and Black Terns visit southern West Virginia. Redstart, 47:152.

POLAND, J. L.
   1936. Upland Plover found breeding in Berkeley County, West Virginia. Auk, 53:444.
   1938a. Unusual shorebirds in Jefferson County, West Virginia. Wilson Bull., 50:59.
   1938b. A preliminary list of the birds of the Eastern Panhandle. Redstart, 5:64–75.
   1938c. Waterbirds at Leetown, West Virginia. Auk, 55:127–129.
   1939. Ruddy Turnstone in West Virginia. Auk, 56:76.
   1941. Additions to the Eastern Panhandle bird list. Redstart, 8:88–92.

RIVES, W. C.
   1890. A catalogue of the birds of the Virginias. Proc. Newport Nat. Hist. Soc. Doc. 7, Newport, R. I.
   1898. The summer birds of the West Virginia spruce belt. Auk, 15:131–137.

ROBBINS, S. B.
   1975. First confirmed record of Chuck-will's-widow for West Virginia. Redstart, 42:56–58.

SAMUEL, D. E.
   1969. House Sparrow occupancy of Cliff Swallow nests. Wilson Bull., 81:103–104.
   1971. The breeding biology of Barn and Cliff Swallows in West Virginia. Wilson Bull., 83:284–301.

SCHORGER, A. W.
   1955. The Passenger Pigeon. Univ. Wisconsin Press, Madison.

SCOTT, W. D.
   1872. Partial list of the summer birds of Kanawha County, West Virginia. Proc. Boston Soc. Nat. Hist., 15.

SHEARER, D., AND M. SHEARER
   1975. Unexpected night sound. Redstart, 42:59.

SHIELDS, L., AND A. SHIELDS
   1948. Prothonotary Warbler's nest in Wood County, West Virginia. Auk, 65:454.

SHIELDS, T. E.
   1955. A sight record of the Eared Grebe, Ohio County, West Virginia. Redstart, 22:29.

SHREVE, A.
   1966. Sharp-tailed Sparrow at McClintic Wildlife Refuge. Redstart, 33:64.
   1968. Harris Sparrow at Charleston. Redstart, 35:60.
   1977. Territorial Short-billed Marsh Wren in Kanawha County. Redstart, 44:94–97.

SHREVE, MRS. HARVEY (= A. SHREVE)
   1964. Parasitic Jaeger in West Virginia. Redstart, 31:11.

SHORT, L. L., JR.
   1963. Hybridization in the wood warblers *Vermivora pinus* and *V. chrysoptera*. Proc. 13th Internatl. Ornithol. Congr., 1962. pp. 147–160.

SIMS, A., AND W. R. DEGARMO
   1948. A study of Swainson's Warbler in West Virginia. Redstart, 16:1–8.

SMITH, J. L.
   1965. The Passenger Pigeon in West Virginia. Redstart, 32:94–96.
   1976. Young male Harlequin Duck at Bluestone Dam, Hinton, West Virginia. Redstart, 43:73.
   1980. Decline of the Bewick's Wren. Redstart, 47:77–82.

STARK, A. C.
   1874. "Chestnut-sided Warbler." Amer. Naturalist, 3:756.

STEWART, R. E., AND C. S. ROBBINS
   1958. Birds of Maryland and the District of Columbia. N. Amer. Fauna, 62.

SURBER, T.
   1888. "From West Virginia" Oologist, 5:11.
   1889. Birds of Greenbrier County, West Virginia. Hawkeye Ornithologist and Oologist, 2:1–3.
   1898. Two species new to the list of birds found in West Virginia. Auk, 15:61.

SUTTON, G. M.
   1928. Untitled note. Cardinal, 2:105.
   1933. Birds of the West Virginia Panhandle. Cardinal, 3:101–123.
   1937. Notes from Brooke County, West Virginia. Cardinal, 4:117–118.

TANNER, J. T.
   1952. Black-capped and Carolina Chickadees in the southern Appalachian Mountains. Auk, 69:407–424.

TAYLOR, W.
   1926. Status of Yellow-headed Blackbird (*Xanthocephalus xanthocephalus*) on the Atlantic Seaboard. Auk, 43:241.

TRAUTMAN, M. B., AND M. A. TRAUTMAN
   1968. Annotated list of the birds of Ohio. Ohio J. Sci., 68:257–332.

VOSSLER, B.
   1967. Brown Creepers nesting in Ohio County. Redstart, 34:24.

WALL, A.
1884. Untitled. Amer. Field, 22:32. (Unexamined but given in Brooks, 1938).
WAGGY, C. D.
1973. Breeding ecology of the Canada Goose at the McClintic Wildlife Station. Unpubl. M. S. Thesis, West Virginia Univ.
WARD, L.
1948. A Marsh Hawk nest in Canaan Valley. Redstart, 16:14–15.
WEIMER, B. R.
1935. Holboell's Grebe at Bethany, West Virginia. Cardinal, 4:17.
WEST, R., AND T. SHIELDS
1935. Some bird records for the Northern West Virginia Panhandle. Redstart, 2:26–28.
WEST VIRGINIA DEPARTMENT OF NATURAL RESOURCES
1982. 1981 West Virginia Big Game Bulletin.
WETMORE, A.
1937. Observations on the birds of West Virginia. Proc. U. S. Natl. Mus., 84:401–441.

1939. Western Olive-backed Thrush in West Virginia and Tennessee. Auk, 56:477.
1940. Notes on woodpeckers from West Virginia. Auk, 57:113–114.
WIMSATT, W. A.
1939. Black Vulture and Duck Hawk nesting in Maryland. Auk, 56:181–182.
1940. Early nesting of the Duck Hawk in Maryland. Auk, 57:109.
WILSON, A., AND C. BONAPARTE
1931. American Ornithology.
WRIGHT, M. B.
1963. Bohemian Waxwings at Morgantown. Redstart, 30:22.
WYLIE, B.
1974. Green Heron migration. Redstart, 41:118–119.
YENKE, W. H.
1952. Stilt Sandpiper in Ohio County, West Virginia. Redstart, 20:18.

INDEX TO BIRD NAMES

Accipiter cooperii 45–46
    gentilis 46
    striatus 45
Actitis macularia 56
Aegolius acadicus............ 68–69
Agelaius phoeniceus 156
    p. arctolegus 156
    p. phoeniceus 156
Aimophila aestivalis 144–145
Aix sponsa 33–34
Alectoris chukar 166
Ammodramus caudacutus 150
    henslowii 149–150
    h. henslowi 150
    h. susurrans 150
    leconteii 150
    savannarum 149
Anas acuta 35
    americana 37
    clypeata 36
    crecca 34
    discors 35–36
    penelope 36–37
    platyrhynchos 35
    rubripes 34–35
    strepera 36
Anser albifrons 31–32
Anthus spinoletta............ 110
Aquila chrysaetos 48
Archilochus colubris 71
Ardea herodias 27
Arenaria interpres 57
Asio flammeus 68
    otus 68
Avocet, American 55
Aythya affinis 38–39
    americana 37
    collaris 38
    marila 38
    valisneria 37
Barn-Owl, Common 67
Bartramia longicauda 56–57
Bittern, American 26
    Least 26–27
Blackbird, Brewer's 158
    Red-winged 156, 159
    Rusty 157–158
    Yellow-headed 157
Bluebird, Eastern 103, 112
Bobolink 13, 155–156
Bobwhite, Northern 14, 51
Bombycilla cedrorum 110–111
    garrulus 110
Bonasa umbellus 50
    u. monticola 50
    u. umbellus 50
Botaurus lentiginosus 26
Brant 32
Branta bernicla 32
    canadensis 32–33
    c. interior 33
    c. maxima 33
    hutchinsi 33
Bubo virginianus 67
Bubulcus ibis 28

Bucephala albeola 40–41
    clangula 40
Bufflehead 40–41
Bunting, Lark 148
    Painted 143
    Snow 155
    Indigo 142–143
Buteo jamaicensis 47
    lagopus 47–48
    lineatus 46
    platypterus 46–47
    swainsoni 47
Butorides striatus 28
    s. virescens 28
Calamospiza melanocorys 148
Calcarius lapponicus 155
Calidris alba 57
    alpina 59
    bairdii 58
    fuscicollis 58
    himantopus 59
    mauri 57–58
    melanotos 58–59
    minutilla 58
    pusilla 57
Campephilus principalis...... 76
Canvasback 37
Caprimulgus carolinensis ... 69–70
    vociferus 70
Cardinal, Northern 140–141
    Red-Crested 166
Cardinalis cardinalis 140–141
Carduelis flammea........... 163
    hornemanni............... 163
    pinus 163–164
    tristis 164
Carpodacus mexicanus 161–162
    purpureus 161
Casmerodius albus 27
Catbird, Gray 108–109
Cathartes aura 42–43
Catharus fuscescens 104–105
    f. fuscescens 105
    f. salicicola 105
    guttatus 106–107
    g. faxoni 107
    minimus 105
    m. bicknelli 105
    m. minimus 105
    ustulatus 105–106
    u. almae 106
    u. swainsoni 106
Catoptrophorus semipalmatus 56
Certhia americana 90–91
    a. americana 91
    a. nigrescens 91
Ceryle alcyon 71–72
Chaetura pelagica 70–71
Charadrius hiaticula 54
    melodus 54
    semipalmatus 54
    vociferus 54–55
Chat, Yellow-breasted 138–139
Chen caerulescens 32
    c. atlantica 32

    c. caerulescens 32
    hypoborea 32
Chickadee, Black-capped ... 13, 87–88
    Boreal 13, 88–89
    Carolina 14, 88
Chlidonias niger 64
Chondestes grammacus 147–148
Chordeiles minor 69
Chuck-will's-widow 69–70
Circus cyaneus 44–45
Cistothorus palustris 101
    p. dissaeptus 101
    p. iliacus 101
    platensis 101
Clangula hyemalis 39
Coccothraustes vespertinus 165
Coccyzus americana 66
    erythrophthalmus 65–66
Colaptes auratus........... 74–75
    a. auratus 75
    a. borealis 75
    a. luteus 75
Colinus virginanus 51
Columba livia............... 64
Contopus borealis 76
    virens 76–77
Conuropsis carolinensis 65
    c. ludoviciana 65
Coot, American 53
Coragyps atratus 42
Cormorant, Double-crested 26
    Great 25–26
Corvus brachyrhynchos 86
    b. brachyrhynchos 86
    b. paulus 86
    corax.................... 87
    c. principalis 87
    ossifragus 86
Coturnicops noveboracensis 51
Cowbird, Brown-headed 159
Crane, Sandhill............ 53–54
Creeper, American Brown ....
    .... 13, 90–91, 94
Crossbill, Red 13, 162–163
    White-winged 163
Crow, American 86
    Fish 86
Cuckoo, Black-billed 15, 65–66
    Yellow-billed 15, 66
Cyanocitta cristata 85
    c. bromia 85
    c. cristata 85
Cygnus buccinator........... 31
    columbianus 30–31
    olor 31
Dendragapus canadensis 13
Dendroica caerulescens 122–123
    c. caerulescens 123
    c. cairnsi 123
    castanea 129
    cerulea 130
    coronata 123–124
    discolor 127–128
    dominica 126
    d. albilora 126, 127

fusca 125
kirtlandii 127
magnolia 121
palmarum 128–129
p. hypochrysea 129
p. palmarum 128–129
pensylvanica 120–121
petechia 120
p. aestiva 120
pinus 127
potomac 127
striata 129
tigrina 122
virens 124–125
Dickcissel 15, 143
Dolichonyx oryzivorus ... 155–156
Dove, Mourning 64–65
Rock 64
Dowitcher, Long-billed 59
Short-billed 59
Dryocopus pileatus 75–76
Duck, American Black ... 34–35
Harlequin 39
Ring-necked 38
Ruddy 42
Wood 33–34
Dumetella carolinensis ... 108–109
Dunlin 59
Eagle, Bald 7, 13, 44
Golden 48
Ectopistes migratorius 65
Egret, Cattle 28
Great 27
Snowy 27–28
Egretta caerulea 28
thula 27–28
Eider, King 39
Elanoides forficatus 44
Empidonax alnorum 78–79
flaviventris 77
minimus 79
traillii 78–79
virescens 77–78
Eremophila alpestris 81–82
a. alpestris 82
a. hoyti 82
a. praticola 82
Eudocimus albus 29
Euphagus carolinus 157–158
cyanocephalus 158
Falco columbarius 49
peregrinus 49
sparverius 48–49
Falcon, Peregrine 49
Finch, House 161–162
Purple 13, 161
Flicker, Northern 74–75
Flycatcher, Acadian 14, 77–78
Alder 13, 78–79
Great Crested 80
Least 13, 79
Olive-sided 13, 76
Scissor-tailed 81
"Traill's" 78–80
Willow 78–79
Yellow-bellied 13, 77
Vermilion 80
Fulica americana 53

Gadwall 36
Gallinago gallinago 59–60
Gallinula chloropus 53
Gallinule, Common 53
Purple 52–53
Gavia immer 23–24
stellata 23
Geothlypis trichas 136–137
t. brachydactylus 137
t. trichas 137
Gnatcatcher, Blue-gray ... 14, 103
Godwit, Hudsonian 57
Goldeneye, Common 40
Goldfinch, American 164
Goose, Blue 32
Cackling 33
Canada 32–33
Greater White-fronted ... 31–32
Snow 32
Goshawk, Northern 13, 46
Grackle, Common 14, 158–159
Grebe, Eared 25
Pied-billed 24
Horned 24–25
Red-necked 25
Grosbeak, Black-headed ... 142
Blue 14, 142
Evening 165
Pine 160–161
Rose-breasted 13, 141–142
Grouse, Ruffed 50
Sharp-tailed 166
Spruce 13
Grus canadensis 53–54
Guiraca caerulea 142
Gull, Bonaparte's 62
Great Black-backed 63
Herring 62
Laughing 61
Ring-billed 62
Haliaeetus leucocephalus ... 44
l. alascanus 44
l. leucocephalus 44
Harrier, Northern ... 13, 43, 44–45
Hawk, Broad-Winged 43
Cooper's 45–46
Marsh 45
Pigeon 49
Red-shouldered 43, 46
Red-tailed 43, 47
Rough-legged 47–48
Sharp-shinned 13, 43, 45
Sparrow 49
Swainson's 47
Helmitheros vermivorus 132
Heron, Great Blue 27
Green 28
Green-backed 28
Little Blue 28
Hirundo pyrrhonota 84
rustica 84–85
Histrionicus histrionicus 39
Hummingbird, Ruby-throated ... 71
Hylocichla mustelina 107
Ibis, White 29
Icteria virens 138–139
Icterus galbula 160
spurius 159–160

Ixobrychus exilis 26–27
Jaeger, Parasitic 61
Jay, Blue 85
Gray 13
Junco hyemalis 154–155
h. carolinensis 154
h. cismontanus 154
h. hyemalis 154
h. montanus 155
Junco, Dark-Eyed ....
.... 13, 16, 17, 154–155
Kestrel, American 43, 48–49
Killdeer 54–55
Kingbird, Eastern 14, 81
Western 80–81
Kingfisher, Belted 71–72
Kinglet, Golden-crowned .. 13, 16, 102
Ruby-crowned 102–103
Kite, American Swallow-tailed 44
Kittiwake, Black-legged 63
Lanius excubitor 111
ludovicianus 111–112
l. ludovicianus 112
l. migrans 112
Lark, Horned 81–82
Larus argentatus 62
delawarensis 62
marinus 63
philadelphia 62
atricilla 61
Laterallus jamaicensis 51
Limnodromus griseus 59
scolopaceus 59
Limothlypis swainsonii 132–133
s. altus 133
Limosa haemastica 57
Longspur, Lapland 155
Loon, Common 23–24
Red-throated 23
Lophodytes cucullatus 41
Loxia curvirostra 162–163
c. bendirei 163
c. benti 163
c. minor 163–164
c. neogaea 163
c. sitkensis 163
leucoptera 163
Magpie, Black-billed 85–86
Mallard 35
Martin, Purple 14, 82–83
Meadowlark, Eastern ... 156–157
Western 157
Melanerpes carolinus ... 72–73
c. carolinus 73
c. zebra 73
erythrocephalus 72
Melanitta nigra 39
fusca 40
perspicillata 39–40
Meleagris gallopavo 50–51
Melospiza georgiana ... 151–152
g. ericrypta 152
g. georgiana 152
lincolnii 151
melodia 150–151
m. euphonia 151
m. melodia 151
Merganser, Common 41

Hooded 41
Red-breasted 41–42
Mergus merganser 41
serrator 41–42
Merlin 49
Mimus polyglottos 109
Mniotilta varia 130–131
Mockingbird, Northern 14, 109
Molothrus ater 159
Moorhen, Common 53
Mycteria americana 29
Myiarchus crinitus 80
c. borealis 80
c. crinitus 80
Myiopsitta monachus 166
Night-Heron, Black-crowned . . 28–29
Yellow-crowned 29
Nighthawk, Common 69
Numenius phaeopus 57
Nuthatch, Red-breasted 13, 89–90
White-breasted 90
Nyctea scandiaca 67–68
Nycticorax nycticorax 28–29
violaceus 29
Oldsquaw 39
Oporornis agilis 135–136
formosus 135
philadelphia 136
Oriole, Baltimore 160
Northern 14, 160
Orchard 159–160
Osprey 43, 44
Otus asio 67
a. asio 67
a. naevius 67
Ovenbird 17, 133–135, 159
Owl, Barred 68
Great Horned 67
Long-eared 68
Northern Saw-whet 13, 68–69
Short-eared 68
Snowy 7, 67–68
Oxyura jamaicensis 42
Pandion haliaetus 44
Parakeet, Carolina 7, 11, 65
Monk 166
Paroraria coronata 166
Partridge, Chukar 166
Gray 166
Parula americana 119–120, 127
Parula, Northern 96, 119–120
Parus atricapillus 87–88
a. atricapillus 88
a. practicus 88
bicolor 89
carolinensis 88
c. extimus 88
hudsonicus 88–89
Passer domesticus 165–166
Passerculus sandwichensis . . . 148–149
s. labradorius 149
s. mediogriseus 149
s. savanna 149
Passerella iliaca 150
Passerina ciris 143
cyanea 142–143
Pelecanus erythrorhynchos 25
Pelican, American White 25

Perdix perdix 166
Perisoreus canadensis 13
Phalacrocorax auritus 26
carbo 25–26
Phalarope, Northern 51
Red 61
Red-necked 61
Wilson's 60–61
Phalaropus fulicaria 61
lobatus 61
tricolor 60–61
Phasianus colchicus 50
Pheasant, Ring-necked 50
Pheucticus ludovicianus 141–142
melanocephalus 142
Phoebe, Eastern 79–80
Pica pica 85–86
Picoides arcticus 74
pubescens 73–74
p. medianus 74
villosus 74
Pigeon, Passenger 11, 65
Pinicola enucleator 160–161
e. eschatosus 161
Pintail, Northern 35
Pipilo chlorurus 144
erythrophthalmus 144
e. arcticus 144
e. erythrophthalmus 144
fuscus 144
Pipit, Water 110
Piranga ludoviciana 140
olivacea 140
rubra 139–140
Plectrophenax nivalis 155
Plover, Black-bellied 54
Piping 54
Ringed 54
Semipalmated 54
Lesser Golden 54
Pluvialis dominica 54
squatarola 54
Podiceps auritus 24–25
grisegena 25
nigricollis 25
Podilymbus podiceps 24
Polioptila caerulea 103
Pooecetes gramineus 146–147
Porphyrula martinica 52–53
Porzana carolina 52
Progne subis 82–83
Protonotaria citrea 132
Pyrocephalus rubinus 80
Quiscalus quiscula 158–159
q. ridgwayi 159
q. stonei 158
q. versicolor 159
Rail, Black 51
Clapper 51
King 51–52
Virginia 52
Yellow 51
Rallus elegans 51–52
limicola 52
longirostris 51
Raven, Common 13, 87
Recurvirostra americana 55
Redhead 37

Redpoll, Common 163
Hoary 163
Redstart, American 14, 131–132
Regulus calendula 102
satrapa 102–103
Riparia riparia 83–84
Rissa tridactyla 63
Robin, American 107–108
Sanderling 57
Sandpiper, Baird's 58
Buff-breasted 59
Least 58
Pectoral 58–59
Semipalmated 57
Solitary 56
Spotted 56
Stilt 59
Upland 14, 56–57
Western 57–58
White-rumped 58
Sapsucker, Yellow-bellied 13, 73
Sayornis phoebe 79–80
Scaup, Greater 38
Lesser 38–39
Scolopax minor 60
Scoter, Surf 40–41
White-winged 41
Black 39
Screech-Owl, Eastern 7, 67
Seiurus aurocapillus 133–134
motacilla 134–135
noveboracensis 134
Setophaga ruticilla 131–132
Shoveler, Northern 36
Shrike, Loggerhead 14, 111–112
Northern 111
Sialia sialis 103–104
Siskin, Pine 13, 163–164
Sitta canadensis 89–90
carolinensis 90
c. cookei 90
Snipe, Common 12, 13, 59–60
Somateria spectabilis 39
Sora 52
Sparrow, American Tree 145
Bachman's 15, 144–145
Chipping 145–146
Clay-colored 146
Field 146
Fox 150
Grasshopper 149
Harris' 153–154
Henslow's 15, 149–150
House 165–166
Lark 14, 147–148
Le Conte's 150
Lincoln's 159
Savannah 13, 18, 148–149
Sharp-tailed 150
Song 150–151
Swamp 13, 151–152
Vesper 15, 18, 146–147
White-crowned 153
White-throated . . . 12, 13, 152–153
Sphyrapicus varius 73
v. appalachiensis 73
v. varius 73
Spiza americana 143

Spizella arborea 145
    pallida 146
    passerina 145–146
    pusilla 146
Starling, European . . . 14, 72, 112, 159
Stelgidopteryx serripennis 83
Stercorarius parasiticus 61
Sterna antillarum 63–64
    a. antillarum 64
    a. athalassos 64
    caspia 63
    forsteri 63
    fuscata 64
    hirundo 63
Stork, Wood 29
Streptopelia risoria 166
Strix varia 68
Sturnella magna 156–157
    neglecta 157
Sturnus vulgaris 112
Swallow, Bank 15, 83–84
    Cliff 13, 84
    Northern Rough-winged 83
    Tree 13, 83
    Barn 84–85
Swan, Mute 31
    Trumpeter 31
    Tundra 30, 31
    Whistling 31
Swift, Chimney 70–71
Tachycineta bicolor 83
Tanager, Scarlet 14, 140
    Summer 14, 100, 139–140
    Western 140
Teal, Blue-winged 35–36
    Green-winged 34
Tern, Black 64
    Caspian 63
    Common 63
    Forster's 63
    Least 63–64
    Sooty 64
Thrasher, Brown 109–110
Thrush, Gray-cheeked 105
    Hermit 13, 17, 106–107, 122
    Swainson's 13, 94, 95, 105–106
    Wood 107
Thryomanes bewickii 92
    b. altus 92
Thryothorus ludovicianus 91–92
Titmouse, Tufted 89
Towhee, Brown 144
    Green-tailed 144
    Rufous-sided 144
Toxostoma rufum 109–110
Tringa flavipes 55–56
    melanoleuca 55
    solitaria 56
Troglodytes aedon 92–93
    a. aedon 93

    a. baldwini 93
    troglodytes 93, 101
    t. hiemalis 101
    t. pullus 101
Tryngites subruficollis 59
Turdus migratorius 107–108
    m. achrusterus 108
    m. migratorius 108
    m. nigrideus 108
Turkey, Wild 50–51
Turnstone, Ruddy 57
Turtle-Dove, Ringed 166
Tympanuchus phasianellus 166
Tyrannus forficatus 81
    tyrannus 80
    verticalis 80–81
Tyto alba 67
Veery 13, 104–105
Vermivora celata 118
    chrysoptera 117
    lawrenceii 118
    leucobronchialis 117–118
    peregrina 118
    pinus 116–117
    ruficapilla 118–119
Vireo flavifrons 114
    gilvus 114
    griseus 112–113
    g. noveboracensis 113
    philadelphicus 115
    solitarius 113–114
    s. alticola 114
    s. solitarius 114
    olivaceus 115–116
Vireo, Philadelphia 13, 115
    Red-eyed 17, 115–116
    Solitary 113–114
    Warbling 114
    White-eyed 14, 112–113
    Yellow-throated 14, 114
Vulture, Black 8, 14, 42
    Turkey 42–43
Warbler, Bay-breasted 129
    Black-and-white 130–131
    Black-throated Blue . . . .
        . . . . 13, 97, 122–123
    Black-throated Green . . . .
        . . . . 15, 17, 124–125
    Blackburnian 13, 17, 125
    Blackpoll 129–130
    Blue-winged 14, 116–117, 118
    Brewster's 117–118
    Canada 13, 138
    Cape May 14, 122
    Cerulean 14, 130
    Chestnut-sided . . . .
        . . . . 7, 13, 17, 96, 120–121
    Connecticut 135–136
    Golden-winged 15, 117, 118
    Hooded 14, 137

Kentucky 14, 143
Kirtland's 127
Lawrence's 118
Magnolia 13, 16, 97, 121
Mourning 13, 98, 136
Myrtle 124
Nashville . . 12, 13, 14, 95, 119–120
Orange-crowned 118
Palm 128–129
Pine 14, 127
Prairie 127–128
Prothonotary 15, 132
Sutton's 9, 116, 126–127
Swainson's 9, 14, 99, 132–133
Tennessee 14, 118
Wilson's 138
Worm-eating 14, 132
Yellow 120
Yellow Palm 129
Yellow-rumped 13, 123–124
Yellow-throated 14, 98, 126
Waterthrush, Louisiana . . 14, 134–135
    Northern 12, 13, 134
Waxwing, Bohemian 110
    Cedar 110–111
Whimbrel 57
Whip-poor-will 15, 70
Wigeon, American 37
    Eurasian 36–37
Willet 56
Wilsonia canadensis 138
    citrina 137
    pusilla 138
Wood-Pewee, Eastern 76–77
Woodcock, American 60
Woodpecker, Black-backed 13, 74
    Downy 73–74
    Hairy 74
    Ivory-billed 76
    Pileated 75–76
    Red-bellied 14, 72–73
    Red-headed 14, 72, 112
Wren, Bewick's 14, 92
    Carolina 14, 91–92
    House 92–93
    Marsh 101
    Sedge 13, 101
    Winter 13, 93, 101
Xanthocephalus xanthocephalus . . 157
Yellowlegs, Greater 55
    Lesser 55–56
Yellowthroat, Common 136–137
Zenaida macroura 64–65
Zonotrichia albicollis 152–153
    leucophrys 153
    l. gambelii 153
    l. leucophrys 153
    querula 153–154